Biology and Christian Ethics

This stimulating and wide-ranging book mounts a profound enquiry into some of the most pressing questions of our age, by examining the relationship between biological science and Christianity. The history of biological discovery is explored from the point of view of a leading philosopher and ethicist.

What effect should modern biological theory and practice have on Christian understanding of ethics? How much of that theory and practice should Christians endorse? Can Christians, for example, agree that biological changes are not governed by transcendent values, or that there are no clear or essential boundaries between species? To what extent can 'Nature' set our standards? Stephen R. L. Clark takes a reasoned look at biological theory since Darwin and argues that an orthodox Christian philosophy is better able to accommodate the truth of such theory than is the sort of progressive, meliorist interpretation of Christian doctrine which has usually been offered as the properly 'modern' option.

Orthodox Christianity and sensible biological theory alike can agree that we are sinners, that every individual is an end in itself, and that the true values to which we should direct ourselves transcend the needs of survival.

STEPHEN R. L. CLARK is Professor of Philosophy at the University of Liverpool. He is the author of *Aristotle's Man (1975)*, *The Moral Status of Animals* (1977), *The Nature of the Beast (1982)*, *Civil Peace and Sacred Order (1989)*, *Animals and their Moral Standing (1997)*, *God, Religion and Reality* (1988) and *The Political Animal* (1999), as well as articles in *Philosophy*, *Inquiry*, *Philosophical Quarterly*, *The Monist* and others.

NEW STUDIES IN CHRISTIAN ETHICS 17

General editor
Robin Gill

Editorial board
Stephen R. L. Clark, Stanley Hauerwas,
Robin W. Lovin

Christian ethics has increasingly assumed a central place within academic theology. At the same time the growing power and ambiguity of modern science and the rising dissatisfaction within the social sciences about claims to value-neutrality have prompted renewed interest in ethics within the secular academic world. There is, therefore, a need for studies in Christian ethics which, as well as being concerned with the relevance of Christian ethics to the present day secular debate are well informed about parallel discussions in recent philosophy, science or social science. New Studies in Christian Ethics aims to provide books that do this at the highest intellectual level and demonstrate that Christian ethics can make a distinctive contribution to this debate – either in moral substance or in terms of underlying moral justifications.

Other titles published in the series

1 KIERAN CRONIN
Rights and Christian Ethics

2 IAN MCDONALD
Biblical Interpretation and Christian Ethics

3 JAMES MACKEY
Power and Christian Ethics

4 IAN S. MARKHAM
Plurality and Christian Ethics

5 JEAN PORTER
Moral Action and Christian Ethics

6 WILLIAM SCHWEIKER
Responsibility and Christian Ethics

BIOLOGY AND
CHRISTIAN ETHICS

STEPHEN R. L. CLARK

University of Liverpool

CAMBRIDGE
UNIVERSITY PRESS

PUBLISHED BY THE PRESS SYNDICATE OF THE UNIVERSITY OF CAMBRIDGE
The Pitt Building, Trumpington Street, Cambridge, United Kingdom

CAMBRIDGE UNIVERSITY PRESS
The Edinburgh Building, Cambridge CB2 2RU, UK   www.cup.cam.ac.uk
40 West 20th Street, New York, NY 10011–4211, USA   www.cup.org
10 Stamford Road, Oakleigh, Melbourne 3166, Australia
Ruiz de Alarcón 13, 28014 Madrid, Spain

First published 2000

Printed in the United Kingdom at the University Press, Cambridge

Typeset in Baskerville 11/12.5pt   System 3b2   [CE]

A catalogue record for this book is available from the British Library

Library of Congress cataloguing in publication data

Clark, Stephen R. L.
Biology and Christian ethics / Stephen R. L. Clark.
p. cm.
Includes bibliographical references and index.
ISBN 0 521 5613 0 (hardback) ISBN 0 521 56768 8 (paperback)
1. Christian ethics. 2. Biology – Religious aspects – Christianity.
3. Ethics, Evolutionary. I. Title
BJ1275.C55 2000
241′.64957–dc21   00-023025 CIP

ISBN 0 521 56131 0 hardback
ISBN 0 521 56768 8 paperback

Contents

General editor's preface

This book is the seventeenth in the series New Studies in Christian Ethics. A number of books in the series have combined philosophical and theological skills as this book does, notably Kieran Cronin's *Rights and Christian Ethics*, Jean Porter's *Moral Action and Christian Ethics*, Garth Hallett's *Priorities and Christian Ethics* and David Fergusson's *Community, Liberalism and Christian Ethics*. In addition, the wider issues of biology have also been the concern of Michael Northcott's well received *The Environment and Christian Ethics*. All of these books closely reflect the two key aims of the series – namely to promote monographs in Christian ethics which engage centrally with the present secular moral debate at the highest possible intellectual level and, secondly, to encourage contributors to demonstrate that Christian ethics can make a distinctive contribution to this debate.

Stephen Clark's reputation both as a philosopher of real distinction and as a Christian ethicist is very high. He is a very productive author who always writes thought-provoking books which challenge many dominant orthodoxies. His early books soon established that his was an unusual and distinctive voice – notably his *The Moral Status of Animals* (1977) and *The Nature of the Beast* (1982) – with a particular concern about animals and the environment. His interest in the philosophy of religion and in theological concerns was clearly established in his subsequent books *From Athens to Jerusalem* (1984) and *The Mysteries of Religion* (1986). His most famous ambitious project to date has been the three volumes *Civil Peace and Sacred Order* (1989), *A Parliament of Souls* (1990) and *God's World and the great Awakening* (1991). They are by no means easy books – highly literate and lyrical in style – but offer many sharp and unexpected insights. His next book, *How To Think About the Earth* (1993), focused upon some of the ecological issues of his early books. Until he wrote the present book, I regarded *How To Think About the Earth* as the most significant theological book to have emerged in the recent ethical debate about ecology.

His new book *Biology and Christian Ethics* clearly develops from the issues examined in these earlier books. It responds to the challenges of such writers as Richard Dawkins and E. O. Wilson, and to such issues as social Darwinism, orthogenesis, species essentialism, 'selfish genes', human biotechnology, and (crucially) ethical anthropocentrism. He approaches these writers and issues as a philosopher and theologian, rather than as a scientist; however, his earlier writings show that he has the intelligence to read carefully in areas other than his own. He is well able to unmask some of the implicit ideological commitments of those who imagine that they carry none.

The challenge that Stephen Clark offers here is a double one. A large part of what he writes is a challenge to those who claim too much in the name of science. By reducing ethics simply to evolutionary or socio-biological impulses writers such as Dawkins and Wilson produce a highly distorted account of what it is to be a moral (let alone a religious) human being. In the process, so Stephen Clark successfully argues, they proffer a highly questionable series of 'scientific' explanations. Even Darwin, as will be seen in two chapters that follow, was given to some scientifically and ethically flawed claims in his paradigmatic account of evolution.

The other challenge is to scientists and theologians alike. Stephen Clark argues that many of us have a deeply distorted and contradictory relationship with other animals. In his theological account of creation all animals are our neighbours. Scientists should not, he believes, regard them as the proper subject of experiments, let alone biotechnological manipulations, and the rest of us should not eat them. Instead, we should learn to value and respect them as neighbours who share to a greater or lesser degree many of the qualities and capacities that we regard as characteristically human. Stephen Clark's own theological commitment to both ecology and vegetarianism is apparent at many points of his argument.

On almost every page of this book there are distinctive, challenging and creative insights. In short the book is a delight.

ROBIN GILL

Preface

My first extended work of philosophy was a study of Aristotle's ethics in the light of his biology (*Aristotle's Man*). My second was an impassioned work on the moral status of non-human animals (*The Moral Status of Animals*), and my third, a more decorous study of non-human experience and motivation, in the light of current biological theory and ethological reports (*The Nature of the Beast*). Later books were directed rather at cosmological and epistemological aspects of the philosophy of religion, though almost all of them also made some glancing reference to our biological nature, and to the treatment of non-human animals and our 'environment' (see especially *How to Think about the Earth*). Various essays on non-human animals have been collected in *Animals and their Moral Standing*, and on the political life of the *human* animal in *The Political Animal*. Other papers on matters relevant to this present volume include 'The Lack of a Gap between Fact and Value' in *Aristotelian Society Supplementary Volume* 54.1980, pp. 245ff.; 'Sexual Ontology and the Group Marriage' in *Philosophy* 58.1983, pp. 215–27; 'Richard Dawkins's *Blind Watchmaker*' in *Times Literary Supplement*, 26 September 1986, pp. 1047–9; 'Orwell and the Anti-Realists' in *Philosophy* 67.1992, pp. 141–54; 'Does the Burgess Shale have Moral Implications?' in *Inquiry* 36.1993, pp. 357–80; 'Natural Goods and Moral Beauty' in D. Knowles and J. Skorupski, eds., *Virtue and Taste: essays on politics, ethics and aesthetics in memory of Flint Schier* (Blackwell: Oxford 1993), pp. 83–97; 'Tools, Machines and Marvels' in Roger Fellows, ed., *Philosophy and Technology* (Cambridge University Press: Cambridge 1995), pp. 159–57; 'Environmental Ethics' in

Peter Byrne and Leslie Houlden, eds., *Companion Encyclopedia of Theology* (Routledge: London 1995), pp. 843–70; 'Objective Values, Final Causes' in *Electronic Journal of Analytical Philosophy* 3.1995, pp. 65–78 (http://www.phil.indiana.edu/ejap/); 'Ecology and the Transformation of Nature' in *Theology in Green* 3.1995, pp. 28–46; 'Status and Contract Societies: the non-human dimension' in *National Geographical Journal of India* 41.1995, pp. 225–30; 'Natural Integrity and Biotechnology' in Jacqueline A. Laing and David S. Oderberg, eds., *Human Lives* (Macmillan: London 1997), pp. 58–76; 'Making up Animals: the view from science fiction' in Alan Holland and Andrew Johnson, eds., *Animal Biotechnology and Ethics* (Chapman & Hall: London 1997), pp. 209–24; 'Platonism and the Gods of Place' in Tim Chappell, ed., *The Philosophy of Environmentalism* (Edinburgh University Press: Edinburgh 1997), pp. 19–37; 'Objectivism and the Alternatives' in E. Morscher, O. Neumaier and P. Simons, eds., *Applied Ethics in a Troubled World* (Kluwer: Dordrecht, Boston and London 1998), pp. 285–94; 'Pantheism' in David E. Cooper and Joy A. Palmer, eds., *Spirit of the Environment* (Routledge: London 1998), pp. 42–56; 'Is Nature God's Will?' in Andrew Linzey and Dorothy Yamamoto, eds., *Animals in Christian Religion* (SCM Press: London 1998), pp. 123–36; 'Understanding Animals' in Michael Tobias and Kate Solisti Mattelon, eds., *Kinship with the Animals* (Beyond Words Publishing: Hillsborough, Oreg. 1998), pp. 99–111; 'Dangerous Conservatives: a reply to Daniel Dombrowski' in *Sophia* 37.1998, pp. 44–69; and 'Conducta decente hacia los animales: un enfoque tradicional' in *Teorema* 18/3.1999, pp. 61–83.

These and other papers have been read at conferences, to students and to philosophy societies in the United Kingdom, the United States, India and the Netherlands. An earlier version of chapter 6, on 'The goals of goodness', composed for the Anglo-Indian Convivium in Panchgani in January 1998, was published in *Studies in World Christianity* 4.1998, pp. 228–44. One brief paper, 'Deconstructing Darwin' was originally delivered at a conference on Ethics at Yale University, and is due to be published by Rowman and Littlefield in the Proceedings of that conference. It has served as a basis both for the Alan

Richardson Lecture at Durham University in spring 1999, and for this volume. The first full draft of the book was composed during a happy period as Alan Richardson Fellow in the Department of Theology at the University of Durham. I am extremely grateful to the Richardson Committee, to the Department of Theology and to Van Mildert College for giving me the opportunity to devote myself whole-heartedly (or as whole-heartedly as can reasonably be managed) to a single project, as well as access to a different University Library. I should also express my gratitude to the Arts and Humanities Research Board and the University of Liverpool, who together enabled me to take a whole year's sabbatical (part of it spent at Durham). Gillian and Verity allowed me both physical and mental absence despite the extra burdens this placed on them; Gillian, Samuel and Alexandra contributed commentary and information from their own expertise.

Other philosophers, theologians and scientists have influenced me over many years through their writings and their emailed or spoken word, especially George Berkeley, G. K. Chesterton, Vernard Eller, Marshall Massey, Mary Midgley, Simon Conway Morris, Oliver O'Donovan and Plotinus. There have certainly been many others, most of whom would probably not wish to be associated with anything I have chosen to learn from them! Amongst the many whose wisdom I now miss, I count my cousin David Phillips of Ellesmere, and my friends Flint Schier, Hilary Torrance and Michael Vasey. Finally, I should also like to thank Robin Gill and the Cambridge University Press for encouraging me to undertake and complete so large an enterprise.

Introduction

It has been an axiom for Christian anthropologists (that is, for Christians reasoning about human nature) that human beings are animals of a peculiar kind: 'spiritual amphibia' who are the meeting point of 'merely biological' and 'merely angelic or intellectual life'. It has also been axiomatic that human beings were particularly important to God, and that their appearance in the world was by special creation (even if that did not take place as literal-minded readers of the Book of Genesis might suppose[1]). Many Christian thinkers have also placed great stress on 'natural law', which is what 'nature has taught all creatures', as the basis for moral exploration. All these ideas have been called into question by recent biological theory and observation. It may be that some of them, and some related concepts (e.g. species essentialism), need to be abandoned; others need only to be reformulated, and a few need merely to be reasserted against the errors of our age.

Some writers have suggested that none of this is true: 'science' and 'religion', it is said, have entirely different provinces and operate by entirely different rules. Nothing about our biological history and nature, so they say, has any relevance to any 'religious' claim: science deals with 'facts' and religion only with 'values'. That claim is not unreasonable, though I believe it to be false; but if there is such a distinction, that itself

---

[1] 'The basic error of fundamentalism is something from which neither rabbinic midrashists nor church fathers suffered: it is a refusal to recognize the variety of styles and genres of statement in the Bible, and therefore to realize that the divine Truth, which both Jewish and Christian faith ascribes to the Bible, comes to us in many modes, some of them essentially symbolic', Robert Murray, *The Cosmic Covenant* (Sheed & Ward: London 1992), p. xviii.

demands a rigorous reformulation of traditional Christian discourse. Perhaps 'religion' is what Marx suggested: 'the opium of the people, *the heart of a heartless world*'.[2] It depicts a possible future, not an actual past. Those who make the distinction frequently confuse it with a quite different one: 'science' has no limit to its enquiries, accepts no explanation as complete, and takes nothing merely 'on authority', whereas 'religion' can only be a matter of unquestioning faith, dependent on the authority of sacred texts and persons.[3] My own experience is that scientists are as obdurate in their convictions as anyone, and that the institutions of peer review and academic rivalry have often made it difficult to question fundamentals.[4] 'Believers' and academic theologians, in my experience, are no *less* ready to subject their convictions and prior assumptions to critical enquiry – which is not to say that *anyone* is eager to do so.

The axioms of traditional Christianity, and the problems posed by modern biological science, are significant for more than Christendom. All the Abrahamic faiths[5] have very similar conceptions of our presence in the world. Indeed, it is difficult to find any tradition in which something like those axioms is not affirmed. In some archaic religions non-human animals are also denizens of the spirit world, and human beings, just as such, are nothing special, though a particular tribe may be. In Hindu

---

2 Karl Marx, in his *Criticism of Hegel's Philosophy of Right*, tr. Annette Jolin and Joseph O'Malley (Cambridge University Press: Cambridge 1977); the point is not that religion is a delusion, but that it is a dream. Unfortunately human dreams have a way of coming true in ways that we might not wish.

3 The claim is made, for example, by Steve Jones in *In the Blood: God, genes and destiny* (HarperCollins: London 1996), p. xvii.

4 It is axiomatic, for example, that *all* knowledge is either good, or at least neutral, and only the uses of it (which are someone else's fault) can be bad; that all knowledge must be founded on repeatable experiments that demand no especial virtue to complete or understand; that the increase of human knowledge is enough to justify any amount of merely animal distress; that any sign of public disapproval merely shows that 'the public' needs to be better educated about scientific values. None of these claims strike me as obvious.

5 These include Rabbinic Judaism, the various Christian churches, and Islam: all trace their beginnings to the historical example of Abraham, and are, in broad terms, ethical monotheisms. I do not mean to invoke that chimera, 'the Judaeo-Christian tradition'. See W. Cantwell Smith, *The Meaning and End of Religion* (SPCK: London 1978; first published 1962).

religions, distinctions of caste and cult may matter more, in a way, than any difference of species. In Buddhism the human world is only one of six distinct realms of being (the others being the worlds of animals, gods, demons, hungry ghosts and hell), and enlightenment lies in realizing our non-identity with any form we briefly wear: all forms are empty of significance. But all these notions, in usual practice, come round to the same three axioms: as human beings we do more than eat, drink, mate and sleep – we also dream, think, worship and aspire; our being thus human gives us a special relationship with cosmic reality; how we are to behave has something to do with how things generally do behave. Even those creeds that urge us to transcend or correct nature have some vision of the better way which demands that we take *some* judgements as merely given. Even those biologists who have most sought to contradict tradition often find it hard to change. Nature is something we both defy and follow, and 'human nature' demands that we inhabit other worlds of meaning than the merely biological. If we did not, however could we have formulated modern biological theory? As Chesterton observed, only human beings really notice that they resemble other creatures, and so differ from them even in their similarity. 'The fish does not trace the fish-bone pattern in the fowls of the air; or the elephant and the emu compare skeletons.'[6] Even those biologists who insist that human beings are only another variety of animal find it reasonable to use non-human creatures in ways that they would shrink from using other humans.[7] I do not say that they are right to do so.

So questions about our history and nature are of more than parochial interest. How can we preserve, or can we preserve, the notions which have so far sustained us all? How can we accommodate ourselves, as we have conceived ourselves, within the theories that our best scientific endeavour has endorsed? And what follows if we cannot? What follows, in particular, for our conduct towards other creatures, whether human or

---

[6] G. K. Chesterton, *The Everlasting Man* (Hodder & Stoughton: London 1925), p. 307.

[7] Chesterton himself, it is only fair to add, entirely disapproved of vivisection (see 'Christmas' in *All Things Considered* (Methuen: London 1908).

non-human, and for our plans for the future? What difference, especially, must evolutionary theory make?

Adam Sedgwick, Professor of Geology at Cambridge from 1818 to 1873, regarded Charles Darwin's theory of 'evolution through natural selection' as an ill-grounded, and dangerous, speculation. In his *Spectator* review in 1860, he expressed his

'deep aversion to the theory; because of its unflinching materialism; because it has deserted the inductive track, the only track that leads to physical truth; because it utterly repudiates final causes, and thereby indicates a demoralized understanding on the part of its advocates. By the word, demoralized, I mean a want of capacity for comprehending the force of moral evidence, which is dependent on the highest faculties of our nature. What is it that gives us the sense of right and wrong, of law, of duty, of cause and effect? What is it that enables us to construct true theories on good inductive evidence? Theories which enable us, whether in the material or the moral world, to link together the past and the present. What is it that enables us to anticipate the future, to act wisely with reference to future good, to believe in a future state, to acknowledge the being of a God? . . . By gazing only on material nature, a man may easily have his very senses bewildered; . . . he may become so frozen up, by a too long continued and exclusively material study, as to lose his relish for moral truth, and his vivacity in apprehending it.'[8]

Sedgwick saw a genuine difficulty, a genuine threat, and therefore resisted the theory. Others have believed that we could accept the theory and still accommodate all that we need of old humanity (however much that is). A few, as I have indicated, have thought that we should simply hold 'the realm of science' and 'the realm of religion' apart – a doctrine which Aquinas denounced (in the shape of Siger of Brabant's Two Truths Theory) some centuries ago.[9] According to that account, it is as unreasonable to expect 'religious' or 'moral' truth to agree with

[8] Adam Sedgwick, 'Objections to Mr Darwin's Theory of the Origin of Species' (7 April 1860); reprinted in David L. Hull, ed., *Darwin and his Critics* (University of Chicago Press: Chicago and London 1983), pp. 159–66, esp. pp. 164–5.

[9] It was this, by Chesterton's account, that roused Aquinas to a last great burst of fury (*St Thomas Aquinas* (Methuen: London 1933), pp. 106ff.). Since Chesterton is now too often supposed to have been 'a mere journalist', and therefore unreliable, it is worth adding that Etienne Gilson found it reasonable to say that this was the best book ever written on Aquinas (M. Ward, *Gilbert Keith Chesterton* (Sheed & Ward: London 1944), p. 526); this seems fair comment.

'scientific' truth as to criticize '*Xena: Warrior Princess*' for obvious anachronism and physical implausibility (whether it is science or religion that is to be compared to *Xena*).[10] My own suspicion is that the doctrine of 'Many Truths' amounts to exactly the sort of polytheism that Abrahamists have always resisted: there can in the end be only *one* claim on our devotion and belief. But whatever the intellectual or psychological solution may eventually be, at least the question must be asked: how human, how religious, how Christian can a biologically informed intelligence now be? Conversely, how much of biological theory, observation and practice can we justly entertain?

That question clearly strikes some people as offensive. Surely, they say, we have a duty to the Truth, which transcends any other ethical or religious demand. Surely, we must have learnt by now that 'science' cannot be halted or suppressed, and that it should accept no premises upon the authority of any sacred text. We must 'cut loose the natural history of mankind from the Bible, and place each upon its own foundation, where it may remain without collision or molestation'.[11] But it is worth recalling what Josiah Nott was demanding, in his 'lectures on niggerology': the right to preach that there were many different human species, with no necessary similarity or shared compassion. Is it *obvious* that people have a right to spread whatever tales they wish, and that there are no other duties than one 'to the Truth'? Is it *obvious* that there is only one route to the Truth, and that we must abandon everything else to reach it? Is it *obvious* that those who abandon an older authority then owe their thoughts to nothing but the Truth? Is it even *obvious* that all truths should be taught, as a matter of course, to children, against their parents' wishes, and irrespective of the effect such

---

[10] 'For the three hundred years prior to Tycho [Brahe], science and religion had coexisted on terms under which science was to be regarded as merely a collection of "likely stories" – stories that could be interesting in their way, but from which it was completely inappropriate to expect any real picture of the physical world', Victor E. Thoren, *The Lord of Uraniberg: a biography of Tycho Brahe* (Cambridge University Press: New York 1990), p. 275, after Edward Grant, 'Late Medieval Thought, Copernicus and the Scientific Revolution', *Journal of the History of Ideas* 23.1962, pp. 197–220.

[11] Josiah Nott, cited by Stephen Jay Gould, *The Mismeasure of Man* (W. W. Norton & Co.: New York 1981), p. 70, from W. Stanton, *The Leopard's Spots* (University of Chicago Press: Chicago 1960), p. 119.

teaching has? Is it not, on the contrary, obvious that even 'great scientists', let alone the common kind, are frequently moved by prejudice, and would often have done much better to pay attention to an older and more liberal tradition? Devotion to the Truth makes sense if we suppose that it is *God* who is that Truth. But why should we devote ourselves to a Truth that is, expressly, not divine?

Much of what follows will, I hope, be relevant to any humane intelligence. But it may also be true that Christian tradition allows one further question. The majority of Christian thinkers have probably followed Greek, and Hebrew, precedent in supposing that Christ revealed what all of us, in our heart of hearts, already know. He is called the *Logos* because He is the one through whom we are *logikoi*.[12] At the least, the new commands of God are consistent with the ones revealed through human reflection upon nature and society. If biological theory now casts doubt on common sense, it also casts doubt on Christendom. But some theologians have entertained the diffi- cult suggestion that all merely human thought is sin: 'natural religion' amounts to devil worship, secular virtues are but splendid vices, and the Christian revelation is that we were always wrong. On these terms (however difficult they are to formulate, let alone to face), a sound biological understanding which contradicted common sense might, paradoxically, confirm the Christian view – except, of course, that 'sound biology' is as impossible for sinners as 'sound religion'. God and Nature are sometimes, in many traditions, almost the same thing. In others, and notably in some Christian sects, they are almost opposite things. A dim reflection of that opposition appears to haunt even some atheistical biologists, who speak of fighting back against 'the selfish gene' in the name of higher, or at least more amiable, values (without explaining where these values come from, nor how we might hope to succeed).[13]

There may be a truth to learn even from such Manichaean

[12] The aphorism is owed to Origen, cited by M. F. Wiles, *The Spiritual Gospel* (Cambridge University Press: Cambridge 1960), p. 93.

[13] See S. A. Barnett, *Biology and Freedom* (Cambridge University Press: Cambridge 1988), pp. 136ff. for an appropriately acerbic response.

stories[14] – but one simple answer was given by Augustine long ago, to those who believed themselves uniquely inspired by a God with nothing to say to anyone else. They must concede that at least they owed their knowledge of the alphabet to human beings, and so their knowledge of the revelatory scriptures. If Fact and Value really were inscrutably distinct, we could never find out Value: 'if God is not in Nature, He is not in you', as Plotinus warned those who thought themselves exalted above all natural things.[15] Conversely, we can value nothing that the facts of our nature make impossible for us. If we cannot sensibly trust ourselves, we cannot even trust our own best image of the trustworthy. If we can identify something as deserving greater trust than any ordinarily human voice, we cannot simultaneously suppose that we are thoroughly perverse. And finally (for the moment), any supposed Fact which really had no Value would not be worth believing.

In brief, we cannot sensibly adopt a theory which entails that we could never have the intellectual or moral virtue to discover or to recognize its truth. Any doctrine of 'total depravity' (however plausible it sometimes seems) implies that we could not recognize its truth. It follows that God cannot have left Himself without witnesses, even if the witness is often disturbed or cloudy. It also follows, so I shall suggest, that a *strictly* Darwinian biology cannot sensibly be considered true. If it were, we could neither have the wit to find it out, nor any duty to admit it if we did.

The issue before us is to discover or determine what we are, and what we are for. Traditional believers – amongst whom I count myself – suppose that there are answers to those questions, and that they can be found by prayerful examination of

---

[14] Manichaeanism is one of a select group of consciously devised religions: its founder, Mani, supposed that the world of our present experience was created by one of a pair of deities, and that it was the *other* god who was responsible for our grasp of real virtue, and our only hope of escape from misery. David Lindsay's *Voyage to Arcturus* (Gollancz: London 1965; first published 1920) is a fine literary exposition of the system, and one informed by contemporary biological theory.

[15] Plotinus, *Enneads* II.9.16, 26–8; the chapter in question is entitled, by Plotinus' follower, Porphyry, 'Against the Gnostics'. I have used A. H. Armstrong's translation throughout: *Plotinus*, vols. I–VII (Loeb Classical Library, Heinemann: London 1966–88).

the Word of God in Scripture – and the world. Less traditional believers, reacting against the follies that have often been taught as gospel, believe instead that the answers are not for us to discover, but rather to decide. The question is not (for them) about our present world, but about the world to come, and its coming rests on human enterprise. Humanity is a bridge between the unmeaning world of brute biology and the future, happy world of humane artifice. I am myself less optimistic about the sort of world that human beings, unaided, will create, but also less enthralled by any *present* order than conservative believers are. It is precisely because I think our nature is imperfect that I distrust the plans of those who would remake it. Conversely, it is because I catch occasional glimpses of a redeemed humanity that I can believe we are not bound for ever within the circles of this world.

CHAPTER I

The development of Darwinian theory

SAMENESS AND DIFFERENCE

Civilized people, almost everywhere, believe that people are unlike dogs, cattle, sparrows and ants. People decorate and clothe themselves; they build houses, fences, roads and monuments; they tell elaborate stories about their personal and communal history, and sign their names to contracts. Most civilized people also assume that people matter more than 'animals', although they do not agree what treatment that importance warrants. Tales about tribes who treat human beings as property, or as meat, simply support our own conviction that we ourselves are civilized. Tribes who seem to regard monkeys, crocodiles or cows as their superiors, or at least as 'sacred', almost make us suspect that 'savages' like that are not *really* human (and so may be treated with the same contempt that they, we think, display).

Such humanism is itself a strand in all the Abrahamic faiths, as also in the sort of atheism which thrives in a post-Abrahamic culture. The first point to be made about the humanism of civilized humanity is simply that it was always compatible with the equally obvious truth that people are very *like* dogs, cattle, sparrows and ants. Obviously, we are born, eat, drink and die. We also jockey for position, make up to potential mates and allies, mark out our territories, defend our young, and (ants apart) play games. It has always been obvious that people are mammals (like dogs and cattle), vertebrates (like dogs, sparrows, crocodiles and trout), and animals (like dogs, ants, worms and jellyfish). Our very shapes are so alike that we can imagine easy transformations, of human to wolf or dolphin. These similarities pick out real classes. There is no real class of (for example) yellow things (although a great many things are yellow), since there is no true generalization about all yellow things beyond the merely tautological (that they are yellow). Being mammalian, or vertebrate, or animal, entails many other properties, which allow real, useful classifications. It does not follow that such classes have real essences, as though all and only mammals, for example, had a particular set of properties. Perhaps there is no property that all and only mammals have – but there is still good reason to distinguish mammals and birds.

Common sense identifies real species and real kinds of creature. Their existence suggests that there are a limited number of ways to be, variously realized in the world of nature. Similarly, there are many crystalline forms, having discoverable similarities and differences. Individual crystals may have different sorts of symmetry. Briefly: a crystal has a *centre* of symmetry if every face of the crystal has a similar face parallel to it; it has as many *planes* of symmetry as there are ways of dividing the crystal into portions which are mirror images of each other; if it is rotated around an *axis*, it may reach a position where all its parts are congruent with the original position only after a complete (360-degree) rotation, or at earlier points. This last phenomenon identifies the axes of rotation: it turns out that crystals can return to congruence after movement through 360, 180, 120, 90 or 60 degrees, and there may, correspondingly, be four sorts of axis of rotation (dyad, triad, tetrad and hexad; there is no pentad axis,[1] and a full 360-degree rotation is possible for anything). Summing up these different symmetries identifies seven crystal systems (a cube, for example, belongs to the same system as octahedrons and rhombic dodecahedrons).[2]

---

[1] There are, however, aperiodic 'quasi-crystals', returning to congruence after a 72-degree rotation, which have been identified as possible analogues of DNA; see Paul Davies, *The Fifth Miracle: the search for the origin of life* (Penguin: Harmondsworth 1999), pp. 244–5.

[2] For the record: triclinic crystals have only one axis of rotation (that is, they return to a congruent state only after rotating through 360 degrees); monoclinic have one diad axis only; orthorhombic have three diad axes; tetragonal have one tetrad axis only; cubic have four triad axes; trigonal have one triad axis; and hexagonal have one hexad axis. Other symmetries are mathematically related to those limitations. This

Further analysis identifies thirty-two crystal classes (helped along by yet another symmetry: how many alternate rotations and inversions return the crystal to a congruent state?), and a total of 230 'space groups' distributed among those thirty-two classes. Crystals of different substances will inevitably belong to the same limited number of systems, classes and groups. Not all actual crystals will be 'well formed': 'the size and shape of individual faces of a crystal are purely incidental features determined merely by the conditions of growth of the particular crystal under consideration, but the angular relationships of these faces reveal the underlying crystallographic symmetry'.[3] Crystals, in brief, can be classified, and characterized as more or less 'well formed' (that is, revealing the underlying symmetry on the surface), without anyone supposing that they have an historical or genealogical relationship (as indeed they do not). Similarly, it seems not to have occurred to anyone until a couple of centuries ago that the 'family resemblances' of living creatures are caused by family relationships.

Occasional traces of that idea do surface. Aristotle, though he is commonly supposed to have fathered the notion of unchanging, distinct species, actually identified many hybrid or intermediate kinds, and saw that, for example, seals could helpfully be described as 'deformed quadrupeds'. It is possible that he entertained the thought that all living creatures arose from hybridization and 'deformity' from an original, more perfect stock. If so, he thought the stock was human: human form, in Aristotelian science, is the template for all other creatures.[4] The idea is not wholly absurd: it is quite often noted that humans present a relatively unspecialized shape, and that any vertebrate embryo, at least, looks a bit like an undeveloped human.[5] That

information is drawn from F. C. Phillips, *Introduction to Crystallography* (Longmans: London 1963, third edition). Further details can be discovered in other standard works, together with many pretty pictures: crystals are almost as beautiful as living things – but not, I suspect, because they are symmetrical.

[3] Ibid., p. 18.

[4] I argued for this interpretation of the Aristotelian texts in my first book, *Aristotle's Man: speculations upon Aristotelian anthropology* (Clarendon Press: Oxford 1975).

[5] Though the similarities were exaggerated by theorists like Haeckel; see Mike Richardson, *Anatomy and Embryology* 196.1997, pp. 91–106 and elsewhere (a reference owed to Simon Conway Morris).

apes are 'degenerate' people (as Buffon suggested[6]) is an idea
with some emotional appeal. It might even, if we count the
immediate ancestors of hominids as people, be almost true:
chimpanzees and the other great apes may have evolved from
an upright, relatively large-brained biped a lot more like us
than like modern chimps. But the theory that *everything* is descended from the Ur-Human is now little more than a curiosity,
and was never a central preoccupation. Where we all came
from was of less significance than what we are all like now.

So biological taxonomy was once like crystalline taxonomy,
and the human shape often reckoned the most 'perfect' realization of the structure underlying other kinds, whether that was a
strictly genealogical claim or not. Men – and it usually was,
exactly, *men* – revealed the underlying symmetries of living
things (top, bottom; front, back; right, left; male, female) that
were variously distorted in the growth of other creatures.
'Man', according to William Whewell, 'is the most perfect and
highly endowed creature which ever has existed on the earth.'[7]
Alternatively, different sorts of life could be identified, and
different 'perfect types', just as a perfect cubic crystal is different
from a perfect tetragonal crystal. Perhaps all living creatures
aspire to be human (as it were); perhaps there are different
aspirations, and the different kinds are different for ever. Either
way, there is an identifiable archetype for each real class of
creature, as Richard Owen, who discovered the class of dinosaurs, reasoned.

To what natural or secondary causes the orderly succession and
progression of such organic phenomena may have been committed,
we are as yet ignorant. But if without derogation to the Divine Power,

---

6 Reported by Owen in 'Darwin on the Origin of Species', *Edinburgh Review* 11.1860,
   pp. 487–532; see David L. Hull, ed., *Darwin and his Critics* (University of Chicago
   Press: Chicago and London 1983), p. 197.
7 William Whewell, *Of the Plurality of Worlds* (John W. Parker & Son: London 1854),
   p. 210. Whewell, a great polymath and philosopher, was Master of Trinity College,
   Cambridge from 1841 to 1866. Robert Chambers, who advanced an evolutionary
   theory before Darwin, actually thought the same thing: 'Man . . . as type of all types
   of the animal kingdom, the true and unmistakable head of animated nature upon this
   earth', Chambers, *Vestiges of the Natural History of Creation* (1844; reissued by Leicester
   University Press: Leicester, and by Humanities Press: New York, in 1969), p. 272.

we may conceive such ministers and personify them by the term *Nature*, we learn from the past history of our globe that she has advanced with slow and stately steps, guided by the archetypal light amidst the wreck of worlds, from the first embodiment of the vertebrate idea, under its own ichthyic vestment, until it became arrayed in the glorious garb of the human form.[8]

Goethe professed a similar notion:

Every animal is an end in itself; it comes forth perfect out of the womb of Nature, and perfect are its offspring. All limbs develop themselves according to laws everlasting. Even the rarest of forms preserves in secret the archetype . . . These are bounds no god can extend, and Nature respects them, for only through such limitations has perfection ever been possible.[9]

The appearance of form, refracted and reflected in the natural world, may not always suggest the notion of design. It does suggest the real existence of intellectually discoverable structures, and that in turn may demand the real existence of an eternal intellect. All attempts to dispense with 'real forms' by suggesting that they are only simplified descriptions of a world where nothing is the 'same' from one point or instant to the next (as if the structures of matter – say, the crystal systems I described above – had no more real existence than the signs of the zodiac) founder on the impossibility of describing such a thought and on the success of scientific theory. If material structures were no more real than zodiacal signs, we could not sensibly use the thought of them for engineering purposes. If they were only our projections, we could not even identify ourselves, or the very words we use, as real. No scientific realist can reasonably deny that there are true descriptions, nor that their truth precedes our statement of them. But no one *need* suppose that 'the mind of God' has any particular plan for the material or any other world (let alone that we know what it is).

---

[8] Richard Owen, *On the Nature of Limbs* (van Voorst: London 1849), cited by Whewell, *Plurality of Worlds*, p. 373. Owen was Hunterian professor of comparative anatomy from 1836 to 1856, and superintendent of the natural history collections at the British Museum from 1856 to 1883.

[9] Goethe, *Selected Works*, ed. D. Links (Penguin: Harmondsworth 1964), p. 152; cited and translated by Robert Murray, *The Cosmic Covenant* (Sheed & Ward: London 1992), p. 158.

Matter takes on form, in all manner of beautiful and entangled ways. Matter itself is the consequence of form: its last diminished reflection. Plotinus, whose system may be the culmination of Greek philosophical enquiry, reckoned that the world extended over space and time was the reflection of eternal form: of course the same forms turned up in different places; of course those forms were hierarchically arranged, so that nothing could be mammalian without also being vertebrate, and nothing vertebrate without also being animal. Of course, not every fantasized chimera could in fact exist. There need be no *design* in this, and certainly no earlier planning phase: horned animals do not have horns 'to defend themselves'.[10] The animals in question are horned because that is what their form requires; one might as well suppose that snowflakes have six arms to grasp the wind. There are simply a limited number of ways to *be* (which is also, to be beautiful), and those ways have discoverable connections.

So the dominant assumption in biology until late in the nineteenth century was that the material world, at any particular time, provided a cross-section of the manifold forms of beauty. Philosophers in the Abrahamic traditions thought that the world had a real beginning, that it was finite both in time and space. Those influenced by Stoic thought concluded that, despite appearances, the reason for all things' existence was to do people good. Mice help to keep us tidy; bed bugs stop us lying in bed too long. But the mainstream view remained far closer to Plotinus' than is now remembered. All living creatures, like diamonds and snowflakes, exist because there are a limited (but very large) number of ways to be, to be beautiful, to declare God's glory. Their resemblance to each other did not suggest, but neither did it preclude, a genealogical relationship. In humankind, it was often thought, the highest beauty possible for extended, temporal things was born. Less anthropocentric theorists acknowledged that oaks, whales and ants were just as perfect 'in their kind' as people.

---

[10] Plotinus, *Enneads* VI.7.10.

The dominant view amongst pagan philosophers was that the world has always been much the same as now, amongst Abrahamic philosophers that it had a definite beginning. In either case, they needed no special explanation for the similarity of living things, any more than for the similar similarities of rivers, mountains, stars and crystals. These are the shapes the world embodies, since otherwise there would not be a world at all. Not all philosophers agreed. Stoics sought to do without 'real forms', preferring to insist that mechanical causation linked the world together in the only possible way. Epicurean philosophers, who sought to explain things as the chance-led coagulation of atomic bits, drew on an insight of the early philosopher and mystic, Empedocles, to 'explain' existing forms: they were just the remains of every possible combination of limbs and organs, risen from the fruitful earth. Aristotle pointed out, in criticism of Empedocles, that limbs and organs were already organized as elements within a larger whole, and that the successful reproduction of viable combinations (on which Empedocles depended) ignored exactly what most needed explanation – namely the similarity of parent and child.[11] There could never have been separate limbs and organs that just chanced to fit together and somehow reproduced whole bodies. The imagined parts that sprang up from the earth were already functioning organisms; if any such organisms demand an explanation then so did they. Existing organisms, Aristotle added, are not put together like artifacts, but grow according to a pre-existing pattern; why should it ever have been different?[12]

Nothing can reproduce itself that is not already a living creature, capable of growth and self-repair. Growth and reproduction, indeed, could be classed together as moulding

[11] Much the same difficulty arises for modern Darwinian theory: 'before Darwinian evolution can start, a certain minimum level of complexity is required' (Davies, *Fifth Miracle*, p. 118).

[12] Lyell's principle, that we should not invoke any processes in explanation of the past that we cannot discover in the present (*Principles of Geology*, 1830, p. xii; see David L. Hull, *The Metaphysics of Evolution* (SUNY Press: New York 1989), pp. 66–7), is sometimes supposed to count in favour of evolutionary change; it is at least as likely to count against it (see below).

available matter to a particular form. Even if new forms came into material existence by the juxtaposition of earlier existents (whole bodies, as it might be, by juxtaposing limbs and organs), it would not be by chance that some such new forms functioned: there must already have been a readiness to work together according to a pattern 'known' to all parties. The limbs must not expect that every other part of the new whole will work just like a limb. Each cell in a multicellular organism must recognize its place within the larger whole, because it contains the template for that larger whole. 'For Kant and the Rational Morphologists [that is, Cuvier, Geoffroy, Richard Owen] . . . an organism was a self-organizing entity whose parts existed for one another and by means of one another.'[13] The idea was Aristotle's too. We now know (or at least suspect) that there have been significant alliances between disparate organisms in our past. Each eukaryotic cell is itself a colony organism, housing bacteria (the mitochondria) that took up residence in larger prokaryotic cells a billion years ago.[14] Perhaps, *pace* Aristotle, every living organism owes its ancestral origin to such conjunctions – but it would still be significant that some worked (and others, by hypothesis, did not), and that they had discovered a reproducible form. The easiest explanation would be that each cooperating part already had a share in the form which was to come to be: two sorts of bacteria could learn to live together because they shared a form (or in our terms, because they both retained traces of a common ancestor).

It is now so *obvious* to educated eyes that all of us are relatives, that we can hardly understand how anyone could have failed to see that horses walk upon their toes, and birds flap their arms to fly. How could anyone not have realized that these homologies were marks of shared descent? How could Whewell have been content to say that 'the skeleton of a man and of a sparrow have

---

[13] Stuart A. Kauffman, *The Origins of Order: self-organization and selection in evolution* (Oxford University Press: New York 1993), p. 7.

[14] Lynn Margulis and Dorion Sagan, *Microcosmos: four billion years of microbial evolution* (University of California Press: London and Berkeley 1997, second edition), pp. 129ff. Prokaryotes, strictly speaking, are now known to belong to two distinct groups, archaebacteria and eubacteria, each as different from the other as either from the eukaryotes which went on to produce multicellular life-forms like ourselves.

an agreement, bone for bone, for which we see no reason, and which appears to us to answer to no purpose'?[15] We are of course aware that some similar organs (eyes, for instance) have evolved independently in several different lineages: the eyes of the octopus are like our own, but not because our shared ancestor (long before the Cambrian) had eyes like that. Embryologically, an octopus's eyes and a mammal's are formed from quite different tissues.[16] No ancestral bees ever built cubic honeycombs, or tetrahedral: any pile of balls will fall into a hexagonal order, and shape the cells accordingly.[17] As it happens, bees are related – but we need more evidence than similarity in hive construction. The homology of human and sparrow skeletons *might* be a similar by-product of engineering efficiency (though I would myself agree that the genealogical explanation is more attractive).

Engineering requirements, or the forms of life, were thought sufficient to explain convergences. Perhaps they explain more than we now suppose – or at least it was not absurd to think so.

The claim that certain limitations of structure inherent in nature explain the relatively few basic patterns that anatomists find in the structure of living organisms was far from implausible at the time.

---

[15] Whewell, *Plurality of Worlds*, p. 330. The claim is not as absurd as it may seem; at any rate, some biologists consider, for example, that the identity of the so-called '9 + 2' array of microtubules in bacterial cell-whips and in the spindles linking chromosomes during mitosis is just one of those things for which we do not know the (engineering) reason. Others suspect a genealogical tie, but the case is unproven; see Margulis and Sagan, *Microcosmos*, pp. 139, 145.

[16] Fascinatingly, it now seems that there is common genetic underpinning, in the *Pax-6* gene and other master-control genes; first announced by Rebecca Quiring et al. in 'Homology of the Eyeless Gene of Drosophila to the Small Eye in Mice and the Aniridia in Humans', *Science* 265.1994, pp. 785–9. Some have concluded from this discovery that the eye did not, after all, evolve on many different occasions: all eyed creatures may turn out to be descended from a single eyed ancestor. This is not to say that *Pax-6* is a gene 'for' eyes, even if the addition of that bit of DNA may, in particular circumstances, result in 'optical monsters' with ectopic eyes. The point is rather that genomes often appear to contain unrealized potentials which can, somehow or other, be turned on.

[17] The point was made by Samuel Haughton ('Biogenesis', *Natural History Review* 7.1860, pp. 23–32, reprinted in Hull, ed., *Critics*, pp. 217–27; see esp. pp. 225–6), who also points out that the solitary humblebees from whom social bees are supposed to have descended (as being fitter) still survive (and so, presumably, were not less fit at all). This assumes too readily, and wrongly, that fitness is an absolute quality.

Explanations in terms of common descent were also plausible. And of course nothing prevents an anatomist from combining the two.[18]

Science-fiction writers, seeking to imagine alien worlds, usually suggest that very much the same range of creatures will exist 'out there' as here. They have this much reason, that our present account of biological history suggests that after every mass extinction new creatures appear that look much like the old, even though they have evolved from different stock. If particular chemicals and their crystalline forms no longer existed there would still be crystals of a similar kind. Things like wolves and dolphins have evolved repeatedly, without occasioning much surprise. Whether things like people are predictable as well, is moot. The popular view in the mid nineteenth century was that there were bound to be alien intelligences 'out there'; Whewell thought it unlikely.[19]

Our predecessors, seeing that creatures superficially unlike each other may nonetheless be significantly the same, accepted this as a fact no more surprising than the similarity, with difference, of rocks, rivers, snowflakes, clouds. The world explores the possibilities. When geological strata showed that still other creatures, like and unlike, had existed once, this did no more, at first, than show new variants on an accepted theme. The same forms are displayed in different regions, with distinctive traits; why not in different periods too? It was not even absurd to wonder whether the rocks themselves were direct copies of the eternal forms: such marks need not be evidence of past life, but only of a universal tendency to take on certain shapes. That, after all, is now the first assumption when we notice complex shapes on other worlds: not that they are signs of life, but only that lots of things 'look living' – especially to people with our sympathies. Those who claimed to see a skeleton in the rocks may once have been no more, nor less, convincing than those who claimed to see a human face upon

---

[18] Hull, *Metaphysics*, p. 72. See also Philip Ball, *The Self-Made Tapestry: pattern formation in nature* (Oxford University Press: Oxford 1999), on the power of *mathematical* explanations of bodily structures.

[19] See Stanley Jaki, *Planets and Planetarians: a history of theories of the origin of planetary systems* (Scottish Academic Press: Edinburgh 1978).

the sands of Mars. Why should pebbles not look like trilobites if frost patterns look like ferns? And if they were after all the relic of such living creatures, this only enlarged the bestiary a bit.

To summarize: the similarities of shape and faculty between different sorts of creature (including us) do not of themselves *demand* a genealogical explanation. Even the apparent existence of now-vanished forms, attested by the fossil record, does no more than increase the range of manifested forms. Once we admit the possibility that parents might have had dissimilar offspring then the fact of our present dissimilarities no longer counts against our literal relationship. Perhaps the nested forms within which extinct and extant organisms can be located are themselves represented genealogically: the logical relationship of animal to vertebrate to mammal to primate is reflected in the passage from some Ur-animal in the long ago to something like *Pikaia*, to a milk-secreting reptile, to a tree-shrew. Each creature contains, potentially, the families that spring from it – though the force of that 'potentially' needs clarifying. Were we ourselves that Ur-animal, when we were 'in' the Ur-animal? It had long been imagined, after all, that all of his descendants were stacked up in Adam's loins, like Russian dolls, waiting to be released into convenient wombs. Even if that were not literally true, might the future be strongly contained within each earlier ancestor? Or was this only to say that the earlier creatures might possibly have descendants of another sort, or else might not? Darwin, replacing archetypes by ancestors, pointed to the possibility that the ancestors we share only with each other (we human beings, we vertebrates) might not themselves be verte-brate or human. Anything at all might have issued from those ancestors, if time and chance had played a different game.[20] Do we *know* that this is true?

---

[20] The difference between strong and weak potential, between a power and a mere possibility, has not yet been completely analysed; we recognize the distinction between a child's *potential* and what might possibly happen to her. The original 'types' of non-Darwinian evolution had potential; Darwinian 'types' have only possibilities.

CHARLES BABBAGE AND CATASTROPHES

Those, like Aristotle, who supposed that the world has always been much the same as now, and that there were no 'first generations', could also think that catastrophes were always leaving just a forgetful few to build the world again. Maybe, in those catastrophes new variants appeared. What went before was no less perfect of its kind – a notion that survives in Sedgwick: 'the reptilian fauna of the Mesozoic period is the grandest and highest that ever lived'.[21] But where did the new kinds come from? To suppose, like Empedocles, that they just sprouted from the earth would seem absurd to any Aristotelian, especially in the wake of Pasteur's refutation of 'spontaneous generation'. If that was possible, so might be pebbles that looked like trilobites: eggs not quite hatched! Aristotle himself conceded that it looked as if shellfish did sprout from nothing, but the basic rule of Aristotelian biology was that living organisms are begotten only by living organisms, of roughly the same sort. If this was a difficulty for any notion of repeated special creations, it was equally a problem for the beginnings of terrestrial life: 'coincidentally, just when Pasteur was proving that contemporary microbes were not generated spontaneously, evolutionary theory required the spontaneous generation of ancient microbes'.[22]

Perhaps God or Nature sometimes does initiate a brand-new world, without any contribution from the old. Cuvier's division of earth's history into the pre-Cambrian, Palaeozoic, Mesozoic and Cenozoic was a step away from the notion that all possible variants must exist.[23] Instead there were four distinct aeons and their associated fauna and flora: cross-sections through the realm of being, or particular ways of realizing all the forms there are. According to Whewell 'each group may, in a general manner, be considered as a separate creation of animal and

---

[21] Adam Sedgwick, 'Objections to Mr Darwin's Theory of the Origin of Species' (7 April 1860); reprinted in Hull, ed., *Critics*, pp. 159–66; see pp. 162–3.
[22] Hull, *Metaphysics*, p. 34; Lyell's principle should have excluded this.
[23] Kauffman, *Origins of Order*, p. 5.

vegetable forms'.[24] 'In what manner, by what agencies, at what intervals, they succeeded each other on the earth'[25] are serious questions. The fauna and flora of successive ages might have been quite different, but it became clear that 'the change from one set of organic forms to another, as we advance in time, is made, not altogether by abrupt transitions, but in part continuously'.[26] How exactly new species came to be, so Whewell thought, we have no present evidence:

We might feel ourselves well nigh overwhelmed, when, by looking at processes which we see producing only a few feet of height or breadth or depth during the life of man, we are called upon to imagine the construction of Alps and Andes; – when we have to imagine a world made a few inches in a century. But there, at least, we had *something* to start from: the element of change was small, but there *was* an element of change: we had to expand, but we had not to originate. But in conceiving that all the myriads of successive species, which we find in the earth's strata, have come into being by a law which is now operating, we have *nothing* to start from. We have seen, and know, of no such change; all sober and skilful naturalists reject it, as a fact not belonging to our time.[27]

This is not to say, as T. H. Huxley sneeringly suggested, that 'a half-a-ton of inorganic molecules might suddenly coalesce as a live rhinoceros',[28] but rather to confess our ignorance of how the new creatures came. Others were prepared to suppose that at the end of ages the survivors of the old began to beget and bear new sorts of creature. In those privileged eras the rule of life ('like father, like son') was bent, but not broken. The first bird hatched from a reptile's (or more probably a dinosaur's) egg.

This speculative scenario would be more plausible if it were true that an organism's character depended not only on its

---

[24] Whewell, *Plurality of Worlds*, p. 161.
[25] Ibid., p. 163.   [26] Ibid., p. 172.
[27] Ibid., p. 176. Whewell here expresses what was to be a major obstacle to the acceptance of Darwin's theory – namely, the lack of inductive support.
[28] T. H. Huxley, *Lay Sermons, Addresses and Reviews* (Macmillan: London 1870), p. 375; cited in Hull, *Metaphysics*, p. 67. Huxley and his successors have repeatedly insisted that there is no 'non-miraculous' alternative to Darwin's theory. This is, historically, false – though it should also be noted that biological theory and observation cannot possibly exclude the occurrence even of miracles.

parents' characters but also on the wider environment. So of course it does – but the variations caused by changes in the environment are not, or so we now suppose, necessarily appropriate to that environment. Once again, it is still part of folk biology that new generations will be better fitted to a new environment. We expect that children born in India will be better suited to India than their European parents were. We expect laboratory-bred mice to be better adjusted to laboratory life than 'wild' animals would be. What could make this true? It may be that selection has done its work very quickly, but theory suggests that such effects are gradual, and very slow: we expect farm and laboratory animals to be far better adapted to their environment than selection would suggest is true.[29] Perhaps appropriate antibodies and hormones are passed to the young while they are in the womb. Maybe these adjustments happen more easily in neonates than in adult forms. But this is to assume that the adjustments are already part of the organism's repertoire, and do not constitute the making of a new kind. This is, incidentally, why industrial melanism in moths does not provide the long-awaited example of Darwinian speciation. So if we take catastrophism seriously it must be that the new shapes were already available, part of the existing biogram which had not previously had a chance to be expressed.

This seems to have been Robert Chambers's thesis. In his *Vestiges of the Natural History of Creation*, first published anonymously in 1844, he proposed that natural developments could *seem* discontinuous, even though it was the same underlying principle at work. Borrowing from Charles Babbage's *Ninth Bridgewater Thesis* he formulated a puzzle which has in modern times been associated with Nelson Goodman's second riddle of induction, and with Wittgensteinian difficulties about 'following a rule'. Babbage asked us to conceive a calculating machine, operating strictly 'by rule', which generated the numbers 1, 2, 3, 4, 'and so on', all the way, by single-unit steps, to 100,000,001.

---

[29] Artificial selection may be faster, because more exact and ruthless, than 'natural': a laboratory or farm animal that would not play its owner's game would not leave many – or any – offspring. In nature there is often a different game to play. But even artificial selection is dependent on the chance arrival of helpful variations.

The obvious inference is that it will continue 'in like fashion' – yet the numbers that follow are instead 100,010,002; 100,030,003; 100,060,004; 100,100,005; 100,150,006, 'and so on' until the 2672nd term. The rule has not changed – but until we passed the hundred million mark there could be no way to distinguish the actual rule from the obvious one. Similarly, Babbage and Chambers reasoned, what seems like a discontinuity in the natural record may only reveal that something else was going on than we had supposed. The very same creatures that were once dinosaurians always had the potential to give birth to birds: dinosaur and bird are simply different appearances of the same nature.

Unsurprisingly, Chambers's work was severely criticized. One reason Darwin was so slow to publish was that he did not want to suffer the anonymous author's fate. The criticism, modern mythology notwithstanding, came from geologists and biologists, not or not only from biblical literalists. T. H. Huxley, later self-appointed 'Darwin's bulldog', was amongst those critics; ironically, it was Chambers himself who bullied Huxley into taking the public stage against Samuel Wilberforce, Bishop of Oxford from 1845 to 1869. That much-mythologized encounter, in its turn, was not between science and religion, but an episode in late nineteenth-century scientific debate.[30] Wilberforce's criticisms of Darwin were standard fare, best expressed by Fleeming Jenkin.[31] As David Hull has pointed out, much of the general opposition to Darwin, as to Chambers, was to their neglect of inductive method: the theory of evolution by natural selection was not a generalization from any – let alone many – observed instances. It was as if someone were to claim that all swans were white, without ever having found a single

---

[30] 'The standard account is a wholly one-sided effusion from the winning side, put together long after the event, uncritically copied from book to book, and shaped by the hagiographic conventions of the Victorian life and letters', Sheridan Gilley, 'The Huxley–Wilberforce Debate: a reconsideration' in Keith Robbins, ed., *Religion and Humanism* (Blackwell: Oxford 1981), pp. 325–40, esp. p. 332. I am grateful to Sheridan Gilley for providing this reference.

[31] 'The Origin of Species', *North British Review* 46.1867, pp. 277–318; reprinted in Hull, ed., *Critics*, pp. 303–44.

swan that was.[32] Chambers's position was even more dangerous: not only could he produce no actual examples of new species emerging from the old, his exposition of Babbage inevitably threw doubt on all inductive generalization. If the evidence that emeralds are and will be green is just the same as the evidence that they are and will be *grue* (that is, green until time t, and blue thereafter), we can never have empirical evidence that they will be green, not grue, after t, any more than we can know from one step to another when some 'obvious' formula will prove unreal.[33] In order to make the natural record rational, it must have seemed that Chambers had abandoned reason. Oaks always produce acorns, but what an acorn is depends on circumstance. The computer was never really acting on the program 'n* = n + 1'; acorns were never what we thought they were, for when the moment comes they will open their wings and fly.

The Babbage–Chambers paradox deserves much more attention: my suspicion is that it can be answered only by a strong, and non-empirical, commitment to taking certain formulae as genuinely universal. But it is understandable that catastrophism of whatever kind seemed less than satisfactory. Different forms were manifested in the fossil record (or the same forms manifested differently). Either there were entirely fresh beginnings or the new creatures were descended from the old. How, as it were, did they know when, and how, to change? Perhaps the transformation was programmed from the beginning, or perhaps there was a sudden intervention by superior power. But either of these postulates looked likely to make all inference vain.

FORMAL AND FINAL CAUSES

Sedgwick criticized Darwin for repudiating final causes, but Darwin was doing no more than fulfil the Enlightenment

---

[32] And incidentally denying that swans were a natural kind in any case, so that generalizations about them could only be accidental; see chapter 5, on natural kinds.

[33] Nelson Goodman, *Fact, Fiction and Forecast* (Oxford University Press: New York 1983, fourth edition); there is a very large philosophical literature on this problem.

demand. Aristotle had distinguished four ways of answering the question 'why?': the so-called Four Causes. 'Why does that green lump look like a frog?' 'Because Jo (its efficient cause) moulded it to amuse her children (final cause), or because it has got a shape which stereotypically reminds us of a frog (formal cause).' 'Why is it sticky?' 'Because it is made of Plasticene (material cause).' Similar answers, so it seemed, could be given to questions about living things: indeed, without some grasp of what an organ was 'for' it would be impossible to say what it was at all. We do not just chance to use our eyes to see: that is what eyes are for, and what eyes are. Aristotle himself did not conclude that someone had those purposes in mind, but only that the organs of living creatures had identifiable functions that helped to explain their presence in the organic whole. Very occasionally, he suggested that a creature's structure or be- haviour had a wider function: sharks roll on their back to bite because it gives their prey a chance to get away.[34] Notoriously, he supposed that plants existed for animals to use, and animals for us – though the remark is less significant in context than it came to seem.[35] It was a later philosophical school that prac- tised an extreme anthropocentrism, finding congenial meaning in the existence of bed bugs, tempests and the smallpox virus. A thing's 'function' is the most important thing that things 'of that sort' do – and it was obvious that nothing could be more important than ourselves! The enterprise gave 'final causes' a bad name: by insisting that the gods did everything for our sake, so Spinoza said, 'the philosophers have made the gods seem as insane as men'.[36] More sophisticated versions of 'the reason why' (that everything is for God's glory, or to manifest eternal beauty in the world of time) avoided arrogant folly, but left us

[34] Aristotle, *Historia Animalium* 8.591b25–6; it is indeed important for any predator, or parasite, that it be not *too* efficient, but it is difficult to see how anything but the efficiency of its prey can prevent this happening. A superlatively efficient predator will do better in the short term even if the result is extinction. The real warning is not for sharks, but for people.

[35] Aristotle, *Politics* 1.1256b15ff. The underlying point could be put differently: without animals, we would die, and without plants, all animals would die. The very fact that we are, ecologically speaking, useless is the mark, for Aristotle, of our higher value!

[36] Spinoza, *Ethics*, tr. S. Shirley, ed. S. Feldman (Hackett: Indianapolis 1982), p. 58 (pt. 1, appendix).

without any idea what God's glory might require, unless we suppose that intellect is infallibly linked to beauty, or that we have His revelation. Since we do not know what He intends, nor how He goes about it, final causes have to be excluded.[37] Knowing what happens (at least so far as spatial alterations go) is much easier than knowing why. The point was not that there *were* no final causes, but that we had no grasp on what they might imply.[38]

Enlightenment philosophers concluded that final causes have to be ignored, and that formal causes give no information. Molière's jesting assertion that opium puts people to sleep because it has a 'dormitive faculty' (that is, a way of putting people to sleep) was taken to show that 'formal causation' is no explanation at all. Efficient causation fared no better. A few philosophers, like George Berkeley, argued that our only empirical grasp of causation was as *action*, or *efficient* cause: the only causes we knew about were ourselves, and other 'spirits'. David Hume observed that we had no empirical grasp of causal power at all: all we could ever see was that things like *this* do follow things like *that*. But the dominant model of explanation came to be the Stoics' reworking of material cause: one thing causes some effect in another only by pushing or pulling in quantifiable ways. Only material, extended objects can be causes. It followed, even before Darwin, that forms and final causes cannot explain biological variety. New species do not emerge to maintain beauty, nor because the forms demand expression at that particular locus. Even crystals take the shape they do as an effect of 'material' causation, because their atomic or molecular bits are pushed and pulled just so. Somehow new species do emerge, and prosper. Somehow, they get their start from some ancestral stock of a somewhat different character. But how?

---

[37] 'We shall entirely reject from our Philosophy the search for final causes; because we ought not to presume so much of ourselves as to think we are the confidants of His intentions' R. Descartes, *Principles of Philosophy*, tr. V. R. Miller and R. P. Miller (Reidel: Dordrecht and Boston 1983), p. 14 (part 1.28). And *Philosophical Letters*, ed. A. Kenny (Clarendon Press: Oxford 1970), p. 117: 'we cannot know God's purposes unless God reveals them'.

[38] Traditional believers might dispute this: surely we know that God intends us to be holy, free and loving? The problem may still be that we do not know what this means.

We now imagine that the chief significance of Darwin's rejection of 'final causation' lay in his rebuttal of the anthropocentric notion that the universe and all terrestrial history were aimed at *us*. That was certainly often Whewell's view. He was so impressed by the intellectual, moral and spiritual powers of humankind that he could see no *better* reason for the world than our creation.

After the long continued play of mere appetite and sensual life, there came the operation of thought, reflection, invention, art, science, moral sentiments, religious belief and hope; and thus, life and being, in a far higher sense than had ever existed, even in the slightest degree, in the long ages of the earth's previous existence.[39]

But the range of final causation was often wider: Richard Owen argued, apparently with some effect, that there *must* be intelligent life on Jupiter, with eyes to see, since otherwise the moons of Jupiter would have no purpose.[40] Whewell responded that they might have the very same purpose as our own moon had in all the ages when there was no intelligent life on earth. In saying so, Whewell himself acknowledged that God might have other beauties in mind than ours. Speaking of the beauty of snowflakes, flowers and crystals, he enquires

What are we to conceive to be object and purpose of this? . . . They are there, it would seem, for their own sake; – because they are pretty; – symmetry and beauty are there on their own account . . . Because there is rule, there is regularity, and regularity assumes the form of beauty. . . God delights in producing beauty.[41]

Owen, and others, had supposed that the expanse of stars and planets would be 'waste' if they were lifeless. Whewell replied that if its being the site of organization and organic life vindicated a spot's existence, it could as well be vindicated as the seat of attraction, of cohesion, of crystalline processes.[42] He might have added that the whole notion of 'waste' or 'wasted energy' is utterly inappropriate in the context of an infinite

---

[39] Whewell, *Plurality of Worlds*, p. 393.

[40] Cited, and disputed, by Whewell, ibid., pp. 51, 299.

[41] Ibid., pp. 360, 362. Plotinus was better advised, in denying that mere regularity was the same as beauty: 'A living face is more beautiful than a dead statue', *Enneads* VI.7.22.

[42] Whewell, *Plurality of Worlds*, p. 207.

Creator. God loses nothing by spreading the world so wide. But Whewell's main comment is apt: the God who contains the archetype of Humanity may also contain innumerable others, and have many other purposes in mind. Whewell, like other Enlightenment philosophers, thought it unwise to think we had an exhaustive account of God's purposes or methods. That the world (including interstellar dust and male nipples) had some point or other, he did not dispute: we should not try to guess what the world 'must' be like merely to give it a point we could imagine.[43]

His caution was commendable. But Darwin denied, implicitly, what Whewell still believed. In rejecting final causes, and reinterpreting 'functions',[44] Darwin was not only denying anthropocentric interpretations of the natural world: those had been disputed for centuries, as they were by Whewell's critics. 'To imagine ourselves of so much consequence in the eyes of the Creator, is natural to us, self-occupied as we are, until philosophy rebukes such conceit.'[45] Darwin was denying that it mattered whether things were beautiful at all: nothing comes to be, or persists in being, because it is good that it should do so. Nothing comes to be or persists in being even because it is good

---

[43] Even Descartes, who sometimes seemed to be prepared to deduce an entire world system from his own first principles, actually insisted that the world he had imagined was only a world God possibly could have made: which one He had *actually* made was not to be learnt by introspection only. 'Seeing that [the parts into which matter is divided] could have been regulated by God in an infinity of diverse ways, experience alone should teach us which of all these ways He chose' (*Principles*, p. 106 (part 3.46)). And *Principles*, p. 286 (part 4.204): 'just as the same artisan can make two clocks which indicate the hours equally well and are exactly similar externally, but are internally composed of an entirely dissimilar combination of small wheels: so there is no doubt that the greatest Artificer of things could have made all these things which we see in many diverse ways' even if He had a single purpose.

[44] A 'function' nowadays – as that the heart's function is to pump blood – is that feature of the organ's activity which played a crucial part in its 'natural selection'; see Ron Amundson and George V. Lauder, 'Function without Purpose: the uses of causal role function in evolutionary biology', *Biology and Philosophy* 9.1993–4, pp. 443–69 (reprinted in David L. Hull and Michael Ruse, eds., *The Philosophy of Biology* (Oxford University Press: Oxford 1998), pp. 227–57), for discussion of the different senses given to the term. Present functions, the present object of selective pressure, need not be the evolutionary explanation of the original organ: feathers, perhaps, were once just thermal regulators. Either way their importance is not what we once thought.

[45] Whewell's critics, as reported by Whewell, *Plurality of Worlds*, p. 66.

for the organism, or the species, or the great globe itself. What Sedgwick saw was that this elimination of objective, causally effective value, left us without a clue. The Babbage–Chambers paradox was ignored, and their theories about evolutionary change denounced, because they seemed to make rational enquiry impossible. Darwin's idea made rational enquiry value-less, and arguably impossible. Fortunately, he managed to conceal the implication.

DARWIN'S DEMOLITION OF SPECIES

Babbage's catastrophism – the suggestion that the *very same* principles extended over time can lead to radically and unpre-dictably different conclusions – is in danger of destroying inference. The opposing, uniformitarian, doctrine proposed that nothing happened in the past that cannot be seen to happen now. Taken literally, it is a foolish limitation: why should we suppose that everything that ever happens has also happened nearby in the brief span of our lives? It certainly does not follow that because no asteroid or comet has crashed into us during recorded history, then such things never happen – particularly since its happening would probably end recorded history. It is clear that there have been serious catastrophes, eliminating most of the then-existing species. Some commenta-tors have suspected that most evolutionary change takes place after those catastrophes, as the survivors branch into new niches. But uniformitarian presuppositions still remain. If comets have not crashed, small meteors have; maybe we have not seen the continents collide, but something like such episodes can be modelled now. Catastrophes are only interruptions, and whatever happens afterwards is no different in *essence* from the everyday slow variation that Darwin proposed. Many lineages were abruptly ended, but the survivors soon filled up the space.

If new species are not responses to a changed environment, whether by celestial forms or by the formulae innate in living organisms, where do they come from? Darwin's earliest critics commented that his title, *The Origin of Species*, was a misnomer: strictly, he never explained how any new species came to be,

precisely because he denied that *species* were significant.[46] In
the old view, species are interbreeding populations of creatures
that share, or seek to share, a distinct form. Any individual of a
species may be maimed, deformed, perverted, but no such
alteration will transform the species. There are variations
within the species which do not constitute deformity at all, and
some such variations prosper in particular environments.
Speckled moths survive much better on soot-darkened trees,
and give way to whiter cousins when the air is clean. Such
familiar truths do not prove that any new species can be formed
by natural selection – unless a species is no more, essentially,
than a variety. On Darwin's account a species is only a set of
populations united by a common ancestor and barred from
interbreeding with other populations,[47] and so perhaps preserving – or drifting to create – a different range of characters. Dog
breeders have produced all manner of varieties from the
ancestral stock, but all such breeds are *dogs*. Accordingly, so
critics said, the analogy with artificial selection proved nothing:
we have never created a new species. But suppose that all
existing dogs save Irish wolfhounds and chihuahuas were
exterminated: the remaining stocks could never – without
surgical intervention – share descendants, and would be different species. A species, then, is only a variety that has lost its
chance to interbreed with others of its sometime kin. No
essential change occurs in wolfhounds or chihuahuas when
their cousins are killed: beforehand they were one species, but
not thereafter.[48]

Darwin's insight, or insistence, was that there were no
species, in the old sense, at all. There were no distinct kinds,
resembling each other solely by convergence to particular

---

[46] 'Perhaps a less elegant but more apposite title for Darwin's book would have been *On
the Unreality of Species as shown by Natural Selection*'; Elliot Sober, *The Philosophy of Biology*
(Westview Press: Boulder, Colo. 1993), p. 143.

[47] This concept of a species clearly cannot apply to asexual organisms, which reproduce
by cloning. It is also probably too restrictive in botany and bacteriology.

[48] There are similar cases in nature, notably 'ring species' such as the different
populations of Arctic gulls which would be identifiable as different species if only
their Scottish populations were considered. See Morton Beckner, *The Biological Way
of Thought* (Columbia University Press: New York 1959), pp. 61ff.

forms. The appearance of such kinds was a product of the death of all the intervening organisms. Once this step is understood we can see why industrial melanism has seemed, to Darwin's supporters, to clinch the case, but seemed, to his critics, to be quite irrelevant. The Darwinian account treats all variations alike. The older view supposed that difference *between* kinds was of another order – and did not necessarily equate a *species* with a *kind*.

That last point is implicit in the story I have been telling. The ancient claim was that there were a limited (though immensely large) number of real ways of being, which were constantly reflected in the biological world, very much as the different crystal classes are. Crystals, for some purposes, may be classified by their chemistry (as sodium chloride or ammonium sulphamate). For other purposes, they can be classified as cubic or orthorhombic or the rest. Their material roots are one thing, and their form another (though their molecular structure too turns out to be a function of the mathematical possibilities). Convergent species converge on one form or template, but are unlikely to achieve it so successfully as to be able to interbreed. In one way they display the same *species*, the same 'lowest form'. Wider groupings, kinds, are such that variation in their properties creates new varieties: the 'same' limbs or organs are heavier, smaller, thinner and the like. Difference between such kinds is of another order: it is not that squids have *larger* limbs than seals, but that they have an entirely different body plan. In a sense, they do not even have larger *eyes* than seals, since the organs are formed from different tissues and by different stages.

That there are such radically different kinds is 'obvious': no imagined routine of stretching or squashing could produce a squid from a seal, whereas just such stretchings and squashings could transform at least the model of a seal into the model of a walrus or a dog. 'We cannot fit both beetle and cuttlefish into the same framework, however we distort it; nor by any coordinate transformation can we turn either of these into one another or into the vertebrate type.'[49] Perhaps those

---

[49] D'Arcy Wentworth Thompson, *On Growth and Form*, ed. J. T. Boner (Cambridge University Press: Cambridge 1961; first published 1917), p. 321.

transformations, to be realistic, will be some simple mathematical function, as Thompson suggested. Organisms are transformed holistically, not by an arbitrary change in one limb or organ at a time.[50] Once again, Darwin transcended everyday experience. Variation within a breeding species could produce apparently different breeds, although those variations could be bred back to the norm. Variations within a wider 'species' or kind could be conceived as larger transformations of relative shapes and sizes. Variation between such kinds might also have their origin in some ancestral form. Oak tree, squid and seal are utterly different, but even they may show similarities that could be clues to a shared ancestor that looked very unlike them all. Of course, their similarities might be simple necessities, independently discovered. But they might also be inherited. Where Owen saw nested archetypes, Darwin posited ancestors.[51] We are alike because we are related.

This conviction is now so firmly fixed, at least among educated Westerners, that we can hardly conceive it otherwise. It is difficult even to remember that there are several Darwinian claims: that we are related to each other; that our differences are accumulated gradually; that natural selection is the explanation for those differing accumulations. That there was ever any alternative to any of these claims is almost impossible to recall. 'Obviously', all opposition to the Darwinian theses must have been reactionary, and is now the province of the ignorant or stupid ('or wicked, but [he would] rather not believe that'[52]). The slightest suggestion, on the part of a respectable academic, that 'creationists' might have a point to make, is greeted with alarm or wondering contempt. Even those who reveal, in

[50] Which opens up the un-Darwinian possibility that radically different forms *might* emerge in a single generation, rather than being the product of innumerable tiny changes.

[51] Charles Darwin, *The Origin of Species* (Dent: London 1971; first edition 1859) pp. 413, 420; see C. Patterson, 'Introduction' in C. Patterson, ed., *Molecules and Morphology in Evolution: conflict or compromise* (Cambridge University Press: Cambridge 1987), pp. 1–22, esp. p. 3.

[52] So Richard Dawkins, in the *New York Review of Books*, cited by Alvin Plantinga, *Books and Culture*, May/June 1996, at <http://id-www.ucsb.edu/fscf/library/plantinga/dennett.html>.

practice, that they are influenced by old ideas, now do not dare to say so. Science-fiction writers, as I remarked before, tend for all sorts of reason (including dramatic convenience) to depict alien worlds that are full of the same sorts of living thing as we encounter (including bipedal vertebrates with familiar faces and a human language). In the older view, this might be expected just because the template of human life was the eternal Word. Nowadays it demands a different explanation, which is usually given by 'panspermia', whether natural or directed. Francis Crick, one of the founders of modern genetic theory, has proposed that someone (a galactic civilization, say) infected the early earth with the seeds of life, and so there are many things like us 'out there'. The story depends, of course, on thinking that those early seeds strongly contained the outcome, rather than (as seems more likely) making this outcome possible along with indefinitely many others. Why it is easier to believe, without a shred of evidence, in such galactic engineers, than in the infinite intellect of God, who knows?

The danger perceived in Darwin's theory was that he ignored the template (or the templates). Others had explored the possibility that there were family trees, linking all existing creatures and those of earlier ages in a genealogical web. But the dominant view was that there must still be distinct kinds, because there were different ideal forms. Humankind was one such kind, unlike and like all others. Hybrids were sometimes possible, and even 'throwbacks' (not necessarily to an ancestral form, but to a more general type). Defects were failures of the relevant form to master matter. Ideally, we might conclude, we should all look alike: our differences are defects.[53] Ideally, so some might hold, there would be nothing living but the Human Form; others, and even on occasion Whewell, might agree that there were other noble forms than Man. Darwin's theory demands a different reckoning – though he himself continued to expect that distinctions grew more definite over time. The

---

[53] Though that was not Plotinus' view: *Ennead* v.7.1.18–23, 'No, there cannot be the same forming principle for different individuals, and one man will not serve as model for several men differing from each other not only by reason of their matter but with a vast number of special differences of form.' Difference is not always defect.

gap between the ape and human exists because the intervening creatures are extinct: some day the apes and 'the savage peoples' will be extinct as well, and the gap between the baboon and a humanity superior even to the Caucasian will be comfortingly wide.[54] That humankind itself would divide into many species, genera, families (and that the most prolific might not even be the most intelligent) is an idea that he only hinted at. Of all his ideas it is the one we most need to understand, and answer.

DARWIN'S EARLY CRITICS

I have sketched the background to Darwin's insight at such length because it is now so commonly assumed that the opposition was from biblical literalists or 'the established Church'.[55] All budding scientists are taught to believe that science itself took shape as part of the rebellion against an established order. It is widely supposed that 'in the Middle Ages' (a period flexibly extended from Augustine until Francis Bacon) people believed (and 'the Church' desired them to believe) that the earth was flat, that the sun went round the earth, that everything began six thousand years ago, and that Aristotle had all the answers to all 'scientific' questions. Clerical or religious opposition to Charles Darwin, typified in the unfortunate Bishop Wilberforce, and since associated with 'the Monkey Trial' in Arkansas, is all part of a conspiracy to keep control. No doubt such conspiracies do exist. The paradox is that 'scientists' now claim just the same authority as priests once did, to determine what is rationally believed: it is undeniably agreeable to have the pleasure both of

---

[54] Charles Darwin, *The Descent of Man* (Princeton University Press: New Jersey 1981; a facsimile of the 1871 edition), vol. I, p. 201, citing Schauffhausen, *Anthropological Review* (April 1867), p. 236. The belief that black men were closer to the apes, attested in Darwin's German popularizer, Haeckel, and elsewhere, is a lot closer to Darwin than his admirers think; cf. A. Kelly, *The Descent of Darwin: the popularization of Darwin in Germany 1860–1914* (University of North Carolina Press: Chapel Hill 1981), p. 117; D. Gasman, *The Scientific Origins of National Socialism* (Macdonald: London 1971).

[55] Davies, *Fifth Miracle*, p. 248, for example, speaks of the 'very public clash between Darwin and the Christian Church' (apparently thinking of the debate between Huxley and Wilberforce). Davies himself, unknowingly, lends his support to many of the criticisms mounted against Darwinism.

being respected sages and of identifying in imagination with persecuted rebels. Outsiders may perhaps be excused for wondering whether our most militant 'scienticists' would have been heretics or inquisitors if they had lived some centuries ago.

The historical truth is that no one in the 'Middle Ages' thought the earth was flat.[56] Dante's *Divine Comedy*, indeed, explicitly depends on an earth that is not. That the earth went round the sun was a notion advanced by clerics (Nicholas of Cusa, and Copernicus), largely on the aesthetic ground that the sun would make a more glorious centre for the world, and widely accepted in advance of empirical evidence as part of a Renaissance cult of human intellect. Heliocentrism did not humiliate us by removing us 'from the centre' (that is to say, the bottom[57]) of the world; on the contrary, it exalted us (especially in Giordano Bruno's heresy) by showing that we were already sailing through the heavens, and could reach beyond the scenery to real causes. That the earth was made, and history began, a relatively short time ago was a story told in the context of an infinite Creator. Only a moment separates us from our world's beginnings. The earth is an infinitesimal point in comparison with the heavens.[58] Our history is but an instant in comparison with God's eternity. A similar notion is regularly popularized in the comparison of world history to a single year: humankind arrives a moment or so before midnight on 31 December. Whewell, like George Berkeley a century earlier, criticized those who used the Hindu and Egyptian Scriptures to suggest that humankind had been around for many tens of thousands of years longer than the Hebrew Scriptures seemed to say. They were right to criticize, even though, in the event, it

---

[56] Cosmas Indicopleustes (*c.* 548) produced a text which proclaimed that theory, partly on the basis of literal-minded exegesis of the Scriptures – but there are eccentrics in every age. It would be at least as easy to locate bizarre opinions in present-day popular literature as in that of the Middle Ages: it does not follow that they are widely believed. That Columbus had to persuade influential flat-earthers appears to have been a legend invented by Washington Irving; see Owen Gingerich, 'Astronomy in the Age of Columbus', *Scientific American* (November 1992).

[57] 'The lowest depths of the universe', according to Augustine, *Sermones* 18, 1.

[58] Boethius, *Consolation of Philosophy* 2.7: 'that is, compared with the magnitude of the celestial sphere, it may be thought of as having no extent at all'.

has turned out that we had underestimated the length of human prehistory. Aristotle, and even Aristotelians, claimed no complete or infallible knowledge of the world, but part of Renaissance ideology derived from the rediscovery of Platonism as an alternative to Aristotelian common sense. Platonism gave more credit to mathematical speculation than Aristotle ever did, and provided a reason to believe that human beings could uncover hidden truths. 'The Intellect of Man is a spark of the light by which the world was created'.[59] One of the many ironies of history is that it was this Platonism which later seemed to be opposed to Darwinism, though it was itself the source and excuse for science. Darwin offered an ideology that was in many ways more congenial for established authority than the Platonic.[60]

The Church, at any rate of England, soon accepted Darwin as an honourable and creative man, and most scientists soon professed themselves converted – though they did not always agree to *Darwin's* theory. 'The view of evolution that was popular among scientists in the second half of the nineteenth century was saltative, directed, and progressive'.[61] Some of those who thought of themselves as Darwinists expounded the

[59] Owen's paraphrase of the Cambridge Platonist, Nicholas Cudworth, as cited by Whewell, *Plurality of Worlds*, p. 375.

[60] It is widely supposed that Plato defended 'the class structure', and urged unfailing obedience to the 'upper' classes, on the basis of a deliberate lie to the effect that they were of a more noble 'metal'. On the contrary, Plato explicitly rejects the claim of 'aristocrats' to be the better rulers. Only those who have been shown, experimentally, to be courageous and compassionate, clear-sighted and incorruptible individuals, can be trusted with such power: in their absence, *no one* has authority to rule. Darwin, on the other hand, was taken to suggest that the upper classes had already proved their fitness.

[61] Hull, *Metaphysics*, p. 53; that is, they assumed that new species emerged rapidly and that later kinds were better than those they replaced. Darwin, so we now suppose, proposed a different theory. Denys Cochin, a French Catholic scientist turned politician, remarked approvingly that though Darwin 'offers us monkeys for ancestors, at least he promises that we will not have them for children', *L'Evolution et la vie* (Paris 1886), pp. 269–70 cited by Harry W. Paul, *The Edge of Contingency: French Catholic reaction to scientific change from Darwin to Duhem* (University Presses of Florida: Gainesville 1979), p. 67. It is worth recalling that Darwin's theory could itself be viewed as an evolving individual: there is no eternal 'essence of Darwinism' which must be shared by all, and only, Darwinists any more than there is an 'essence of Abrahamism', or 'mammalkind' (see Hull, *Metaphysics*, pp. 268–9). I shall have more to say about essences below.

same theory as those who thought, more plausibly, that they were anti-Darwinists! His critics found fault with his theory not because it contradicted Genesis but because it was too speculative for their taste, because it abandoned any notion that the way things *should* be affected how things were, and because (at least in his successors' hands) it identified whatever was most 'noble' in humanity with what was thought ignoble, and offered no real hope of progress except to oppressors. We cannot easily now appreciate the degree to which 'apes' struck civilized observers as loathsome parodies of the human. Precisely because they looked 'almost human' it was difficult not to see what they were doing as base: bestial in a far more real sense than what was done by less human-seeming beasts. We have ourselves been coached to believe that chimpanzees are friendly and amusing innocents – to the point where it comes as a shock to realize that they can also be cannibalistic, infanticidal, violent, abusive and neglectful (just like us). The thought that *we* are apes is likely now to be associated with the thought that we could manage quite well in small, anarchical communities (with lots of sex). In the nineteenth century (not necessarily less realistically) it meant that we are selfishly and sensually indifferent to nobility, that all our rhetoric about the grandeur of humanity is only an ape's breast-beating (and probably that we *want* lots of sex).[62] According to Whewell,

The thoughts of Rights and Obligations, of Duty and Virtue, of Law and Liberty, of Country and Constitution, of the Glory of our Ancestors, the Elevation of our Fellow-Citizens, the Freedom and Happiness and Dignity of Posterity, – are thoughts which belong to a world, a race, a body of beings, of which any one individual, with the capacities which such thoughts imply, is more worthy of account, than millions of millions of mollusks and belemnites, lizards and fishes, sloths and pachyderms, diffused through myriads of worlds.[63]

Darwin clearly implied that human beings are simply a set of primate populations, having the characters that chanced to help

---

62 See Glendon Schubert and Roger D. Masters, eds., *Primate Politics* (Southern Illinois University Press: Carbondale and Edwardsville 1991), for a discussion of the changes in political fashion that are reflected in changes in ethological description.

63 Whewell, *Plurality of Worlds*, p. 368.

their ancestors to breed, and owing nothing to any objective beauty.[64] But in that case, Whewell's praise is only panegyric.

The simplicity of Darwin's theory now conceals from us the moral and metaphysical difficulty of what he said. On the one hand, science was held to be inductive, that is, it progressed by forming useful, law-like generalizations from accumulated instances. On the other hand, despite a century's distrust of formal and final causes, it was widely supposed that there were distinct ways of being, or ways of being beautiful, to which the natural world was constantly approximating. Physicists in the grip of that idea sought out 'beautiful equations' whose scope went far beyond the observations. Darwin did the same, so introducing deduction to biology, while also denying the efficacy of just those beautiful forms on which the physicists, implicitly, relied. Darwin also spoke at length of the 'nobility' displayed in human compassion, while simultaneously arguing that only incompetents would choose their worst stock to breed.

Berkeley's comment on the possible effects of an earlier form of scepticism seems appropriate:

The morals of a people are in this like their fortunes; when they feel a national shock, the worst doth not shew itself immediately. Things make a shift for a time on the credit of old notions and dying opinions. But the youth born and brought up in wicked times, without any bias to good from early principle or instilled opinion, when they grow ripe must be monsters indeed. And it is to be feared, that age of monsters is not far off.[65]

Why should we suppose that any ingrained, 'natural' morality will be enough to maintain civility, once our young are taught that there are no true 'objective' values, and that our 'instincts', if we have them, are only the survivors of a Darwinian winnowing? 'What beauty can be found in a moral system, formed, and governed by chance, fate or any other blind,

---

[64] There is a certain oddity in the phrase, since we now constantly suppose that 'the objective or objectifying gaze' is one that denies all value to its object (which cannot therefore be perceived as beauty).

[65] George Berkeley, 'Discourse to Magistrates', *Works*, eds. A. A. Luce and T. E. Jessop (Thomas Nelson & Son: Edinburgh 1948–), vol. VI, p. 221; see also 'Alciphron', ibid., vol. III, pp. 130–1.

unthinking principle?'[66] If the young are taught that they are only animals, will they not behave as they think 'animals' behave? Why *should we not* be alarmed?

But what exactly was the theory Darwin proposed? Seeking an explanation for the survival of particular variations, he read (he later said) Thomas Malthus's grim suggestion, first published in 1798, that any population vastly outstrips its food supply (a little oddly, since its food supply is just another such population), and that almost all the creatures of a given generation therefore starve to death. 'Man tends to multiply at so rapid a rate that his offspring are necessarily exposed to a struggle for existence, and consequently to natural selection.'[67] Malthus's later editions acknowledge that this is not always happening, and therefore conclude that there are devices in place to slow down such population growth.[68] In nature, nothing breeds until it has an appropriate territory or social place; in human society, the poor should exercise restraint.[69] But suppose that Malthus's first grim prophecy is correct. In that case, Darwin saw, it would be the creatures with some slight advantage over others that would leave most living offspring. In so far as their advantage was transmitted to their offspring, there would be more with that trait in the next generation. Creatures that breed without the resources to take care of their young can only leave *any* descendants by leaving so many to fend for themselves that a few will manage to survive. The alternative is to take care of only the few they have. So by infinitesimal stages the population would 'improve'. Each surviving generation would, on average, be 'fitter' than the one before. That 'fitness' might reside in almost anything: strength, craftiness, endurance, or mere fecundity.[70] Almost any trait, in

---

[66] Euphranor speaks; 'Alciphron', ibid., p. 128.

[67] Darwin, *Descent*, vol. I, p. 185.

[68] David Stove, *Darwinian Fairytales* (Avebury: Aldershot 1995) is not entirely fair to Darwin in making Darwinism dependent on the truth of Malthus's first account. Even if population pressure rarely has that stark effect, it is still true that creatures are not equally successful in their attempts to breed.

[69] Darwin, *Descent*, vol. II, p. 403: 'both sexes ought to refrain from marriage if in any marked degree inferior in body or mind'.

[70] It is clear that Darwin initially had in mind those characters and practices which did the *individual* some good. But of course by those criteria it might happen that

appropriate circumstances, can explain greater success as a breeder. Consider, for example, phenylketonuria. In our ordinary environment, this condition is 'unfit', since sufferers are damaged by normal dietary doses of phenylalanine. The problem can be contained by imposing a strict diet, low in phenylalanine and high in tyrosine. This is, by present standards, unpleasant and expensive.[71] But if our dietary environment were to be changed, it would be the rest of us, who probably need phenylalanine, that suffered and failed to breed. There may be traits that are 'absolutely unfit', but we cannot always know just what they are: most 'unfitnesses' are relative.[72]

Generalizing the idea, we find that, given three conditions, evolutionary change is inevitable.

(i)   Individual members of a species have different properties.

(ii) Some individuals, because of their different properties, have more offspring than those with others.

(iii) Offspring resemble their parents.

Huxley, reading the suggestion, thought how silly it was not to have seen it for himself. In fact, others had made the same

impoverished Irish were less *fit* than Scots, and yet had many more children. As Mr. Greg puts the case [so Darwin tells us]: 'The careless, squalid, unaspiring Irishman multiplies like rabbits: the frugal, foreseeing, self-respecting, ambitious Scot, stern in his morality, spiritual in his faith, sagacious and disciplined in his intelligence, passes his best years in struggle and in celibacy, marries late, and leaves few behind him. Given a land originally populated by a thousand Saxons and a thousand Celts – and in a dozen generations five-sixths of the population would be Celts, but five-sixths of the property, of the power, of the intellect, would belong to the one-sixth of Saxons that remained. In the eternal "struggle for existence", it would be the inferior and *less* favoured race that had prevailed – and prevailed by virtue not of its good qualities but of its faults' (Darwin, *Descent*, vol. I, p. 174, citing W. R. Greg, *Fraser's Magazine* (September 1868), p. 318. Stove, *Darwinian Fairytales*, p. 46 points out that Greg was actually arguing *against* Darwin, and that the article is entitled 'The Failure of "Natural Selection" in the Case of Man'. The properly Darwinian theory was that fitness was proved by successfully outbreeding rivals: the fit are those that survive to breed because of some inheritable trait. That final phrase, insisting that there must be a *reason* for success, is what rescues the theory from tautology.

71 According to Philip Kitcher, *The Lives to Come* (Allen & Unwin: London 1996); see E. Nichols, *Human Gene Therapy* (Harvard University Press: Cambridge, Mass. 1988) for recipes. It is worth observing that the 'unpleasantness' of the recipes might be remedied by hiring better cooks.

72 Which is why Stephen Jay Gould's conviction (expressed in *Wonderful Life: the Burgess Shale and the meaning of history* (Penguin: Harmondsworth 1991)) that those creatures of the Burgess Shale who seem to have left no descendants were really just as fit as those that did cannot be substantiated.

discovery, including Alfred Wallace, whose manuscript triggered Darwin's own publication, and Edward Blythe, whose published work Darwin had almost certainly read (and never acknowledged).[73] Richard Owen's comment was perhaps a little ungracious, describing the theory as

no very profound or recondite surmise; it is just one of those obvious possibilities that might float through the imagination of any speculative naturalist; only, the sober searcher after truth would prefer a blameless silence to sending the proposition forth as explanatory of the origin of species, without its inductive foundation.[74]

But he had a point, and perhaps some excuse for his annoyance, since Darwin had chosen to suggest that the *only* alternative to his theory was a belief in special, miraculous creation (whereas Owen believed, and had said, that there was another explanation in the theory of archetypes). Whewell too had noticed something similar, that the *extinction* of species could readily be explained by 'natural causes' (ones still working in the world we know).[75] It is not so clear that their origin can be explained like this. The idea, for example, that there were once plant forms fitted to years of different lengths (and only the ones that chanced to match the actual length of the terrestrial year survived) struck Whewell as 'too gratuitous and extravagant to require much consideration'.[76] Rather than suppose that all imaginable forms existed (and were culled), it is better to suppose that only some imaginable forms are genuinely possible, and required.

But let us grant that creatures of a given kind do vary, and in such a way that they manage to leave, on average, more offspring than their fellows. Let us also grant that the character

---

[73] See Loren Eiseley, *Darwin and the Mysterious Mr. X* (Dent: London 1979); Erasmus Darwin also has a claim to have originated the idea.

[74] Owen, 'Darwin', in Hull, ed., *Critics*, p. 195.

[75] Whewell, *Plurality of Worlds*, p. 178.

[76] Whewell's *Bridgewater Treatise, Astronomy and General Physics considered with reference to natural theology* (William Pickering: London 1833, second edition); cited by Hull, *Metaphysics*, p. 33. The suggestion that there have been or are indefinitely many other universes, mostly inhospitable to life, might be regarded as an equally gratuitous hypothesis for the explanation of this universe's fitness for such living things as us; see J. Barrow and F. Tipler, *The Anthropic Cosmological Principle* (Clarendon Press: Oxford 1985) for a lengthy discussion of associated problems.

that won them this advantage is transmitted to their offspring, and continues to make them fit. It does not follow that the population will change indefinitely, however long the process lasts. Suppose that speed is a survival characteristic for antelopes, and slower antelopes are eaten. It does not follow that there will, in each generation, be antelopes faster than there were before, until they are breaking the sound barrier as they fly. No antelope (so far as the argument has yet gone) will ever be faster than the fastest antelopes were before. All that has happened is that there will be fewer slow ones. As Fleeming Jenkin[77] said in his review of *The Origin*, the notion of indefinite variation 'seems no more accurate than to conclude that because we observe that a cannonball has traversed a mile in a minute, therefore in an hour it will be sixty miles off, and in the course of ages that it will reach the fixed stars'.[78]

A separate problem, also posed by Jenkin, was that superior variations would almost certainly be lost. Offspring resemble their parents, yes, but in any sexual species, they resemble *both*. Suppose a shipwrecked mariner, of plainly superior type, secured a high position among the natives of the land. No doubt his qualities 'would certainly tend very much to preserve him to a good old age', and he might have many offspring from his many wives. 'Yet he would not suffice in any number of generations to turn his subjects' descendants white.'[79] Jenkin's example, though racist, is not silly: any inherited characteristic is likely to be lost to view – unless, as Mendel was to show, it happens to depend on one particular allele in the genetic code. In that case, the variation might be replicated perfectly in some proportion of the top dog's descendants, and they too will succeed (though they probably will not be white).

Or at least they will succeed if the same character is still the fittest. Darwin's insight was that domestic animals are bred to

---

[77] 1833–85; Professor of Engineering at Edinburgh from 1868.
[78] Jenkin, 'Origin of Species', pp. 277–318, see Hull, ed., *Critics*, p. 306.
[79] Jenkin, 'Origin of Species' in Hull, ed., *Critics*, pp. 315–16; Jenkin here assumed, like Darwin, that the 'white race' was superior in wit and energy to any other. Whewell, as we shall see, did not.

exhibit the character we want because we choose which animals will breed, and *carry on until we have the effect we want*. It does not follow that this will happen in nature unless the very same character continues to have the edge, for natural causes, for long enough, irrespective of other characters. Once again, do we know this to be true?[80] We may believe that a sparrow's world is very much the same as yesteryear, and that much the same characters will give a sparrow an advantage (even when other sparrows have them too). But this may be an illusion. Actually, life changes all the time, and what served our grand-parents (or the sparrow's) well enough may now not do as well. If the situation is the same, then selection tends to preserve the existing norm, cutting off careless, lazy, unattractive sparrows. If the situation is rapidly changing, perhaps different sorts of sparrow will get their chance – but in that case, it is not clear that the *same* characters will be in demand for long enough to change the species. In fact, the very success of a variation over a little while may make it less successful later on. Animals of the kind game-theorists call 'hawks' (which always seek to get the upper hand against their kin) will profit only as long as they are not facing hawks: when hawks face hawks they will lose more often than their meeker kin, the 'doves'. The net effect may be to ensure that most animals back down sometimes. Many species have stayed much the same for millions of years.[81] Many species have vanished without trace. Is it obviously true that others will be gradually changed, and how?

If there are to be novel species the rate of sustained, one-directional selection must be 'just right', and there must be *new* variations, not previously part of the species' repertoire, for

---

[80] Maynard Smith recognizes the difference between natural and artificial selection: 'In nature more than one phenotypic trait is exposed simultaneously to selection . . . Selection in nature may be intermittent, or may reverse its direction . . . The response to artificial selection depends on genetic variability already present, whereas in evolution there *must* be, in the long run, a balance between the exhaustion of variability by directional selection and its generation by mutation' (J. Maynard Smith, *The Evolution of Sex*, Cambridge University Press: Cambridge 1978, p. 12; my italics).

[81] Oddly, some commentators then say that they are 'stagnating', like *Australopithecus*, and it becomes important to locate some sudden change that started up the evolutionary race once more.

selection to work on. 'But this theory of the origin of species . . . simply amounts to the hypothesis that, from time to time, an animal is born differing appreciably from its progenitors, and possessing the power of transmitting the difference to its descendants. What is this but stating that, from time to time, a new species is created?' [82]

Jenkin's question was only answered decades later, with the (partial) unravelling of the genetic code. Phenotypic characters (that is, the characters displayed by individual organisms) often depend precisely upon particular bases in the nuclear or mitochondrial DNA of the fertilized cell from which the creature grows. However urgent it is that antelopes speed up, nothing demands that any such change occur (though even scientists who thought that they were Darwinists sometimes failed to see this truth). But if it did, it would have some chance of survival. There must still be physical limits, but the process of random change and rigorous selection may perhaps evade them. Antelopes may never travel faster than sound, but – if their lineage survives at all – they have some chance of changing. Perhaps, indeed, that is exactly what they have done: once upon a time, their ancestors were not antelopes, and moved more slowly. The problem remains of tracking, in imagination, the route by which each novel variation gained sufficient advantage over others to spread through a population. Once upon a time, a population of vaguely mice-like creatures produced a sport who jumped from twig to twig. In successive generations, other appropriate changes offered themselves (each helpful enough to give its owner an edge) until at last the sometime 'mice' were bats. Over the same period other descendants of the 'mice' frolicked in the surf, and slowly bred their descendants to be whales. We can *believe* this, but imagination falters when asked to conceive how each new trait first happened and then spread through *the very same population*. The only available reply is to say 'It *must* have done', because in fact there are bats and whales (and tigers, antelopes, porcupines and people) who bear the evidence of their own relatedness.

[82] Jenkin, 'Origin of Species' in Hull, ed., *Critics*, p. 318.

The modern myth is that Darwin *proved* we were all related, and that our variations were selected as the fittest available within each lineage. Nature is doing, more consistently, what we now do to our domestic cattle – and ourselves. Locking up and executing criminals, so Darwin said, is breeding us a law-abiding race (or would do, if we sterilized the Irish too).[83] In fact, Darwin proved no such thing, and his theory, after its first success, fell into disrepute for decades, partly because he had no answer to Jenkin's arguments.[84] 'Anyone', he said, 'whose disposition leads him to attach more weight to unexplained difficulties than to the explanation of a certain number of facts will certainly reject my theory.'[85] Many did, though they did not always realize they had. Variation only occurs up to some limit; unique mutations, if they occur, would be swiftly absorbed back to the norm; natural selection for new kinds must be

[83] Darwin, *Descent*, vol. i, p. 172: 'malefactors are executed, or imprisoned for long periods, so that they cannot freely transmit their bad qualities. Melancholic and insane persons are confined, or commit suicide. Violent and quarrelsome persons often come to a bloody end. Restless men who will not follow any steady occupation – and this relic of barbarism is a great check to civilization – emigrate to newly-settled countries, where they prove useful pioneers.' Ernest A. Hooton, and others, wished the strategy to be more ruthlessly employed. 'The elimination of crime can be effected only by the extirpation of the physically, mentally, and morally unfit, or by their complete segregation in a socially aseptic environment' (*The American Criminal* (Harvard University Press: Cambridge, Mass. 1939), vol. i, p. 309, cited by Stephen Jay Gould, *The Mismeasure of Man* (W. W. Norton & Co.: New York 1981), p. 111). So did Ernst Haeckel and his Monist League: 'The "redemption from evil" [for the ill, deformed and criminal] should be accomplished by a dose of some painless and rapid poison' (*Wonders of Life* (Harper: New York 1904), pp. 118–19, cited by Gasman, *National Socialism*, p. 95).

[84] See Peter J. Bowler, *The Eclipse of Darwinism: anti-Darwinian evolution theories in the decades around 1900* (Johns Hopkins University Press: Baltimore and London 1983); G. K. Chesterton was right to think that Darwinism was then in decline, and right to insist that it was Darwinists who had to prove their case against doubters (*Fancies versus Fads* (Methuen: London 1923), pp. 186ff.). He was also right to ask about 'the survival value of features in their unfinished state', even if he was wrong to equate this with the question of what to do with 'half a wing'. That there *must* have been a path from the wingless to the winged condition, and that each step *must* have given an evolutionary advantage, is even now an article of faith, not an empirical observation.

[85] Charles Darwin, *Origin of Species*, p. 453. How a *false* theory could explain anything, and why we should not regard the 'difficulties' as refutations, remained unanswered. Admittedly, successful scientific theories often do pass through a period when they raise more problems than they, putatively, answer. See Paul Feyerabend, *Against Method: outline of an anarchistical theory of knowledge* (New Left Books: London 1975).

neither too slow nor too quick;[86] each step upon the labyrinthine routes from mouse-like thing to bat, whale, antelope,
tiger, porcupine and person must somehow have been advantageous for the very same population. At the end of Darwin's
theory we are left with the old miracle: somehow or other, new
species are created. The enormous rhetorical power of Darwin's
theory (compounded of Darwin's persona, the weight of detail
and the unvoiced rejection of causally effective form) helped to
sustain it, as a curiosity, until Mendelian genetics seemed to
provide an answer to some (not all) of the problems. Even now,
many who *think* they are Darwinists only believe that living
things are relatives, and have missed the really distinctive
features of the theory.

One further gloss: Darwinism, as first expounded, claimed
that human races varied in their competence and virtue. That
savage tribes will vanish from the world, and that the *poor* or *the
Irish* should (unless the noble Anglo-Saxon foolishly prevents
their passing), is repeatedly affirmed in *The Descent of Man*. It is
easy to believe that this was only a passing fancy, to which even
humane intelligences in Victorian Britain were not quite
immune. It is worth recalling that Whewell wrote far otherwise:

We have good reason to believe that there is no race of human beings
who may not, by a due course of culture, continued through generations, be brought into a community of intelligence and power with the
most intelligent and powerful races. This seems to be well established,
for instance, with regard to the African Negroes . . . And we cannot
doubt that, in the same manner, the native Australians, or the
Bushmen of the Cape of Good Hope, have human faculties and
human capacities.[87]

We may be prone to regard ourselves as standing at the summit of
civilization; and all the other nations and ages, as not only occupying
inferior positions, but positions on a slope which descends until it
sinks into the nature of brutes. And yet how little does an examination
of the history of mankind justify this view! . . . How different have
been the forms of civilization among the Chinese, the Indians, the

---

[86] It may be that the organisms themselves define the direction, by their persistence in
particular strategies: the role of 'choice' was emphasised by Alistair Hardy, *The Living
Stream* (Collins: London 1965).

[87] Whewell, *Plurality of Worlds*, p. 182.

Egyptians, the Babylonians, the Mexicans, the Peruvians! And yet in all, how much was displayed of sagacity and skill, or perseverance and progress, of mental activity and grasp, of thoughtfulness and power.[88]

Even from . . . an abject race [debased and degraded under adverse conditions], if a child be taken and brought up among the comforts and means of development which civilized life supplies, he does not fail to shew that he possesses, perhaps in an eminent degree, the powers which specially belong to man.[89]

Darwinism was suspect not only as a theory which demanded more imaginative credulity than many could muster, but as an ideological defence of racist and antagonistic attitudes. For exactly the same reasons, it appealed to many.

THE MENDELIAN SYNTHESIS

Darwinism fell into disrepute for many years, in part because of its ideological associations, and in part because of the unanswered questions about the source, and stability, of the variations necessary for evolutionary change. When it was at last revived, in conjunction with Mendelian genetics, one feature of Darwin's own account turned out to be entirely wrong. Darwin had assumed that an individual's own character and behaviour might affect what its offspring inherited. Obviously, this might, in part, be true. Facts and fables about, for example, congenital syphilis, suggested that children might indeed be damaged, and their children's children, by what parents did. The stock would be damaged by drunkenness, debauchery, disease and degradation. It was implicit in Darwin's class consciousness that the children of those who had risen in the world must be of better stock than those who had not: to have risen at all is proof of an innate superiority, but also a guarantee that one's children will be better still. Later generations, released from ignorance and avoidable disease by the Welfare State and the Education Act, are likelier to believe that the poor were never 'genetically

---

[88] Ibid., p. 185.
[89] Ibid., p. 188; those in search of such an 'abject race' might consider the Ik described, and – probably unfairly – vilified, by Colin Turnbull in *The Mountain People* (Cape: London 1973).

unhealthy'. On the contrary, by Darwin's theory, they had been bred to be clever, strong and prolific. It was the aristocrats who married heiresses who were doing their stock more damage.[90] But his theory, on this point, seems not to have influenced his views.

We civilized men do our utmost to check the process of elimination; we build asylums for the imbecile, the maimed, and the sick; we institute poor-laws; and our medical men exert their utmost skill to save the life of every one to the last moment. There is reason to believe that vaccination has preserved thousands, who from a weak constitution would formerly have succumbed to smallpox. *Thus the weak members of civilized societies propagate their kind.* No one who has attended to the breeding of domestic animals will doubt that this must be highly injurious to the race of man. It is surprising how soon a want of care, or care wrongly directed, leads to the degeneration of a domestic race; but excepting in the case of man himself, hardly anyone is so ignorant as to allow his worst animals to breed.[91]

The aspiring middle classes, and the *deserving* poor, were best of breed.

Weismann's Law distinguishes *soma* and *germ plasm*.[92] Almost nothing that an individual organism does or suffers will affect its seed. Over the course of a lifetime the genes carried in each living cell will suffer damage, from chemicals or chance radiation. They will also, it seems, grow old, as *telomeres* (which is to say, *end bits*) break off or decay from the end of chromosomes. It is, it seems, the gradual removal of those *telomeres* which tells the cell to stop dividing (and so die). Cancerous cells, in contrast, do not turn off. Living cells with damaged genes hand on the damage to the cells into which they divide, and the whole

---

[90] An heiress, by definition, is likely to be an only child; the aristocrats were therefore selecting their mates from relatively infertile families. 'Noble families are continually cut off in the direct line' (Darwin, *Descent*, vol. I, p. 170). Francis Galton, Darwin's cousin, suggested that breeding from such heiresses had another effect, by filling the House of Lords with people 'characterized by a more than common share of shrewd business capacity, possibly also by a lower standard of commercial probity than at present' (*Memories of my Life* (Methuen: London 1909), pp. 314–15, cited by Gould, *Mismeasure*, p. 76). It is possible that this is a joke.

[91] Darwin, *Descent*, vol. I, p. 168; my italics.

[92] So reproducing the division between the organizing Form and Matter. The parallel, indeed, goes further: the transcendent, unaffected Form affects Matter via the *immanent* Form, just as DNA affects the *soma* via RNA.

organism ages, misbehaves, grows cancerous or senile. Similar damage is also done to the cells that are specialized to produce gametes, but those gametes are checked more carefully before their combination is allowed to produce a new member of the species. If too much damage has been done the sperm or the ovum does not function at all; even fertilized ova may not survive their testing. If some damage has still been done (but insufficient to abort the embryo), at least there will (in most sexual species) be two copies of each chromosome, and the new organism will most probably grow up much like its parents (and without their acquired flaws).[93] Weismann's Law is not absolutely true. Bacterial populations, in particular, may be able to transmit acquired immunities to subsequent generations,[94] and viral infections may affect the genome. It may even be that Chambers was right to suspect that environmental stimuli could activate unusual patterns of growth and behaviour, which are then passed on to later generations.[95] But popular belief in the effects of sudden surprises, too much education, or personal depravity is apparently unsound. We can all be glad to believe that every child is a new beginning, unhampered by its parents' errors – except, unfortunately, that its parents bring it up.

There is no need to describe the genetic apparatus in any detail: there are multitudes of popular expositions, and annual

[93] This is one reason to be nervous about the transfer of nuclear genetic material from an adult organism into a deliberately emptied zygote: the material transferred has almost certainly been seriously damaged, and the failure rate for such experiments in cloning is enormous; on which, see below. The Roslin Institute's Dolly (the first animal cloned with a nucleus taken from an adult sheep) is, so far, healthy; whether the loss of *telomeres* will affect her ageing, or her offspring, is so far unknown.

[94] Bacteria reproduce asexually, but also exchange genetic information by 'transduction'. Some even excrete DNA, to be ingested by chance passers-by. From which it follows that a 'war on germs' is one of the most foolish strategies that we could have. Bacteria, in effect, are far more like a *single* population than a bunch of species, and are equipped to adapt themselves far faster than we can. Some recent science fiction explores the thought of what 'intelligent' bacteria could be like: Greg Bear, *Blood Music* (Gollancz: London 1986); Orson Scott Card, *Xenocide* (Legend: London 1991), and *Children of the Mind* (Tom Doherty Associates Inc.: New York 1996).

[95] 'The members of a clone of *Daphnia* can have different morphologies: for example, they develop spines in the presence of predators. The change in morphology is adaptive; it occurs in response to an environmental stimulus; and once it has occurred, it is transmitted through the egg. Almost certainly, it is caused by changes in gene activation and not by changes in the base sequence', John Maynard Smith, *Evolutionary Genetics* (Oxford University Press: Oxford 1998, second edition), p. 11.

revisions of the Geneticists' Bible for professionals who wish to know the current state of theory.[96] Briefly, all living organisms known to us depend on the same genetic code, constructed from four chemical bases arranged in the molecules collectively identified as DNA. Bases A (adenine) and T (thymine) are paired, as also C (cytosine) and G (guanine). When the molecule is unzipped, appropriate bases from the cellular environment join up with each unzipped half, and the molecule is thereby reduplicated. It is the linear arrangement of the bases that in turn determines what particular proteins are manufactured: messenger RNA is a copy of DNA (except that T is replaced by U (uracil)). Each triplet of bases (AAC or AGA or AGC, and so on), except the three which act as 'Stop Codons', thereby determines the production of an amino-acid which in turn combines within the cellular environment to form polypeptides, proteins and so, eventually, the expected organism. The matter is made more complex in that the bases can, at least in some organisms, be read from a different starting point, and so simultaneously give the code for different proteins. It has also turned out that not all the triplets have a phenotypic effect. In eukaryotes, some stretches of DNA (introns) are automatically snipped out from the mRNA before they generate the proteins they would otherwise determine. According to some estimates, indeed, almost all the several billion bases in the human genome are 'junk DNA'. This cannot be entirely true. If there are too many repeated 'introns' on the chromosome the organism may be variously damaged (as in the case of Tay-Sachs syndrome). It has also been suggested that the presence of large amounts of 'junk DNA' (whether introns, or the mass of DNA that is not even translated into mRNA) may explain why some species have remained more or less unchanged for many millions of years. In either case, the unexpressed DNA is having some effect, even though no proteins owe their existence to it. In eukaryotic organisms, the nuclear DNA is not the only genetic determinant: mitochondrial DNA, inherited in the

[96] For example, Christopher Wills, *Exons, Introns and Talking Genes* (Oxford University Press: Oxford 1992); Steve Jones, *The Language of the Genes* (Flamingo: London 1994); Kitcher, *Lives to Come*; Davies, *Fifth Miracle*.

maternal line, also has effects on the proper working of the newly created organism.[97]

Any of the original bases might be replaced in either of the paired chromosomes (one from each parent), or in the mito-chondria. In many cases this has no effect at all, since the third base in a triplet is often redundant, so that several different triplets code for the same amino-acid – a fact which sometimes allows mutations to accumulate that would otherwise have been eliminated early.[98] Even if the resulting triplet encodes a different amino-acid, there may be no phenotypic effect, since the other chromosome carries the original base. Even if both are altered, this may make no difference to the function of the resulting protein, since similar codons result in similar amino-acids. Parts of either or both chromosomes can be reduplicated, or reversed, or eliminated, with various effects. Elimination of a base may be especially damaging, since all subsequent codes will be altered (by removing the second A, say, from a line reading AGT ACT GCT CGA, we would instead have AGT CTG CTC, and so on). What is strange is that so many of these arbitrarily altered and miscopied strings can still result in viable organisms. Some changes do have lethal, or at least severe, effects, but most seem to allow the amino-acids to fold up into functioning proteins. This present volume has far fewer char-acters than the human genome (indeed, the library from which you borrowed it may well have fewer characters), but I could hardly hope that it would survive the excision, reduplication or reversal of any substantial part of them, let alone that the resulting volume would be better written or contain more truths. It probably would not even contain more falsehoods. The genome is amazingly robust, as though the proverbial monkeys managed to type Shakespeare's plays with new and broadly acceptable variants every day.

These arbitrary alterations in the code are the source of

---

[97] The fertilizing sperm inserts a little paternal mitochondrial material, but this seems to be eliminated early in the cell's division.

[98] And so makes it possible for natural selection to do more than stabilize existing successful types: so S. Ohno, *Evolution by Gene Duplication* (Springer Verlag: New York 1970).

variation. Does this amount to saying, with Jenkin, that the neo-Darwinian theory is just that new species sometimes emerge and prosper? That may be so. But the dominant version of the theory would deny it: the phenotypic changes caused by piece-meal variations in the genome are likely to be small, and most will be disadvantageous (in the sense that the resulting organism may be too ill to breed at all). The subtle changes that we have so far managed to identify are not quite so lethal, at least as long as there are better versions on the other chromosome. Because such alterations have no very bad effects they can be carried on to another generation. In some cases, they might even (as single copies) have good effects. It seems that either of two small alterations helps their organisms to resist malaria. But when the organism receives copies of those genes from both of its parents, it suffers from either sickle-cell anaemia (among those of African descent) or thalassaemia (in Mediterranean stock). The various alterations that lead, in double dose, to cystic fibrosis, may similarly offer some protection against cholera. Possessing the gene as a heterozygote does no damage at all, and may do good; possessing it as a homozygote, in two copies, may be lethal. Many Ashkenazi, similarly, carry the genes for Tay-Sachs syndrome, but their children will only suffer the disease if they chance to receive copies from both parents. The Ashkenazi community has been able to avoid the problem by testing the young and keeping careful records, and strongly discouraging marriage between two carriers. We may all, even without such records, discourage cousins from marrying each other, since they are likelier to carry some matching bases that might have damaging consequences for a quarter of their children.[99]

The most convinced neo-Darwinists, who do not necessarily represent majority opinion among biologists although they dominate the media, demand that *every* variation have an edge against its rivals, before it can expand into the local gene pool. Each infinitesimal step must be in the right direction, or it will be unmade. It is strange that the demand be made, since it

[99] I confess to some hesitation about this, since my father's parents were first cousins.

renders evolutionary change even less imaginable. It seems easier to suppose that many alterations are neutral in their effects (if they have phenotypic effects at all), until they chance to accumulate, and be evoked, in some suitable environment (so that something like Chambers's hypothesis is true). We do not need to suppose that literally every widespread character was always or ever advantageous. The only surprise would be if it had been lethal at an early age. Huntington's disease (resulting from two copies of an altered base) permits its victims, as well as its heterozygotic carriers, to breed. Till recently, it need not even have been true that Huntington victims had fewer descendants than the norm. Maybe they did not even have much shorter lives. Even now, implausible as it might seem that anyone who knew the risks would wish it, victims might even seek to have *more* offspring, early, so as to have a better chance of a long line. Attempts to prove that common characters are, technically, advantageous (or recently were) seem to depend on thinking that Darwinian evolution must be at an end, that everyone and everything is perfectly adapted. Faced by the obvious absurdity of that claim, advocates may say instead that once we were: back before industrialization, agriculture, or the end of the last Ice Age, we were 'in harmony'. Our modern ills are the effect of trying to run a global, industrial civilization with creatures bred to be hunter-gatherers in the tropical rain forests.

This strange belief in a pre-agricultural Eden, and its associated therapies, is a topic for another occasion. One further modification of the neo-Darwinian theory seems important (though some have held, I think mistakenly, that it is rather an alternative to neo-Darwinian theory). Small populations snatched from disaster by no wit or power of theirs may happen to share some character more plentifully than a larger population. That character may have been neutral, or even disadvantageous even in its heterozygotic form, and yet be sufficiently plentiful as to determine that small population's way of living. If only some Irish, say, survived a world disaster, it would not be unreasonable to expect a larger number of redheads in all future generations than if only Japanese survived,

even though being redheaded confers no obvious advantage
(and may even be associated with higher levels of skin cancer in
late middle age than brunettes suffer).[100] Even without disasters
of that magnitude, in small populations 'genetic drift' will fix
some types 'by chance'.[101]

Again, even though Mendelian inheritance avoids the
'blending problem' which Darwin's critics raised, it is still true
that many characters (height, skin colour, hairiness) may be
governed by so many alleles that the effect of promiscuous
mating is to blend them all. We expect the future generations of
a multi-racial Britain to be a prettier colour than the present
pallor. That they are also likely to be taller is presumably
explained by better nurture (though this improved environment
may also reveal what was hitherto concealed: that some lines
are always likely to breed shorter adults than some others).
Similarly, if domestic dogs were left alone to breed, we can
expect that most of them will end up looking much like
mongrels. The distinctive traits of wolfhound, terrier, bulldog
and chihuahua are saved because their breeding pools are
artificially confined. It follows that evolutionary change is
easier, swifter and more distinctive in relatively smaller populations, where the accidental traits can be preserved even if they
are not, in themselves, advantages. It is probable that many
new species owe their origin to accidental isolation when a river
flooded, or an avalanche cut off the only exit from a valley, or a

---

[100] Human beings, it should be added, are astoundingly alike, perhaps because we
passed through an evolutionary bottleneck not very long ago. Richard Lewontin has
suggested that 'if the holocaust comes and a small tribe deep in the New Guinea
forests are the only survivors, almost all the genetic variation now expressed among
the innumerable groups of over four billion people will be preserved' (cited by
Gould, *Mismeasure*, p. 323). But this is just to say that the Founder Effect has *already*
had its way!

[101] 'In a finite population, the frequencies of different types will fluctuate from
generation to generation, in the absence of natural selection . . . [and] one type will
ultimately become fixed by chance', Maynard Smith, *Evolutionary Genetics*, p. 26. In a
parthenogenetic population of N individuals it will be only 2N generations before
all the members of the population will be descended from *one* of the original
population, whether or not that single individual had any heritable character that
made it recognizably fitter than the rest. 'Mitochondrial Eve', the postulated
ancestress in the maternal line of all living human beings, was no fitter than her
sisters.

pregnant finch was blown to the Galapagos.[102] Catastrophists may have been right to think that change was associated with a global die-off of the earlier kinds, but genetic drift within small populations does not need global disaster to have a global effect. What was once one species easily becomes a multitude, if only the population is broken up, by chance. As long as those mouse-like creatures who were our ancestors were only one breeding population, the routes by which they became both whales and bats seem unimaginable. If skinny-dipping led to more offspring than any other technique, how was it that leaping from twig to twig did too?[103] But if the mouse-like creatures were already, accidentally, split up, with somewhat different characters, by chance, that had hitherto been neutral, the history is easier to conceive.

In fact this story helps to answer the question Darwin did not: how do *species* happen? Why is it that populations stop being able to breed with other populations of the very same stock? One answer may be just that differences accumulate if the populations are kept separate for long enough: differences sufficient to make courtship, copulation, or successful fertilization difficult. It may then be 'advantageous' not to waste time and effort courting those who are likely to be too different. Perhaps Darwinian evolution gives an edge to those not tempted by miscegenation. But it would surely be just as plausible to suggest that a creature capable of breeding that bit more widely than its rivals would have extra chances.[104] Specialized species, maybe, should not risk producing hybrids, less capable of their refined activities; but the hybrids themselves might be the better generalists, and so absorb the

---

[102] Darwin varied in his views about the importance of geographic isolation (Hull, *Metaphysics*, p. 235), presumably to elevate the significance of *selection* over *genetic drift*. Not all Darwinians agree.

[103] Not to mention eating grass, eating the grass-eaters, burrowing after worms and beginning to compose their family tree.

[104] Octavia Butler's *Xenogenesis: Dawn, Adulthood Rites, Imago* (Gollancz: London 1987, 1988, 1989) conceives an extraterrestrial species that is equipped to breed with *any* other species to produce hybrids with that same capacity. Presumably they must be shape-changers, and perhaps have conscious control of their own biochemical condition. It is tempting to say that no such creature could *evolve*, but that would be to place limits on Darwinian evolution that Darwinists are loath to concede.

specialists. Are generalists less choosy in their mates? Do generalists or specialists leave more descendants?

To those questions I have no empirical response – except to observe that a *speciating* lineage is likelier to leave more descendants, over the long run, than a lineage which keeps itself one species, whether generalist or specialist.[105] The mouse-like things from whom all mammals are descended have descendants as the stars of heaven. If there is a sibling species left undivided since that day, we can be sure that there are fewer individuals of that sort than there are other mammals.[106] By turning into several different species, a population also slows down the spread of viral and bacterial infection. And even if one species turns out to be vulnerable to changing circumstance, the rest may not be. So it may be that we can plausibly conclude that *speciating* is itself a Darwinian advantage, and that most presently existing species will retain the tendency to speciate if they can. More crudely, most creatures will prefer to mate with other creatures like (though not too like) themselves, and thereby create a gene pool that effectively isolates them from a wider group within which evolutionary change is slower. The alternative, to refuse to speciate, is preferred when generalists are what we need to breed, or when the environment is both unvaried and unchanging.

Darwin himself, and many of his contemporaries, fondly expected that there would one day be a Caucasian species (and perhaps a Mongol). The other human species would have joined the Neanderthal. There are racists, of whatever variety,

[105] In the cichlids of the East African Rift lakes, for example, 'the two sets of jaws, fine-tuned according to food habits, allow each species to occupy its own very specific ecological niche. In this manner, hundreds of species can co-exist without directly competing. If instead these cichlids had tried to exploit the same resources, most would have been driven to extinction', Melanie L. J. Stiassny and Axel Meyer, 'Cichlids of the Rift Lakes', *Scientific American*, February 1999, pp. 44–9, esp. p. 48. It may be true that the species-making tendencies of individuals would, in some circumstances, be less fit than the species-preserving tendencies of other individuals, in which case the fitter *species* would not last long enough to prove its fitness. But I do not see why this should be universally true.

[106] This will not always be true at every taxonomic level: there are, for example, more individuals of *Homo sapiens* than there are of all the species of *Pan*. But our species is still a very varied one, and scattered – perhaps *more* varied than are *Pan paniscus* and *Pan troglodytes*.

now who hope to avoid miscegenation, and create new species in their images. It is not long since we were prepared to hunt Australian natives to extinction, and cheat native Americans of their claims under every treaty that we swore. Perhaps we did the same to Neanderthals, and all the other hominids whom we recall in folklore as dwarves, goblins, elves and ogres. Our original sin, perhaps, was to refuse our brothers and sisters the title and entitlements of *humanity*.

CHAPTER 2

Moral and metaphysical assumptions

IDEOLOGY AND TRUTH

It is hardly surprising that Darwinian ideology and Darwinian theory aroused debate. Any orthodox believer must accept that there can in the end be no opposition between truth and truth. If this is how we have evolved, so be it. But our emotions were soon engaged, on either side. Whewell's comments on another theory (that the heavens swarm with life) are apt:

This is a stupendous view of the greatness of the creation; and, to many persons, its very majesty, derived from magnitude and number, will make it so striking and acceptable, that, once apprehended, they will feel as if there were a kind of irreverence in disturbing it. But if this view be really not tenable when more closely examined, it is, after all, not wise to connect our feelings of religious reverence with it, so that they shall suffer a shock when we are obliged to reject it. I may add, that we may entertain an undoubting trust that any view of the creation which is found to be true, will also be found to supply material for reverential contemplation. I venture to hope that we may, by further examination, be led to a reverence of a deeper and more solemn character than a mere wonder at the immensity of space and number.[1]

Whewell's warning, of course, could also be directed at those who believe that evolutionary change must have been guided by Platonic archetypes, or that all life sprang fully formed from the ground (though they will have different reasons from a reverence for magnitude and number). But the fascination of the Darwinian and neo-Darwinian story should also not be under-

[1] William Whewell, *Of the Plurality of Worlds* (John W. Parker & Son: London 1854), pp. 222–3.

estimated. It has an appeal of its own, a 'grandeur' of its own, and one that has affected even orthodox religious. All of a sudden, features that had seemed incomprehensible now turned out to be a sign of shared descent. All of a sudden, we were told – though not openly by Darwin himself – that our common characteristics were 'all for the best'. Rich and poor were exactly where they were bound to be – or they would be soon. Suddenly, we could believe that terrestrial history was immensely longer than the days of Europe (as we had earlier realized that the world is also larger). It is almost as exciting to *realize* that we are mammals, and have millions of non-human kin as competent in their way as ourselves, as it would be to encounter extraterrestrial intelligence. Plenty of believers have concluded that it is *right* to believe in neo-Darwinian evolution – not just because it fits the facts, but because it fits their own religious views. Plenty of self-styled non-believers have been deeply moved by its magnificence.

But others, not unreasonably, had doubts, and have them still. Darwin himself condemned (though he also used) 'the principle of exclusion', the thought that once we have eliminated the impossible, whatever remains is true.[2] This might be true in the abstract – but we have no guarantee that we have thought of all the real alternatives.[3] The fact that the housemaid and the Colonel *could not* have done it, does not prove that the butler did, unless we can show that no one and nothing else did either. The argument from Occam's razor is also flawed: the fact that only the butler could have done it *by himself*, does not establish that he did. In either case, if we would be damaging the household or the village with our suspicions, we might reasonably keep quiet. Even those who insisted that the Lord had made the earth in six days only, and Adam from the dust of

[2] Darwin, *Autobiography*, ed. Nora Barlow (Collins: London 1958), p. 84, cited by David L. Hull *The Metaphysics of Evolution* (SUNY Press: New York 1989), p. 38.

[3] Which is why we should be wary of evolutionary theorists who insist that such-and-such *must* have happened. Steven M. Stanley, for example, argues that *Australopithecus afarensis must* have spent a lot of time in the trees, since otherwise they would all have been eaten (*Children of the Ice Age: how a global catastrophe allowed humans to evolve* (W. H. Freeman & Co.: New York 1996), pp. 87–8): perhaps they tasted bad? This is not an altogether frivolous suggestion: that is how shrews survive. But there may be many other more authoritative or comforting explanations.

the ground, had more than 'fundamentalist' concerns. It had been the believers who had long maintained the unity of humankind against the claims of 'science'.[4] Mythographers of science occasionally sneer that 'the Church' debated whether women, or American Indians, 'had souls', as though 'the Church' wished to deny the claim: the point was that women, and American Indians, *did* 'have souls', and all were fully human. The Spaniards whom Darwin so despised took the trouble to debate their treatment of the Indians, and drew the true conclusion that they merited the same respect as any human creature.[5] Those who claimed otherwise were 'free-thinkers' or court philosophers, disposed to argue that only the fully 'rational' (North European) male deserved respect. Not unreasonably, believers suspected Darwin or his followers of a similar fancy. What Genesis declares is that male and female are one flesh, that all human peoples are created from one stock, that children shall not be sacrificed, nor folk enslaved for ever. Even if some tribes were granted higher status, this was not because of any innate character. Even if brothers were rivals, they might hope for peace. Some stories spoke of God's judgement against particular peoples, and later books appeared to suggest that Israel might be His tool in this, even to the point of excusing genocide. The stories swiftly came to pose problems

[4] Louis Agassiz (1807–73, of Harvard University), one of Darwin's opponents (and himself the one to identify the evidence for the Ice Age), claimed that Negroes, Mongols and Caucasians *must* be different species, but not because of anything the Bible claimed (since in fact it said the opposite): his opposition to evolutionary theory was also not clearly founded on a biblical Christianity, but on ideological prejudice and the supposed results of 'science'. See Stephen Jay Gould, *The Mismeasure of Man* (W. W. Norton & Co.: New York 1981), pp. 42–50; and A. Hunter Dupree 'Christianity and the Scientific Community in the Age of Darwin' in David C. Lindberg and Ronald L. Numbers, eds., *God and Nature: historical essays on the encounter between Christianity and science*, (University of California Press: Berkeley 1986), pp. 351–68.

[5] 'Today it is becoming increasingly evident that no other nation made so continuous or so passionate an attempt to discover what was the just treatment for the native peoples under its jurisdiction than Spaniards', Lewis Hanke, *Aristotle and the American Indians* (Hollis & Carter: London 1959), p. 107; see also Anthony Pagden, *The Fall of Natural Man* (Cambridge University Press: Cambridge 1982). Hanke also quotes 'the prominent Quaker John Archdale' who claimed, in the eighteenth century, that 'Providence had reserved the extermination of the Indians for the "*Spanish* Nation, and not for the *English, who in their Natures are not so cruel*"' (Hanke, *Aristotle*, p. 100; my italics).

of interpretation (which I shall not address), but it should at least be noticed what the sins were that called for judgement. We can learn from Ezekiel what it is to turn one's back on the laws: the man of violence 'obeys none of them, he feasts at mountain shrines, he dishonours another man's wife, he oppresses the unfortunate and the poor, he is a robber, he does not return the debtor's pledge, he lifts his eyes to idols and joins in abominable rites; he lends both at discount and at interest. Such a man shall not live'.[6] Consider also the offence of passing children through the fire 'to Molech' (or 'as a burnt offering').[7] Consider the iniquity of Sodom: '*This* was the iniquity of your sister Sodom: she and her daughters had pride of wealth and food in plenty, comfort and ease, and yet she never helped the poor and wretched.'[8] Perhaps *all* of us are variously 'degenerate', since Ezekiel and the other prophets regularly report that Israel, which is all of us, has done worse than Sodom. The evolutionists proposed instead that 'the greater part of the human race must be considered as being lapsed or declined from the original type. In the Caucasian or Indo-European family alone has the primitive organization been improved upon'.[9]

Earlier attempts to show that women, or American Indians, or Negroes, or the Irish were not quite human at least conceded that there were common goods, and that a civilized humanity might aspire to share them. The Darwinian synthesis declared instead that none of us was guided by a glimpse of real beauty, nor the wish to share our goods. The qualities selected over evolutionary time were those that gained an advantage for the self, or for its offspring. Even self-sacrificial heroism or parental care is only preserved because the relatives of heroes and of caring parents prosper; or, to put it more realistically, heroes and caring parents are dupes. The prosperous are easily

---

[6] Ezekiel 18.10–11.   [7] 2 Kings 23.10.

[8] Ezekiel 16.49–5. The sin of Sodom, in short, was not 'sodomy', but callousness in the use of wealth and power.

[9] Robert Chambers, *Vestiges of the Natural History of Creation* (1844; reissued by Leicester University Press: Leicester, and by Humanities Press: New York, in 1969), p. 309. Darwin abandoned 'the original type', but his judgements on the different races made the same distinctions.

convinced that they deserve their wealth. Irish and 'blacks' and 'dagoes' were defined as lesser breeds, susceptible to vice and superstition. By creating a 'liberal', mercantile economy, the Anglo-Saxon has established a proper testing-ground, as long as he is not led astray by 'noble folly' (which is what Plato's Thrasymachus called justice[10]).

Present-day Darwinism, though less overtly racist, has similar ideological overtones. 'Unselfishness' cannot last long, except as a rhetorical device: the only lasting strategies are ones that favour our close relatives, or secure a swift return. Ideals of nobility are only tricks. Fidelity is equally fictitious: males are bound to be promiscuous;[11] females may be choosier, but have good reason to bind as many males, consecutively or simultaneously, as possible. Natural inhibitions against incest, cannibalism, infanticide and lies are merely weak restrictions against wasting time. 'Morality has no other demonstrable ultimate function than to keep human genetic material intact.'[12] The theorists who urge us all to be Darwinists sometimes disclaim these morals (as Huxley also did); it is not clear why, nor how.

There are Darwinian variations. Peter Kropotkin's demonstration of the possibilities of mutual aid was one of the earliest responses to an ideological individualism.[13] Malthus's nightmare scenario, of mass starvation and the ethics of desperation, is not a permanent reality.[14] Famines do occur, but most lives are lived in times of plenty (obviously, since living things are *themselves* the plenty[15]). The most successful strategy, Kropotkin urged, is very rarely to trample down one's rivals: at all levels of biological interaction (molecular, individual, collective) the

[10] Plato, *Republic* 1.348d.
[11] Amongst fruitflies 'the female is extremely discriminating; in contrast, a male will dance with and attempt to mount a blob of wax on the end of a bristle, moved in an appropriate side-to-side way and then held still', J. Maynard Smith, *The Evolution of Sex* (Cambridge University Press: Cambridge 1978), p. 168.
[12] E. O. Wilson, *On Human Nature* (Harvard University Press: Cambridge, Mass. 1978), p. 167.
[13] *Mutual Aid* (Heinemann: London 1902); Kropotkin (1842–1921) was a Russian prince, an experienced natural historian, and an anarchist.
[14] See Daniel P. Todes, *Darwin without Malthus: the struggle for existence in Russian evolutionary thought* (Oxford University Press: New York 1989).
[15] A point made by I. I. Mechnikov (1845–1916); ibid., pp. 87–8.

most successful agent is the one that best makes friends, and best makes itself invaluable to others. Tyrants, rapists, murderers do not prosper; even murderous tribes, in the end, do not prosper.

But even this response ignores the problem. Such strategies survive because they work: they survive, that is, because the strategists, in the long run, leave more offspring than their rivals can. Recent accounts of the Darwinian theory identify 'the genes' as what survives (whether in literal offspring, or amongst our kin). 'The genes', it is said, determine strategies, and always select the ones that will work 'the best' (that is, will have most chance of preserving genes). There is considerable confusion in the language used. Genes, it is said, are 'selfish', because the ones that survive are those that managed to leave most carriers in each generation. That there are such metaphysical 'genes' at all may seem surprising: all that empirically exists is DNA, or particular bits of DNA curled up inside the cells. The idea that any physical bit of DNA *survives* fertilization, division, and the subsequent creation of the new creature's gonads is obscure. All that survives are copies, accurate or not. Even if genes desired offspring, they would not be strictly selfish: only philoprogenitive. Desiring nothing, they perhaps determine (or the processes of natural selection, 'choosing' among the phenotypic effects of the whole genome, determine) just what strategies are likeliest to be common. Those strategies do not have to be 'selfish' even if the genes are 'selfish': they may benefit other organisms with or without those genes, and may do so with no ulterior motive.[16] The idea that 'self-sacrificial behaviour' needs some special explanation, or even that deliberate celibacy needs a special explanation, does not bear enquiry.

Those who model themselves on predators forget that there are always fewer predators than prey: large, fierce animals are rare, and ones that prey on large, fierce animals are rarer still. To that extent, it is possible to preserve some sort of humane society even amongst Darwinists. Those who mockingly insist

---

[16] As David Hull remarks, 'there is no reason why a book must be named *The Selfish Gene. The Altruistic Organism* would do as well and be no more misleading' (*Metaphysics*, p. 284); it would, admittedly, be much less 'sexy'.

that kindly and cooperative creatures are bound to be targeted, and defeated, by the unscrupulous are being naive. There are other ways of winning than the use of violence and fraud, and many ways to disarm the dangerous. But despite these answers the ideological effect of neo-Darwinism has been to ratify the claim that only idiots or hypocrites are 'altruists', and that the 'real motive' of all action is self-interest. 'Given a full chance to act in his own interest, nothing but expediency will restrain [anyone] from brutalizing, from maiming, from murdering – his brother, his mate, his parents, or his child. Scratch an "altruist" and watch a "hypocrite" bleed'.[17] Weirdly, it is headline news if meercats, who habitually stand on guard to warn their kin of danger, turn out to be in less personal danger than it might seem: 'really' they are not altruists after all! And if they were, they would be dupes. It is axiomatic that any pretence of loving concern for strangers must be a lie, since our genes will not allow us to squander resources that might instead assist the carriers of those genes. It is not necessary that we *want* to spread our genes throughout the population, but all that we do want must be meant to serve that goal (or else be a by-product of some dangerous mutation).

VIRTUE AND NOBILITY

The pleasure principle (namely, that enjoyment is the only real good) is now so widely, and unquestioningly, believed that it is often difficult to remember that virtue used to be *opposed* to pleasure. Or if that formulation seems to be too shocking, what mattered was our motive, not success. The ethically right act is done for the right reason – which is, to be doing the right thing. The skilful archer, so the Stoics said, is not exactly aiming to hit the target, but to be aiming, pulling the bow, releasing the

---

[17] M. H. Ghiselin, *The Economy of Nature and the Evolution of Sex* (University of California Press: San Francisco 1978), p. 247. Ghiselin did well to put some of these words in inverted commas: it would have been even better to have avoided them all entirely. The claim that murderous selfishness is inevitable is indeed, as David Stove suggested, an incitement to crime (Stove, *Darwinian Fairytales* (Avebury: Aldershot 1995), p. 74). It is also an assertion with no proper basis in the *scientific* theory that Ghiselin and others defend.

arrow in a way that usually or often would. Modern students are baffled: what can the archer be aiming at if not the target? How can she not be disappointed in her efforts if she misses? If the target is only trivial, we might accept that the real goal is to hit the target in the proper manner: having someone pick the arrow up and ram it in the bull's-eye does not count. But if the goal, say, is to kill the deer (or the enemy archer), any way that works will do. Life is not a game, and success excuses all. It follows at once that moralists who wish to 'keep the rules', no matter what the outcome of their acts will be, are bound to seem irrational. At best, obedience to such rules may be worth enforcing if obedience, in general, does have 'good' results (that is, it achieves what we desire). Unilateral disobedience will then be thought 'unfair', though all of us will recognize it as a reasonable act. The moral is: do not get caught.

But in the older view, we act 'for beauty'. Other creatures may be beautiful, but only human beings, it was thought, can know they are, and only human beings can act in order to be beautiful. What happens afterwards is gloss. Life *is*, in a way, a game, if by that is meant that our goal is not exactly to secure a certain state of affairs. The football is not left within the goal. The arrow is taken from the target. And whatever we accomplish in a wider sphere, we know that life goes on. Does it matter if the child who is saved from drowning dies next week? Or if she grows up to be a villain? In one way, obviously so; but in another, no. There are actions that we do regardless of their cost, and of their probable outcome. We do not regret them if they turn out 'badly'. Or rather, we did not regret them, in the days when we knew beauty. 'Any prudent person would have told Frodo that Gollum would certainly betray him, and could rob him in the end. To "pity" him, to forbear to kill him, was a piece of folly, or a mystical belief in the ultimate value-in-itself of pity and generosity even if disastrous in the world of time.'[18] Certainly pity, to be pity, 'must be directed to the good of its

[18] J. R. R. Tolkien, January 1956, *Letters of J. R. R. Tolkien*, ed. H. Carpenter (Allen & Unwin: London 1981), p. 234; see also p. 202, on the apparent 'irrationality' of Gandalf's self-sacrifice.

object. . . [and not] exercised *only* to keep oneself "clean" '.[19]
But it remains a virtue even if its object is not benefited, and
even if there is little or no chance of visible reward. For saints,
something matters more than visible success. That they will,
after all, succeed must be by grace, and not by their design.
Which is what Plotinus said, elaborating Aristotle's dicta:[20] the
value of real virtue does not lie in *successful* action. We cannot
guarantee overt success in anything we try to do, and worrying
about it makes us less likely to succeed. Conversely, those who
lack *pity* also lack good reason for what they do, and that lack
can be shown in actions which also have no strictly painful
effects: 'the person who boils the flesh of lambs or kids or any
other young animal in their mother's milk, shows himself
cruelly brutal in character and gelded of compassion, that most
vital of emotions and most nearly akin to the rational mind'.[21]

The Enlightenment abandonment of final causes was a
methodological device, founded in a commendable humility
about our chances of unravelling God's reasons for His acts. But
what science chose to ignore (for its own purposes) became
ignorable: if science knew nothing about such value, how could
values ever be known at all? In the guise of archetypes, such
final or formal causes were still significant. When Darwin
changed those archetypes to ancestors, and even made it
evident that some ancestral types were nothing like their
descendants,[22] the last lone ghost of beauty disappeared.
Lineages last for many reasons, but their being, variously, 'fit'

---

[19] Ibid., p. 330.   [20] Plotinus, *Enneads* VI.8.5.

[21] Philo, *Virtues* 144, commenting on Exodus 23.19 and Deuteronomy 14.21; see Murray,
The Cosmic Covenant (Sheed & Ward: London 1992), p. 117. It may be that the
commandment in question ('not to boil a kid in its mother's milk') originally had
some ritual significance, but it was early interpreted as ethical.

[22] Interestingly, this discovery had already been made, in the field of Indo-European
linguistics. It had always been obvious that very different languages (French, Italian,
Spanish, and so on) had evolved from Latin. William Jones's lecture to the Royal
Asiatic Society of Bombay in 1786 presented the evidence that there was a lost
language ancestral to Latin, Greek, Sanskrit and Persian, since the resemblances
were unlikely to be demanded by any purely 'rational' account of how to speak (since
other people spoke quite differently, and still made sense). We can now trace both
wheel and *cakra* back to a proto-Indo-European word, $k^w e k^w lo$-s, very unlike either. See
Bruce Lincoln, *Death, War and Sacrifice* (University of Chicago Press: Chicago 1991),
pp. 1–2.

has nothing to do with being beautiful. Indeed, being beautiful is without effect at all – unless by way of sexual selection. It is not only 'nature' that selects successful breeders: so do potential mates (though of course their judgement is subject to Dame Nature's rule). 'Being beautiful' is only having a character that will attract a mate, or – by extension – any sort of attentive care. We used to care for children, and admire that care, because we thought it beautiful, and them. Now, so Darwin led us to suppose, we think them beautiful because we care for them. It is not that we condemn infanticide because we think it is wrong, nor because we reckon children worth the cost: we think it is wrong because we love our children. We do not love them because we see that they are lovely: we think them lovely, because not doing so might leave us with fewer children. Beauty is not a feature of the world that has its own effect on us: instead, it is a projection of the emotions that we feel for merely Darwinian reasons. Even our tendency to believe that beauty is a causally important power, an objectively real datum, is engineered by genes that get an 'advantage' from our fond delusion.[23]

Some moralists have thought it did not matter. Loveliness and dignity are an obvious part of *our* experienced world. In judging that a child is lovely why should we need to think her loveliness would survive our loss of love? Why should an imagined beauty that persisted even if we never cared for it be relevant to anything we cared for? The only evidence we could have that a joke is funny is that people laugh at it; what would be the point of claiming that my jokes are *really* funny, although no one laughs (not even me)? Their being funny just is the fact that we laugh. The beauty of children just is our loving them. The beauty of noble deeds is the admiration they excite. Realizing this should make no difference: 'Parents are no more likely to stop loving their children once they understand the role that such feelings play in the perpetuation of their genes than they are to cease enjoying orgasm once they understand its

---

[23] Michael Ruse and E. O. Wilson 'Moral Philosophy as Applied Science: a Darwinian approach to the foundations of ethics', *Philosophy* 61.1986, pp. 173–92, esp. p. 179.

evolutionary role.'[24] On this account, 'unweaving the rainbow' does not damage beauty; on the contrary, some have thought, it adds new levels of enjoyment when we realize what is 'really happening'. But Hull's claim is plausible only because we have already abandoned older ideologies. It is implicit in this claim that parental love and orgasm are just natural events, owing nothing to the beliefs and projects of particular human beings, and without any cognitive significance. All Dante *really* wanted was to get Beatrice into bed, and nothing would have altered in his heart if he had come to believe that Beatrice was not a unique and immortal beauty. Romantic love is easily deconstructed; why should we suppose that we will still feel it once we have realized its origin? Parental love is also, in large part, an artifact. Consider it a device, deployed by infants, to secure themselves: the unfortunate birds whom cuckoo-chicks control would feel quite differently if they could wake up. Is parental love, even as a 'natural' feeling, so secure? Parents have been known to shake or strike their children, to abandon them or kill them, without obvious qualms. No doubt those patterns of behaviour too can be made to seem the 'fitter': we had better unload unsatisfactory children and start again, especially if they might not be ours. Even if we manage to endure the costs of caring, there will come a moment when we wish them gone. Is it obvious that sacrificial care will long outlast the discovery that children are cuckoos? Even before we noticed, our care was less than perfect: knowing that the passing enjoyment of parental love is only a trick to keep us careful of our genes, will we really be as caring? 'Natural affection is nothing: but affection from principle and established duty is sometimes wonderfully strong'.[25] Johnson elsewhere remarks on his own brief compassion for horses being driven too hard, and his entire unwillingness to call a halt.[26] 'Principle and established duty', enforced in civilized society, can carry affection and compassion with them: without that aid, our own transient delights come first.

[24] Hull, *Metaphysics*, p. 258.
[25] Johnson (20 April 1778), James Boswell, *Life of Samuel Johnson* (Clarendon Press: Oxford 1953), p. 1227.
[26] Johnson (20 July 1763), ibid., p. 309.

In the older ideology, we were held to our duty by the conviction that the care we felt, and the objects of that care, were beautiful. Doing the right thing because we saw it to be right is likelier to lead to action than our passing fancies, especially when we know those fancies' roots. When modern Darwinists urge us to rebel against 'the selfish genes' they cannot appeal to any higher standard than our own desires. In which case, it will probably be the stronger and more self-focused wishes that are preferred to any difficult devotion. 'Who is not tempted', Epictetus said, 'by attractive and wide-awake children to join their sports and crawl on all fours and talk baby talk?'[27] But this is a passing fancy, no more a judgement of right reason than the wish to swing the brats against the nearest wall.[28] Epictetus, I should emphasize, supposed that there was a right way of behaving, revealed in part in what was 'natural'. Having been guided to that one right way by the pleasure that we sometimes get from it, we can sustain it even through its pains. It is one thing to do something because it is right, or beautiful, or noble. It is quite another to do it because we enjoy doing so. Is it even the same thing that we enjoy once we have given up the thought that it is right to do it? Do we even enjoy it just as much when we have realized why we once did?

Sedgwick was right to think that Darwin's theories subverted normal moral sense. If Darwin was right that beauty, or moral beauty, had no part to play in making us have the feelings that we did, any more than it determined what the forms of life might be, then our feelings could have no more weight than their immediate strength could give them. Moderns fail to see the problem because they have already forgotten what was meant.

As it is not for those to speak of the graceful forms of the material world who have never seen them or known their grace – men born blind, let us suppose – in the same way those must be silent upon the

---

[27] Epictetus, *Discourses* 2.24.18.

[28] One of the most heart-breakingly beautiful of psalms (beginning, 'By the waters of Babylon we sat down and wept') concludes as follows: 'O Babylon, Babylon the destroyer, happy the man who repays you for all that you did to us! Happy is he who shall seize your children and dash them against the rock' (Psalms 137.8–9). That verse is now rarely read, or sung, in churches.

beauty of noble conduct and of learning and all that order who have never cared for such things, nor may those tell of the splendour of virtue who have never known the face of Justice and of Moral-Wisdom beautiful beyond the beauty of Evening and of Dawn.[29]

This may still not seem too disagreeable. Once we acknowledge that different judgements are no more than proposals, stemming from our programmed sympathies and lusts, we can begin to negotiate decency, without supposing that we thereby lose our grip on principle. In wars of principle the other side is always *wrong*, and who could compromise with open error? Even Darwinists, who might have learnt more liberal ways, can bear no compromise with 'creationists': the least concession ends in open war. Witness an exhibition at the Natural History Museum in London in 1981, in which it was briefly conceded that, as a matter of fact, some people think that Darwinism is not a completely satisfying account of natural history. The result was an abusive editorial in *Nature*, demands for the Director's resignation, and the removal of the offending, factual statement.[30] Obviously, Darwinists believe not only that their theory is correct, but also that it is wrong to give a cultural space to any opposition, irrespective of the wishes and opinions of those who pay the taxes. Even if people were wrong to think that Darwinism is an imperfect theory, they would have some right to a say in what is done with it. And in fact it does not seem that they are entirely wrong.

On any account (Darwinian or otherwise), it is likely that human beings will always think their opponents are in the wrong (even if no one is 'really' in the wrong). People who have abandoned any claim to knowledge of objective beauty do not become more liberal on the instant. On the contrary, if I believe that there *is* a real beauty, then I will admit I might be wrong about it, just as I might be wrong about tomorrow's weather or the price of gold. If there is no real truth, I cannot be wrong, and therefore need not listen to those who disagree with me.

[29] Plotinus, *Enneads* I.6.4, in S. MacKenna's trans. (Faber & Faber: London 1969, 4th edn) 59..
[30] The story is told by Phillip E. Johnson, *Darwin on Trial* (Intervarsity Press: Downers Grove, Ill. 1993, second edition), pp. 135ff.

Precisely because my moral judgements are projections, I can demonize all those who disagree.

Subjectivism preceded Darwin. In abandoning the appeal to final and to formal cause in scientific enquiry, and in deciding that reality could only be known through science, the founders of modernity had stipulated that no moral judgements could be factual. What Darwin added was the test of time. If moral judgements are proposals, then the only question is: who wins? There is no point in proposing strategies that nobody can live by, or that will self-destruct. Perhaps we will not be *wrong*, but we will still be dead.

My point here is not to challenge the technique entirely: it might be a good idea to live in ways that have some chance of being sustained. Tyranny is only a short-term strategy: what tyrants ever left their power to their grandchildren? But proposals vindicated only by success seem to miss the point: save this child from drowning, because a habit of child rescue, suitably promoted, is a better bet long-term than any policy of child neglect; do not rape that youngster, because a habit of mistreating youngsters results in fewer grandchildren to care for one's old age. Are we to conduct proper clinical trials to determine if this guess is true? Or shall we just wait to see if child molesters are gradually eliminated from the species? How likely is that, if such child molesters possess (as it seems they do) such natural virtues as charm, cunning and a grasp of their own 'needs'? Even if they themselves have no descendants their *characters* persist as easily as those of saints.

Decent people, no doubt, do not need to worry. Decent people do what they do because they want to do it, and are fortunate in their desires. Those with larger or more perverse imaginations may still be troubled by what happens when the young are told that there are no real, objective values; that moral rhetoric is only a device to control the relatively disadvantaged; that enlightenment consists in seeing through such lies; that the final standard of success is how many copies of themselves they leave, at whatever cost to others. If all that is true, it hardly requires much cynicism to suspect the motives of those who teach it as the truth. If it is not true, why teach it?

Either way, my sympathies can lie with citizens of Arkansas (and elsewhere in the United States) who see their money spent on teaching children what they see as lies, without an opportunity to challenge them.[31] Ardent Darwinists claim, simultaneously, that 'science' contains no metaphysical or religious implications, and that 'science' refutes 'superstition'. Sometimes the theory of evolution through natural selection is held to be compatible with the existence of real value, and a real God. At other times, and more consistently, the harder line is pushed: that values are projections, terrestrial life a cosmic accident, and all attempts to deny these claims are priestcraft. Sometimes it is suggested that Darwinian theory need not vindicate greed, infidelity and oppression. At other times the message is as clear that only open selfishness is honest – an ethical proposal that receives no challenge because it is concealed as 'science'.

CIVILIZATION AND SIN

'Natural selection follows from the struggle for existence; and this from a rapid rate of increase.'[32] Since Darwin immediately goes on to deplore the sad result when 'the struggle for existence [is not] sufficiently severe to force man upwards to his highest standard', and 'a few wandering savages' occupy 'enormous areas of the most fertile land .. capable of supporting numerous happy homes' it seems strange that he continued to believe in any such constant natural increase, or in natural selection. Elsewhere he contends only that 'man *tends* to increase at a greater rate than his means of subsistence; consequently he is *occasionally* subjected to a severe struggle for existence, and natural selection will have effected whatever lies within its scope'.[33] On these terms evolutionary pressure must only be

[31] See Langdon Gilkey, *Creationism on Trial: evolution and God at Little Rock* (Winston: Minneapolis 1985) for a theological critique of 'creationism', and Ronald Numbers, *The Creationists: the evolution of scientific creationism* (A. A. Knopf: New York 1992) for a historical account of American creationism. J. M. Spier, *An Introduction to Christian Philosophy* (Craig Press: Nutley, N.J. 1966) is an outline of the Dutch philosopher Dooyerweerd's philosophical anthropology.

[32] Charles Darwin, *The Descent of Man* (Princeton University Press: New Jersey 1981; a facsimile of the 1871 edition), vol. I, p. 180.

[33] Ibid., vol. II, p. 387; my italics.

intermittent: much of the time human (and probably other) populations are well within the carrying capacity of their habitat, and there will be no struggle for existence to eliminate the less fit. This does not mean that evolution stops dead: it may still be true that heritable characters which offer even the slightest increase in the number of viable descendants will spread through the population. We simply have no way of saying what those characters might be, especially since even *neutral* characters will also spread.

Believing that there must be such a struggle, we initiate it. The civilized races, remember, will soon exterminate such savages as still persist – or perhaps, on a lighter note, absorb them, if it turns out that all sub-species are interfertile (but that is not what Darwin says). Whatever heritable traits stand behind the civilized races' greater energy, inventiveness, rapacity and lack of self-control will certainly infect the later generations of our species. It is not certain that this will be good for us, nor that we shall not 'regress'. The Greeks 'who stood some grades higher in intellect than any race that has ever existed' still 'retrograded from a want of coherence among the many small states, from the small size of their whole country, from the practice of slavery, or from extreme sensuality, for they did not succumb until "they were enervated and corrupt to the very core"'.[34] The *meaning* of history, so Darwin apparently believed, lay only in the 'the great stream of Anglo-Saxon emigration to the west',[35] the triumph of the Anglo-Saxon code.[36]

Evolutionism of this 'progressive' kind is probably what most Darwinists preferred. The great sin of the Victorians, as Chesterton remarked, was that they thought that history ended

---

[34] Ibid., vol. I, p. 178, citing W. R. Greg, 'The Failure of "Natural Selection" in the Case of Man', *Fraser's Magazine* (September 1868), p. 357. Darwin adds that the Holy Inquisition lowered, through selection, the general standard of intelligence in Europe. He offers no evidence either that this has been the effect, or that the Inquisition's victims were in fact predominantly 'intelligent'.

[35] Darwin, *Descent*, vol. I, p. 179, quoting Zincke's 'Last Winter in the United States' (1868, p. 29).

[36] One of the many paradoxes of human history is that American creationists, opposing Darwin, may sometimes share his belief in the manifest destiny of the Saxon tribes. Others of Darwin's critics do not.

happily, because it ended with them.[37] Our ancestors were
fishes (tree shrews, apes and savages) but we are at once a
different *kind* than they, and one that exists to put aside our past.
Standard works on evolutionary history, until very recently,
assumed that there *had* to be all those earlier ages before the
first true humans could get up and walk. In that moment we
escaped from 'nature'. The idea long preceded the Victorians.
It was 'a mixed up and bestial existence' that some god saved us
from, giving us understanding, language, agriculture, shelter,
sea-voyages and trade, and augury.[38] Previously, they had been
at the mercy of the wild beasts,[39] beings whose way it is to
prevail over each other by violence. Their union, of the weak
against the strong, brought us the art of politics, of which
warfare is a part.[40] Until then the stronger killed and ate the
weaker; but the weak banded together, and now seek to resolve
their differences by law.[41] The war with beasts (and with human
outlaws who make beasts of themselves) is fundamental to
human civil order.[42] Without law and order we should all be
savages, undiscriminating in our casual affections, violent in our
revenges, and philistine in our attitude to art and science alike.
Because they thought that we would be like that without the
constant presence of the law, generations of Europeans have
convinced themselves that non-Europeans actually were like
that. So Darwin on the inhabitants of Tierra del Fuego: 'their
expression was wild, startled and distrustful. They possessed
hardly any arts, and like wild animals lived on what they could
catch; they had no government and were merciless to every one
not of their own small tribe.'[43]

The new progressivism identifies vice with being behind the

---

[37] G. K. Chesterton, *Chaucer* (Faber & Faber: London 1932), p. 38.

[38] Euripides, *Suppliants* 201ff. (Theseus speaks).

[39] Dicaearchus, fr. 67: Cicero, *De Officiis* 2.5.

[40] Plato, *Protagoras* 322b.

[41] Ps. Lysias, 2.18–19; W. K. C. Guthrie, *History of Greek Philosophy*, vol. III, (Cambridge University Press: Cambridge 1969), p. 74.

[42] T. Cole, *Democritus and the Sources of Greek Anthropology* (American Philological Association Monograph 25.1967), p. 124.

[43] Darwin, *Descent*, vol. I, p. 404. Stove, *Darwinian Fairytales*, p. 75, points out that we know, from the personal testimony of one who lived with them, that Darwin was completely wrong.

times, by failing to domesticate the natural. Sin is, for us, behaving 'like an animal'. Sin in the older view is pride, insistence on a private world, the conviction that 'all things are mine'. The type of sin for the older view is Lucifer; for the newer, it is the savage, or the ape.[44] For the older, salvation is through repentance, turning back; for the newer, 'reason'. Some fantasists have even encouraged the thought that 'science' will one day make a god to resurrect us all (so it is really important to keep the research grants rolling).[45]

Which is a more plausible picture? Is 'sin' just acting thoughtlessly, or violently, or without due regard for current fashion? Is virtue just not acting on the spur of sudden lust or temper? Is it a coincidence that *thoughtless* crimes (or ones that we consider thoughtless) are not the ones that civilized people relish? The ages of torture are the ages of high civilization.[46] Civilized people, whose dress, diet, and manner of speech are calculated to be as different from naked savages as they can make them, have been the ones to break the most commandments. Even their occasional beneficence (as it did not take sociobiologists to see) is more to do with their own high opinion of themselves than to do others good. There is no need to reckon that only the civilized are sinners, but the notion that to be civilized is to be free of sin would be funny if it were not so painful. The Holocaust was not a return to 'savagery', or something only 'animals' could do; on the contrary, it required enormous thought (both technical and managerial) and devotion to a 'new world order'. The Nazis acted out the advice that Western intellectuals had given: to dispose of the 'retarded', whether these were imbeciles, or sodomites, or Jews, or gypsies:[47]

At some future period, not very distant as measured by centuries, the

---

[44] Cesare Lombroso supposed, for example, that 'we can identify born criminals because they bear anatomical signs of their *apishness*'; Gould, *Mismeasure*, p. 124 (my italics).

[45] Frank Tipler, *The Physics of Immortality: modern cosmology, God and the resurrection of the dead* (Macmillan: Basingstoke 1994).

[46] G. K. Chesterton, *Short History of England* (Chatto & Windus: London 1917), p. 87; Chesterton did not intend this as a compliment.

[47] See S. A. Barnett, *Biology and Freedom* (Cambridge University Press: Cambridge 1988), pp. 141ff.

civilized races of man will almost certainly exterminate and replace throughout the world the savage races. At the same time the anthropomorphous apes, as Professor Schauffhausen has remarked, will no doubt be exterminated. The break [between man and his nearest allies] will then be rendered wider, for it will intervene between man in a more civilized state, as we may hope, than the Caucasian, and some ape as low as a baboon, instead of as at present between the Negro or Australian and the gorilla.[48]

That is why, so G. Stanley Hall suggested, there is a gap between the fossil apes and us: our ancestors eliminated all the 'missing links'.[49] H. G. Wells looked forward with relish to sweeping away 'those swarms of black and brown and dirty-white and yellow people'.[50]

So the idea that sin is 'living like an animal', and civilization is the path to virtue, is implausible. But is the opposite view any better? Is civilization itself the source of sin? Progressivists do not have to believe (although they may) that *we* are the end of history: perhaps humanity, as Nietzsche said, is only a rope between the beast and superman.[51] Back in the old days, human beings were hominids: we lived, like our close relatives, in family groups and troops, most probably selecting new members from the pool of banished males. No doubt we squabbled and remembered fancied slights. No doubt, as soon

---

[48] Darwin, *Descent*, vol. I, p. 201, citing Schauffhausen, *Anthropological Review* (April 1867), p. 236. Darwin, on balance, reckons that there is only one, variegated human species – but he also supposes that 'the Negro and the European are so distinct that, if specimens had been brought to a naturalist without any further information, they would undoubtedly have been considered by him as good and true species' (*Descent*, vol. II, p. 388). Once again: some of Darwin's creationist opponents have had the same prejudices – but the dominant form of biblical Christianity has insisted that we are one family.

[49] Paul Crook, *Darwinism, War and History* (Cambridge University Press: Cambridge 1994), p. 143, citing 'Recreation and Reversion', *Pedagogical Seminary* 22.1915, pp. 510–20.

[50] Crook, *Darwinism*, p. 101, citing H. G. Wells, *Anticipations* (Harper & Brothers: New York and London 1902), p. 212: 'And for the rest – those swarms of black and brown and yellow people who do not come into the needs of efficiency? Well, the world is not a charitable institution, and I take it they will have to go. The whole tenor and meaning of the world, as I see it, is that they have to go.' Strangely, Wells's admirers are prepared to excuse or explain away remarks by Wells that they would find unforgivable if they had been made, say, by Kipling (as in fact, of course, they were not).

[51] F. Nietzsche, *Thus Spake Zarathustra*, tr. A. Tille and M. B. Bozman (Dent: London 1933), p. 7.

as language had emerged, we lied about our prowess, cheated our friends and fantasized whole worlds to walk in on long winter nights. We had, in short, our own peculiarities. Sometimes we went to war, as chimpanzee troops sometimes do, for reasons that we can now only guess. If we had perished then, no alien archaeologist could have told that we were ever 'human' (from which it follows that we actually do not know how many 'human' species lived before us).

Civilization, settled life, created different classes. Some worked immensely harder than 'savages' ever had, while others invented leisure.[52] Living in larger units, we had to discover more than family affections and unwritten law to keep the wheels turning. Domestication and civilization came together:[53] we bred ourselves, and coached ourselves, to do what was not 'natural'. Other species have succeeded 'better': social insects invented castes (or 'castes') before us, and use chemical controls to keep the colony, the swarm together; rats respond to body odour only, not to individual identity. We have not yet discovered the right rules, nor bred them into us. So far, we are experiments in living, and will be surpassed. It may be that our civilization has been a long detour, and supermen will be a lot like savages. It may be, as has often seemed, that our future lies in caste society. It may be that there is something else to come (as must be the Abrahamic, and specifically the Christian hope). The sins of civilization, in any case, are not less than those of savages. It is neither literal bestiality nor savagery indeed that *civilized* folk should fear.

Virtue – as every moralist since Socrates has noticed – is not hereditary, and even Darwin usually only *hopes* that it may perhaps become so.[54] It does not follow that it is not persistent. The prophets of the past have realized that, left to ourselves, we may indeed become fat, lazy and indifferent to the pains of others, and only rouse ourselves for the sake of our own kin. It has been their claim that something new is always being intruded into history and the natural world, the radical claim

[52] Marshall Sahlins, *Stone Age Economics* (Tavistock Press: London 1972).
[53] See Chambers, *Natural History of Creation*, p. 337.
[54] Darwin, *Descent*, vol. I, p. 104.

that virtue is not measured by expectable, worldly triumph. They have claimed, in brief, that the world of nature is not closed, that something different interferes to remind us whence we came, that we are not the end. They may, of course, have been mistaken: perhaps their words are only mental microbes of the sort that interfere in a decent Darwinian 'progress'. But as before, this claim is as metaphysical, and as value-laden, as its opposite. Those of us who hold to the faith have at least this comfort – that it is not the expectably successful who have left their mark most clearly on our history. When the great, self-praising emperors are dead, it is the wandering Aramaean, summoned at seeming random from the nations of the Middle East, or the mendicant princeling who abandoned palace, wife and child to seek enlightenment, or the Crucified Himself, who have preserved such images of decency as we still have.

METAPHYSICS AND THE THEORY OF KNOWLEDGE

Darwin's refusal to consider the 'idealist' option as a possible account of evolutionary change turned on his conviction that it was not 'scientific'. He was correspondingly disturbed that so many scientists, and philosophers of science, considered that his own approach was 'unscientific' too. Their principal objection was that he had abandoned 'the inductive path'. To Whewell, for example, it seemed ridiculous to postulate the past existence of all manner of lost varieties, each differing from the next by infinitesimal degrees, rather than accept the present fact of discontinuous kinds. That issue, and the putative existence of natural kinds, will concern me in chapter 5; it has a claim to be the most serious and puzzling question about evolutionary change, and one that is still neglected. The form in which it troubled Darwin himself was that the 'fossil record' itself was discontinuous; that judgement has been altered a little by a century's work. Whereas Darwin had found the fossil record difficult to deal with, modern Darwinists often rest their case on its supposed completeness: we can, it is supposed, trace many lines through millions of years of variation, and so show how the beginnings were unlike their ends. The issue is not so easy.

It is no surprise (or need not be) that Darwin's discovery was founded, like many others, upon error. 'Dare sound Authority confess that one can err his way to riches?'[55] Columbus sailed for the Spice Islands because he had convinced himself that the earth's circumference was much smaller than all educated opinion said. He was mistaken, but triumphant. Similarly Darwin was convinced that the earth had *not* been subject to any global disasters, that the effects of habit could be inherited, and – against contemporary evidence – that there had been plenty of time for gradual alterations to add up to the world we know. It has turned out instead that Lamarck was almost entirely wrong; that the earth has several times been wrecked by meteor strike, volcanoes and biological mutation; and that the actual duration of animal life has been much shorter than we might at first imagine. We have not had four thousand million years to develop from an imagined 'simple form', since multicellular development of the animal kind began not much more than half a billion years ago.[56] Once things at last began to get a little complicated, it happened very quickly. If Darwin had known all this for sure, he might have been even more diffident about his publication. Even now, many defences of the theory often amount to no more than the assertion that things *must* have happened like that (because there is no decent alternative theory), and the failure to discover many, or any, *gradual* changes in the fossil lines is no more than one would expect. Because we are absolutely sure it happened, we can find easy explanations for our failure to uncover actual cases. It is unfortunately common for a fossil to be identified as a 'missing link' only to be revealed a little later as, at best, a *relative* of some creature still unknown. *Archaeopteryx* was not the *ancestor* of birds, nor *Australopithecus* of hominids: they *must* have been the cousins of some great unknowns who simply did not leave their bodies to be fossilized for us. Absence of proof is rarely proof of

---

[55] W. S. Auden, 'The History of Science', *Collected Shorter Poems 1927–57* (Faber: London 1966), pp. 305–6.

[56] Multicellular *algae* appear a billion years ago; it may be that the animal line is older than we can at present show, and that there was a long, pre-Cambrian process to explain what seems like a sudden eruption of complex form.

absence; so Darwinists are entitled to maintain their case, even in the face of problems which might have troubled Darwin more. Even when the modern synthesis, incorporating Mendel's observations, put Darwinism back in centre stage, it could be argued that theorists had been lucky. Very few phenotypic characters would have been so accommodating as Mendel's peas had been. Good fortune led through error and untypical results to fixing neo-Darwinism as the *obvious* truth.[57] Early criticisms *must* have been disarmed (and sometimes actually have been).

Examining the metaphysical roots of this success is often judged improper. The claim that 'science' is free of metaphysics, and that 'scientists' make no metaphysical nor value judge-ments, is as sloppy a lie as any. Notoriously, the topics scientists think worth discussing, and the methods they employ, embody theories about the world, and about what is valuable (sometimes contentious ones). In some fields, there is also a clear preference for *beautiful* theories, as being more likely to be true (though why?) than ugly, clumsy or arbitrary ones. The beauty that is intended is intellectual, not sensual: it would presumably be wrong (ethically as well as factually) to prefer a sexually stimu-lating theory!

Modern science began in the Enlightenment endeavour not to appeal to final and to formal causes (though mathematical formulae have usually been exempt, and beauty keeps breaking in). This was at first a methodological precaution, but quickly became an ontological assumption. Scientists or would-be scientists are assured that only material causes can be real – forgetting that they themselves, by any ordinary rule, are more than material entities. The laws of logic and inductive inference are obeyed by rational agents. Empirical observations and control experiments are items in a scientific life that do not correspond to anything 'in nature'. Scientific theories may only

---

[57] I do not dispute that later work has established that – broadly – Mendelian inheritance is a fact; my point is only that, as so often in the history of science, we have been lucky. If Darwinism were not true of biological evolution a version might still be true in the history of ideas: ideas are produced at random, survive the early years by luck, and proliferate at the expense of other ideas which survived the early cull. Not all lost ideas have ever been fully tested, any more than all lost mutations.

be about material things (perhaps), but they are not themselves material. It may be true that intentionality and experience can somehow be identified with measurable events in matter. Perhaps the stages in a logical argument, if they are to be convincing, must be mapped in a sequence of neurological changes in an appropriately configured brain. But what matters to the argument is that logical laws are not broken. Even lousy arguments, to be convincing, have such neurological equivalents. Even badly designed experiments obey appropriate laws of physics. It is more significant that they disobey 'the laws of science' – or even the laws of the land.

Huxley objected to Robert Chambers's use of 'laws' as entities or active archetypes: 'a *Logos* intermediate between the Creator and His works'.[58] If laws are not actually active, of course, they are not *explanations* either. As Wittgenstein was to remark, it is the essence of the modern error to suppose that 'the laws of nature' *explain* what happens, rather than recording it.[59] But if they do not explain, what does? That the 'laws of physics' are everywhere the same (or that elementary particles are everywhere the same) is an extraordinary fact (or wild assumption). Philosophers who appeal instead to 'causal powers' may be on the right track, but there remains a question why those powers are everywhere the same, or grounded in a hidden order. 'Scientific' rejection of such explanatory norms rests only on the determination not to think of things like these. If there were such archetypes as Chambers, or Owen, imagined then the processes of evolutionary change might be appreciably easier to believe. There is a more immediate obstacle to their existence: chance variation is as likely, so it seems, to go in any direction, and not just the way that organisms might themselves prefer. Here the issue is the *metaphysical* rejection of such formal

---

[58] T. H. Huxley, 'Review of *Vestiges of the Natural History of Creation*' (*British and Foreign Medico-Chirurgical Review* 19.1854, pp. 425–39), p. 427, cited by Hull, *Metaphysics*, pp. 71–2. That there is such a *Logos*, of course, is orthodox in any Abrahamic faith, though only Christians believe that it *is* God, or that it ever became flesh (as John 1.1–14).

[59] A remark discussed by M. O'C. Drury, *The Nature of Words* (Routledge & Kegan Paul: London 1973).

and final causes, archetypes and intermediate Reason. If they do not exist, does Intellect itself?

The issue is a serious one. All that we can empirically observe are present effects whose causal origins – no doubt for compelling reason – are spread out through time. Another Victorian critic of evolutionary theory, and the fossil record, drew out the implication. Faced by fossil evidence (or what was said to be evidence) of an earlier age than any he believed was real, Philip Gosse enquired how we could tell the difference between a real and virtual past.[60] Suppose we knew (by observation and reliable witnesses) that God had made a mature oak tree, but had not bothered to create its earlier stages. If the tree were then cut down, its inner rings would still give evidence of all the seasons that it might have suffered. Even if we did not cut it down, we might reasonably infer what winds had blown, what squirrels nested in its trunk, and so on. Even an imaginary 'perfect' tree, symmetrical in all its parts, would merely testify to quiet times. In creating that particular tree, God would inevitably have created a phantasmal past. If He were similarly to create the white cliffs of Dover, or a coalfield, a close inspection would reveal an inner structure from which a fantasy of calcium-secreting animalcules, or decayed vegetation, could be derived. The only thing instantly created that would carry no phantasmal past would be something utterly unlike the things we ordinarily encounter: a 'singularity' whose past cannot be extrapolated or imagined. It follows that no amount of fossil-bearing rocks, containing the images of things that might have been or yet might be, can actually establish that the past was real.

Of course, Gosse's observation, like Babbage's, casts doubt on science. Nothing we can now observe, or now recall, establishes that the world did not begin five minutes ago, or fifty years. All we can say is that it *seems* to have existed long enough to build up sedimentary rocks containing fossils. If none of that

---

[60] Philip Gosse, *Omphalos* (J. van Voorst: London 1857). Gosse's argument has been sympathetically discussed by Jorge L. Borges, *Other Inquisitions 1937–52* (Washington Square Press: Washington 1966), pp. 22–5. It has not been the preferred solution of creationists, not even of those who would rather postulate a relatively 'young' earth.

was real, why should the evidence be so consistent? Might one oak, as it were, not give a different history from its neighbour? Strictly, we do not know that it does not – since any wildly inconsistent result would only tend to cast doubt on the character of the maverick, or render that particular dating mechanism unreliable. But why should there not be a consistent, virtual past? An author who begins her work *in medias res* (as every human author does) will usually conceive a wider world than any she has troubled to write down or to invent. Perhaps she will write the 'prequel' later.[61] By granting the same skeleton, or the same DNA, to sparrowhawk and sparrow, God signifies our spiritual bond, whether or not He made their imagined ancestors. Even if we abandon God, it is conceivable that the world, our world, sprang into being with a complex structure, full of things of the same kind as would thereafter have a past.[62] What grounds the conviction that this must be false? As far as I can see, it must be metaphysics. Perhaps God 'would not do that kind of thing'? But who can tell what God would do except by intuition or by revelation? Gosse could reply that God had revealed that He had. If the revelation is unbelievable (and certainly some found it was), it can only be because we 'know' that the world, and God, is *rational*.

Methodologically, science depends on supposing that the sample of existence we encounter is a true sample of reality, and one that is intelligible in human terms. If we suppose that things once happened differently from now (however rational, in the abstract, that thought is), we lose our right to think that we have adequate samples. In the nature of the case, of course, we can never demonstrate *empirically* that we do, or did. So once again, it was expectable that Gosse's answer was not widely believed. The *method* of science excluded it – but that cannot make it false, unless we already know that science is the only road to truth. I

---

[61] I have suggested elsewhere (*God's World and the Great Awakening*, Clarendon Press: Oxford 1991), that God might indeed have begun the world at Bethlehem, or Calvary, and composed its history 'later', very much as Olaf Stapledon's Star Maker does (*Star Maker* (Methuen: London 1937)).

[62] Those who insist that the universe could 'just have happened' are actually in a weak position to deny this possibility; see my *God, Religion and Reality* (SPCK: London 1998).

referred in my introduction, disdainfully, to the notion that there could be Two Truths, not to be compared. I remain committed to the thesis that there is One Truth only. But it does not follow that there is only one route to It, nor even that we can always tell what 'truths' are inconsistent. Darwin himself had *faith*, insisting that there was time enough for life to have evolved its wild variety although the physics of his day made it impossible that the sun should have been burning for so long. In other words, he denied, implicitly, that *physics* was the only route to Truth. Because he 'knew' life had evolved over ages, he 'knew' that the world must have allowed the event, although there was no theory, at the time, to offer a plausible mechanism for how it had.

The assumption that science is possible (let alone complete) is made more problematic by Darwinian theory. Our reasoning abilities were never required to cope with the real world: other predatory species prosper well enough without them, and our closest relatives are almost extinct despite their cleverness. It is premature, at least, to claim that reason is what we needed to survive, because it made us acquainted with reality. 'Success in reproductive competition may accrue to those who misperceive the world, and who act to the detriment of others.'[63] It does not follow, even if it were true that we get some advantage from our grasp of local conditions, that those capacities would also be enough to make us acquainted with past ages or the distant stars. Squirrels and wolves are clever enough to cope with ordinary problems, but show little sign of the sort of mind we think we have. Our wits were needed, so it is plausible to think, precisely to cope with each other's wits. We *hope* that they also cope with wider worlds.

The following makes a plausible, if still uncertain, story. Ancestral apes, already capable of recognizing individuals and manipulating their relationships, were doing very well until a rival primate line, the Old World monkeys, acquired the ability to digest unripe fruit (the apes only managing ripe fruits). Deprived of their main food (as red squirrels by grey), some

---

[63] Ghiselin, *Economy of Nature*, p. 139.

apes wandered out of the woods onto the plains of Africa, gradually standing upright and shedding body hair to cope with increased sun. To survive out on the plains, our ancestors needed to work in larger groups (perhaps to cope with predators, or to gain access to water holes in larger territorial ranges than smaller groups can easily manage), and therefore to be able to handle vastly increased complexities of individual relationship. We needed to be able to remember more individuals, and their relationships with each other, and could also no longer rely on social grooming (like other primates) to maintain our attachments. Comparing the proportional size of neocortex in many mammalian species and the usual size of their immediate groups, Robin Dunbar[64] identifies a close relationship: the larger the usual group, the larger the relative size of neocortex. Extending the line, he proposes that the normal human group is roughly one hundred and fifty strong, and cites anecdotal and statistical evidence that this is the usual number of human individuals any of us can recognize and remember. Keeping so many in our heads, and in our hearts, requires an expansion in our memory capacity, and an innovation in our grooming practice. Instead of physical grooming (in pairs), we began to engage in gossip (in groups of five or six). We have language, in brief, not because we needed to identify things in the world (the bison by the waterhole) but because we needed to keep up to date with what our friends and family were doing, and to reassure each other of our continuing attachment. Our theory of mind blossomed: we needed to know not only what another thought about ourselves, but what she thought another thought about a third. On the evidence, other apes also have theories of mind, but ours allow for far more levels of intensionality (and so for deliberate fiction). Because we understand more clearly that another's point of view is not our own, we can also form the idea of a world that is more than any one finite person's point of view.

Dunbar further speculates that we have invented soap operas – and perhaps religions – to provide a substitute for the shared

[64] Robin Dunbar, *Grooming, Gossip and the Evolution of Language* (Faber: London 1996).

networks of known faces that city dwellers can no longer count upon. Once our organizations have grown so large that we can no longer know, on a personal level, any large number of our fellow members, we need to invent new mechanisms of control: we no longer defer to our dominants because we know them well, but because they hold the office (and the magic ornaments) that can attach us to them. When we can no longer trace connections that will reassure us that some new-met person can be trusted, we rely instead on some shared fictional experience. Discovering how another feels about a well-known soap, or particular characters within that soap, is a way of finding out how we should feel about that other. Dialects, like fandom, also identify the groups where we can feel at ease, the people who have been socialized like us.

> The men of my own stock,
> They may do ill or well
> But they tell the lies I am wonted to,
> They are used to the lies I tell.
> And we do not need interpreters
> When we go to buy or sell.[65]

We may expect that social, gossiping animals like us will be equipped to recognize each other's thoughts and feelings. We spend most of our time, once ordinary hungers are satisfied, chatting with each other and about each other, or even about fictitious characters. Relatively unsociable types, delighting in mathematics or gadgets or even in non-human animals, are mildly despised as nerds, or diagnosed almost as autistic. Such nerds are protected, sometimes, in the social group, and it is to them that we owe most technical and theoretical progress. The theatre of their minds is occupied by numbers and by shapes, instead of by the latest doings of Aunt Gladys or the imagined deeds of Xena. But why should the ability to count, or fiddle, or create imagined worlds, create the kind of mind appropriate to the 'way things are', any more than the ability to recall what Aunt Jemima said to Joey at Kate's wedding about what Kate

---

[65] Rudyard Kipling, 'The Stranger', *Collected Verse 1885–1926* (Hodder & Stoughton: London 1927), p. 534.

had said to Joey's father at the funeral? Nothing in the speculative history of how nerds and gossips were selected gives .us good reason to expect an intellectual insight into 'how things are'. Medieval philosophers of science, and – sometimes – Descartes, were content to say that all our theories were no more than stories. Theories were devices to help us cope with appearances, not true accounts of what was real. Only the renewed conviction that the human intellect was somehow in tune with the Divine licensed Galileo and others to contend that our best theories were real observations. That theory – though the Inquisition justly deemed it dangerous – at least makes sense. How can it make sense to suppose that an unexpected primate has the mind of God if there is no god to guide us? Nobody denies that our sensory apparatus limits us to perceive a tiny, useful sliver of the wider world; what grounds our conviction that our intellect knows no limit?

The 'hidden world', invisible to our senses, poses another problem. The materialist assumption is that only extended things are causes, and that they have, themselves, no properties like warmth or beauty.[66] The point is sometimes obscured by claiming that, for example, temperature just *is* a measure of the activity of lesser bits, and that the interior of stars must obviously be 'hot'. But the 'heat' intended is not what we feel: if there were inhabitants of such stellar interiors, they would experience it as no hotter, no more dangerous, than we do a summer's day. Nor is the *beauty* of the crystals or the living things we see identically the same as regularity. Perhaps there are some properties that extend from merely material things into the worlds we know; maybe material crystals have exactly the same *structure* as the ones we see. But that claim, commonsensical – and Aristotelian – as it may be, demands some care. Once we have divided, in our thought, the world (or worlds) that we experience and the one, first world, how are we to compare the two? By hypothesis, the world of our experience has been produced (as have innumerable other worlds) by the

[66] 'The Wall is not white; the fire is not hot etc. We Irishmen cannot attain these truths', George Berkeley, *Philosophical Commentaries* B392, *Works*, ed. A. A. Luce and T. E. Jessop (Thomas Nelson & Son: Edinburgh 1948), vol. I.

motion of material bits. We cannot *observe* that matter in a certain state produces mind, because all observations are an effect of mind. But equally we cannot deduce that matter must exist if mind is to exist, since *matter* has been defined as having no mind at all. If matter in a particular state produces mind, this must be a brute fact – and brute facts have to be learnt by observation. Nothing in the material properties explains why mentalistic properties (such as qualia, or intentions) should exist, and we cannot point, within our experienced worlds, to any brute and unexplained conjunction of the two. We may imagine that we can see, for example, how some chemicals are associated with particular motions in another creature, and infer from this that the association must exist in us as well. But of course, those observations are just that: conjunctions of one set of observations with another.

It follows that if 'matter' and 'the material world' are to avoid being 'metaphysical', we had better not distinguish mind and matter quite so clearly. Matter without mind is the phantom Plotinus called it,[67] and in that case, it makes no sense to talk as if there was a material world before the evolution of mind. If anything evolved, they evolved together.

In all these ways, contemporary evolutionary thought at least makes life more difficult for scientists. Babbage and Gosse were ignored because their theories seemed to show that we had no hope of discovering any truth. Darwin was criticized, initially, for denying the existence of those natural kinds that critics thought were vital to the intellectual enterprise. The problems with Darwinian (and more broadly, materialist) theory have not yet been solved. It follows that we should hesitate to teach our young that Darwinian or neo-Darwinian theory is the only rational way: if it is true, there is some reason to suspect that there is no *rational* way at all. Nor is it obvious that the theory is compatible with moral or political virtue. It was widely supposed in Darwin's day (but not, you will recall, by Whewell) that

[67] Plotinus, *Enneads* III.6.7; see my 'Plotinus: body and soul' in Lloyd P. Gerson, ed., *Cambridge Companion to Plotinus* (Cambridge University Press: Cambridge 1996), pp. 275–91, and 'A Plotinian Account of Intellect', *American Catholic Philosophical Quarterly* 71.1997, pp. 421–32.

'savages' or 'blacks' or even the Irish would be closer to 'the ape' than are more civilized humanity. It was widely supposed that there are 'defective' humans who would, in nature, perish, but are preserved on sentimental pretexts. It is still widely believed that there is nothing wrong in using 'animals' for culinary or experimental purposes, and widely taught that humans are animals too.

How shall we come to terms, or even to grips, with this?

NATURAL VICE AND VIRTUE

Whether or not we are all related, it is certain that we are all alike. Although the Stoics were inclined to say that pigs were only mobile meals, with souls instead of salt to keep them fresh,[68] they also knew that pigs defended their young. Precisely because they were not quite 'rational', they did not have the dangerous opportunity to act 'unnaturally'. Other commentators, more generously, saw that 'animals' were often moved by just the same emotions as ourselves. Dogs could be angry (and perhaps indignant), loyal and affectionate. They could be taught to keep the household rules, and sometimes seized the chance to break them. They could give good examples of courage and fidelity to their masters, even if their courage was not rooted in right-doing. De Waal, in a recent study of chimpanzee behaviour,[69] plausibly insists that our ancestors were guided by gratitude, obligation, retribution and indignation long before they developed enough language capacity for moral discourse. Moral discourse, and the law, are ways of resolving conflicts which would not exist at all unless we were already attached to others, capable of forming long-term alliances, cautiously respectful of authority, and resentful of those who cheat. De Waal's object here is twofold. On the one hand, he conceives moral motivation as something founded in

---

[68] According to Claudius the Neapolitan 'a hog is not useful for anything but food' (Porphyry, *De Abstinentia* 1.14). According to Chrysippus it is only a 'walking larder', made for nothing but sacrifice (ibid., 3.20).

[69] Frans de Waal, *Good Natured: the origins of right and wrong in humans and other animals* (Harvard University Press: Cambridge, Mass. 1996)

emotional responses that we share with other primates, other mammals. On the other hand (and for that very reason), he thinks the 'right' morality is one that works with those emotional responses, not against them. Whereas the early Dawkins claimed that we alone can pit ourselves against the selfish replicators which would cause us to behave rashly, egoistically or cruelly,[70] De Waal correctly observes that the metaphorical selfishness of genes does not imply that the creatures which they build are selfish: on the contrary, genes may do far better in the replication stakes by causing creatures to be, ordinarily, unselfish. 'Kin selection' and 'reciprocal altruism' are both mechanisms that will help the genes that (partly) lead them to be more widely replicated than those that program ordinary egotism. As the later Dawkins also argues,[71] conditional cooperators are almost always 'fitter' than cheaters (with whom no one cooperates for long). It does not follow that our motives for cooperation are always 'self-serving': on the contrary, we may more usually be guided by affection, loyalty, or shame. Nature, so to speak, does not rely on our knowing what will be 'the best' for us or for our genes: it gives us interests that generally do the work. Motive and evolutionary function are distinct (but what does knowing the function do to our motivation?).

Such motives can be detected, except by those self-blinded by Cartesian theory or embarrassment at seeming anthropomorphic, in our closest kin. The young and weak are treated with more forbearance (save in extremity), and are sometimes helped even by those not closely related to them. Alliances survive occasional quarrels or betrayals, but only after a show of indignation and a careful reconciliation. Different species (and different groups) have different styles of hierarchy. Interestingly, De Waal was able to show that even rhesus monkeys (whose hierarchical style is bullying) could learn the gentler style of stump-tailed macaques (by placing young rhesus with a company of stump-tailed): the rhesus do not simply imitate the stump-tailed, but begin to use their species codes of dominance and reconciliation in a friendlier and less obsessive way.

[70] Richard Dawkins, *The Selfish Gene* (Oxford University Press: London 1976), p. 215.
[71] Richard Dawkins, *The Blind Watchmaker* (W. W. Norton & Co.: New York 1986).

Whether the new style survived when the gentled rhesus were reintroduced to ordinary rhesus society, is not revealed. Chimpanzees in a rage may inflict serious injury on each other or on human 'friends', and later reveal compunction and concern for the effects. They may also, of course, treat passing colobus as clubs or missiles, and do not, it seems, repent. De Waal concludes from this that our concern for creatures of another species both is *and should be* limited,[72] though his own anecdotes make clear that other apes imagine he is their friend. He allows himself a brief and inexplicit barb against an experimenter who chose to blind some rhesus in order to see how well they coped, and what forbearance or concern the other rhesus would display: it raises questions, so he says, about the taxonomic limits of compassion. Alternatively, it raises questions about the obdurate stupidity of certain scientists.[73] His own experimental subjects, he assures us, are treated decently – *but he will not put up with disobedience from them*. It almost seems that he supposes that the animals should do what they are told: rats (he reports another experimenter's jokey conclusion) are a 'morally bankrupt species' because they only obey the experimenter's prohibitions when they think they have to. By implication, people who internalize a tyrant's orders, are being 'moral' – whereas the rest of us might reasonably think that, for that very reason, they are not.

But of course there is some strength in the suggestion. Our virtue is not always rooted in right-doing. Our courage, loyalty and decency are often no more than that of dogs: channels of our devotion to identifiable objects. When we defend our young it is often not to do right, but an immediate answer to their perceived vulnerability (or our property rights in them). Other responses to that perception are also possible, and may be

---

[72] He does not say why. Nor does he explain why 'granting rights to apes' (that is to say, protection from the predatory attacks of human beings) should be considered 'patronizing' or 'contemptuous'.

[73] If this seems harsh, consider it as a counter to the complacency of scientists who believe that 'scientists, on the whole, are amiable and well-meaning creatures. There must be very few wicked scientists. There are, however, plenty of wicked philosophers, wicked priests and wicked politicians' (Peter Medawar, *The Hope of Progress* (Methuen: London 1972), p. 87). I see no reason to suppose that scientists are so unlike other people.

deadly: why else are we now so nervous about putting a child's beauty on display? The impulses of natural virtue may sometimes (often) lead to sin. So may the internalized orders of our guardians or tyrants.

In the past, we could believe – at least if we were not misled by moralizing contempt – that 'animals' were 'innocent': their natural impulse made them do exactly what God and Nature wished them to. Our error lay in disregarding or perverting natural impulse rather than in failing to resist it! As far as 'innocence' is concerned, our later and more careful observations have revealed that animal nature can be 'perverse' as well. Baboons are observably fond of baboon cubs. They like their contact and their company – but this is not necessarily good for the cubs. The impulse to seize them may at least distress them, and might result in their death. Sometimes we may even suspect a genuine malice: a cub killed, by seeming chance, is one less rival for one's own cub's future. Early reports of wolf or lion or chimpanzee behaviour have often emphasized their family affection – but later accounts reveal conspiracies to kill, infanticide and cannibalistic war. Either animals behave badly too, or their behaviour is not 'really' bad. It is the second hypothesis that often seems most popular, but why?

One answer is simply that we should avoid passing judgement on creatures whose lives are largely opaque to us. Our past excesses in *blaming* other peoples for anything they do that is different have sometimes led to panicky pardons for clitoridectomy, suttee and slavery. Our sympathies are not quite universal. Some creatures are excused and others not – partly no doubt because some creatures are more present threats to us. Consider mink: when several thousand mink were recently (in 1998) released from British mink farms (allegedly by animal-rights protestors), they were alternately patronized and demonized. Many were so unused to freedom that they crept back to their cages, or died on the roads. But those who chanced to survive were somehow transmuted into dangerous predators, killing for the sake of killing, and were therefore themselves to be killed on sight. It seemed that mink were unnatural, un-British beasts – although there has been a feral population in the British Isles for decades, and they do no more than any animal to survive.

When other animals, in their proper place, hunt down their prey, it is natural. Wild dogs who burrow into a living wilde-beest, or lions who kill and eat another lion's cubs, are doing 'what comes naturally'. The mink, outside their proper place, are perceived to be unnatural. Cannibalistic chimpanzees lie at the edge: either this is part of the chimp biogram and 'natural', or it signals a disturbance in the troop, perhaps upset by decades of human observation and encroachment.

So animals in their proper place, and doing what is expected of them, must be 'innocent'. Animals outside their place, and seeming to defy the laws of natural, local virtue, are depraved. Is 'doing what comes naturally' good or bad? Is that a silly question?

CHAPTER 3

Trying to live in nature

THE BALANCE OF NATURE

Talk of 'nature's balance, or 'nature's way', idealizes the way things are apart from human 'interference'. This serves a sound rhetorical purpose when seeking to restrain exploiters. Overuse of herbicides and insecticides, and especially of substances that do not decay – at least for many ages – into harmless forms, may devastate the land. Overuse of fertilizers, and the casual disposal of chemically contaminated slurry, may ruin waterways and the aquifer. Dumping poisonous waste where poorer people live, or the other – non-human – nations of the living earth, combines stupidity and callousness. Such acts may be as genocidal in effect, or even in intention, as Hitler's or Pol Pot's – and should be judged as harshly. The lands between the Tigris and Euphrates were once fertile. Easter Island was once a wooded isle. Adding the giant Nile perch to Lake Victoria 'to increase fishery yields' has reduced the cichlid population by a factor of ten thousand – and much of the lake, bereft of algae eaters, is now anoxic.[1] Cutting down the rainforest to clear land for crops may win a crop or two – but most of the nutrients were in the trees themselves, and the thin soil left exposed soon bakes hard.

Doing things differently, in other words, may have very bad results: existing creatures, exposed to a new challenge, may be forced into decline (and all the predators and parasites who fed on them will also suffer). Neighbouring creatures, better used to

[1] Melanie L. J. Stiassny and Axel Meyer, 'Cichlids of the Rift Lakes', *Scientific American*, February 1999, p. 49.

the new conditions, may intrude, and either survive or not. The net effect may be an absolute desert, or (more probably) a desert as far as humans are concerned, or (at best) a very different land. Absolute deserts, utterly devoid of life, are rare: indeed, it is doubtful if they ever exist on earth at all, since any newly vacated niche would be a target for bacteria, fungi, quick-flowering plants and all manner of small beasts. We might consider the result a tip, a swamp, a midden or industrial landscape – but it is not dead. For two and a half billion years the most conspicuous results of life were layers of microbial mats, stromatolites, that might be thirty feet in height. Their era passed when atmospheric oxygen increased from 0.0001 per cent to 21 per cent in 'the greatest pollution crisis the earth has ever endured'.[2] If there are thriving ecosystems around hot sulphur springs far down in the ocean's darkness (as there are), it would be silly to underestimate the resilience and colonizing power of living things.[3] Bacterial populations would probably have the edge: their reproduction is far faster than that of most eukaryotes, and successful lineages could infect the others with appropriate skills. But there are plenty of eukaryotes that would also prosper: notoriously, cockroaches could probably survive a nuclear winter.

This is not to say that there have been no disasters. There have been, it seems, several mass extinctions in earth's history – and we are almost certainly living through the sixth mass extinction of which there is any record. The first five such extinctions, attested by fossil evidence, occurred at the close of the Ordovician (440 million years ago), the Devonian (365 million years ago), the Permian (245 million years ago), the Triassic (210 million years ago) and the Cretaceous (66 million

[2] Lynn Margulis and Dorian Sagan, *Microcosmos: four billion years of microbial evolution* (University of California Press: London and Berkeley 1997, second edition), p. 108. I should add that stromatolites may have fallen prey to grazers, and that it is not certain that there was in fact a single, catastrophic increase in oxygen.

[3] Actually, it has been suggested that those creatures are not colonists so much as native inhabitants, and very much like our earliest ancestors: 'The record of the genes suggests that [the common ancestor of all present-day life-forms] lived deep beneath the Earth's surface, at a temperature well above 100 °C, and probably ate sulphur' (Paul Davies, *The Fifth Miracle: the search for the origin of life* (Penguin: Harmondsworth 1999), p. 165).

years ago). At the end of the Permian, it seems, at least three-quarters of marine species were extinguished. In all cases it took many millions of years for a similar diversity of species to be restored (the most extreme view is that it can take a hundred million). It seems that no phylum has been eliminated in any of these extinctions, but some have been seriously reduced in size and in variety. The present mass extinction began back in the Pleistocene, with the emergence of *Homo sapiens*. It may be that climate changes have also had an influence, but it seems very plausible indeed that human beings, in Eurasia, Australia and the Americas, drove many higher vertebrates to extinction. That, after all, is what we have done in historical time, or even living memory, on every island we have visited. We do not merely hunt animals to extinction, but so change their habitats as to deprive even creatures we have no interest in hunting of any chance of survival. Present estimates of species loss are usually founded on the figures for the acres of rainforest cleared for temporary cultivation, and informed guesses of the number of distinct species (chiefly invertebrate) to be found per acre. In some cases, space is made available for the arrival of opportunistic species (such as rats, pigeons or people); in others, an even more drastically simplified ecosystem is all that can survive. As I write, it has suddenly become evident that the common sparrow is in decline in the British Isles, for no obvious reason. E. O. Wilson's estimate is that the rate of species loss is between a thousand and ten thousand times the usual.[4] We do not know – and probably will not know until it is far too late – if too many key species are being eliminated for the whole to survive in any form hospitable to us. 'One planet, one experiment'.[5]

The problem may be a worse one than before: on previous occasions, the problem went away. Whether it was a meteor or a volcanic eruption that exterminated dinosaurs, there was a time when the skies cleared again, temperatures returned to 'normal' and the survivors proliferated into vacant niches. If

[4] E. O. Wilson, *The Diversity of Life* (Harvard University Press: Cambridge, Mass. 1992), p. 280.
[5] Ibid., p. 182.

human beings went away the same would happen.[6] But we can guarantee that we will not go quietly, and only a worldwide, radical change of heart will even slow our work. That alteration cannot be only a change of rhetoric: it would have to entail a willingness, on the part of the most powerful peoples, to do without the liberties we have come to take for granted. In fact, it is probable that it is already far too late: even if we all cut back on heat, light, transport, factory food and all the fruits of power, the global temperature would go on rising; bacterial and viral evolution will continue (and the diseases or biochemical readjustments that this brings). Our most realistic task will be to learn to cope with this, not to avoid it.

A 'balance of nature' is the current ratio of prey and predator, the present limits of different local systems: alterations in any area (as it might be, building a dam, killing off mosquitoes, or introducing goats) is likely to have large-scale effects whose sum we cannot calculate. Perhaps some new 'balance', of whatever merit, will eventually be achieved. It may not include us. Those who point to the utterly unprecedented numbers of our species, and their power, to show that we will triumph anyway should consider the case of the American passenger pigeon: 'the vast flocks of these pigeons being the most extraordinary aggregations of animal life of which we have any knowledge'.[7] The last passenger pigeon died early in this century.

But could we ever have expected otherwise? Is it true that there have ever been long stable periods in which nothing large scale changed, the Eden of romantic fancy? That there are catastrophes is clear, and some of them have been global. Does it follow that 'catastrophism' is correct, that most of the earth's history is placid and unchanging? Gradualists, like Darwin, disagreed. We fantasize about 'the cycles of Cathay' or the unchanging order of an English village – but the truth is that

---

[6] Not necessarily quite as Dougal Dixon has imagined, in *Life after Man: a zoology of the future* (Granada: London 1981); in fact, almost necessarily not, since any prediction of chance alterations must be vain.

[7] William Benjamin Carpenter, after Wallace and Audubon, in *National Review* 1860, cited in David L. Hull, ed., *Darwin and his Critics* (University of Chicago Press: Chicago and London 1983), p. 99.

most such orders are only recent inventions, read back into an unknown or forgotten past. Some commentators still believe that there are human tribes, in Amazonia or Papua New Guinea, which have lived unchanged, 'in balance', since their ancestors arrived some twenty to forty thousand years ago. But why should we believe this, any more than we believe that nineteenth-century English squires preserved the code of chivalry, or that modern 'Druids' were the builders of Stonehenge[8]? The Tupi-Guarani Indians of Amazonia themselves remember that their ancestors were once obedient citizens of something like an Inca or an Aztec empire, and chose to renounce the state.[9] The Navaho of the southwestern states of the USA may speak as if they have lived in and around New Mexico since the First Beginning – but they also know very well that they have been settled there for less than two centuries. Our century has been full of change, in the human and the natural world, and we contrast this, ignorantly, with 'then'. But any detailed look at history and the natural world suggests that every century, and every life, has endured change. We are free to imagine that life 'then' was stable only because we know too little of the changes.

In brief, the world is always changing, and the notion of a world 'in balance' is a fantasy of how things would be if they knew their place. It is sometimes called 'Platonic', but this is to miss Plato's point entirely. So far from saying that there was once a time when everything was unchangingly ideal, Plato insists that everything in the phenomenal world is always changing, including any 'ideal city'. The only age or world which stayed 'ideally' the same would be one controlled from moment to moment by the hand of God. In that imagined age, things would be entirely, laughably different;[10] the only world we have is one in which ideals are variously, incompletely,

---

[8] See Mark Girouard, *The Return to Camelot: chivalry and the English gentleman* (Yale University Press: New Haven and London 1981); Ronald Hutton, *Pagan Religions of the Ancient British Isles* (Blackwell: Oxford 1991).

[9] See Pierre Clastres, *Society against the State*, tr. R. Hurley (Urizen Press: New York, 1977).

[10] The fantasy is developed in his *Statesman*; see C. Rowe, ed., *Reading the Statesman: Proceedings of the Third Symposium Platonicum* (Academia Verlag: Sankt Augustin 1995).

realized, and the moment passes. So far from wishing to keep things as they were, or as we fantasize they were, a Platonist will welcome each new version of an eternal beauty which cannot ever be complete in time. It may still be a very bad idea to introduce goats, rats, pigeons or people to a prosperous island, but not because there was 'a balance of nature' which should be preserved. Even there, the world was already changing.

But suppose there were a 'balance', and the greater part of earth's history was composed of 'quiet' days. In those ages, framed by the *end* of ages, evolutionary change was slow. Most selection helped to preserve the norm, and not to create new sorts of creature – though if by accident it ever did, that was enough to end the age in question. Atheistical biologists may think that this is what 'religious' believers want – an age in which things knew their place, in obedience to high command. Perhaps there is some truth in this: the 'religious', statistically, are often conservative, and tend to think of time as a gradual or catastrophic fall from grace. That there was a perfect age, sometime, is almost as strong a prejudice in the religious as a belief in a Communist utopia is in the Marxist. Atheistical biologists of an humanitarian sort may also suspect that anyone who admires such 'peaceful', 'balanced' ages must be danger-ous.

For balance consists in this: that the populations of prey, predator and parasite maintain much the same ratio over time. 'Surplus' deer are cropped by wolves; if there are too few deer, the wolves will starve; if there are too few wolves, the deer will starve. The Malthusian tragedy is avoided because all popula-tions are kept below the level where they would endure a catastrophic dieback. It is also avoided because lower-status deer do not risk trying to take food from high-status deer: even in a famine, when – momentarily – there are too many deer for the available resources, it is not true that all the deer starve equally. Higher-ranking deer may survive in health while others starve, or fall prey to the wolves.

This story is idealized: most probably there are always *little* tragedies, when whole populations starve, and rescue comes too late. Whatever local differences there were in such a population's gene pool will be lost. Remember the passenger pigeon – and perhaps the sparrow. But let us suppose that the 'balance' often is preserved, perhaps with the help of internal parasites, viral infections and migrating birds. Let us say that almost every disturbance automatically results in alterations elsewhere in the system which bring the whole back on track – unless that disturbance is massive, sustained, deliberate (that is to say, it is human). The effect is to ensure that many different kinds of being, each with their own beauty, all survive, though individual organisms are often diseased, hungry, fearful and, eventually, dead. Let us even agree that wildly fluctuating systems contain more misery overall than 'balanced' ones, and may collapse entirely (to be replaced, in time, by utterly different creatures doing much the same).

Any such system, in its way, is beautiful, in that the creatures it contains are beautiful. But how can it be ideal? Do we approve of *human* populations being kept 'in balance' like that? On those terms some sufficient number of lower-ranking persons starve or are sacrificed to predators. Perhaps long ago and far away those predators were wolves or tigers, but it has long been true that the most successful predators are people. All the tricks of hierarchical domination can be invoked to balance the population. In most mammalian species, it is a minority of males that breed: most youngsters are banished to the fringes, where they contend with predators and rival tribes. In most mammalian species, infanticide, especially of lower-ranking cubs, is rife. If 'balanced nature' is beautiful, so I suppose is ancient order.

Low-ranking deer, no doubt, are only deferential because, in general, it pays: a low-ranker has more chance of feeding, and breeding, in the end if it does not annoy the higher ranks too much. A deference that usually pays may be suicidal in famine conditions (but only a few such deer, goaded beyond endurance, would survive rebellion anyway). Human beings prefer to rationalize their fear: rich and poor conspire to convince themselves that status is significant. Thersites has no business challenging Agamemnon, even though he is right.[11] War,

---

[11] Homer, *The Iliad* 2.211ff.

pestilence and famine all demand a reasoned justification (and are given it). Religious structures, typically, are used to make the 'balance' bearable. Irreligion, in one of its many facets, is rooted in indignation.

Indignation itself proclaims that things are not as they should be, and is misplaced if there is after all *no* way they really should be. A merely personal irritation rarely fuels much more than a determination to *replace* the oppressor. Being willing to replace *oppression* is a different matter. So where should we get the impetus to resist 'the balance' or the stamina to endure it? '*Honest* indignation', Blake said through his visionary Isaiah, 'is the voice of God'[12] – but we are all too familiar with the effects of 'righteous' indignation (on the soul of the believer as well as the outer world) to agree entirely.

There seem to be three possibilities. The simplest, enshrined in rhetoric about the balance, is to suppose that nature's way is best, and rebellion is at least absurd (and might be sin). The second is to rebel against nature, and hold to an ideal of mutual affection that has never been fully realized on earth. The third is to reckon that nature is indeed the best it can be, but that we need to learn a different lesson. Each of these familiar ways (which I shall label 'naturist', 'Manichaean', and 'Plotinian') itself has many variants, and all may be found in one and the same thinker (as in Darwin, for example).

Naturism is the belief that nature is as it should be, and as we should be as well. Romantic naturism tends to play up the 'softer' side of life: beauty, and family affection, are the norms to follow, and human beings err when they replace such natural impulse with rational discipline. More hard-boiled naturists acknowledge violence, hierarchy and speciation as the natural norms: discipline is the law all must acknowledge. For a romantic naturist, buggery is a simple hedonic practice, an expectable expression of affection (especially among young males not yet admitted to the breeding group). For the hard-boiled, buggery is a dominance ritual, enforcing relative status – perhaps on those same young males. A third variety of naturist

12 William Blake *Marriage of Heaven and Hell*, plate 12, *Complete Writings*, ed. Geoffrey Keynes (Oxford University Press: London 1966), p. 153.

denounces buggery as 'unnatural', a practice that appears, they say, only in disturbed, 'unbalanced' communities. All naturists agree that nature's way is best, but their disagreements may suggest that their account is not empirical.

Manichaeans emphasize how wicked the world is. The balance I have sketched and the wild *imbalance* that is the more literal or common truth involve (they say) each creature's seeking the edge on others, to control or to destroy. Rather than do what probably comes naturally (in suppressing rivals, seizing all available goods, impregnating – if we are male – as many females as we can) we should accept the curbs of law and morality. Whereas a hard-boiled naturist would think of morals as destructive mental microbes when they seemed likely to lead on to extinction or degeneration of the stock, a Manichaean, in principle, would prefer not to survive if the cost of survival is to live 'like beasts'.

Evolutionary change depends on natural selection and the result – we are told – is that no 'really' altruistic character survives for long. Nepotism and market skills perhaps provide an occasional imitation, but the law of life insists that no one give a sucker an even break. Nature compels both cruelty and indifference. Even the ties of affection, which romantic naturists admire and some Manichaeans exalt against more 'natural', domineering instincts, are only devices to secure the future of particular genes. Even the pose of Manichaean distaste, we might suspect, is only an excuse for giving oneself airs. The Manichaean, by knowing that everything (else) is evil, can use it without limit. The paradox involved in despising others for doing what one does oneself (but justly, since they deserve no better) has rarely troubled anyone for long. An only slightly more pressing problem is the intellectual puzzle: if evolution guarantees that we are never fair, nor altruistic, why do we think that is *wrong*? The answer, obviously, is that it pays us better if *others* try to be fair and altruistic: we spread the infection by believing it, and have learnt to believe we are altruistic even when (which is always) we are not.

Some Manichaeans, in short, are really naturists: nature requires a pretence of virtue, which we should only subvert in

secret conclaves. We *ought* to repress the 'animal within', but we
are only animals ourselves: the only virtue we can actually
achieve is verbal. But there are perhaps alternatives. The first
and simplest is to adopt a metaphysical dualism: the ancient,
actual Manichaeans believed that this world was the realm of
evil, but that God had managed to intrude small particles of
light within the dark. God (which is eternal value) fights the
darkness, though the only victory is likely to be escape. We
recognize the wrongness of the world of nature, despite our love
and longing for it, because we are particles of light in darkness.
There is no hope of changing nature: whatever we do will be
controlled by evolutionary forces, and will survive only if it
happens to promote some lineage's interest (perhaps, as before,
by giving an acceptable excuse for tyranny, or giving us strength
enough to endure being tyrannized until we can ourselves be
tyrants once again).

The dream of heaven is of a place where all goods are
compatible, and wolves lie down with kids. Here on earth, here
and now, one creature's good often demands another's ruin, but
every lineage stands to gain by enforcing a fair field. Mutual
hostility will not pay as well as peace. Perhaps that remains a
dream: the fact that a cooperative way of life would pay us all
seems not to prevent our being antagonistic now. Natural
selection is not forward-looking: whatever gets an edge here
and now will win, even if that victory is Pyrrhic. But the fact
that we can *dream* of heaven is itself some reason to believe that
there is something other than nature's way. God's reason for
creating, or the world's excuse for being, may be, as tradition
says, to display the forms of being: all the ways, that is, of being
beautiful. Those ways, those forms, are somehow, in eternity,
compatible, but cannot, it seems, exist all at the same time here
without discovering how hard it is to be. As Augustine said,
there is nothing bad about there being scorpions; the difficulty
comes when mammals and scorpions come together.[13]

Once metaphysical dualism is reinstated, however weak the

---

[13] Augustine, *De Moribus* 2.8.11: scorpions, he pointed out, do not do *themselves* any
harm; see also *City of God* 11.22. See Gerald Bonner, *St Augustine of Hippo: life and
controversies* (Canterbury Press: Norwich 1986, second edition), p. 206.

influence of that Other World, the naturalistic bias of evolutionary theory is in question. If we can know things that do us, and our genes, no good (in the usual, material sense), then there is some causal influence from outside the world. Darwin thought the way of the ichneumon wasp was inconsistent with there being a loving God (in any ordinary sense of 'loving'). Was he merely squeamish, or did he suppose that he *recognized* a wrong? What possible good would being squeamish do? What advantage did that squeamishness give whatever genes determined, in Victorian Britain, that he would feel squeamish? A cynical analysis (as above) is that the pose brought honour, and no cost at all. But if his judgement was sincere, and rational, it required that he have an insight evolution should deny. Once that is granted, why should we suppose that the Other World (of Value) has influence only on the higher mental processes of Victorian gentlemen? Might it not also influence all manner of things, even if its influence is often swamped by this world's cares? May not the influence, exactly, be that of Forms, providing ideals of beauty to each mortal thing?

DOES HUMANKIND HAVE A COSMIC ROLE?

If we resist that dualism then 'value judgements' can only be the proposals or the strategies I described before, and had better be realistic, in the sense that they be ones that have some chance of being adopted, and successfully acted on. Unfortunately, we are programmed to believe that catastrophes do not happen: after all, we have never been able to do much about them, and those tribes – if any ever existed – who lost heart have long since gone. We are also programmed – like every other creature – to prefer immediate benefits to any long-term advantage. Evolutionary change cannot allow the diminution of inclusive genetic fitness in the short term for the putative sake of an increase generations later. Whether we compete or cooperate, our inclination will be to cope, and not concern ourselves with millennial disasters. Even the Manichaean insight, as expressed by Huxley, that there are duties which transcend our natural inclinations, may not help: that thesis, after all, is exactly that *nature*, just as such, is not worth much. In any case, we demonstrate our own superiority by not weeping over mass extinctions.

On this account, it is no part of the general human mindset to mind much about the loss of biodiversity, or the welfare of the other creatures that, together, make the earth. Conservationism is a mental microbe, or leakage from a natural human wish for mostly fruitful pastures. If it ever truly competed with respect for our own lineage, it would be eliminated. Genuine biophilia is impossible.

Of course, empirically, there are devoted biophiles – though Wilson, who coined the term, appears to find it quite compatible with biophilia to fumigate whole islands (and so, probably, eliminate whole species) for experimental purposes, and advocates the farming of turtles, iguanas, and anything else that is tasty, so as to give people a reason not to kill them all. More generally, I am always astonished by the speed with which romantics turn from praising God's grandeur and the glories of nature, to masticating His factory-farmed creatures. Biophiles and zoophiles should perhaps be prepared to make some little sacrifice if they are to be thought sincere. But the mere existence of self-proclaimed, and even consistent, biophiles does not entirely rebut Ruse and Wilson's doctrine – that our morals can have no other function than species-survival. On that latter account, the mass extinction we are living through (as well as the intensive agriculture which is partly responsible for that extinction) is of no moral interest. The fully engineered biosphere, if we can manage it, would embody all the values we can expect to have.

Rational creatures of the human kind are challenged (or so I shall conceive below) to find a way to find, incorporate and control the many minds and moods they have inherited. The whole world, it could be said, is being challenged to find its way towards God's holy mountain; it is not *now* a unity, except in that the same challenge is heard throughout. In either case (the self and the 'whole earth'), the ways we have found so far are rarely harmonious: some goods are squeezed out, and others are perverted.

The most familiar attempt to give an Abrahamic, or explicitly Christian, account of evolutionary history (and its future) has been Teilhard de Chardin's, though very similar accounts have also been offered that do not mention his name.[14] The central notion of these accounts has been that evolution has a direction. There may be eddies, backdrafts and whirlpools, but there is (it is said) a general increase in 'complexity'[15] and 'cerebraliza-tion'. There may be backward lineages that do not grow more complex or cerebral, but where there is development, it is in that direction. All modern vertebrates have larger, 'better' brains: sixty-five million years ago, the 'brightest dinosaur', *Stenonychosaurus*, had a smaller brain than an ostrich.[16] The 'encephalization quotient' rises all the time: by and large, it is better to be 'brighter'. Increasingly, the problem is to improve our grasp upon a complex future, and that future lies with mind. Lineages that cannot cooperate will perish,[17] and the eventual outcome, as far as we can see, is the transformation of all available substance into mind.

This story is not only Chardin's. Olaf Stapledon, a seminal science-fiction writer from Merseyside (1885–1950), advanced a similar story in *Star Maker* (and elsewhere), though he retained a healthy suspicion that any such Universal Mind would find

[14] See especially Teilhard de Chardin, *The Phenomenon of Man*, tr. B. Wall (Collins: London 1959); R. C. Zaehner pointed out the convergence between Chardin's work and Sri Aurobindo's in *Evolution in Religion* (Clarendon Press: Oxford 1971); Charles Birch and John B. Cobb, *The Liberation of Life* (Cambridge University Press: Cambridge 1981) is better based on Whitehead. See Claire Palmer's *Environmental Ethics and Process Thought* (Clarendon Press: Oxford 1998) for a careful, critical study of Whitehead's contribution to the 'metaphysics of environmentalism'. I share Palmer's doubts about the merits of this approach.

[15] Darwin borrows Von Baer's account of that sort of progress, identifying increased complexity with increase in the differentiation and specialization of an organism's parts (*The Descent of Man* (Princeton University Press: New Jersey 1981; facsimile of the 1871 edition), vol. I, p. 211). Von Baer, in turn, had borrowed it from Aristotle.

[16] Christopher Wills, *The Runaway Brain: the foundation of human uniqueness* (HarperCollins: New York 1993); quite how we know it was the brightest, I leave others to enquire.

[17] Stephen Budiansky, *The Covenant of the Wild: why animals chose domestication* (Weidenfeld & Nicolson: London 1992), argues that only domesticable species will survive, and thence infers that we are entitled to do almost what we please to species that we have already tamed; this used to be the defence of slavery, that *slaves* (or *servi*) had been spared (*conserved*), not slaughtered, and so owed their life, and perpetual service, to their captors. See Thomas Wiedemann, *Greek and Roman Slavery* (Routledge: London 1988; first published 1981).

itself as distant from the One as any unassuming wombat (or perhaps as close). The infinitely great is not a very large number: even a Mind that exceeds ours (whatever that would mean) by a factor of a googolplex to one (that is to say, 10^{googol}, where a googol is 10^{100}) is no closer to the infinite. Science fantasists who imagine some future when our descendants, whether our natural offspring or the electronic children of our brains, can utilize the energy of galaxies are suffering from an ignorant gigantism, a belief that things are better when they are bigger. Some recent fantasies, imagining what life is like for really intelligent eubacteria, at least point towards the splendours of the immensely *small*. But either school has a confined idea of Mind.

For what *is* Mind, in the sense imagined here? What is the direction that we are asked to accept, the dimension in which there is, we are told, improvement? Crudely, what's later in time, and bigger, will be better; but what is it? Consider first complexity. The basic elements, on present theory, have been forged, successively, in the Big Bang, and in the interiors of first-generation stars. Organic chemicals have, possibly, been formed in interstellar dust and cometary material. Biochemistry came later still, and with it came the possibility of reproduction with variation. 'Errors of transcription' in the genetic code will guarantee the existence of more and more variations, with longer and longer strands of DNA. Significant differences develop over time, allowing increasing possibilities of inter-action. Where there are more elements, there are more compounds; where there are more varied organisms, there are more ways for organisms to relate. There may be periodic 'simplifications', but the trend is towards complexity, by the mere accumulation of permitted errors. How much of the DNA will have any phenotypic effect, we cannot tell. 'Can it really require five times as much DNA to specify a newt than a man, or 500 times more DNA to specify a fritillary than a cress plant?'[18] Probably not: the remainder may record past options, now disused, or be parasitic, or be a fairly harmless error. Perhaps they are *future*

---

[18] John Maynard Smith, *Evolutionary Genetics* (Oxford University Press: Oxford 1998, second edition), p. 201.

options, lying in wait for changing circumstances – but that is a non-Darwinian thought. The result is an increased variety of genotype, which may in turn lead to an increased variety of phenotypes (as presumably it actually has).

At some point, these increased complexities demand that successful organisms cannot be fully automatic. There are no longer simple strategies to cope with a limited range of options, since those options are changing and developing all the time. Organisms have to notice more, remember it, and calculate the odds. Increasingly they must deal with other calculating entities, and run through their choices, in a practice mode, before they take the risk of action. Where earlier organisms only needed to sense immediate situations and follow simple patterns, later organisms also sense interior theatres, or populate their own sensorium with different paths through life. Eventually, the story goes, they learn to recognize each other as thinking things, and seek to uncover the world as it is for all (or for all the creatures they must mind about). Our future development will be to try all possible variations on the theme of imaginative, 'rational' interaction, and the next step 'up', the step that sets the agenda, will be 'the noosphere', the shared sphere of experience and action. Our present fear must be that a mechanical or insect-like intelligence will be the winner – but that requires a longer story.

Is there any truth in this account of cosmic and terrestrial history, and is it something Abrahamists should welcome? We certainly cannot always claim that there are more sorts of creature *now* than ever before. Mass extinctions guarantee that there are often many less. It has been argued that there were more *sorts* of creature, more body plans, in the Cambrian than ever before or since.[19] Nor can we always claim that the creatures *now* are more intelligent, more social, more complex in their physiology and their relations than their ancestors were

---

[19] Stephen Jay Gould, *Wonderful Life: the Burgess Shale and the meaning of history* (Penguin: Harmondsworth 1991); Simon Conway Morris, *The Crucible of Creation: the Burgess Shale and the rise of animals* (Oxford University Press: Oxford 1998) plausibly suggests that this claim is exaggerated: the Cambrian creatures belong to familiar phyla after all.

before. Despite Darwinian folklore Sedgwick was most probably correct that dinosaurs were as splendid a fauna as ever
before or since. There is a 'minimal and substantial level of
complexity in all free-living organisms', such that it is difficult
to point to any contemporary creatures which are really 'primitive'.[20] And if there are no 'primitive' creatures *now*, how do we
know that there ever really were? We cannot even be sure that
intelligent creatures like ourselves are bound to arrive late on,
and then survive to set the agenda for all later creatures. On the
one hand, we do not know how likely intelligence of our sort is,
nor even how often it has happened so far; on the other, it is at
least overconfident to insist that we cannot be extinguished.
Remember the passenger pigeon. The end of an age, for all we
know, is imminent, and the most intelligent life hereafter may
be squirrels.[21] No plausible story can be deduced from merely
Darwinian theory to suggest that human intelligence is inevitable, nor that it is, in the end, an advantage. The likelier we
imagine that it is that living creatures develop everywhere, the
likelier we have to suspect it is that 'human' intelligence is very
rare, and usually self-destructs. If it was not like that, the
universe would be full of 'human' intelligence by now. And if it
is, where are they?

Of course, there are ripostes to this. If we choose to believe
that 'human' intelligence is probable, then it may be (variously)
that the envoys are already here, that we live in a celestial
backwater or slum, that it is still too early in cosmic history for
the eventual network to exist. If we choose to believe it is not,
we may still say that it had to happen *somewhere*; why not here?
Maybe it will be, literally, *human* intelligence that someday fills
the stars with meaning, even if they have none now. None of
this rests on any empirical observation or well-grounded theory:
it is simply a way of making old-style religion respectable, while
doing without the grounds for such religion. The Galactic

---

[20] Stuart A. Kauffman, *The Origins of Order: self-organization and selection in evolution*
(Oxford University Press: New York 1993), p. 294.
[21] I do not mean that squirrels will evolve into space-travelling intelligence (as Margulis
and Sagan, *Microcosmos*, suggest might happen to racoons if we were gone), but that
squirrels show the sort of cleverness that actually is useful here and now, and have no
need of 'humanness'.

Empire or the Universal Mind that some say *must* eventually exist is a transformation of religious myth – but Abrahamic religion at least had the merit of having arguments, of reason and experience, to believe its truth.

Suppose (as seems quite plausible) that the story of terrestrial life is *not* a story of increased complexity nor of increased intelligence, and that there is no reason to believe in any Galactic Empire or evolved Super Mind. Earthworms and crabs 'are not our ancestors; they are not even "lower" or less complicated than humans in any meaningful sense. They represent good solutions for their own way of life; they must not be judged by the hubristic notion that one peculiar primate forms a standard for all of life'.[22] Suppose there was no reason to expect the emergence of 'human' intelligence, nor any reason to suppose that, now it exists, it sets the agenda for all time to come. Does it follow that 'old-time religion' must be false? That is clearly the assumption made by many atheistical biologists: humanity happened 'by chance', and no one or nothing aimed the world at us. What is strange about this conclusion is that the Abrahamic faiths had always said that nothing required God to raise humanity, or Abraham. Both were abrupt, 'miraculous' occasions, and neither need be permanent. To ask whether God had us 'in mind' from the beginning may receive different answers. Even those Abrahamists who answer 'yes', do not thereby say that everything inevitably led to us: on the contrary, the story could intelligibly have gone many different ways.[23] If God made Adam from the dust of the ground, and Abraham's people from 'a wandering Aramaean', it can hardly be because He *had* to do it. Nothing in Abrahamic theism says that God made many worlds like ours, or that He did not. As far as theory is concerned, who knows?

22 Stephen Jay Gould, *The Mismeasure of Man* (W. W. Norton & Co.: New York 1981), p. 318.
23 Which is why Gould's claim, in *Wonderful Life*, that 'accident' determines many crucial stages in terrestrial evolution, creates no particular problem. See Wolfhart Pannenberg, *Toward a Theology of Nature: essays on science and faith*, ed. T. Peters (Westminster/John Knox Press: Louisville, Kentucky 1993), p. 76: 'On the basis of the Israelite understanding of God . . . the experience of reality is characterized primarily by contingency, particularly contingency of occurrences. New and unforeseen events take place constantly that are experienced as the work of almighty God.'

I do myself, by temperament, find it more plausible that God made many witnesses to His play, and that that is why our 'human' intelligence exists at all. It is slightly more likely that there are things like us in a world created and maintained by God – and especially the Incarnate God – than in a world indifferent to our being. To that extent, the discovery of human intelligence 'out there' would lend a little empirical support to theism.[24] But the argument is not conclusive: perhaps God does not need more than one humanity; maybe there is a Galactic Empire after all, 'by chance', and it sows life on all the worlds it can to be checked up on later. Perhaps we are living in the millennial gap between investigations.

The story of the Empire has some merits. This is not because it is true or plausible (I suspect it is neither) but as a way of distinguishing ideals. It is significant that in order to make the story work at all we have to accept all manner of possibilities (such as instantaneous communication) which mainstream theory bans. Stapledon was more honest in invoking 'spiritual' connections; modern fantasists have to rely on tachyons, worm-holes and the Bell–Rosen–Podalsky equations. Plainly, we *want* there to be a single, integrated cosmos; the question is, what sort?

Communal living can suppress variety, surpassing all free-living forms because it makes full use of all the talents the free livers had. Hives can do everything that solitary bees can do, and also ensure that it is done on time. That ideal of human harmony, when everyone knows her place and does the job assigned by ancestral habit, has often been acclaimed. Even those who think it helpful to retain 'wild stock', in case of unprecedented challenges, only require another caste, which must not be permitted to control the hive. If ever the Hive were

---

[24] If a certain observation A would be more likely if an hypothesis H were true than if it were not, then that observation makes the hypothesis more likely to be true, assuming that the hypothesis has some prior plausibility, irrespective of the observation. See my 'Extraterrestrial Intelligence, the Neglected Experiment', *Foundation* 61.1994, pp. 50–65. Davies, *Fifth Miracle*, pp. 255–6 also suggests that the search for extraterrestrial (or extra-solar) life is 'the testing ground for two diametrically opposed worldviews' – though he seems himself to prefer what is effectively a romantic pantheism to theism.

truly universal, nothing would ever happen to disturb its order, and the small 'wild' populations would be given new, programmed tasks. There would be no need to *force* the component creatures: they would willingly do what the Whole required, whether by chemical, electrical or para-physical controls. Atheistical philosophers regularly enquire why God, if He exists, has not already made the Hive. On the other hand, science-fiction writers, imagining that outcome, regularly attribute it to mechanical or insect-like intelligence, and prefer 'the human'. In this, they may be right, and at least more orthodox.

Absorption into an Overmind or Hive is often supposed to be the religious dream.[25] By reckoning God's will to be done (not ours) and His laws written in our hearts, we seem to say that what is good is that we should act just so, without effort or complaint: we should, that is, be puppets – as perhaps we already are. Sin is wanting to have things *our* way, and hanging on to the good we knew before rather than welcoming the equal good of what comes next. If we were wise we would welcome everything, and regret nothing – not even the loud complaints at fate we made when we were foolish. Twisting the story round again, the dream of cosmic unity might either make us content with things here and now, or give us our excuse to remake things. Perhaps that is what the Whole requires of us, to engineer a world that actually is consciously designed, and excludes pests. The world that there will be is the technosphere, because the world that there is has made us to make it.

Two simple but inadequate replies are possible. We cannot in fact create a fully engineered biosphere, with nothing in it but those creatures we have recognized as needful, under appropriate control. We have evolved within the context of four thousand million years of biochemical evolution; we simply do not know what our lives in fact depend on. As well imagine us surviving without heart or lungs or liver as imagine us without the living world that supports and embraces us. Eliminating insects (if this were possible) would also eliminate

---

[25] Arthur C. Clarke infected a generation of science-fiction readers with the idea, in *Childhood's End* (Sidgwick & Jackson: London 1954).

the flowering plants that depend on them, and most of our basic foodstuffs. Reconstructing all the processes that together deliver proteins, trace elements, enzymes is entirely beyond us, and would require a research programme we shall never even think of affording until we absolutely have to – by which time, with the destruction of the existing biosphere, it will be far too late (since we shall then have no model even of a partly working system).

Secondly, many or most of us would probably not like to live in any such engineered biosphere. We like to surround ourselves with living, independent creatures, whose presence signals to us that all is well. It would be too much to say that all of us delight in just the same landscapes (those appropriate, perhaps, to Neolithic hunter-gatherers). But very many, in all nations and classes of society, desire *some* sort of 'natural landscape' (even if we have to have it landscaped). Living in an airport terminal (even with carefully positioned aspidistras) would not be the form of life we relish.

So we cannot create a fully engineered biosphere, and would not much like it if we could; what we desire is the health of the whole system, shared with other living creatures. We prefer it, perhaps, because that is what, in the past, has always served our health. No one wishes to live amongst waste products, nor in a land that cannot bear fruit. We estimate the value of the land to us by the sight of its own fruitfulness. But for that very reason we will seek to use its fruits, increase its fruitfulness, and defend them from creatures we identify as pests. We may perhaps be induced to set aside an acre or two as 'wilderness', but not at the expense of farming land. When we realize that those few acres are inadequate to save the species who once shared the land, we sigh – but not for long. In brief, the love of 'natural landscape' is inadequate to save us from an overuse of land, because its basis is, most probably, in the wish to use land to the limit. And as usual, we do not know that we have reached that limit until we are have passed it.

When Babylon has fallen, 'there no Arab shall pitch his tent, no shepherds fold their flocks. There marmots shall have their lairs, and porcupine shall overrun her houses; there desert owls

shall dwell, and there he-goats shall gamble'.[26] 'The whole
world has rest and is at peace; it breaks into cries of joy. The
pines themselves and the cedars of Lebanon exult over you:
since you have been laid low, they say, no man comes up to fell
us'.[27] The land shall have the Sabbaths we denied to it.[28] As I
remarked some years ago:

> The natural historian of a future age may be able to point to the
> particular follies that brought ruin – chopping down the tropical
> rainforests, meditating nuclear war, introducing hybrid monocultures,
> spreading poisons, financing grain-mountains, and rearing cattle in
> conditions that clearly breach the spirit of the commandment not to
> muzzle the ox that treads out the corn.[29] The historian whose eyes are
> opened to the acts of God will have no doubt we brought our ruin on
> ourselves, that it is God's answer to the arrogant.[30]

Sometime in the next century, we will have pulled so many
threads out from life's tapestry that the whole begins to fray. We
have already made inevitable a climate change that is likely to
drown millions and starve millions more. The bacterial and
invertebrate population of the planet will no doubt adjust.
Human beings have been trying to live 'at the top of the food
chain', as if they were large carnivores, despite the obvious
truth that carnivores are always scarcer than their prey. We
have been trying to secure things for ourselves despite the
obvious truth that everything we have and relish is the product
of a system that we do not understand and cannot replace. The
only sort of species that has much hope of survival is one
without delusions of grandeur, but those delusions were once
helpful fictions, and we seem to be stuck with them. We will not
even attempt to change until it is too late. We will not avoid
catastrophe, because we do not, we cannot, believe in it.

An older moral and historical tradition would not find this
unfamiliar. Although I have offered reasons why, perhaps, we
have been *biologically* disposed to think that everything will
always be as it is, our predecessors had good reason to dispute
it. The evident fact that life is always changing, and that no

---

[26] Isaiah 13.20– 1.   [27] Isaiah 14.7–8.
[28] Leviticus 26.34.   [29] Deuteronomy 25.4.
[30] In *How to Think about the Earth* (Mowbrays: London 1993).

work of human hands will last, was all too obvious. Plotinus addressed the issue of the fall of cities, arguing that such losses will make little difference, and that new generations, *better* than their parents, will arise.[31] The point was not, as it might be for progressivists, that present calamity was vindicated by a future gain, but that the Good shines glancingly through life in time. It is in the present that we touch eternity, not in some distant aeon when the world is strange. Plotinus also recognized both the beauty of the material world, and its incompleteness. Whereas naturists can find no standard outside time, and Manichaeans distrust the roots of every impulse that we have, 'Plotinians' consider this a fractured, but not a wholly broken, world.

We are imperfect, incomplete, and no more like a beautiful woven web, but like a bundle of cords knotted together and flung into a corner. It is said that the world was once all perfect and kindly, and that still the kindly and perfect world existed, but buried like a mass of roses under many spadefuls of earth.[32]

Plotinus himself did not suppose that all the things that we regret were actually evil. Often we should consider life a children's game: it is wrong to be a bully, but it is also wrong to let oneself be bullied.[33] The fault lies in the attitude, rather than in the event itself. In this, Plotinus was closer to the ancient philosophical norm than modern moralists. The issue here is that, in looking toward the world where everything is at one, he did not look back to the past. Our dream of 'Eden' is a world where nothing is at odds. We represent it to ourselves as a 'peaceable kingdom', God's holy mountain where 'none shall hurt or destroy'. Interestingly, there are two slightly different images. In one, the peace we hope to enjoy, or think that once we did, is peace *from* any wild animals: our shepherd keeps the predators away from us. In the other image, we have peace *with* the wild things, for every thing that is displays the form of beauty which is parodied here now.[34] Who knows which is

---

[31] Plotinus, *Enneads* III.2.18, 14ff.

[32] W. B. Yeats, *Mythologies* (Macmillan: London 1959), p. 104; I discussed the passage further in *Civil Peace and Sacred Order*, (Clarendon Press: Oxford 1989), pp. 29–30.

[33] Plotinus, *Enneads* III.2.8.

[34] Robert Murray, *The Cosmic Covenant* (Sheed & Ward: London 1992), p. 39; see Philo, *Rewards and Punishments* 87–8; see also *Special Laws* 2.190–1.

intended in Isaiah's prophecy? The wolf and the kid make friends, and the lion shall eat straw like the ox:[35] have the lion and the wolf been *tamed?* And is that different from being suppressed? The answer to that question turns on our notion of real natures, and of the Divine.

Pheidias, so Plotinus said, depicted Zeus as He would look if He were ever to be embodied,[36] complete in Majesty – and with a thunderbolt. 'The wrath of the lion', Blake said, 'is the wisdom of God'.[37] It is wise to remember that the Divine may be our Judge – as long as we do not suppose that *our* judges are divine. But there is another image of the Divine that may be better for us: the Lamb that was slain 'before' the world was made, and as a condition of its making. The one by whom we are called to account has been and is our victim. In 'the balance of nature' it is not the predator, but the prey, which stands in for God.

METAPHYSICAL FREEDOM IN A MATERIAL WORLD

Stoic philosophers, who held that everything was just as it must and should be, were consistent in rejecting 'essences', though they seem not to have made the connection between these two assertions. If the good is realized as much in an egg's being eaten as in its hatching, then there is a sense in which it never was an *egg* (a thing to hatch) at all. Only our ignorance concealed from us the ways in which it was bound to have a different destiny from other eggs. In claiming that pigs were only locomotive meals, Stoics denied that the goal, the *telos* of pigs could be frustrated by their being tethered, fattened up and killed. Human beings being what they are, it was the Stoics' anthropocentrism that had most effect, but Stoic doctrine applied to us as well: whatever it is that human beings variously do or suffer is only what *must* be. It is not 'against human nature' to be enslaved, since the good of all, apparently, demands they be. Of course, the good may also demand that we

---

[35] Isaiah 65.25.   [36] Plotinus, *Enneads* v.8.1.
[37] Blake, *Marriage of Heaven and Hell*, plate 8, *Complete Writings*, p. 151.

complain, or make a show of complaining, but, once wise, we will not.

An egg that will be eaten is not in fact the same sort of thing as an egg that will hatch out. Of all the seeming turtles that run down the beach, only a few are *turtles* (fated to swim out to sea): the rest are lunch. Only a few human beings will have 'the mind of God', and act as they know God would have them act, because they will it too. Only the wise, that is, are masters: the rest of us are slaves, possessions, mere material, because we are only *acted on*, and never, of our *own* will, act. The most that we can hope for, if He wills it, is that we are willing slaves.

It may at first appear that Stoic ethics are just the sort of religion that most atheists despise: here is one version of the conservative doctrine that 'whatever is, is right', and the demand that we surrender any individual desire. God demands – and gets – an absolute obedience. 'Freedom' is only the knowledge of necessity. Even atheists and rebels have their part to play – as vessels doomed to destruction. God wills 'the good', but no one's individual good, since there are no individuals as such at all. But strangely, the selfsame Stoicism has been the guiding force of Enlightenment atheism. There is nothing outside the universe, the intricately woven system of material forces, and that universe is rigorously determined. There are no active forms to which mere matter variously aspires, but only differing shapes of matter, no more distinct than different shapes in Plasticene. Although we struggle to remain in being as the beings we are (or thought we were), that is only the effect of material motions outside our control. Living creatures and living lineages are much like water, creeping across a hillside. We can no more survive our deaths than rivers can survive their drying up – in fact, much less, since *rivers* at least carve beds for future waters.

Recent biological theorists have sometimes argued that 'the problem of free will' has been definitively settled – by biology. Our behaviour is as much the outcome of our genes as is our bodily structure, even though we cannot always tell exactly what the connections are. Structures, indeed, are only forms of behaviour. An accidental change in a single codon may guarantee disease, mental illness or 'immoral conduct'. Other changes may only alter the odds of being infected (with disease, neurosis or criminality), but we still will not be *free*: it will not in any significant sense be merely 'up to us' what we are like, or what we do. Nor will it ever be true that we 'could do otherwise', even if there were some randomizing factor in the effects of any particular altered codon. Of course, we might still *feel* free, in the sense that we do not feel coerced. In the old vocabulary, 'freedom of spontaneity' may, sometimes, be ours, but 'freedom of indifference' never. It is not clear that biological theory makes much difference here. E. O. Wilson's story of the bee that, in a way, *feels* free, even though its behaviour is precisely predictable by anyone with the necessary clues (about the position of the flower patch, the hive, and the bee's load of nectar), is no more than a cuter version of the Stoics' stone that rolls downhill in obedience, as it might imagine, to its own desire to fall. 'Falling freely' is, emphatically and obviously, *not* doing something that it is in our power to halt by the mere exercise of our will. It does not immediately follow that there is no room at all for any other sort of 'freedom'.

Libet's observations are also frequently cited to establish that our 'wills' are not our own.[38] It appears that the neurological events associated with an action actually begin, irrevocably, a little before an agent realizes that she has made her choice. Since those neurological events are supposed to be the mere results of earlier biochemical exchanges, it appears that all that we do is just such another result. Whether those events are strictly determined, as the Stoic or Laplacean view would hold, or indeterminate, as Epicureans think, makes no real difference. The two views actually coincide in one of the most baroque of serious physical speculations: the Many Worlds hypothesis. By this account, all physically possible outcomes actually happen, even if new disconnected worlds must be created to accommodate all inconsistencies. Either my typing [HAROLD] at this point was unconditionally determined by my biochemistry, or else

---

[38] See Benjamin Libet, *Neurophysiology and Consciousness* (Birkhauser: Boston, Mass. 1993); see Daniel Dennett, *Consciousness Explained* (Penguin: Harmondsworth 1993), pp. 154ff.

there are as many 'worlds' as are needed to accommodate all possible and incompatible ways of filling in the space between the square brackets. Such speculations go well beyond our evidence. Even the Libet observations are far less compelling than some recent theorists contend. It is difficult not to suspect that the experiments are sloppily designed, and the margin of error considerably greater than the gap identified between the neurological event and the conscious decision. But even if there is such a gap, so what? We are all already aware that our *decisions* are often made before we realize: the moment when we know we have decided on one course of action is the moment we have begun it. It does not follow that it was not *our* decision. On the contrary, acts like that are far more truly *ours* than those we consciously and doubtfully select. The issue still is: who are we?

If Enlightenment atheism is a version of Stoicism, may it not be that theism and Stoicism, despite appearances, do not mix? It may seem a strange conclusion. The God identified by Paul as that in whom we live and move and have our being[39] was first addressed like that by the Stoic Cleanthes. The writings of Epictetus and Aurelius have inspired theistic moralists for centuries (and atheists too). It has been, by contrast, the Epicurean image of atoms colliding in the void that has seemed more irreligious. For Epicureans all that it is worth living for is quiet pleasure, without any picture of a single, ordered world: for Epicureans there is no 'universe', nor any good beyond the moment's joy. Epicureans share with modern science a strongly atomistic methodology, and a belief in uncaused 'swerves', statistically expectable but unpredictable in any particular case. Stoics have insisted that nothing can ever be uncaused, or out of line, and that the only *substance* is the universe itself. The differences are real, but either creed has often offered moral inspiration on the one hand, and irreligion on the other.

Neither Stoic nor Epicurean ontology allows for the existence of real individuals of the kind we mostly believe in. Neither admits the possibility of any causation beyond the material.

---

[39] Acts of the Apostles 17.27–8, after Cleanthes; see A. Long and D. Sedley, eds., *The Hellenistic Philosophers* (Cambridge University Press: Cambridge 1987).

Both agree that the only thing we can hope for is to be content with what in fact occurs, and that the only desirable 'freedom' is 'to go with the flow', whether or not that flow is utterly determined. Epicurean irreligion is obvious and explicit: to worship the unhuman, and forget quiet pleasures, is a source of pain. Stoic irreligion is more insidious.

What is it 'not to be a slave'? What is it to be 'a friend of God' if not (as it is for Stoics) simply to will what 'God and Nature' wills? What is it to inhabit an infinite universe? The Stoics' universe, remember, is a finite one, doomed to repeat its transformations in an endless cycle (so that the wise, and Nietzsche, welcome the thought that every episode will be repeated endlessly, or that past and future meet). The Epicurean universe is infinite, but no *universe* at all: all possible worlds exist somewhere (as speculative physicists also sometimes suppose). In either case all possibilities are realized, and probably many times. So part of the opposite answer is just this: not everything strictly possible occurs. What actually is, is chosen – but by whom? A single choice, that of 'God and Nature', returns us to the Stoic theme, where we are limbs of God (equivalently, robot servants of the 'selfish gene'). Avoiding that scenario requires that there are many, unrelated choices, as there are many, unrelated goods. Pigs really are denied their own real good, in being confined, castrated, killed. Slaves are denied their honour, not just occasional comforts. 'According to most philosophers, God in making the world enslaved it. According to Christianity, in making it, He set it free.'[40] Can liberty be misused? Of course – but any system which prefers 'security in right doing' must in the end demand a slave economy, in which the only 'liberty' worth having is to be content with what there is already. If what matters on the other hand is *liberty*, even if we use it ill, we should not expect the outcome to be ordinarily good. The liberty of 'the children of God' described by Paul, is not a Stoic freedom of spontaneity, but being unbound creators.[41] In our present state, the good that we intend to do is

[40] G. K .Chesterton, *Orthodoxy* (Fontana: London 1961; first published 1908), p. 77.
[41] J. L .Segundo, *Grace and the Human Condition*, tr. J. Drury (Maryknoll: New York 1973), discussing Romans 7.21–2; Segundo looks beyond the all-too-familiar reading which

overcome in action: things turn out badly, because the material is intransigent – as Plotinus also thought. The encouraging joke turns out to have been an insult, the consoling hug a sexual advance. In a real sense, we never know the effect of anything we do: we do not know what we are doing, or what we will be taken to have said. As Plotinus argued, the intransigent material is itself the cumulative effect of form: everywhere we are confronted, challenged and confined by the hardened effect of action. The material world, in one way, is the effect of slowly cumulating choices; in another, it is exactly what no one in particular chose. *Liberty* would be to get the effect we wish.

Some versions of 'genetic determinism' (like Darwin's) have included the claim that there is nothing to be done about 'genetic failures': imbeciles and criminal psychopaths alike are 'fated' to be fools and villains. It would therefore be a waste of time to seek to cure or educate such people. They should at least (as Wendell Holmes demanded) be forcibly sterilized. If they involve any substantial cost to the body politic, they should be put down (no doubt, 'humanely'). As I have remarked before, the Nazis did hardly anything that they had not been urged to do by the intellectual leaders of the modern world. That experience has been enough to give such 'genetic determinism' a bad name. The truth is that any genotype may have many different phenotypic expressions: even identical twins are not precisely alike in all respects, whether they are brought up together or not. More recent hopes of 'genetic engineering', once they move beyond the simple excision of a dangerous allele, are also likely to be naive about the relationship of genotype and phenotype, and would be disastrous for our lineage if they did succeed. Lineages that are culled too vigorously lose their chance to adapt to novel situations. To do that to ourselves, at the very time that we face vast changes, would be folly. But 'environmental determinism' may be just as bad. Notoriously, it was part of Soviet ideology that there were other, better ways of manipulating phenotypes than through selective

equates Paul's problem with the weakness of our will. We are not slaves to sin merely because we cannot control our own desires and tempers, but because even in doing rightly, as we think, we end up doing wrong.

breeding. Soviet ideologues expected to be able to achieve, in a single generation, changes that their Western counterparts insisted would take millennia. Genetic engineers now hope to realize the Soviet dream by mechanisms based on Western theory. Both sides have an identical conviction: that our behaviour and beliefs are always all and only what must be expected of half-civilized hominids like ourselves. Perhaps it is not possible in practice to predict what any of us would do, under what pressures: the world, we have now realized, is far too complex for Laplace's Demon to extrapolate from present conditions to the past or future. The detail of the universe is beyond our grasp (since elementary particles cannot have specific locations and velocities at the same time), and the calculations needed to follow through from *inexact* information would in any case take longer than the universe will last. We never have more than guesstimates to guide us – and can therefore never actually confirm that any theory that we have is accurate.[42] We must always live with a margin of error large enough to vitiate our certainties.[43] None of this stops ideologues from claiming that our thoughts and actions *must* be caused by the interaction of our genotypes and our environment, even if we cannot say, in detail, how. To suppose that anything else could interfere, would be to give in to 'dualism', and the possibility of 'souls'.

I shall try to examine reasons for our belief in individual, personal being in chapter 5. Perhaps it is indeed a delusion, demanded by the context of our early evolution (namely, gossiping groups). Even animal-trainers, even animal psychologists who believe, or seem to believe, that their victims are as

---

[42] C. S. Lewis, in his allegorical satire *The Pilgrim's Regress* ((Bles: London 1943, second edition), p. 37) causes 'Mr. Enlightenment' to remark, idiotically, that 'if you make the same guess often enough it ceases to be a guess and becomes a Scientific Fact'.

[43] 'W. J. Youden of the U.S. National Bureau of Standards listed fifteen determinations of the Astronomical Unit (the average distance from the Earth to the Sun) made between 1895 and 1961, and observed that each new determination lay outside the limits of probable error reported for the previous determination. Each new determination was based on new techniques and made by different observers and so was subject to a different systematic error', (Gerd Digerenzer et al., *The Empire of Chance* (Cambridge University Press: Cambridge 1989), pp. 82–3, after W. J. Youden, 'Enduring Values', *Technometrics* 14.1972, pp. 1–11.

mechanical as Nicholas Malebranche believed,[44] are better able to deal with them if they *pretend* that they are independent, feeling creatures. By pretending that others are, so some have argued, we create *ourselves* as independent, feeling creatures. But before accepting arguments like this at their face value, it would be as well to consider the metaphysics: what makes it certain that 'dualism' is wrong? What is 'metaphysical freedom'?

'The glorious liberty of the children of God' to which Paul refers is not just being unpredictable, nor yet being liable to random acts of decency. Our agency is constrained, frustrated, or 'necessitated', when we cannot do what we want, when our achievement falls far short of, or is utterly opposed to, our idea. *Achievement* is not in our hands, which is one reason why we prefer to praise the attempt, whatever the eventual outcome. The paradox of virtue, and even pleasure, is that we are most successful when we do not aim, strictly, at *success*. So was Paul being 'Stoical' after all? The strange – and seemingly genocidal – advice that the incarnate Krishna gives Arjuna is to 'do our acts as worship'.[45] Liberty, on this account, would simply be a willed detachment from the results of action, and so to do what 'God and Nature' would have us do, without expecting to understand too quickly what that is. Liberty, in effect, is just the same as fate. Unfreedom is only being at odds with what must be – and just as much enforced by 'God and Nature' as the sage's freedom. So far, scientific or scientistic insistence on our being part of nature is not novel: biological data about our ancestry, or our present physiology, add little to that theme, however interesting they may be in themselves. The puzzle remains, as it was for Stoics, that we cannot, so it seems, do without the category of 'self' even to describe how best to do without it. Insisting on our own way, apart from how things are and will be, is disastrous – so each of us is urged to find another way of seeing and feeling things. Being enlightened is being part

[44] See Leonora C. Rosenfeld, *From Beast-Machine to Man-Machine* (Octagon Books: New York 1968, second edition).

[45] *Bhagavad Gita* 3.9: 'save work done as a sacrifice, this world is in bondage to work', S. Radhakrishnan and C. A. Moore, eds., *Sourcebook in Indian Philosophy* (Princeton University Press: New Jersey 1957), p. 113; see R. C. Zaehner, *Our Savage God* (Collins: London 1974), pp. 89ff.

of 'how things are': in one way, we could never not have been, and in another, we must make an effort not to 'get in the way of the works'.[46] Standard criticism of Stoic theory always turned on this: that they seemed to assume that we *were* selves in the very moment of persuading us that we were not.

Religion, looking 'back' or 'up' to heaven, does not require us to believe that all is well here and now. On the contrary, we readily see that many creatures do not get to live the life which they would enjoy. Welfarists insist that one of the 'Five Freedoms' domesticated animals should have is the freedom to express their normal behaviour.[47] Epictetus imagines how a captive bird might speak: 'my nature is to fly where I please, to live in the open air, to sing when I please. You rob me of all this and then ask what is wrong with me?'.[48] The assumption is partly that they will otherwise be 'frustrated' (that is to say, in pain), but also that they are thereby denied enjoyments, and that the world is a little less diverse and beautiful. The extinction of species is also resented partly because of the unknown risks – to us – involved in any catastrophic alteration of the biosphere, but also because less varied biospheres are less beautiful. That loss is not made good by zoos: an isolated, 'denatured' animal does not display the form of being whose loss, through species extinction, is regrettable.[49]

The Stoic requirement that we 'be ourselves' by not identi-

---

[46] 'In ordinary beings there is the constant effort to attain stability, to overcome inner contradiction, and so to become more organized and more coherent. The Tathagata [a label of the Buddha] is not disturbed by the succession of things. He is not caught in the parts of the mechanism', J. H. Woods, 'Integration of Consciousness in Buddhism' in *Indian Studies in Honour of C. R. Lenman* (Harvard University Press: Cambridge, Mass. 1929), p. 137.

[47] Those freedoms, originally proposed in the Report of the Brambell Committee, identify ideals against which farming and other practices should be assessed. The 'Fourth Freedom', to express normal behaviour, differs from the others, which are all expressed in terms of freedom *from* assorted ills.

[48] Epictetus, *Discourses* 4.1.24. Stoics were usually unsympathetic to the cause of animals, but Epictetus was a great enough philosopher to be laudably inconsistent.

[49] This is not wholly to condemn existing zoos. The actual individual animals can rarely be released 'back to the wild', because they have not got the necessary skills, and their former habitat has possibly been destroyed. It may, sometimes, be possible to think of zoos as 'holding pens', where refugees can wait, and learn, until there is a place for them outside. See Stephen St C. Bostock, *Zoos and Animal Rights* (Routledge: London 1993).

fying ourselves with any material gain is paradoxical, but not entirely without precedent. Zoo animals, so to speak, are 'not themselves', and neither are any diseased or disabled creatures. But the Plotinian challenge is a greater one: we do not altogether know, by observation, what those forms of being are. We do not know what such creatures would do, if free, because the whole creation is subject to sin: it is not only human beings who are trapped, and do not succeed in doing what they *would*. What is the liberty that the whole creation wants? What is the world where wolf and kid are friends? What is it that empirical wolves and kids remind us of, or symbolize? What is *our* liberty? Are 'diseased or disabled' animals any *less* themselves than apparently 'able' ones?

The power to live up to our ideals, or choose among them, may be one allowed for by our physical make-up and environment. But it is not to be equated with mere physical possibilities. To be free or unfree does not depend on whether there is or is not a clear causal track from chemistry to politics. The real issue is whether we are *entities* at all, and to that question biology returns no answer. Our belief that we are entities depends on our believing ourselves *obliged* to do what actually we need not do. If there are no such obligations, there are no *errors* either. But it does not follow that, believing this, we shall be more humane. The thieving slave remarked, intelligently, to Zeno that, on Zeno's terms, he could not help the fact that he had been *born* to steal. 'And to be flogged', Zeno replied.[50]

Adapting ourselves, our attitudes, to 'what must be' may be the best that creatures like us can manage for ourselves. By not *desiring* what we cannot have, or cannot count on having, we shall be less constrained. But Liberty, or Creativity, is something more. If it exists, it is something supernatural. But there is one respect in which Darwinian theory actually offers an insight hidden from more traditional theories. On the older, Platonizing theory of evolutionary change, there are always limits, and something to live up to. Although Plato himself would have no difficulty in supposing that there are many forms of beauty

---

[50] Diogenes Laertius, *Lives of the Philosophers* 7.23 (Long and Sedley, eds., *Hellenistic Philosophers*, vol. i, p. 389, 62E); the story may be apocryphal.

so far unrealized in this world here, it is always natural to assume that everything that can be has already been. Both Stoics (and their circular universe) and Epicureans (and their infinitely many worlds) are actually committed to that view. Darwinists, by contrast, can conceive that the future is wholly open: we cannot tell – and even an angelic intellect entirely conversant with the present state of things could never tell – what will happen next. Codons are changed, reversed, reduplicated, moved, potentially, in an infinite number of ways, and have entirely unpredictable effects. The supply of living forms is inexhaustible. Just as any native speaker can create intelligible sentences that no one has ever used before, so living creatures also can produce entirely novel life-forms from the same simple codes. That freedom is no more than an image of Paul's liberty, but it may serve as a reminder that there might be reasons why some Christians have preferred to be Darwinists, than accept what they thought was Plato.[51]

INDIVIDUALS AND THE GAME OF LIFE

A broadly 'Plotinian' approach to life allows us to believe that things are neither wholly bad nor wholly good. It also permits a less 'holistic' view of things than other philosophical schools have offered. Neither a determined nor an undetermined universe is friendly to the sort of 'freedom' that we often wish (or fear). In a Stoic or an Epicurean universe individual decisions are irrelevant – and so are individuals. As Plotinus recognized, no merely material metaphysics can identify real individuals, since 'materiality' is just *extension*. No particular point in the extended universe is ever the *same* as any other, so any identities that there can be must be either strictly *formal* or *unreal*. The boundaries between one thing and the next are equally suspect. Every material thing has many parts, and any attempt to distinguish all its parts from all the other things that are *not* its parts will founder because nothing can exist apart from its environment. Is the air you breathe *part* of your body?

[51] See Arthur Peacocke, *Science and the Christian Experiment* (Oxford University Press: Oxford 1971); K. G. Denbigh, *The Inventive Universe* (Hutchinson: London 1976).

Where does your skin stop? It is not surprising that thinkers operating with a materialist metaphysics have come to celebrate the extinction of 'the self'. All eukaryotic cells are colonies. All multicellular organisms are colonies of colonies. They may differ in the degree of solidarity or permanence they display, but none are different *in kind* from swarms of ants, or slime moulds. What matters is how fast, and how reliably, the changes in one bit can be transmitted to the other bits, and back again. That very notion (of transmission or communication) is itself corroded by the discovery that one bit is not another: even the supposed connections are only arrays of separate bits, through which a wave, as it were, is propagated (and no doubt subtly changed). It hardly matters, from this point of view, whether it was Epicurean or Stoic who got things more right. Either we are swarms of atomic bits or we are sections of a rigid whole. Boundaries between what we call single organisms are no more exact or permanent or helpful than the boundaries between our separate nations. All boundaries are interfaces, and have peculiar properties. Connections within our single organisms are only sometimes more reliable or unequivocal than are the connections between 'separate' things.

One response is to insist, quite plausibly, that the extended world is not the total world. There are other real things than merely material ones, and they plainly have an influence in the world we know. The material world, as it were, is one that is always coming into focus, and the gap between things as they are and things as they reveal themselves in place and time is very much as Plato said it was. The world of logic and real identities is not the world of sense and matter. But the Platonic answer may not be the only one, at least to the question in its most pressing form. Should we welcome the extinction of 'the self'? Some recent theorists have certainly suggested this. Kitcher, for example, suggests that 'the ethereal self' is 'decisively' rebutted by molecular genetics, developmental biology and neuroscience.[52] In this, he speaks for many. Only 'Western' or 'Platonic' or 'Enlightenment' or 'masculinist' thinkers, some

---

[52] Philip Kitcher *The Lives to Come* (Allen & Unwin: London 1996), p. 278.

have said, ever really supposed that there were real entities, real individuals divided from 'the world' and from each other. A sounder realism acknowledges that 'logic' does not work, that there are no single entities with precise locations and distinguishable interests, and that what we take ourselves to be is a function of the biochemical and social context. One form of the doctrine rests on theories about language. The other rests on those theories about the world which I have sketched. On the one hand, no point or bit in the extended world can ever be identical with any other (that, after all, is what makes it the point or bit it is). But for that very reason, on the other hand, there are no firm boundaries between 'this' and 'that', nor anything more than differences of degree between a swarm, an organism or a cell.[53] Any of these may act together on occasion; any may fall apart. None can survive at all without the context of a myriad 'others'.

One problem with expounding that position is of course that the *exposition* at any rate demands that it be one. Even if the world itself is likely to be non-logical, and composed of punctiform particulars in arbitrary arrays, an exposition must be logical and unified. Even if 'the author' is a fiction, it must be a coherent fiction while the chapter lasts. A text in which succeeding sentences were disconnected, contradictory or subtly deconstructive of what was conveyed before, would not (most probably) deserve high marks – though it might indeed be truer to our ordinary ways of thinking than a perfectly consistent text could be. Perhaps rather more great classics of philosophy are more like that than teachers tell their pupils: the closing sentences, perhaps, are not intended to mean just the same as the opening sentences, any more than the destination of a route map is the same as its beginning. Great works transform their readers, and their writers too. But open inconsistency or disconnectedness makes exposition difficult: until

---

[53] Or even a species. 'There are entities commonly classed as organisms that are no better organized than are many species', David L. Hull, *The Metaphysics of Evolution* (SUNY Press: New York 1989), p. 114, after Ernst Mayr, 'The Ontological Status of Species: scientific progress and philosophical terminology', *Biology and Philosophy* 2.1987, pp. 145–66, esp. p. 159.

we see what is excluded by a claim, or what would lead the author to abandon it, how can we see what is said? Styles vary: the more 'literal' the exposition the easier it is to specify what is implied or contradicted; the more 'metaphorical', the harder it is to know what counts as an objection.

The notion of 'the selfish gene', as a way of expounding neo-Darwinian theory, at first sight seems an obvious and clumsy metaphor. 'Being selfish' is being inclined to give one's own wishes greater weight than can be justified. Genes presumably have no wishes, and whether they would give them more weight than they should, who knows? 'Altruistic behaviour', on the other hand, is willingly doing good to others, at some personal cost. Who knows what costs there are for genes, or what 'doing good' to them requires? Even if we arbitrarily equate 'the good of a gene' with its survival, and its behaviour with its biochemical effects, we are no closer to literal discourse. The particular bits of DNA which are the gene (the proximate cause, that is, of a phenotypic difference) do not wholly survive a cell's division. Each subsequent cell will probably contain a replica of the first cell's DNA, but that is 'survival' only in a *formal* sense: roughly the same *pattern* persists, whether or not the identical molecules do. 'Selfishness', in short, seems a wholly inappropriate category to describe genetic change. My wish to have as many children as I can (supposing I had that wish) would not be 'selfish' unless I chose to do so at the unjust expense of others. My actually having many children is not 'selfish' unless I could reasonably and decently have fewer, and the cost of those I have is borne, unwillingly, by others. It is not obvious that a gene's reduplication prevents another gene's: on the contrary, one gene can rarely be copied by itself. It is not obvious that there is a limited 'gene space' for which the genetic patterns (not the particular bits of DNA) compete. Really successful genes, one might suspect, collaborate with every other. Predatory genes, if any exist, which eat up their companions, do not last long.

The 'selfish gene' is a metaphor because we cannot tell exactly what the theory's implications are. It has also served, illogically, to commend the notion that we must expect ourselves to 'be selfish'. Much of the confusion rests on a mis-

reading of the terms deployed. Just as Darwin himself sometimes supposed that 'being fit' was a quality like strength or
sense which left its possessor 'better off' than those 'less fit', so
Dawkins sometimes supposes that 'selfish behaviour' must be
ordinarily good for us. But Darwinian fitness is simply, for some
heritable reason, having more offspring than those without that
reason. The rich do not have more offspring than the poor, nor
even necessarily *surviving* offspring. Behaviour, which is 'selfish',
in the sense Dawkins intends, has nothing to do with selfishness
in the moral sense at all. An ordinarily selfish person might
refuse to give his partner children, because he enjoys his holidays too much, and thereby give another male or another
family the opportunity to breed. Ordinary selfishness would
then be 'genetic altruism', and by Dawkins's argument never
exists at all.[54] 'Genetic selfishness' is simply whatever it takes to
ensure sufficient copies of the gene in subsequent generations.
'Altruistic genes' are only those that make it unlikely that there
will be such copies. It does not follow that there are no such
genes: on the contrary, they might appear in every generation,
by random mutation. Their appearance might even be programmed, if they help 'another' gene to be copied. Suppose, for
example, that a family has a better chance of survival if most of
its youngsters are infertile, and stay around to help a favoured
individual to reproduce. By hypothesis, only the fertile youngster's genes are copied, but they could contain the potential for
a change *in utero*, or consequent on early experience, which
activated the gene for infertility.[55] In practice, it may be that the
same genome produces fertile and infertile phenotypes, but a

---

[54] As it obviously does exist, Darwinians of the stricter kind must then pretend that this
behaviour somehow helps his nephews, nieces and first cousins. A better solution (see
below) is simply to deny that natural selection is so fine-tuned: all that has been
selected is a wish to have one's way, which (in the past) would have had some slight
'advantage'.

[55] It was once fashionable to point to the peculiar features of insect reproduction
(which meant that females were more similar, genetically, to their nieces than their
daughters) to explain the presence of infertile females amongst ants and bees. The
catch is that termites have an identical social structure, with a more familiar
reproductive pattern, and so do naked mole rats. After first asserting that no
mammals could ever live like social insects, evolutionary theorists are compelled to
find new reasons why their theory *should* have made the right predictions.

programmed alteration in the genome also seems a possibility. Is the element that makes for infertility then 'selfish' or 'unselfish'? Which are the 'selfish' animals? As I told the story, you might suppose that the infertile youngsters are being 'altruistic' (or being mugs), but the story could as easily be told another way: one sister is required to bear the family's young, and the rest are spared that labour. The motives and the welfare of the animals may vary; the ways in which particular genes are salvaged, or reappear, will vary too. The genes which cause cystic fibrosis (when received in double dose) may possibly persist because (in single doses) they give some help against cholera and typhoid. The genes (or the duplicated chromosome) which cause Down's syndrome persist (or rather, constantly reappear) because they are a possibility, a likely variant. Neither they nor the phenotypic characters they cause are 'selfish'.

It is necessary to repeat all this at length because the image is such a persuasive one for all of us. Moralizing biologists have taken to insisting that any common behaviour pattern with a heritable component must persist because it has guaranteed more children than any of the alternatives. Whatever we *think* we are doing with our lives, we are *really* acting out the genes' demand for copies. The only acceptable codes for life are ones that our genes will let us live by. It has seemed to follow that we must expect our males to be absent fathers, and our females to be stay-at-homes. It has seemed to follow that we might care, a bit, for kin, and hardly at all for strangers. 'No abstract moral principles exist outside the particular nature of individual species':[56] There are 'taxonomic limits to compassion', and nature is not denied.

But a closer look at what the theory states may perhaps allow alternatives. The problem faced by holists and by atomists alike is simply: why do we *think* we are individuals? If everything that we do is 'really' a by-product of biochemical and physical events that exist because they must, what 'advantage' is there in the illusions of 'free will' and individual,

---

[56] Michael Ruse and E. O. Wilson, 'Moral Philosophy as Applied Science: a Darwinian approach to the foundations of Ethics', *Philosophy* 61.1986, p. 186.

personal agency[57]? What 'advantage' is there in a moral code
at all, if all we do is fixed by non-moral calculations? One
answer is the story I told before: a lineage may last much
longer if most of its members are encouraged *not* to compete
with the breeders. Whether that disinclination actually to
breed is a product of the same genotype, or of a programmed
other, makes no difference to the effect. Creating castes, or
specializing labour, helps the lineage, and its genotypes, to
survive, even if individual organisms thereby lose 'advantages'
that others of their kind enjoy (whether the advantages are
children or the lack of them). This is, in effect, the explanation
Darwin offered for the existence of heroic action: heroes'
relatives do well (or cowards' relatives, at least, do badly). But
heroes, as we understand them, are not the same as ants: ants
may willingly perform whatever acts are needed to preserve
their lineage, but heroes (even if they are willing heroes) are
probably not doing what they wish. The real problem then is
not why we as individuals do things that help our lineage at
some cost to us: the question is, why we do not want to do it.
If parents can be compelled to love their children, why are we
not similarly *compelled* to do whatever it is that helps the
lineage? J. B. S. Haldane's jokey conclusion[58] that everyone
should be willing to die for the sake of two siblings, four half-
siblings or eight first cousins (and so on) reveals the problem:
it is obviously, and immediately, false. Perhaps in other
lineages there are genes that demand such sacrifice, and make
willing dupes. In ours, there is no such eagerness to die for
cousins – and even parental devotion is not always so
extreme.

Human history makes it clear that we do not in fact mind
overwhelmingly and lovingly about our kin. It also makes clear
that some of us, sometimes, can mind about chance-met strangers and creatures much more distantly related. Our feelings
are not obviously and always governed solely by the need to

---

[57] I briefly distinguish these terms: an individual agent might not last longer than the
act in question; a personal agent has a *life* to live, or even a biography to write.
[58] See Philip Kitcher, *Vaulting Ambition: sociobiology and the quest for human nature* (Harvard
University Press: Cambridge, Mass. 1985), p. 79.

preserve our personal genes. If they were it would not matter to 'identical' twins which one of them survived, or bred, or prospered. Moralists often wish that the Law were written in our hearts, and wondered if, in other kinds, it is. 'Bravery is an innate characteristic of beasts, while in human beings an independent spirit is actually contrary to nature".[59] But there are different sorts of independence. All other herds 'obey their keepers more readily than people obey their rulers', as Xenophon also remarked.[60] And the Lord God, to Isaiah: 'The ox knows its owner, and the ass its master's crib, but Israel does not know, and my people do not understand.'[61] I doubt if Isaiah, any more than Xenophon or Plato, intended us to think that this unruly nature was a function of our 'intelligence or self-responsibility'.[62] 'Man is a "tame" animal . . . but his upbringing has only to be inadequate or misguided and he will become the wildest animal on the face of the earth'.[63] 'Of all wild things, the child is the most unmanageable . . . That is why he has to be curbed by a great many bridles'.[64]

Contemporary descriptions of animal (that is, non-human) behaviour tend to support this trope. We are readily convinced that animals do all and only what their 'instincts' tell them, and that those instincts have been created and refined by millions of years of evolutionary success. The parent who looks after her young, and the new male of the pride who kills them, are both programmed with 'successful' strategies, and do not need to

---

[59] Plutarch, *Gryllus* 987b, *Moralia*, tr. H. Cherniss and W. C. Helmbold (Loeb Classical Library, Heinemann: London 1957), vol. XII, p. 501. Plato, *Laws* 1.642 allows his Spartan to say that Athenian virtue is like that: 'they are good not because of compulsion but spontaneously, by grace of heaven'. I made these points in a paper on Plato's *Statesman* for the *Symposium Platonicum*, since reprinted in *The Political Animal* (Routledge: London 1999).

[60] Xenophon, *Cyropaidia* 1.1.2, *Minora Scripta*, tr. E. C. Marchant (Loeb Classical Library, Heinemann: London 1925). Xenophon went on to say that Cyrus managed it, but Plato suggests that he failed because though 'he went on accumulating herds and flocks for [his children's] benefit – and many a herd of human beings too, . . . he did not know that his intended heirs were not being instructed in the traditional Persian discipline (the Persians being shepherds)' (*Laws* 3.695).

[61] Isaiah 1.3; see also Jeremiah 8.7.

[62] As M. H. Mitchell, *The Philosopher in Plato's Statesman* (Nijhoff: The Hague 1980), p. 33.

[63] Plato, *Laws* 6.766.   [64] Plato, *Laws* 7.808.

worry about 'doing right'. Our 'instincts' have gone wrong, and need assistance or correction from the 'moral' law.

So when do 'individuals' occur, and why? Is it true (or only easy to believe) that other animals do not act, for themselves, at all? What sort of 'error' is the failure of our 'instincts' to deliver clear solutions? What is the 'moral law'?

One answer is an ancient one. It may seem at first that predatory and abusive behaviour always has the edge: 'hawks', so-called, win out. Injustice, as Plato's Thrasymachus declared, has better dividends than justice could. 'The rain it falleth on the just and also on the unjust fella, but mostly on the just, because the unjust has the just's umbrella.'[65] Of course, it paid, perhaps, still better on a larger scale, which might require more virtues. Petty thieves cannot compete with statesmen, and statesmen (businessmen, industrialists and priests) depend on allies whom they should not cheat. Anyone who hopes to breed at all must be more than a predator: the choice of mate may be governed by those properties that have proved most 'fit', but what will be 'fit' depends in part, exactly, on the choice of mates. Young males may prove their fitness by displays of strength, endurance, suppleness or wit. They may even show their fitness by displays of sexual charm – the *sons* of charmers, after all, may charm as well, and carry their mothers' genes across the world. Their daughters, on the other hand, may learn to distinguish charm from honest worth, perceiving that distant fathers have not been a help. It is one thing to be able to supplant an alpha male (by strength or treachery); it is another to conciliate or charm the females of the troop. The characters required may not be quite the same, and which will win depends on social changes as the line develops. In times past it might be true that tyrants could, quite literally, be the *fathers* of their countries – but the more success they had in spreading just those characters of brutal strength, the greater the chance that wilier breeds will win. Once any one of us might have had a chance of winning an outright war, if we were bold and strong enough; now *wars* will have no winners.

---

[65] A couplet by Ogden Nash, contributed by Gillian Clark.

One further gloss: thought experiments (or actual experiments) about the relative success of this or another breeding strategy may sometimes seem to suggest that there are distinct breeds. 'Hawks' prosper until there are too many 'hawks' for comfort, and thereafter 'doves' will happily succeed while their aggressive cousins kill each other off. Once there are 'doves' in plenty a rogue 'hawk' will once again get hold of their umbrellas. Further elaboration of the basic game reveals that neither 'hawks' nor 'doves' can dominate the genetic landscape all the time.[66] The more 'evolutionarily stable strategies' are ones that suggest we share, and revenge ourselves on cheats by a simple tit-for-tat. It is likely that the 'fitter' organisms will be ones that can manage all these strategies, depending on the circumstances and their programmed goals.[67] The more complex the relationships, the more we must remember who does what, and the less we can rely on simple impulses of rage or fear. It follows that it is very unlikely that we could attempt to breed out criminals, as Darwin himself supposed we could. It is simply simple-minded to insist, against available evidence, that greedy and cold-hearted millionaires have more descendants, over the long run, than do the poor but honest. It is also simple-minded to suppose that honesty and kindness are reliably heritable characters. According to Darwin, 'some elimination of the worst dispositions is always in progress even in the most civilized nations'.[68] In saying so, he assumes far too rapidly that there is a simple correspondence between phenotype and genotype: the truth is that the same genotype under different circumstances engenders different phenotypes, which will be more or less successful in reproducing their genotype. The enterprise that in one context earns a prison sentence may, in another, earn a peerage – and which has more descendants is another matter entirely.

The other reason why Darwin's judgement, and his com-

---

[66] R. Axelrod, *The Evolution of Co-operation* (Basic Books: New York 1984).

[67] For example, if the proportion of 'hawks' and 'doves' would be stable in the proportion 30:70 then individual hybrids could profit from playing either strategy in that proportion: see Maynard Smith, *Evolutionary Genetics*, p. 128.

[68] Darwin, *Descent*, vol. 1, p. 172.

ments on the undeserving poor, were certainly at fault lies in the absence of a constant context. Let height stand for all: the poor might often be shorter than the rich, but if we really sought to breed for height we should at first find out how tall the poor, if better housed and fed, could be. We do not know what genes 'win' in a fair fight until we have made sure the fight is fair. Darwin could convince himself that a 'bad environment' was at once the consequence and the cause of a 'bad heredity'. In recognizing his error, we can explore the reasons why we need a level field. No one is to be disvalued or humiliated; no one is to be left alone to die; no one is to be abused or cheated or destroyed. In such a context there is some chance of seeing what the different genes will do. Perhaps then we would be in a position to discover if there are heritable factors in the character of those who abuse, cheat, degrade and kill their fellows. Once it is unfashionable to be a fink, the incidence of finks (so far as that is genetically determined) must go down. Until we know who is bound to be a fink (if anyone at all), we cannot 'improve the stock' by imprisoning those who behave as if they are. So may any of us, granted the right context. Darwin's claim that sensible breeders (of domestic cattle) do not breed from their 'worst stock' is true; but sensible breeders take some steps to see that all their stock are properly housed and fed, before they make their decisions.

Are we closer to understanding how there can be individual and personal agency in a world controlled by biochemical events? The metaphysics of such agency will concern me later. Here my object is to try to see how 'selfish genes' might lead to moral laws, and so to moral agency. Darwin's central insight was that heritable changes would accumulate if they had phenotypic effects that made their reproduction even a little likelier. Such changes would be tiny ones, and their effects would be the result of interactions with other heritable elements, and their uterine or extra-uterine context. To visualize the effect, we can imagine 'genes' that aim to have their pattern represented in the gene pool of their lineage, sometimes at the expense of other genes, but as often in alliance with them. The organisms developed as their carriers had better behave in ways that promote those genes' reproduction – but what that is depends on how they behave. In some periods of evolutionary history, perhaps the process did 'fine-tune' the results: even the slightest difference was enough to give, or lose, an advantage, and just about every organism occupied a narrow range of talent. To use an earlier example: few natural antelopes will be either very slow or very fast.[69] But as the reasons for immediate success become more complex there is less reason to expect each talent to be tuned so well. Organisms may do a great deal 'better' if they have an array of responses (whether biochemical or physical or social) to a world more changeable than once it was (in part because it contains such versatile, unfocused organisms). Increasingly, each organism carrying a particular gene will be trying out a range of undetermined strategies to pass on its genome. Even antelopes, whose survival depended on their speed, may now not always *run* for safety's sake. Each organism is a distinct experiment, or set of distinct experiments. Each cooperative stretch of DNA exists not just in many copies, but in many variants. Each stretch, in effect, is trying out those variants to find the profitable lines – and may 'choose' them all by encouraging its organisms to embark on speciation. This will not work if any particular variant dominates the scene too soon. As in Darwin's Britain, any line that demands prosperity for itself at the expense of others, prevents a proper trial of talent. Those lineages that insist (as it were) on a 'fair field' do more to explore the options than those that close it off. So there are more, and more varied, living creatures with that meta-strategy embedded in their genome than there are creatures with the narrow one.

So the sense of individual agency arises from the need to have a fair field for variation. It is not that we first discover we are individuals and thence infer some need to play the game by rule. The game is first established because it provides a wider and more prosperous variety of kinds. If any lineages survive that tried another, they are very few, since they must be

---

[69] Not very slow, because they are likelier to be eaten; not very fast, because the bodily changes needed to accelerate are either not available, or do immediate damage to other bodily functions.

demanding a context and environment all of their own. Successful lineages cooperate to keep the context what it was, and give each other space. I am aware that this will look like 'group selection', the thesis that lineages have the properties they have because it is 'good' for them (as others have suggested that sexual reproduction is).[70] My thesis is a slightly different one. Those genotypes which make for phenotypes that give each other space have more chances of success than those that predetermine more aggressive and rapacious types. Tolerance (so to call it) is less vulnerable to invasion by intolerant mutants than one might suppose, and any such mutants rarer.

In advancing this suggestion, I am remaking a familiar trope. Our sense of self, as human persons, has been traced to interactions with parents, peers and strangers. We recognize ourselves as individuals because we are enlisted in the social game before we have any sense of what is happening. It is the existence of that social and responsive game which, I suggest, has an earlier history. It has been developing as long as life itself. Our personal agency in turn depends on there being many different roles and contexts for our lives together: we are *persons* distinct from any roles we play because we have so many roles to move between. We are persons because our life is personal.

Or to put it differently: in order that creatures be given a reason to keep their word, or whatever other implicit bargain they have made, they need to be blamed, and to blame themselves, if they default. They need to *feel* that past misdeeds

---

[70] Cf. J. Maynard Smith, *The Evolution of Sex* (Cambridge University Press: Cambridge 1978). The general difficulty with group selection seems to be that even if groups or lineages of such-and-such a kind *would* last longer they are too easily invaded by heritable patterns that give a short-term advantage at the cost of swift extinction for the group or lineage. The obvious reply is that something *must* have happened to preserve them, since life is not yet extinct. As Darwin said: 'Selfish and contentious people will not cohere, and without coherence nothing can be effected. A tribe possessing [fidelity and courage] in a high degree would spread and be victorious over other tribes; but in the course of time it would, judging from all past history, be in its turn overcome by some other and still more highly endowed tribe. Thus the social and moral qualities would tend slowly to advance and be diffused throughout the world' (*Descent*, vol. 1, pp. 162–3). He went on to identify the free-rider problem that would seem to make it difficult to construct such victoriously moral tribes in the first place.

are theirs, and therefore need to feel that there is a self to own those deeds. The self I am is created in my belief that I own a past and future. That belief in turn is demanded if this creature here and now is to maintain the game it needs to play. Those who deconstruct that belief, and speak of past or future selves having only an accidental or sentimental connection with this thing here, are engaged in sabotage.[71]

Although a fair field is vital for the game, it does not follow that the game is tranquil. In trying out the experimental forms of life, we should acknowledge that there will be those who try the old, despotic tendencies. If they should win (if only for a while) the future will be thin – until that very lineage or another branches out into the many habitats and ways of life left bare. The moral of the present chapter is just this: it is variety that best serves the imagined 'interests' of our genes, and variety that demands that there be a fair field for experiment.

---

[71] Such persons can accept no binding obligation from their past, nor hope to bind their future. No doubt in practice they are far more ethical!

CHAPTER 4

The biology of sin

JUSTICE AS UNFAIRNESS

Recent biologically informed moralists, after flirting with the ethics of extreme individualism, have instead discovered that there are advantages, even for our genes, in being sociable. It is, after all, a good idea to do each other good, because until recently the beneficiaries were probably our kin, and might, in any case, do us good turns as well. Theft, rape and murder do not pay in the end – or not as well as commerce and seduction. The capacities and impulses to steal, rape and kill are not so self-destructive as to have been stripped away, but other, controlling systems have been evolved to counter them. Dame Nature has not relied on our *good sense* to keep us from such acts: people who only keep inside the law because they are afraid of being caught and punished are always criminals at heart. Remember the bad joke that rats are a 'morally bankrupt species' because they only obey the experimenter's prohibitions when they think they have to. Real moral prohibitions are constructed in our infancy: whatever we need to do to please our parents and our peers, we will learn – especially we will learn to be ashamed. Perhaps there are other social creatures who simply do not desire to do imprudent things: the calculation is completed even before their impulses are triggered. More probably, there can be no such calculation until we have desires, and those desires do not just evaporate in the face of shame, or common sense. Wolves, it has been said, have 'natural' inhibitions: they do not kill defeated wolves who make their surrender clear.[1] But this may simply mean that they do not *want* to kill them: there need be no tension in the wolf's mind between desire and moral inhibition. A longer look at wolves, in any case, suggests that the defeated wolf is not as vulnerable as Lorenz supposed, and that victorious wolves do often kill. Nonetheless, it is apparent that there is such a thing as shame, associated with a wish to appease superiors or to hide from view. If we were *not* ashamed to sin, no doubt we would be happier for a while, but 'sins' (that is, the things we often want to do, but which would in the end be often less than 'fit') would still be less than healthy.

Nothing in this demands that every human tribe, or every human, should feel shame at just the same desires: there may be some things everyone would feel ashamed to do, since they would be less than fit in any circumstance we can imagine. Most animals will probably avoid copulating with close kin, or too familiar kin, since that would be to risk producing offspring with two copies of some damaged gene. Some solve the problem simply, by not wanting to; others feel restraints on their desires. Whether *all* human individuals or human tribes experience or encourage that restraint, who knows? More probably, the focus of our shame is variously fixed in infancy: some would be ashamed to shout or cry; others ashamed to be silent. But shame itself is a necessary element of our inheritance. Children and adolescents who rebel against parental rules in the name of self-expression nonetheless invent their own weird rituals, and 'would not be seen dead' in flowery jeans. Sociopaths who think it clever to cheat or kill still dress the part. Even existential rebels speak their mother tongues, and follow, automatically, the rules of etiquette. Deference is a survival tactic: staying out of the way of those with power to hurt. 'Putting oneself forward' is a risk not lightly undertaken – though those who miss their moment may find themselves passed over, and those who seize it may almost die of shame.

I am here, momentarily, accepting an account of 'sin' as Darwinists do frequently define it. Our 'moral sense', they

---

[1] Konrad Lorenz, *On Aggression*, tr. M. Latzke (Methuen: London 1966).

think, is fixed by what is needed, or has in the past been needed, to maintain the line (*not* 'to maintain the species'). Darwin speculated that the moral sense of people reared like bees would insist that it was their 'sacred duty to kill their brothers, and mothers would strive to kill their fertile daughters, and no one would think of interfering'.[2] Science-fiction writers have indulged themselves in thinking of alien species whose 'moral sense' is similarly alien: who eat their mates, cull their children, or punish those who do them good.[3] Why 'no one would think of interfering' when we have no hesitation about condemning our own and other people's practices in the name of a higher duty, must remain unclear. It certainly cannot be because those aliens are 'of another species', since species, as I shall discuss at greater length in chapter 5, are not 'natural kinds'. The possibility of a higher duty is also something that will exercise me later. For the moment, I am content to work within an evolutionary frame, and speak of 'sin' as if it were a biological mistake.

Shame, deference, embarrassment at 'stepping out of line' and 'being noticed' keep most of us in line.[4] Not being ashamed (or not showing shame), conversely, may be a route to power, though the entirely shameless are so rare a breed that it cannot be a very fertile one. The offspring of high-ranking females, inured to a deference directed, seemingly, at them as at their mothers, are likely to do well enough, but had better recognize the claims of older, high-ranking males if they wish to grow up at all. Humility is a survival tactic; in extreme cases, that humility may be clinical depression (and result, contingently, in suicide). The great mass of humanity are neither forever

---

[2] Charles Darwin, *The Descent of Man* (Princeton University Press: New Jersey, 1981; a facsimile of the 1871 edition), vol. I, p. 73; see M. H. Ghiselin, *The Economy of Nature and the Evolution of Sex* (University of California Press: San Francisco 1978) p. 218.

[3] Amongst the best evocations are the works of C. J. Cherryh: for example, *Hunter of Worlds* (Futura: London 1980), the *Chanur* sequence beginning with *The Pride of Chanur* (Daw Books: New York 1982), and the *Foreigner* sequence beginning with *Foreigner* (Daw Books: New York 1994). In Cherryh's worlds it is still possible to arrive at something more than an armistice. Different sapient creatures can respect each other, despite biological norms.

[4] As Plato allowed his Protagoras to say in the dialogue named after him (*Protagoras* 322cff.).

humble nor forever proud. Most of us defer to others, and also expect deference. Most of us, if we are able, find some setting where we can hope to avoid superiors, or pay them only such mild deference as will keep us safe to command it from our own inferiors. Classes, castes and cliques, in other words, may be sustained internally as well as by superior force: better a large fish in a small pond than a small one, relatively, in a large. Even a large fish, so to speak, may remember being small, and even carry the active memory of *larger* fish to keep it humble. We can be made ashamed not only by the knowing looks of friends and family, but by the remembered images of long ago.

Justice, involving equal respect for all, might be a product of an evolutionary logic. Creatures that pay their debts because they feel they must are likelier not to cheat; cheaters miss the advantages of later cooperation, and so leave fewer descendants. Exactly how the warning voice is heard may be historically contingent: some will feel an immediate shame at the thought of cheating partners; others will be constrained to act as if the good of all involved were of an equal weight with theirs, or as though there were an agent active in them all which did not greatly care *which* body prospered. Perhaps some will feel themselves to be the limbs or organs of a larger agent. Others will emphasize instead their own lone agency, holding individuals to account, including their own self, for what is done. Liberal individualists and liberal communitarians alike have hoped to establish rules of reciprocal, equal justice on the basis of our likeliest feelings. Alternative solutions to the Prisoner's Dilemma and associated games have seemed more brutal:[5] Thomas Hobbes proposed that the only real solution was Leviathan.[6] Unfortunately, there may be *no* solution.

---

[5] The point about the Prisoner's Dilemma is that situations exist where each of two parties has good reasons to act in a way that will have a worse result, in total, than they could have achieved by acting less self-interestedly. They both therefore have good reason to bind themselves against temptation, and the expectation is that evolutionary selection may have done the job for them. There will be an inbuilt resistance, for example, to betraying one's friends. The stronger, and seemingly more reliable solution, is Thomas Hobbes's – to establish Mister Big, who can always threaten worse than any one else can manage, and will therefore *make* us keep our word.

[6] Since all of us will want to have our way, it is inevitable that all of us will clash, and

Justice, in the sense that Aristotle meant, is giving people the respect that is their due, treating equals as equals, and unequals not.[7] Aristotle was also realistic in recognizing that there were many ranges of inequality: in oligarchic communities the criterion by which people are ranked is wealth; in aristocratic, it is inherited nobility; in democratic, citizenship itself – but even that criterion (which seems to mark a division not a gradient) identifies many classes of unequal merit: women, children, slaves, foreigners and outlaws. In actual practice, democratic constitutions, then and now, do not equalize the prospects of the well born and the base. Once upon a time, we knew our place, and it is probable that we still do. Certainly, Darwin thought so. Modern commentators frequently blame Plato for all this, as though he invented class division. The truth is rather that Plato *challenged* standard views, by proposing that the only people who should really occupy the 'highest' class must be those who had proved themselves compassionate, courageous, incorruptible and wise. It was not the upper classes of his day that he intended, nor even 'clever' people.[8] Nor did he suppose that such wise rulers should distribute wealth, or any other external good, according to class membership. He hoped, perhaps, that we could *breed* good rulers, but expressly denied that breeding was enough.

In summary: our species has devised, in line with similar structures in other social species, emotional responses of shame and pride. We are embarrassed to step out of line, to claim what others with more clout might take from us. Exactly what criteria of worth are chosen, and what etiquette, need not be fixed

hardly anyone will get her way: the only way forward, Hobbes suggested, would be to let Another settle all disputes between us, and that Other, or Leviathan, must be the final judge, having all 'rights' that we might have 'in nature' to its way (*Leviathan* (Oxford University Press: Oxford 1976), ch. 14 and elsewhere)). The modern objection to Hobbes's theory tends to be that it is 'totalitarian', since the sovereign power is in the right whatever it does or says. The contemporary objection was that Hobbes permitted rebellion at the very point when sovereigns most need loyalty: when their power is challenged by a plausible alternative.

[7] See Aristotle, *Nicomachean Ethics* 5.1131a10ff.

[8] *Pace* Stephen Jay Gould (*The Mismeasure of Man* (W. W. Norton & Co.: New York 1981), p. 20, 239 and elsewhere), who thinks that Plato wanted 'clever' people to rule, of the kind that an intelligence test might identify.

biologically. Some gestures of contempt or patronage may be worldwide, but others are learnt as language. There will be some who test the limits of their station, in the hope of rising; others invent small groups where they are king; others again accept humiliation as the safer bet. 'He that is down need feel no fall; he that is low no pride'.[9] Perhaps these last will starve in famine times, but they may as easily survive on foods deemed too humiliating by the prouder types. 'Justice', as most people have experienced it, is being shown one's place, and staying there. Those places, in some eras, may be close together; in others, far apart. What is constant is the role of deference. Justice is surrendering to others what they would take, and taking from others what they have to give. Most actual solutions to the Prisoner's Dilemma convince one party that it is wise to bear the cost of the other's betrayal.

Irreligion in this context is rebellion, but just about every rebellion, in historical fact, has only changed the nature of the elite, and left the role of deference intact, replacing the oppressor, not oppression. Samuel Johnson's barbed comment is unfortunately apt:

One day when I was at [Mrs Macaulay's] house, I put on a very grave countenance, and said to her, 'Madam, I am now become a convert to your way of thinking. I am convinced that all mankind are upon an equal footing: and to give you an unquestionable proof, Madam, that I am in earnest, here is a very sensible, civil, well-behaved fellow-citizen, your footman; I desire that he may be allowed to sit down and dine with us.' . . . She has never liked me since. Sir, your levellers wish to level *down* as far as themselves; but they cannot bear levelling *up* to themselves. They would all have some people under them; why not then have some people above them?[10]

Johnson went on to observe that distinction of rank 'creates no jealousy, as it is allowed to be accidental'. What is really horrid is a society where those of higher status are supposed to *deserve* their rank (which is what he almost seemed to believe himself,

[9] John Bunyan, 'Shepherd Boy's Song', *The Pilgrim's Progress*, ed. N. H. Keeble (Oxford University Press: Oxford 1998).

[10] James Boswell, *Life of Samuel Johnson* (Clarendon Press: Oxford 1953), pp. 316–17 (21 July 1763).

at a later date[11]). If on the other hand we did achieve a genuine equality, we would soon 'degenerate into brutes . . . All would be losers were all to work for all: – they would have no intellectual improvement. All intellectual improvement arises from leisure; all leisure arises from one working for another'.[12] Interestingly, and to his credit, he took the opposite view of slavery, as an obvious betrayal of an original equality:[13] deference and inequality of possessions are – he supposed – necessities, if any are to be happy; absolute possession, without redress, is absolutely evil.

There need be no formal contradiction here. Slavery differs from serfdom because the slave is robbed of any family ties: the issue is not, as we now commonly suppose, that slaves are not 'free'. In a way, they are just as free as anyone, with their own duties and opportunities. 'Slavery is the permanent, violent domination of natally alienated and generally dishonoured persons'.[14] Historically, slaves have often been better off, and had more choice, than serfs, or than the poor. Slaves differ from serfs in that the serfs do have their place, their family connections, and their piece of land. Slaves, typically, are captives, 'kept alive' (*servati*) rather than simply killed, and therefore 'owing their lives' to their preservers.[15] This is not to say that they have real duties: no one could expect a slave to obey except from fear of punishment. They cannot even 'give their word of honour' to obey, since they have no 'honour' left.

Stripped of honour, or absolutely shamed, slaves have no shame, since nothing can dishonour them any further. There are slave systems in which slaves *own* slaves, run businesses and pile up savings until they can buy their 'freedom'. But all these seeming possessions are at their masters' absolute disposal: pocket money, not pay. In Roman law, an emancipated slave

---

[11] 'The higher the rank, the richer ladies are, they are the better instructed and the more virtuous', ibid., pp. 995–6 (16 May 1778).

[12] Ibid., p. 514 (13 April 1773); see also p. 736.

[13] Ibid., pp. 877–8 (23 September 1777).

[14] Orlando Patterson, *Slavery and Social Death* (Harvard University Press: Cambridge, Mass. 1982), p. 13.

[15] A related argument is now regularly used to excuse our treatment of non-human cattle: if we had not decided to breed them for food we would have had them killed as pests.

became a citizen; in Greek, no more than a resident alien. In either system *liberti*, freedmen, might still be held to account, required to pay their sometime owners due respect. That subordination was still better than full slavery, not because *liberti* had more freedom, but because they could have families.

Justice is a relationship between those who can be 'friends' but which is more than the ties of affection we associate with friendship. Friends are those who feel they belong together, and who repay each other's gifts. Masters and slaves are not friends (unless they form an attachment which transcends that order), and owe each other nothing, neither honour, gratitude nor apology. Even 'owing my life' is not a cause of gratitude: this just says that I have no life of my own at all. Neither can slaves, *qua* slaves, be friends – and Cato the Elder notoriously took steps to see that none of his slaves could even feel they were. If slaves were allowed the chance to form attachments, recognize their place, feel gratitude to fellow slaves, and so on, the scene is set for a rebellion, or for their transformation into serfs.

That transformation, of slaves into serfs, took place in Europe in the Roman Empire's fall: plantation slaves so mingled with *coloni* ('free' people required by law to keep their place) as to create new family connections and ancestral honour. The same might have happened in the Americas as the flow of new captives ceased: homebred slaves are on the way to serfdom (though all allegiances are still subject to the dreadful pain of being sold on).[16] Modern nations are the heirs of serfdom – accustomed to believe that they should accept the authority of their nation's lords, and the standing of such nation-states as have those lords' approval.[17]

[16] 'It is an old story that the negro slavery of "Uncle Tom's Cabin" did its worst work in the breaking-up of families. But curiously enough, the same story is told from both sides. For the apologists of the Slave States, or, at least, of the Southern States, make the same admission even in their own defence. If they denied breaking up the slave family, it was because they denied there was any slave family to break up', G. K. Chesterton, *Fancies versus Fads* (Methuen: London 1923), p. 128. Chesterton here points out, before Aldous Huxley's *Brave New World*, how 'free love' is the most obvious of all the bribes that can be offered by slave states.

[17] An Aristotelian *polis*, by contrast, is a self-governing community; a nation, by Aristotle's standards, is a collection of willing serfs. I discussed the issue in 'Slaves and Citizens', *Philosophy* 60.1985, pp. 27–46, since reprinted in *The Political Animal*

Is this inevitable? Aristotle remarked that slavery can hardly
be called 'unnatural', since the relationship of domination is
uncovered everywhere, and every civilized society, until the
eighteenth century, had slaves. It may be true, as I am inclined
to think, that the nature of most present and probable members
of our species is such that, as E. O. Wilson says, 'the qualities
that we recognize as most distinctively mammalian – and
human – make . . . a transition [to a permanent slave society]
impossible . . . Slaves under great stress insist on behaving like
human beings instead of slave ants, gibbons, mandrills, or any
other species'.[18] But being a slave, and keeping slaves, are
obviously ways that human beings actually do behave. Other
sociobiologists are also swift to argue that the jostling for
position observed in every social animal (including ants) must
always lead to stratified societies (and usually ones where men
do all the public work, and women stay at home to mind the
baby).[19] Such commentators are seen by others to excuse the
current habits of their own class and country. Back at the turn
of the century D. G. Ritchie[20] mocked those texts 'where
military conquest and social inequalities are expressly defended
as right, because natural; and nothing but contempt is reserved
for those who venture to hope for the abolition of war, who look
beyond the limits of the nation and who dream of a better social
order'.[21] Status, these others hope, is being eroded by contract:
the bargains that desperate brigands – themselves perhaps
escaping slaves – may make to serve their individual interests.
The problem remains: child-rearing can rarely, if at all, be
conducted on such rules. The closest model that we have for

(Routledge: London 1999). I did not, at that time, see the significance of a distinction
between serfs and slaves.

[18] E. O. Wilson *On Human Nature* (Harvard University Press: Cambridge, Mass. 1978),
p. 81, and see p. 199.

[19] As E. O. Wilson himself declared in *Sociobiology: the new synthesis* (Harvard University
Press: Cambridge, Mass.) back in 1975.

[20] Ritchie (1853–1903) was Professor of Logic and Metaphysics at St Andrews, and an
opponent of Henry Salt, socialist and vegetarian, who was, in turn, an influence on
Gandhi (M. K. Gandhi, *An Autobiography: the story of my experiments with truth* (Penguin:
Harmondsworth 1982; first published 1927), p. 59).

[21] D. G. Ritchie, *Darwinism and Politics* (Swan Sonnenschein & Co.: London 1891,
second edition), p. 8.

this is the Ik: a hunter-gatherer tribe displaced from their old range, and reduced, apparently, to a world without compassion or acknowledged honour. Each Ik, apparently, is a pure, short-sighted egoist, and children are abandoned to their own devices, and child gangs, almost as soon as they can walk.[22]

Colin Turnbull's account of the Ik, as has often been observed, is flawed. If mothers do not care for their children, why not abandon them at once? If hunters do not want to share their catch, why do they feel obliged to do so? Honour, shame and status seem to be as present amongst the Ik as anywhere – and especially in the child gangs. If children everywhere invent gang rules, acknowledge rank and roles, humiliate and torture victims, and gang up on vulnerable outsiders, we are bound to suspect that all this is part of a human, or hominid, biogram. Humiliation, more than success, may awaken the sense of being Me, irrespective of my social rank, which slaves have to achieve (or die). It may also simply solidify rank order. Our children always recreate the rules of place and status which good liberals deplore.

As I have said earlier, our best intentions (or at least our new beginnings) are usually twisted into familiar shapes. Revolutions recreate old systems. Emancipated slaves are callous masters. Merchants sidestepping older honours swiftly become the gentry they despised. The same is true of principled drop-outs, who use the slave or merchant as their metaphor, but end by claiming honour as their own. 'Principled drop-outs' once included philosophers, pursuing wisdom rather than honour, riches or a settled life. Cynics and early Christians shared a rhetoric and needed, they thought, no intermediary.[23] Whereas conventional religion, in its recurrent forms, identified high-status individuals as God's viceroys, Cynics and Christians saw

---

[22] Colin Turnbull, *The Mountain People* (Cape: London 1973); Turnbull's account is probably exaggerated, but other commentators (see R. Lee and I. DeVore, eds., *Man the Hunter* (Aldine Atherton: Chicago 1972)), have conceded that hunter-gatherer society at least promotes fewer close and lasting attachments than more settled tribes.

[23] My point is not that Jesus was 'a Cynic philosopher': there is no need to say so. But contemporary pagans might have found it tricky to distinguish different wandering, penniless preachers. See Gerard Downing, *Christ and the Cynics* (Sheffield Academic Press: Sheffield 1988), and *Jesus and the Threat of Freedom* (SCM Press: London 1987).

'the Son of God' as a dishonoured, alienated, murdered individual. In the Christian case the son of God was Jesus; in the Cynic (which is to say the roughest sort of Stoic) it was Heracles, the son of Zeus who *should* have been king, but whom the force of circumstance enslaved. Heracles achieved his labours by ignoring the conventions; Jesus offended all respectable people likewise.

In telling his story of the labourers in the vineyard, Jesus cast doubt on more than economic prudence. Paying the latecomers just as much as those who had borne the labour of the day is unfair because it destroys status, not because it gives the earlier labourers less than was their due. Day-labourers had little enough status as a class:[24] denying them any difference was, in a way, injustice. The *new* way, treating everyone the same, defines a different sort of justice, a little like the liberal, but from a different root. No one is to receive *less* than they need for a decent life. In the words of Leo XIII:

Let it be granted then that worker and employer may enter freely into agreements and, in particular, concerning the amount of the wage; yet there is always underlying such agreements an element of natural justice, and one greater and more ancient than the free consent of contracting parties, namely, that the wage shall not be less than enough to support a worker who is thrifty and upright. If, compelled by necessity or moved by fear of a worse evil, a worker accepts a harder condition, which although against his will he must accept because an employer or contractor imposes it, he certainly submits to force, against which justice cries out in protest.[25]

If everyone is to count the same, irrespective of desert or standing or ability to withstand such pressures, there is an implicit distinction between a creature's *being* and its *qualities*, That difficult distinction demands a different metaphysic (to be discussed below). One familiar way of putting it (that we are equal in our humanity) faces a particular challenge.

The absolute equality of anyone is itself a challenge to old-

---

[24] When Achilles assured Odysseus that he would rather be a day-labourer than a king among the dead (Homer, *The Odyssey* 11.489ff.), he spoke without any actual experience of being a day-labourer!

[25] Leo XIII, *Rerum Novarum* (Encyclical Letter on the Condition of the Working Classes 15 May 1891) §63, taken from the Vatican website: <http://www.vatican.va>.

style religion (and the human norm), which has no doubt that everyone is unequal. Even slaves construct hierarchical arrangements; even the most wretched of the earth can think that others (foreigners, say, or animals) are worse. 'Farm animals', in the seventeenth and eighteenth centuries, 'were a sort of inferior class, reassuring the humblest rural worker that he was not at the absolute bottom of the social scale.'[26] Typically, even the claim to be no more than equals is a bid for superior status, and deeply resented by those patronized. As before, we level down, not up, and find an easy superiority in pretending to be classless.

Within our groups, we find it natural to defer, and to despise. Sometimes contempt is mixed with patronage: we can applaud inferiors who know their place, and grant them our protection. Causing others to *hate* us, after all, is foolish. Tyrants who say, with Caligula, 'let them hate, as long as they fear', leave few descendants in the seats of power.[27] But it is also uncomfortably easy to create an underclass, and enemies outside, who will never fit into the scheme of deference. Slaves, I have already said, are not serfs: instead, they are the enemy within. Dropouts and untouchables alike lie outside society – and foreigners lie further still (unless we have managed to create transnational communities within which all wars are civil[28]). It is customary to suggest that, in war, we must 'dehumanize' our enemy to make it easier to kill them. But the kind of raids that wars have usually been – in search of loot or slaves – are no more moved by hatred than any other sort of hunt. Hunters are more likely to *respect* their prey than hate them. Conversely, the sort of

---

[26] Keith Thomas, *Man and the Natural World* (Penguin: Harmondsworth 1984), p. 50.

[27] Caligula (according to Suetonius, *Lives of the Caesars: Caligula* §30) was quoting the Roman tragedian Accius. Tiberius, according to Suetonius (*Tiberius* §59), preferred to reword the aphorism as 'oderint dum probent': let them hate, as long as they approve. See also Rehoboam, Solomon's foolish son, in 1 Kings 12.11, who forfeited the rule of a united Israel by his threats. Thomas Hobbes was wiser in the advice he gave: even if it is better to endure one tyrannical enemy than return to nature (where everyone is our enemy), no sensible monarch should alienate his subjects, or drive them to the dangerous folly of rebellion.

[28] The term, notoriously, is ironic: a *civil* war should really be one where enemies remember that they will one day be at peace, and wish to trade and marry; in actual fact such wars are lethal, for the reason sketched below.

insults heaped on enemies, even if they draw on animal names, evoke emotions quite unlike the ones we feel for animals: it is one thing to call an enemy 'a pig' and quite another to call a pig 'a pig'. Racist insults identify our enemies, those not of our own group, as scum, the more to be hated because we know they are not of any other kind than us.

It does appear that chimpanzees can also come to see a neighbouring, even a sometime family group, as something to be obliterated, and not just hunted. That carnivorous animals *hunt* other creatures, whether of their own species or another, need be no surprise. Such hunts are not enhanced by hatred. Captives might be sacrificed, with honour, or even enslaved and still not be despised for ever. Even those ancient wars which culminated in triumphant slaughter did not usually resort to rhetoric about 'scum'. Scum is what we call the lowest members of our *own* group, and using that rhetoric, or feeling that emotion, about neighbouring clans and nations, is as much as to include our neighbours in our clan. To feel such emotion, in other words, is not to *distance* the creatures we would otherwise respect and spare: to suppose that we need that distancing effect in order to bring ourselves to hunt or capture our fellow human beings, is to assume too readily that we are bound, in normal circumstances, to respect humanity. But if there is no such inbuilt feeling, in us any more than in chimpanzees, our use of hatred and contempt has a different root. Our ancestors went to war without 'dehumanizing' anyone, because there was no problem about killing or capturing humans, any more than killing or capturing cattle.

Nor was there any problem about *breeding* people, as we have also been breeding dogs and cattle. Natural and sexual selection, in our history, have been joined by social selection. We and our ancestors have collectively decided who shall breed, and when. Sometimes that decision has been reserved for an elite – as Plato proposed that his guardians should decide. Sometimes it has been the heads of households who have negotiated marriages. Sometimes it may even have been left to 'individual decision', led by sexual fancy and ambition. These different arrangements have their own complexities – but they differ less than sometimes it may seem. I shall address 'genetic engineering' in chapter 7. Some commentators seek to distinguish modern efforts of this kind from past eugenic fantasies: nowadays, they say, decisions about what sort of child to have will rest entirely with the parents, rather than with an ideological elite either of National Socialists or American Democrats. But the distinction is naive. The decisions taken by individuals themselves reflect the collective fashion of the day, as much as decisions taken by elites. My own guess would be that people in general often show greater sense, and more compassion, than elites: left to themselves, 'the American People' probably would not have excluded immigrants on the specious grounds that intellectuals enforced.[29] But the intellectuals in their turn were only acting out the class contempt I have suggested is endemic. We are, as Plato told us, something like herd animals, and absorb our ideals from the wider group. 'Government originated as the rule of the eldest who inherited his authority from his father or mother; all the others followed him like a flock of birds, thus forming one single horde ruled by that patriarchal authority and kingship which of all kingships is the most just.'[30]

We have bred ourselves to be both cute and loyal: as childish as our domestic dogs. Perhaps the first members of our genus, *Homo rudolfensis*, were thus 'neotenic' by accident, or what passes for accident. We retain childish features longer than our cousins, which is why chimpanzee cubs are more like human children than adult chimpanzees are like grown humans. But whatever the origin of the trait, we have been reinforcing it for millennia, breeding ourselves to obey the rule. We have not bred out disobedience (as Darwin thought we might) because such disobedience is itself a good – or at least an occasional advantage. The reasons we wanted – or our rulers wanted – us to be childish may also allow us to be childish in ways they did not want.

---

[29] On which see Gould, *Mismeasure*.
[30] Plato, *Laws* 680e: the passage is quoted, and misrepresented as an endorsement of violent conquest, by Karl Popper, *The Open Society and its Enemies* (Routledge & Kegan Paul: London 1945), vol. I, pp. 50, 225.

A STROLL IN THE WORLDS OF ANIMALS AND PEOPLE

The totality of things as they are is ceaselessly refracted and reflected in the experience and significant relationships of all the living things there are. A worm's world is not the same as a spider's – or rather, since both are actually in the world itself, a worm's *Umwelt* is not the same as a spider's.[31] What one sort of creature notices, needs, or is affected by is not what another does. This would be true even if none of them actually *noticed* anything, but only responded with a difference to particular features of the world. Whether there really is, or is not, anyone to notice those particular features, or whether there is anything it is like to be a worm, are wholly beyond 'empirical' enquiry, once that '*empeiria*' is parted from common sense. Commonsensically, it is a feature of our own world that there are many creatures with a view on it. Those 'hidden' aspects of the world are as real to us as are the backsides of objects – or normally so. When the young Laurie Lee (as he remembered later) was first confronted by an equally small young person:

I had a stick in my hand, so I hit her on the head with it. Her hair was springy, so I hit her again and watched her mouth open up with a yell. To my surprise a commotion broke out around me . . . I was intrigued, not alarmed, that by wielding a beech stick I was able to cause such a stir. So I hit her again, without spite or passion, then walked off to try something else.[32]

All he saw, it seems, was the 'mouth opening up in a yell', and not the pain and shocked surprise that yell embodied. We do not ordinarily think such blindness is commendable. But it has been axiomatic for two centuries that only 'value-free observation' is reliable. *Empirical* investigation is looking at things as if they did not matter, and as if our educated moral responses are illusions. There is some reason for the method: we sometimes need to put aside our fears and loathings so as to *see* the things themselves. The story is told, in an apocryphal gospel, that

---

[31] See Jacob von Uexkuell 'A Stroll through the Worlds of Animals and Men' in C. H. Schiller, ed., *Instinctive Behavior*, (International University Press: New York 1957).

[32] Laurie Lee, *Cider with Rosie* (Hogarth Press: London 1959); see my *The Moral Status of Animals* (Clarendon Press: Oxford 1977), p. 111.

Jesus and his disciples saw a dead dog at the roadside; the disciples drew aside with every sign of disgust, but Jesus remarked calmly on the whiteness of its teeth. Aristotle had also insisted that every sort of creature, however trivial, had some-thing wonderful and beautiful about it.[33] To see that beauty we must often put aside our immediate feelings. To understand what *others* mind about, we must often put aside our own projections. But it does not follow that our common sense is always wrong, nor that there are no *proper* feelings, and no way to grasp what others feel. Painters may sometimes choose to look at things as if they were only surfaces or tiny dots: it does not follow that this is what they are.

But the pressure is strong to look 'objectively', and thence conclude that all that can be real is what is seen 'objectively'. Once we exclude our recognition of another's life, and our immediate moral responsiveness, we have nothing to report but 'atoms in the void'. Complex behaviour (up to and including the making of these marks on paper or on a computer screen) can only be the results of biochemical interactions which have no goals, no feelings, and no meanings. Single organisms are only relatively isolated segments of a single biochemical factory. The only difference between the biochemical events currently occupying the brain closest to this computer and those occur-ring as that brain breaks down in terminal convulsions lies in their strange capacity to excite congruent events in other brains. Sentences are only yawns: they are catching.

Very few people (we can reasonably suspect) have ever managed the self-alienating thought, that thought is only a biochemical event, governed only by physical laws. There are plenty who have given this as their opinion (while hurriedly disclaiming any such perverse description), but they invariably end by meaning much less than they say.[34] It is a great deal easier to blame one's opponents' thoughts on biochemistry, but

---

[33] Aristotle, *On the Parts of Animals* 1.645a15ff.
[34] See my 'Minds, Memes and Rhetoric', *Inquiry* 36.1993, pp. 3–16; this was a critical response to Daniel Dennett's *Consciousness Explained* (or, as most of us suspect, *Ignored*). Dennett's apparent deconstruction of our personal existence turns out in the end to be only a set of metaphors.

even that acknowledges the real existence of such thoughts (perverse, unreasonable and ill informed as they may be). Hearing those thoughts, and one's own thoughts, as noise demands a mental discipline as difficult, and more corrosive, even than traditional meditations on one's own decaying flesh. The paradox – that it *is* a mental discipline – is obvious.

That we, at any rate, experience and intend is hardly worth denying. That something biochemical occurs alongside those experiences and intentions, and perhaps alters and conditions them, is also obvious. Action of any kind occurs within the context of innumerable other acts: what we actually *do* is not a function solely of our own will. That the biochemistry itself generates experiences and meaning is no clearer an hypothesis for talk of 'emergent properties' – that is, realities that have no mathematical relationship to the properties alleged to be their causes. The idea that we either have or ever could explain experience and intention by referring to the biochemical events remains incomprehensible. Explanations are demonstrations that one truth follows from another: no such logical or mathematical connection can ever be uncovered in this case. Talk of 'emergent properties' invokes those brute and unexplained conjunctions that tired adults use to silence children: 'well, it just *is*, that's all'.[35]

Experience and intention (or the more traditional trio: *percipere, velle, agere* – to see, to will, to do), as far as we are concerned, are ineradicable givens: we can neither think them away nor explain their being by biochemistry. It was once easier to suggest that 'animals' were empty of that mode of being: their behaviour (or 'behaviour') might more easily be reckoned the *result* of biochemical processes. Their 'behaviour' was reckoned reflex, even though we could not (and cannot) actually spell out the detailed biochemistry that links the arrival of its sense-

---

[35] The standard case invoked to show that there are such properties is water, whose 'wetness' or 'liquidity' is not shared by its component atoms of hydrogen or oxygen. But this is only to say that we do not yet possess a mathematical account of the ways in which those atoms, once combined, behave. That they behave exactly as such atoms should is surely obvious. That water *feels* wet is a different matter – it is indeed exactly the same problem as the conjunction of physiology and feeling: for that there can be no mathematical account, since feelings are not quantifiable.

receptors of a particular pheromone, pattern of light or modu-
lated noise, and an animal's muscles' contracting in a particular
sequence. Such a description would in any case be useless to
anyone wishing to predict behaviour, but its imaginary presence
sometimes serves to blind us to the obvious. In times gone by, in
any case, we could believe that we (which is, we humans) were
special beings: we alone experienced and thought, in a world of
biological robots. All animals could ever do is move 'as if' they
were experiencing, thinking beings, and compassion for them
would be as inappropriate as for the images on cinema screens.
An excessive liking for the spectacle of 'animals in pain' would
be as morally deplorable as a passion for video nasties – but not
because there are real victims there.[36]

Perhaps human beings are a special creation after all, but
there is no good biblical reason to suppose that 'animals' are
not feeling and thinking things. Strangely (or not so strangely)
the chief defence of views like those came not from biblical
literalists (who generally know better) but from the fringes of the
scientific or secular world. 'Animals' do not experience or think
because they do not *talk*. The emergence of language, in the
species or the individual, is apparently miraculous: until an
infant speaks it does not think or feel – though how it ever
learns to speak in these conditions is obscure. This doctrine was
first expounded by the Stoics, who argued that all experience
and intention depended on possessing concepts that could not
be located or identified except through language. Dogs do not
really want to go for walks, nor do they welcome their humans
home, since they have no words with which to express those
wishes or those feelings. A thought is the thought it is because of
the network of other thoughts and possible thoughts which it
implies or contradicts. Lacking the notions of implication or
contradiction, dogs do not understand what they are thinking
(and so have no thoughts). Lacking such thoughts, they cannot
feel – it is said – unhappy, angry, randy or affectionate. If

---

[36] In the case of video nasties, there *may* be victims, since those taking part may be
coerced or corrupted – both categories that demand more than a biochemical
analysis. What if they were computer simulations?

someone occupies my thoughts to the exclusion of all mundane concerns I may not be quite sure if I am angry, guilty or in love: I discover which it is by grasping what other things I would say and do, and what would change my mind. Dogs' feelings cannot be discriminated, and so are not real. It also follows – though neo-Cartesians are rarely bold enough to say so – that animals and human infants do not feel *pain*.[37] The saving on anaesthetics should be considerable.

There is of course (as in most other theories) a truth of which these follies are distortions. We should not assume too readily that animals, of whatever kind, have just the same emotional world as us. On the contrary, different sorts of animal experience different sorts of lives, and live – as before – in different 'worlds'. What counts as an occasion for the same response will also vary unpredictably from one sort to another. Not even other great apes have ever managed to speak, or sign, much more than single symbols. No doubt even those successful signers are, arguably, doing little more than make some mysterious gesture which elicits human compliance. Even very stupid human beings learn to speak, and even speak more fluently than other, brighter people. Speech, in other words, appears to be found only in the one surviving hominid species. Whether Neanderthals spoke, or spoke only in a sort of proto-language like a simple pidgin, is unknown. If they did not, there were people once who buried their dead, made tools (even if of an inferior sort), and had (on the average) larger brains than us – but did not *speak*. We do not need to imagine that great apes, or monkeys, dogs or cats or dolphins, speak or ever would speak as humans do. But the larger thesis, that none of them think or feel, remains implausible.

Like Descartes (and even more like Nicholas Malebranche), the neo-Cartesians adopt their argument because the conclusion suits them: if 'animals' do not think or feel then sympathy for them is mere sentiment. Any meaning that their lives have is

---

[37] Recent attempts to make these arguments plausible include Michael Leahy, *Against Liberation: putting animals in perspective* (Routledge: London 1991) and Peter Carruthers, *The Animals Issue* (Cambridge University Press: Cambridge 1992). Neither author, as far as I can see, makes any attempt to explain how infants *ever* talk.

as much a projection as the lives of toys or trees. Sympathetic concern for animal interests is therefore only a selfish desire to keep one's toys intact. Those whose interests lie in hunting, killing or 'tormenting' them need feel no pangs of guilt, and can portray themselves as properly hard-headed moralists. My complaint is not that they are hard-hearted, but that that their arguments are very bad.

No one without a theory is in real doubt that animals, infants and the deaf-and-dumb have thoughts and feelings. In this, as in other branches of philosophy, the issue is not to prove what everyone already knows, but rather to ask if what they 'know' is false, or at least has problems. Whewell describes a deaf-dumb child to whom some theorists would deny a mind:

No one would look at the change which came over her sightless countenance, when a known hand touched hers, and doubt that there was a human soul within the frame . . . And such modes of communication with her companions as had been taught her, or as she had herself invented, well bore out the belief that her mind was the constant dwelling place, not only of human affections but of human thoughts.[38]

Our customary and unargued judgements that cows are curious, cats playful, and squirrels rather clever, may be wrong.[39] Even 'monogamous' birds most probably are not faithful *to each other*, but to their nest and range. 'Brave' horses probably do not withstand danger for the sake of doing right, or even 'to help their friends', but are roused to battle by the sound of trumpets. Perhaps they cannot discriminate between 'true friendship' and 'affection': it does not follow that they feel neither, nor even that they 'only' feel affection. A monkey who is unwilling to press the switch that simultaneously releases food to him, and an electric shock to another monkey, is at least more compassionate than the human experimenter, even if he

---

[38] William Whewell, *Of the Plurality of Worlds* (John W. Parker & Son: London 1854), p. 189.

[39] Very strangely, some neo-Cartesians profess to be Wittgensteinians, whose other usual move is to deny the possibility of fundamental philosophical challenges to common sense. This is a useful rhetorical gambit, which they resent being used against them.

lacks full understanding of the situation, and is mainly moved by his own discomfort at the sight.[40]

Is language needed for thought and feeling? If it were, it seems impossible to see how anyone could ever learn a language. Infants, observably, can recognize human faces, reach out for what they want, complain of hunger, frustration and banged heads, before they speak. They can also be surprised by discontinuities, and alarmed by night-time terrors. The world of our experience, and theirs, is not composed entirely of present sensations, nor of simple material objects. We inherit worlds more suitable to our condition.

We may, if we like, by our reasonings, unwind things back to that black and jointless continuity of space and moving clouds of swarming atoms which science calls the only real world. But all the while the world we feel and live in will be that which our ancestors and we, by slowly cumulating strokes of choice, have extricated out of this, like sculptors, by simply rejecting certain portions of the given stuff. Other sculptors, other statues from the same stone! Other minds, other worlds from the same monotonous and inexpressive chaos! My world is but one in a million alike embedded, alike real to those who may abstract them. How different must be the worlds in the consciousness of ant, cuttlefish or crab![41]

Alongside presently existing things are the ghosts of memory, dream, desire and fright. Animals as well inhabit worlds that are more than present objects: buried nuts and bones, and hidden pathways, are as much a part of their experience as immediately present things. If they were not, each moment would be a fresh beginning, through which the creature was carried only by an unformed impulse. Even time is represen-

---

[40] The absurdity of saying, simultaneously, that in animals one thing and another cannot be distinguished, and then attributing the *lower* thing to them, was pointed out by Owen Barfield in *Poetic Diction: a study in meaning* (Faber: London 1928); see also C. S. Lewis, *That Hideous Strength* (Bodley Head: London 1945), p. 321, where his enlightened sage declares that '[the resident sceptic] is introducing into animal life a distinction which does not exist there, and then trying to determine on which side of that distinction the feelings of [the cat and the bear] fall. You've got to become human before the physical cravings are distinguishable from affections.' Why Lewis, who opposed vivisection, did not recognize how badly we also treat pigs, sheep and cattle, is – to me – a mystery.

[41] William James, *The Principles of Psychology* (Macmillan: New York 1890), vol. I, pp. 288–9.

table within the landscape of the mind: there is nothing, *pace* Wittgensteinians, impossible about a dog's expecting his master to come home *tomorrow*. The homecoming is placed beyond an imagined darkness, with no need of words to represent that fact. Travelling through the landscape there will come a moment when interior and exterior worlds combine.

Nor is there any need for words to make analogies, or grasp connections. No doubt, some creatures are quicker or cleverer than others: it is not obvious that humans are always either, nor that it is speech that gives anyone the edge. There is indeed some reason to suspect that it is our internal and perpetual chatter that most gets in the way of insight. There may be occasional problems. One dog may have another dog in mind, but be unable to communicate that thought to any other dog. Speech allows the possibility (as does art) of third-person reference. This is not to say that the thought may not be obvious: perhaps the reference is made by acting out the presence, or by making some familiar noise, that brings the absent dog to mind. Confirmation of a common thought can then be given by increased excitement, or a synchronized greeting when the third dog comes. Long before there is speech, there can be mime, impersonation, or reminiscent noises. Before our ancestors spoke (it is as plausible a speculation as any other) they drew pictures, or built snowmen, to give a public showing to their inner thoughts. Exactly how the other animals coordinate their imaginings, and whether or when this is deliberate is not to be settled by armchair theory. It is enough that the arguments against their having 'inner lives' or even sharing those lives are specious. One of the most interesting and difficult of speculations concerns the experience of cetaceans: by mapping the world through sound they make it possible, it seems, to construct phantoms in each other's experience. How we could establish this as *real*, I do not know, but the notion points to an aspect of imagination that we casually ignore. Even talk of an 'inner' life may be misleading: memories, dreams, and phantoms do not exist 'inside' our skulls, or behind our eyes, but 'out there' in the real, experienced world. It is only by a careful discipline that we distinguish phantoms from realities, just as it is only careful discipline that distinguishes our feelings about our friends from those real friends' realities. We reveal those phantoms to each other through art; perhaps cetaceans can manage more direct modalities.

That animals cannot think or feel was always a weird conclusion, partly because human virtue was so often supposed to rest in resisting animal feeling, or at least transcending it. We took it for granted that we knew, in general, how animals feel, because we feel the same. On the one hand, hunger, despair, lust, anger are emotions that may drive us to destruction; on the other, loyalty, affection, parental care and natural courage are dispositions we encourage in ourselves and others, partly by recalling animal icons. When nineteenth-century reformers sought to outlaw bear-baiting, dogfights and cockfights, they were moved by the thought of animals torn to pieces. Some of their opponents chose to speak as if Descartes was right, and animals felt no more than clockwork or rag dolls. But most claimed to appreciate the animals' *courage* (as hunters nowadays purport to admire the *foxiness* of foxes), and urged that the sports should continue, to inure the public to necessary bloodshed, and inspire them to fresh deeds of glory.[42] Banning the sports would make wimps of us all, because we would lose a present inspiration. The animals, it might be hinted, actually deserve the chance to try their strength: that, after all, is what they do in the wild. A later generation easily convinced itself that few fights in the wild are to the death: defeated animals cringe or run away. That observation may be as loaded as the earlier, that fighting animals fight on. The probability is high that some, not all, surrender, and most, not all, victorious animals do not press the point. That they feel similar pride, fury and humiliation is very likely: why should we feel those things if none of our cousins do?

That we have more 'complex' feelings than the ones we share with them may also be believable: being coyly pleased at winning a prize for raffia work, especially when someone else whose grandmother had offended ours had lost despite her

---

[42] 'When Prince Lewis of Baden saw a cockfight at the English court in 1694, he remarked that he would never have guessed that a bird could display so much valour and magnanimity', Thomas, *Man and the Natural World*, p. 183.

bragging, is probably an emotion unlikely to concern a dog –
but most of its core elements are recognizable in any 'higher
vertebrate'. Whether other vertebrates (or animals) have
complex thoughts and feelings of their own, unnoticeable or
incomprehensible to us, is also wholly unknown, and probably,
by us, unknowable.

WOMEN AND MEN AND SAVAGES

The total 'otherness' of other sorts of thing has usually, by male
philosophers, been associated with the 'other' sex, the feminine.
The easiest, and self-congratulatory, approach has been to
suppose that women lack the 'higher' faculties of men, and so
represent a lesser sort of humanity.

Woman seems to differ from man in mental disposition, chiefly in her
greater tenderness and less selfishness . . . Woman, owing to her
maternal instincts, displays those qualities towards her infants in an
eminent degree; therefore it is likely that she should often extend
them towards her fellow-creatures. Man is the rival of other men; he
delights in competition, and this leads to ambition which passes too
easily into selfishness. These latter qualities seem to be his natural and
unfortunate birthright. It is generally admitted that with woman the
powers of intuition, of rapid perception, and perhaps of imitation, are
more strongly marked than in man; but some, at least, of those
faculties are characteristic of the lower races, and therefore of a past
and lower state of civilization. The chief distinction in the intellectual
powers of the two sexes is shewn by man attaining to a higher
eminence, in whatever he takes up, than woman can attain – whether
requiring deep thought, reason, or imagination, or merely the use of
the senses and hands.[43]

Even when women are 'superior' it is only in such occupations
as are suited to a lower, and more 'primitive', society. Men *could*
feel and think like women, by succumbing to a 'womanish'
sentimentality, or love of luxury: 'proper' men are led by a
harder reason. Darwin was certainly not alone in thinking this.
Adam fell, in the rationalizing version of the Fall proposed by
Spinoza, because he listened to his wife, and thought of himself
as like an animal. The restoration, so Spinoza thought, would

---

[43] Darwin, *Descent*, vol. II, pp. 326–7.

come by obedience to the divine Reason: we males should think and act so as to be doing what we *see* is right. The best that women in general can expect is that they should act on the basis of a proper sentiment, and be guarded from excess by a decent husband.[44] Other, more widely educated philosophers even of Spinoza's day, preferred to recognize that there were women as well as men who could think clearly and unsentimentally, and men as well as women whose thoughts were woolly or confused. Amongst Descartes' most intelligent critics and disciples were women who found his rationalism a release. Women were instrumental in encouraging Leibniz, and his critics, to argue their case in detail. What differences there were between the sexes were but superficial.

Later commentators have returned to thinking that men and women may be more thoroughly opaque to each other: that our experience of life both is and is bound to be different, and that we are likely to have dissimilar feelings, strategies and talents. Some seem to return to traditional stereotypes: women for the nursery and kitchen, men for the hunt and war and parliament. Men operate by abstract principles, and women by immediate practicalities. Women are monogamous and men are polygamous. Men are good with things, and women are good at language: hardly any woman ever gets to be a nerd (though it may be admitted that most men do not either). In extreme cases, theorists illogically infer that because most violent people are men, most men are violent people, just as an older generation used to infer that because most nurturing parents are women, most women are nurturing parents – and those who obviously are not are freaks.

The male supremacist version of this story is that patriarchy is inevitable, because men are, overwhelmingly, the logical, the ambitious, and the domineering sex. The radical feminist version is that men should be phased out – as being aggressive, impatient, untidy and impractical. Bisexual exchange is no longer necessary for reproduction. It may be useful to transfer and rearrange genetic information, but that never *needed* to be

---

[44] So Aristotle also taught; see my 'Aristotle's Woman', *History of Political Thought* 3.1982, pp. 177–91, since reprinted in *The Political Animal*.

done in the way most creatures do. The very existence of *male* organisms, contributing no more than DNA to the fertilized zygote, depended on a choice of strategies: leaving one's seed with *someone else* to rear. Like cuckoos, males depend on there being dupes! More generally, once the system is established, it pays to invest in offspring of the *rarer* sex. And so, until now, the balance of the sexes has been even. Hermaphroditic organisms, who infect each other, or female organisms who incorporate another set of genes by viral infection or transduction, might create more egalitarian species. Males are at best redundant, and at worst, dangerous. Is there anything to be said for having two sexes?

The supposed inevitability of patriarchy, founded in the energy and ambition of the 'masculine mind', is more probably a product of selective attention. Male anthropologists – and biologists – have tended to attend to what conspicuous males do. 'Males act, and females are acted on', so whatever it is that females actually *do* stays out of sight. More careful observation, of human and of animal society, has made it clear that female animals are agents too, and may be dominant agencies. We are in no position yet to know what women, and men, will be like in a genuinely open and egalitarian society, where the costs, as well as the benefits, of child care are shared more evenly between the sexes. We can be confident that as long as we are mammalian our children will occupy a central place in the economy, and there will be some mechanism to involve both sexes in their upbringing. In the past it has always been the case that we can afford to lose more males than females. Even if each adult male is formally restricted to one adult female at a time, any losses will be made good in a generation. A shortage of males, if it were seriously an issue, could always be alleviated by permitting more polygynous arrangements. A shortage of females is always a more cogent check on rising population.[45] The result has usually been that young males wander away, or

---

[45] Which might explain the widespread practice of female infanticide more plausibly than merely social factors, having to do with the expense of providing dowries. Breeders know how to limit herds, and have bequeathed the practices we all once used.

are thrown out of home, while females stay with mothers and
aunts to rear another generation. Males may be invited back as
singletons or as hierarchical cohorts. Even amongst primates
there are several distinct patterns of relationship: pair-bonding
gibbons, polygynous gorillas, squabbling chimpanzee clans.
Similar patterns exist in human history, but 'marriage' of
whatever kind is not the same as the ties of courtship or co-
parenthood.

Marriage indeed can serve as a test case for all comparisons
of human and non-human ritual and established role. Samuel
Johnson believed that savages had no thought beyond the
moment's pleasure, and so no culture, compassion or fidelity.
The opinion was founded on incorrigible ignorance on the one
hand, and personal insight on the other. If savages really were
beings without culture, that is how they would be: 'it is so far
from being natural for a man and a woman to live in a state of
marriage, that we find all the motives which they have for
remaining in that connection, and the restraints which civilized
society imposes to prevent separation, are hardly sufficient to
keep them together'.[46] To the response that a man and a
woman might enjoy each other's company, and have fewer
grounds for quarrelling in 'uncivilized' society, Johnson replied
that there would always be disagreements about what to do,
and no long-lasting affection. Ghiselin reached a similar conclusion: 'marital relationships in a state of nature are purely
matters of expediency, and there exist no laws imposing justice
or moral responsibility upon them'.[47]

There is some reason to acknowledge that hunter-gatherer
groups are not held together by any strong ties of loyalty:
finding family life a strain, individuals may wander off to
attach themselves to other groups. If any competent adult
(however old that is) has access to the relevant skills required
to live at ease in a well-explored milieu, why should they put
up with tedious or irritating company? A similarly fluid
population exists in some parts of the Western world, lacking
any serious bond to locality, family or institution. Whether this

---

[46] Johnson (28 March 1772), Boswell, *Johnson*, p. 473.
[47] Ghiselin, *Economy of Nature*, p. 152.

is Johnsonian savagery, or only a different cultural choice, who knows? The question is: do we need marriage, and the family line? If Johnson is right, that hardly all the weight of civilized society will serve to keep marriages together, and that left to our 'savage' selves we would live, and eat, and copulate just where and when we pleased, what is the point of leaving the 'savage' state?

Johnson's own reply turned on the 'obvious' advantages of having higher goals than pleasure. 'What a wretch must he be, who is content with such conversation as can be had among savages!'[48] – though there is no record of Johnson's having had such conversation. More seriously, he might insist that savages have no compassion (any more, he thought, than brutes or children do): having such compassion, they might be constrained to care for children, parents and old friends beyond the sensual moment.

But why are we so disinclined to do the things we need to do to live? 'That [the Indians] help some of their children is plain; for some of them live, which they could not do without being helped.'[49] Children may not need so long a period of dependency as we now impose on them, but mere personal affection may last less long than is needed. Human mothers may need more help than other primates merely to give birth: they must have had cooperative assistance long before high culture, from other females in their lineage and from such males as were 'attached'. Why are those affections not strong enough to serve? Or if they are, why do we need the law?

The older answer was that our impulses are now disordered. Back before the Fall – whether that was an historical event or not – we wanted what it was right to want, and need not struggle.[50] Some day, after apocalypse, God will 'write His laws

---

[48] Johnson (7 April 1778), Boswell, *Johnson*, p. 912.
[49] Johnson (20 April 1783), ibid., p. 1227.
[50] Steve Jones's belief (*In the Blood: God, genes and destiny* (HarperCollins: London 1996), p. 245) that Christians taught that sex led to our being expelled from Eden is wholly false. In Eden, as Augustine tells us, our desires were not concupiscent. John M. Rist (*Augustine* (Cambridge University Press: Cambridge 1994), pp. 112ff., 321ff.) discusses the many texts in which Augustine explores this issue – though he is perhaps too quick to see residual error in Augustine's suspicion of sexual desire. Our sexuality is now fallen, but was not the occasion of our fall.

in our hearts' again. Between those moments, in historical time, we live by external law, and need the pressure of social sanction to control our impulse. Left to ourselves, we are worse than any beast – though beasts themselves, it seems, are also 'fallen'.

In nature, theorists suppose, the structure and habits of a lineage are those that have served to keep the lineage living. Incompetent and uncaring parents do not leave many young. Quarrelsome and sociopathic adults do not prosper either, since their peers dislike them. Even predators will have good reason not to overkill their prey, and resist the arrival of more eager or bloodthirsty predators. One answer to the problem posed by human folly is that we have kept our sociopaths alive. Johnson supposed that he would himself have perished young: 'a savage, when he is hungry, will not carry about with him a looby of nine years old, who cannot help himself'.[51] He was probably wrong, since 'savages' are as easily charmed by nine-year olds as anyone, and usually live in a vast natural larder. Darwin was also, obviously, wrong to think that the imprisonment or execution of convicted criminals was somehow breeding a more law-abiding species, or that allowing the feckless poor to breed was breeding worse. But the notion still has power to persuade: in nature sociopaths would perish, or not breed. In 'civilized' society, where survival depends far less on individual character, there is less rigorous selection against unsocial traits. Johnson survived despite poor eyesight. Others survived despite being psychopaths.

A further difficulty rests on the rise of empire. As long as people live in local or national groups they are likely to be related closely to almost everyone they meet. Caring for chance-met strangers will be to care for people carrying almost all our genes. Empires, by contrast, depend on large-scale migration, forced or unforced, and lead to vastly heterogeneous populations.[52] Caring for chance-met strangers, in that context, is much less likely to be caring for 'our own', and so is

---

[51] Johnson (20 April 1783), Boswell, *Johnson*, p. 1227.
[52] I acknowledge that casual migrations, even before empire, may have helped to maintain gene flow across the continents: whether it was the wanderers or the settled peoples that predominated long ago, who knows?

vulnerable to invasion by 'sociopathic genes'. Fearing that invasion, we begin to behave like sociopaths ourselves. The more heterogeneous the population, the less eager it will be to maintain welfare rights for all.[53] Empires keep an internal peace by force of arms, where nations are preserved, not flawlessly, by family connections. Empires also *need* their psychopaths – to maintain internal order and to launch attacks on others. Suddenly there was scope for restless, angry, violent people, where there was none before.

So empires, which create the possibility of relationships between distant populations (and so help to avoid the creation of many human species), also make it possible for people to be savages, in ways that our first ancestors were not. Back in the old days everyone could gain, in evolutionary terms, from kindness, and the occasional *unkind* sort were recognized, and confronted. Aristotle was right – though perhaps not for an Aristotelian reason – in identifying imperial subjects as a different breed from those who had lived in small, egalitarian *poleis* for many generations. Perhaps he was also right to say that such imperial subjects showed their 'slavishness' in treating women as slaves, as though they had no serious role of their own to play.[54] Aristotle was almost as sexist and as racist as Charles Darwin (as have been *most* philosophers), but at least he made the attempt to see why different people might have the talents and character they did, at a time when he had no clear counterexamples to his story. Women *did*, in all traditional societies, manage the households, and not public debate. Those who make the same, biological, claim today need to have better arguments for saying that this is what women *must* do, when they obviously do far more.

The argument is that different sexes must have different

---

[53] With luck that problem will not affect the United Kingdom for too long, thanks to miscegenation: in a hundred years these islands will, I guess, be homogeneous again, and eager to provide protection 'from the cradle to the grave' to all our citizens. Populations that remain too heterogeneous will prefer, at best, the 'liberty rights' of classical liberal theory. This is as testable a prediction as any in the social sphere, complicated, as always, by human unwillingness to allow prophecy to be fulfilled; see G. K. Chesterton, *The Napoleon of Notting Hill* (Penguin: Harmondsworth 1947; first published 1904) on the game of 'Cheat the Prophet'.

[54] Aristotle, *Politics* 1.1252b5–6.

strategies. Female mammals can have far fewer offspring than male mammals, and will always be investing more of their time and energy in any offspring than the males do. It has therefore been suggested that, abstractly, male mammals will have more interest in plural copulations than the females do. Once pregnant by one male, a female has a substantial interest in that litter; having impregnated one female, a male can easily impregnate another (and would be wasting his energies by staying faithful). In species where mothers need assistants, she has good reason to get as much support from the father as she can, and so to resent his other litters. The father, conversely, will tend to give as little assistance as he can to any litter (and sometimes none at all). From this theoretical excursus 'new moralists' regularly infer that 'women are monogamous and men are polygamous'. They thence conclude that *successful* men are bastards, whether in praise or fury. As with most such arguments, its fragility is hidden by our preconceptions.

Let us grant the context: that mothers require assistance, which will not all be given by female relatives, and that fathers have, genetically, an interest in the survival of their young. If assistance is vital then it is very unlikely that fathers will manage more than a single litter at a time, and therefore may be attracted to that single service despite occasional temptation to invest elsewhere. Conversely, mothers may solicit help precisely by persuading several males that the cubs might probably be theirs (and the males, correspondingly, may jealously enquire). So women might be polygamous, and men monogamous, with as good a reason. The longer and more arduous the care, the closer male and female investment comes. In some social contexts some males may indeed have immensely more descendants than do females of their generation.[55] The successful father's mother, in that situation, will have at least as many descendants as her son. It may seem to follow that she will

---

[55] Jones (*In the Blood*, p. 94) suggests that one explanation for the homogeneity of the Y-chromosome in African males is that only a few males have been fathers. King Chaka of the Zulus, for example, *literally* fathered his people – though he seems to have felt no affection for them as a result (J. R. Baker, *Race* (Clarendon Press: Oxford 1974), pp. 389ff. on the horrors of Chaka's rule).

value, and other mothers will value, sons (as spreading her genes more widely than her daughters do), but of course the chances of having a successfully breeding *daughter* is greater than of having a successful *son*. And the daughter's son, in turn, may be successful: so the daughter is as great an asset. Having a son at all, in such a case, may be entirely futile: if one male, the king, monopolizes so many, most males have no descendants (or only have nephews and nieces), whereas almost all females do.

Both males and females, briefly, have an interest in promoting more egalitarian structures. It may not seem to matter to females if one male fathers all the next generation, but in that case half their own offspring are likely to be dead-ends, or mere assistants to their daughters' lives. The consequence may be that far more females than males are born or allowed to live, and so there are fewer males to compete for the role of king. In that context, it will be a bad investment to produce females. Plausibly enough, the eventual balance is that just about as many males as females are produced, and a social culture where most adults mate and breed.

Awakening to this situation human beings have options. No human male is as large compared to females as a male gorilla, nor do we easily, as individuals, support two families or more. Kings who monopolize the breeding females of a clan invite a radical and regicidal jealousy. It does not follow that we will always find monogamous arrangements to our taste. In the abstract it might seem more plausible that something like group marriages will be the norm: care of the young is spread around the clan, and any male may be a particular child's father.[56] Philosophers in the grip of theory have even suggested that mothers be kept ignorant of their particular child's identity. More fluid forms, compatible with liberal dreams, may provide some stable home life for the young despite the passage of particular persons. On the other hand, even Tibetans, who had tried a wide range of different forms in their own homeland,

---

[56] I considered the option in 'Sexual Ontology and the Group Marriage', *Philosophy* 58.1983, pp. 215–27, pointing out that in the end such groups are a lot more like a club than like a marriage.

seem to have settled easily into monogamy in their new homes.[57]

Christian moralists have affirmed for centuries that men and women should have no more than one spouse at a time, and be relieved of their commitment only by a death. No one should risk having offspring outside that life commitment, because it is a lifetime's work to care for human young. No doubt 'fatherless' – or even motherless – children can be reared within a close-knit family, and not know the difference, but no one should impose that duty on another. Granted that any copulation carries the risk of pregnancy, the rule against non-marital sex seems necessary. The dreadful array of social obloquy directed against unmarried mothers and their bastard children (and also, though indirectly, against the cads who fathered them) was needed, so our ancestors supposed, because the passion of lust made us forget the world. Better to be ashamed of sinning than bring uncared-for life into the world. Better, perhaps, to force males into marriage than leave the mother shamed.

But if these are the obvious reasons for the laws of marriage, are they now obsolete? The cost was enormous, and the associated slogans about *women's work* have played their part in making the Church obnoxious. Can we not now surpass them? The conviction ignorantly promoted by Margaret Mead, that Samoans enjoyed free adolescent sex, without a thought of consequence, was at the time a foolish fantasy. Samoans, it is clear, were just as judgemental as the rest of us, and fiercely guarded female virginity.[58] Since then we have invented the Samoan fable for ourselves: adolescents (and their elders) reckon it right to copulate without commitment, because the consequences are (mostly) avoidable. They even reckon it right to face the consequences, if they come, without a life-long

---

[57] See William H. Durham, *Co-evolution: genes, culture and human diversity* (Stanford University Press: Stanford, Calif. 1991), pp. 42ff.

[58] Derek Freeman, *Margaret Mead and Samoa: the making and unmaking of an anthropological myth* (Penguin: Harmondsworth 1984) showed that Mead relied on joking adolescents and her own preconceptions to construct a South Sea fantasy of enormous appeal. It is striking that some anthropologists still seem to believe that her informants are lying *now* (in saying that they were lying then). Cf. Margaret Mead, *Coming of Age in Samoa: a study of adolescence and sex in primitive societies* (Penguin: Harmondsworth 1943; first edition 1928).

compact of mutual care and comfort, because they no longer see (or no longer think they see) child care as such a large proportion of their life. Why should people stay together when the rearing's done, and why should they pretend they will stay even that long together, if there are other ways to care?[59]

One further biological gloss no longer seems so relevant. Males remain capable of fathering offspring longer than females can mother them. Social norms, unfairly or correspondingly, allow such older males to impregnate younger women, whereas no older woman can safely date young males without embarrassment. It seems to follow that males are likelier to leave their wives and found a second family. Clearly this happens, no doubt assisted by the creed that everyone should take an individual perspective, and be prepared to start a new life on their own. But women, though they may not start new families, may also abandon old commitments: if males are to be valued only as co-parents, they can be forsaken once the parenting is done. The end of a leasehold is no betrayal.

But the problem all this exacerbates is age. If existing bonds are transient, attachments for use or pleasure,[60] what grounds the duty to care for the elderly? In the past that was one good reason to found a family, that one's children and children's children would care for us in age. Those without descendants might still find a place, as siblings, in some established household. Those aging to a solitary death were pitied whether they were rich or poor. But if we value people for their use, and willingly betray them when their use is done, exactly why should we expect ourselves to be cared for when we in turn are useless? The real or apparent uselessness of aged relatives will concern me later (see chapter 6). Here my attention lies on matrimonial arrangements, and the continued advisability of

[59] One simple answer is the hurt and injury that half-grown children suffer when their parents part: as a university teacher I have had to deal with traumatized adolescents whose parents have seized the chance to destroy the family home as soon as the adolescents leave it for a moment. The claim that quarrelling parents are just as harmful (and had better part) is self-serving: if you are hurting your children by your quarrels, stop.

[60] In Aristotle's taxonomy such attachments are less than those of 'real friendship'; see *Nicomachean Ethics* 8 and 9.

monogamy. Such marriage has been the best available strategy for procreative relationships. Non-marital copulation still carries an enormous risk, still disproportionately borne by women. Changeful and internally promiscuous clans, 'group marriages', have never had much success in child-rearing or mutual care: one might as well entrust child care to a tennis club. The point of a club, after all, is that no greater intimacy is demanded than to pass the time, whereas all boundaries in a stable marriage are just courtesies.

Why is it that people are 'coupling creatures', as Aristotle said, even more than they are 'political'?[61] A couple, specifically (for him) a heterosexual couple, is the bare minimum required for procreation, but other forms are possible, and often actual. In some tribes, procreation is a tribal duty (as, no doubt, copulation is a private pleasure), and the partners' loyalties remain with their own clans: such couples do not live together for life, or even for the days of child care. Any male figures in the lives of children are likely to be uncles more than fathers. But even in such societies it is possible to suspect that couples (not necessarily heterosexual, nor even sexual) form. It is difficult to have more than one intimate: in any threesome one is likely, at any time, to be excluded or frustrated; in any threesome the sense of being an object for a joint discussion by one's partners is liable to get in the way of intimate acquaintance. That there are homosexual, and celibate, couples may only be an echo of the heterosexual marriage – but it may also rest upon a profound requirement of the human psyche.

The Pauline dictum that husband and wife are related as Christ and the Church, or more mystical dicta about God and the individual soul, may readily miscarry. If husbands are as God, then wives must be obedient, and find their purposes in what their husbands wish. 'God is thy Law, thou mine: to know no more is woman's happiest knowledge and her praise.'[62] That way of looking at things has strongly influenced anthropological and ethological discourse. Investigators have read male domi-

---

[61] Aristotle, *Nicomachean Ethics* 8.1162a17.
[62] So Milton's Eve declares: J. Milton, *Paradise Lost* 4.637. Milton's Adam, in his turn, found 'grace in all her steps, Heav'n in her eye' (ibid., 8.488).

nance into all the evidence, and then used that reading to excuse or justify their own domestic rule. Similar complaints can be made against the cult of 'otherness', in which it is always women who are other, because it is men who are talking, or even against the Platonic myth of beauty, where (typically) it is the beautiful boy who must live up to his admirer's phantom. Love, so conceived, is a form of dominance, concealing its own substance by its praise of the beloved.

Pauline and Platonic imagery can be reformed. Whatever the use made of them, both struggled to express a different meaning: the Christ whom husbands are to imitate is one who 'gave His life' to create and to redeem the Church (that is, the body of all faithful people); the beauty that the lover seeks to serve is not his whim, but life itself as an always-new beginning. The relationship of one to the other, as married couples or lovers, is reciprocal: each finds in the other worth that neither can see in itself. Perhaps that is inevitable, since 'worth' or 'beauty' lies in unselfconsciousness. Possession, control and domination are so far from being love as to be love's worst corruption. Paul's advice to us all is to *subject* ourselves to one another, but certainly not to *dominate* each other.[63]

So coupling is a way of losing one's self-consciousness in the intimate recognition of another's reciprocal loss of self-consciousness. Each one's body 'belongs' to the other, as Paul flamboyantly declared: neither, in a Pauline couple, is to hold apart.[64] It is strange that Paul's own careful commentary on the conduct of marriage should ever have been interpreted as hostile. On the contrary, he argues that marriage, especially but not only in a time of persecution, is a cause of pain, but that such mutual dedication is a good, and one not improved by permanent abstinence. It is almost as strange that the phrase 'Platonic friendship' should now be used to mean a mild, asexual affection, when Plato is explicit in his talk of passionate dedication, which is not to be an excuse for any brief copulation. In either case, being motivated and satisfied by copulation is to miss the point (and damage the relationship, and maybe

---

[63] Ephesians 5.21–2.   [64] 1 Corinthians 7.4–5.

the beloved); in neither case is copulation necessarily a mistake. What matters is what is created in the coupling: the new creature which is, for Paul, the couple, and for Plato the restored half-god. The Fall is a falling apart on account of pride. Becoming, or attempting to become, a couple can sometimes be an echo or reminder of the unfallen world.

But this romantic or mystical account of coupling should not be taken too far. It may be true, as Aristotle thought, that people would form couples under almost any circumstances, even if they did not manage to establish 'political communities' – that is, companies of the like-minded prepared to sort out communal problems by discussion, and rear their children to do the same. It may be, as Paul taught us, that husband and wife are, or are to become, 'one flesh'. But there are many other social forms than couples, or than 'nuclear families'. Our Lord spoke harshly of divorce, as tantamount to abandoning one's wife (since it was the husband in contemporary law who was permitted to put aside his wife).[65] There being no other settled state for women, divorce compelled the woman to find another home (unless, of course, she had found one already). He also approved of marriage, as an institution which broke up the bond between parent and child in the name of a new future. But in the kingdom of heaven there is no marriage, and 'family' is found wherever God's will is done. Being born again, 'not of the will of the flesh, nor of the will of man, but of God'[66] marks a final break with any natural tie. 'It is not good for man to be alone',[67] but no one who follows the will of God is thus alone. Saints are hospitable to anyone, having room in their hearts for all. Couples all too often feel no need for any other. The fable that Plato put in Aristophanes' mouth has force: Death slices us in half and leaves us seeking.

SELFISHNESS, SELF-INTEREST, FAMILY TIES AND EMPIRES

Recent reconstructions of our fundamental moral insights or commitments have relied on game-theoretical analyses of ways

---

[65] Matthew 19.3–9. [66] John 1.12–13. [67] Genesis 2.18.

to preserve one's genes. Celibacy will not work, unless we are very kind to our closer relations. Reciprocal altruism is a good idea, if we can be deterred from cheating. Doing good to unrelated others, and with no hope of return, would be best conceived as a way of showing off, rather as peacocks' tails or stags' antlers are proof of manly virtue (if they survive with such a handicap, they must be tough).[68] *Seeming* to do such unrewarded good, at no cost to oneself, is of course a better bet – except that one's dupes may easily resent the trick.

None of this is very new to ethics. That the only reason any of us can have for action is our own good is, notoriously, either obvious or false. Any reason I have for action is of course *my* reason, and success in it is something I desire. It does not follow that I only desire 'success', since what success consists in depends, exactly, on what it is I aim to do. Perhaps my success is simply preserving Crown and Country in good health, at the expense of my own health, wealth, life and reputation. Of course I might deceive myself (and often do): maybe, if pressed, I would choose to preserve my *reputation* for heroic altruism rather than be heroic. But nothing in logic demands that I have no objective desires: wishes that such and such a state of affairs might occur, whether I know of it or not. The desire will still be mine, and I might be wholly callous or unprincipled in its pursuit, but my failing then will not be that I think too much of myself, but that I think too much, for example, of Crown and Country. There is such a thing as being too patriotic for one's country's good, but such patriots are not ordinarily *selfish*.

The conviction that everyone is 'really' selfish, because they always act to help themselves, not others, is sometimes weirdly conflated with the quite different theory that our desires are the ones our *genes* would have us have, so as to spread those genes.

---

[68] Amotz Zahavi, of Tel Aviv University, reports that Arabian babblers (*Turdoides squamiceps*) compete with each other in feeding each other, preening each other, watching over each other, and keeping each other warm by night; after assorted laborious evolutionary explanations for this generosity, he concludes that it *is a signal of the babbler's quality*, a proof that the bird is strong enough to cope with the added burden of being nice to others. Altruism, he misleadingly concludes, 'is simple selfish activity' (Lynn Hunt, 'A Rewarding Tale', *New Scientist*, 6 March 1999, Supplement pp. 8–9).

'Genes', it is said, are 'selfish', in that 'altruistic' genes always act to eliminate themselves (and so are rare). The authors of this claim will sometimes admit to speaking 'metaphorically', and sometimes fiercely deny the charge. Sometimes they suggest that 'altruism' or 'selfishness', in biological circles, are but terms of art, with no more necessary connection to the *moral* use than the 'charm' or 'beauty' of quarks. That last claim must be disingenuous, since its authors move so swiftly between biological theory and moral denunciation – often with very odd results. Challenged in public debate to explain the actions of Mother Teresa and her associates, Dawkins promptly suggests that her behaviour must be motivated solely by her wish for a heavenly reward, without any concern for the strangers that she tends or *pretends* to tend. Dawkins's misunderstanding of Catholic doctrine is one thing. More to the point is his failure to address the *actual* problem for his theory: namely, that such a desire for heaven still does her *genes* no good. There are possible, devious routes by which a celestial motive might be bred into us for a genetic gain. It could also be argued that people like Teresa are indeed exceptional: they exist at one extreme of a range of characters as obviously as great dancers or great logicians. The talents necessary for dance or formal logic may leave the *very* talented with no time to spare for marriage; it does not follow that those talents will be eliminated from the gene pool, since the *ordinarily* talented will continue to find mates.[69] It is interesting that Dawkins misses these obvious retorts, but must immediately seek to sabotage the claim to disinterested charity. It is important, in short, that supposed saints are ordinarily selfish, because Dawkins happens to dislike 'religion'.

But even (or especially) the saints will admit that pride does play a part in all their best endeavours. Real saints, and real philosophers, are willing to seem fools or knaves. Real saints

---

[69] Even if slow antelopes are culled, remember, some antelopes will still be slower than others. Even if very saintly people have no time to spare to breed, ordinarily decent people will still propagate the type, and find, to their surprise, that they have sometimes reared a saint. This is to assume, of course, and only for the sake of argument, that 'saints' have natural dispositions to be saintly. The probability is that this is false: if sanctity is a supernatural grace, it can be bestowed on *any* disposition.

might even be willing to be damned for love[70] – though the paradox of salvation is that such generosity cannot be contained in hell. Unselfconscious generosity is rare. It is very likely that we are often moved by love and hate: we treat strangers kindly because they remind us of our friends and family, and treat them badly for very much the same reason. If fellow-feeling has often been preserved in us because we were related to the fellows that we helped, the self-same apparatus helps us to loathe all those who *look* like kin, but are not. Folk stories about dwarves, elves or ogres may recall the days when there were many hominid species, whom we hated. Our closest rivals are those most like us, without being quite the same. Paradoxically, we may be more kindly disposed to very different creatures than to those who look like parodies of human (that is, our own) shape. In evolutionary terms it may have paid to loathe miscegenation, and to despise the alien.

Once conscious of these confusions, we can reconsider how to justify, and motivate, a care for strangers. We have no assurance that the 'sociable' or 'liberal' emotions are innately stronger than the antagonistic, domineering ones. Struggling to see a fellow-creature as just that instead of as a pest, or loathsome slime, or enemy, we are struggling with our own emotions. Once upon a time, perhaps, the legislators of the Stone Age bound us all together by associating people from many different clans with totem animals. How could we not feel kindly towards those who shared our totem?[71] Our long drift away from archaic religion means that that method is less powerful than it was, but there is still some psychological force in thinking of strangers or potential foes as more like *pets* than people! If this eventually helps us to live as friends, why not? War, after all, is worse, and likely to be a failure even by worldly standards. Once upon a time, perhaps, our tribe could hope to kill the neighbouring males and rape the women. The closer the ties of kinship the

---

[70] Romans 9.3.

[71] I do not intend to resurrect the theory that religion was once all 'totemistic' (a dubious category) – only to suggest that Diodorus may have had a point. In our beginnings the weak banded together under an animal sign (1.90.1), and felt for comparative strangers something of the affection that the *animal* evoked.

more likely that we would display the heroic virtues (and vices) necessary to war. The larger and more varied the population the less likely that we will willingly sacrifice ourselves to spread that population's genes. Neighbourliness and war fever come from the same pot: we are less eager to fight for empire, and less inclined to help our local population. War, at the same time, grows more destructive: if we were to become again such local, neighbourly groups as we once were, and fight with modern weapons for our clan's survival, the chances are that we would all be dead. So instead of caring deeply for our own, and very much less for others, we have begun to care less deeply for more creatures, and seek to keep our hatreds within bounds.

It is unlikely that these cultural shifts owe anything to genetic change. We have been attempting a radical breeding pro-gramme in the last few centuries, by cramming the defenceless poor into huge conurbations. The early years of our industrial cities were marked by childhood diseases that gradually, and well in advance of laboratory-based medicine, became less lethal.[72] Even improvements in working and living conditions were probably of no greater effect than acquired immunities, and natural selection. One consequence of the experiment may have been to eliminate those breeds which retained too clannish sympathies and hatreds: we have been trying, in effect, to breed more 'liberal' people, less moved by ethnic or religious differ-ence, and readier to see a friend within the alien, unfamiliar guise. Unsurprisingly, so far, the attempt is not wholly suc-cessful: the likelier consequence is always that we breed and train new clans. If we did succeed, the side effect would be that we would feel less deeply about *friends* than once we did. If we are not equipped to loathe our opposites, we equally will not be equipped to *love* our friends. As always, distinguishing the 'good bits and the bad' is difficult, and probably destructive. Darnel and wheat should grow together until the Day.[73]

---

[72] Jared M. Diamond, *Guns, Germs and Steel* (Vintage Books: London 1998), plausibly argues that a significant factor in the expansion of European tribes across the world was our bacterial and viral population: we had far more hideous diseases to deliver to the world because our populations had been packed more closely, together with more domestic animals.

[73] See Joachim Jeremias, *The Parables of Jesus*, tr. S. H. Hooke (SCM Press: London

It is also difficult to distinguish cultural effects from the possible genetic drift involved in urban, and then industrial, change. Orlando Patterson's summary:

An industrial society cannot work if people do not change from traditional to more regulated rhythms of work; people must learn to get to work on time, whatever sacred views they may hold about the correct relationship between the rising of the sun and the rising of the human spirit; they must acquire greater literacy, however much such literacy undermines traditional cosmologies; they must acquire specialized skills, however satisfying the activities of the materially self-sufficient person; they must recognize the rights of women to greater independence outside the household economy, however dearly held the traditional sexist views on the matter; they must abandon traditional conceptions of ritual purity with respect to other groups if a modern transportation system is to work; they must accept the rules of bureaucratic structures; they must be willing to migrate from the regions of their birth; they must increasingly abandon familial favoritism in favour of generally accepted standards of competence; they must forego the preservation of a large number of extended kin-ties; and they must accept the inevitable drift toward a more secular view of the world.[74]

They 'must' do these things. But the chances are high that not all will. The idea that our genes are uniquely suited to life in the Stone Age is as romantic an idea as any, and as difficult to prove. That they are already fully suited to the Industrial Age is yet more unlikely. If familial favouritism, say, or caste or national loyalty is as ingrained as it seems, it will take more than wage slavery to wash it out.

The Enlightenment hope was that we could bypass such gradual cultural and genetic shifts. Instead of encouraging an appropriate range of sentiment (the ones we needed to sustain large, cosmopolitan populations in a period of material prosperity and more lethal wars), we might hope to open the eyes of reason, Darwin's 'godlike intellect'.[75] Those who rely on sentiment run risks: the very same features that evoke parental care may also, for example, evoke sexual desire, of the most pre-

---

1972, third edition), pp. 224ff.; darnel and wheat are difficult to distinguish (Matthew 13.24ff.); see also Matthew 25.32.

[74] Orlando Patterson, *Ethnic Chauvinism* (Stein and Day: New York 1977), p. 186.

[75] Darwin, *Descent*, vol. II, p. 405.

datory kind. What matters is that we should see past such cues, to the unknown selves behind them. The Enlightenment, and the Axial Era, hope is that we recognize all *humans* as having the same nature. In the aftermath of the biological revolution that essentialist thesis is now unreliable. If we learn instead to think of the awakening eye in *any* creature, we may consider the possibility of a direct relationship with any chance-met stranger, of whatever kind. Cooperation is a good, enforced by indignation when we are cheated, and shame when we cheat others. It is better to forgive than hold a grudge – but better to hold a grudge for long enough to make our displeasure felt! Plato was right to argue that, despite appearances, the *unjust* do not prosper in themselves or in their progeny. Our *emotions* are not fully geared to live under the eyes of heaven: we *feel* as members of a clan must feel, concerned for our own status and our clan's, and only held from cheating others by fear of failure, or the sense that cheating would be beneath us. Reason suggests that we might pass beyond our personal and clan attachments to a global, unlocalized, impersonal concern. We might give up our lives not just for friends and family, but for the good.

Mackie, writing on Dawkins, argued that game-theoretical analysis suggested that *Christian* ethics was a code for Suckers, and so a danger to the sensible moralists among us. Suckers, because they instantly forgive the Cheats, are keeping the Cheats alive (and cheating) whereas those who play the ancient game of Tit-for-Tat rebuke the Cheats, and drive them out of town.[76] He might as well have criticized *Platonic* ethics: it is no part of justice, on Plato's account, to do harm to *anyone*. Neither Platonism nor the Christian ethics to which Mackie refers are just equivalent to 'being a sucker'. But there is an issue of greater moment here: what relation can there be between the way that Jesus preached, and the laws of earthly virtue? Should we resist evil, by violent means if necessary? Should we return good for evil? Should we forgive the evildoer, no matter how many times the wrong is done?

Polemarchus, in Plato's *Republic*, speaks for natural humanity

[76] J. L. Mackie, 'The Law of the Jungle', *Philosophy* 53.1978, pp. 455–64.

when he says that justice lies in helping one's friends and harming one's enemies. It may require more wisdom than we usually have to know for sure who *are* our friends and enemies: who is it that truly wishes us well, and who intends our harm? But it would seem, to most of us, entirely fair to return evil for evil, and revenge ourselves on those who wish us ill. The prospect of unending feud reminds us that we had better find some way of making peace, by accepting final compensation for the wrongs we have suffered. Perhaps there have been some feuds that ended with the extinction of one side or other, but there is less chance now of finding *all* the associates and friends of those by whom we have been offended. Those who live by the sword do die by the sword as well. That is the origin, so Aeschylus tells us, of the courts, where all sides bring their grievances to be decided, and agree to abide by the judgement. Any of us, of course, may continue, privately, to resent that judgement – but if we oppose it, by seeking private vengeance, we have implicitly declared that the *judges* are our enemies. In the absence of a higher court to decide the issue between us, we are then at war. It seems to follow that the civil peace depends on there being *two* moral systems: the way that private individuals should behave, and the way of state officials (judges, kings and statesmen).

Consider the days when everyone in Israel 'did what was right in his own eyes'.[77] In those days, the gang rape and murder of a visitor's concubine aroused a genocidal fury against the perpetrators' tribe.[78] The tribe of Benjamin was almost wiped out: would have been wiped out entirely, but that the other tribes came slowly to their senses, and did not wish to finish the job.[79] Their solution was to slaughter every male and every non-virgin female in Jabesh-gilead, the one place that had not participated in the earlier genocide, and so provide the survivors of the tribe of Benjamin with wives. In the absence of formal prosecution, and personal responsibility, lynch law rules. Establishing Leviathan, to avoid on-going civil war, is to agree

---

[77] Judges 21.25.   [78] Judges 19.22ff.
[79] 'And the children of Israel repented them for Benjamin their brother, and said, "There is one tribe cut off from Israel this day"': Judges 21.6.

to waive our 'right' to vengeance, on the understanding that Leviathan Himself will act. The state reserves the right of violent revenge. Perhaps it also has a right to 'forgive' offenders, but by doing so it runs the risk of failing in its function. Judges should exact a penalty and recompense for wrong which will be sufficient to avoid lynch law and feud. Niebuhr concluded that Jesus' commandments to His disciples were only given to private individuals, and that public officials might justly do all manner of things that *individuals* might not.[80] The conclusion affects more than rulers. As a private individual, I may not use lethal force against the people who offend me, even if there is no realistic prospect of my bringing them to court. As a servant of the state, a soldier, I *must* use lethal force against 'enemy soldiers' when I am so instructed, and may even act so as to kill or injure 'innocents' so long as I did not aim at their destruction, and used no more force than was reasonably required to win the battle. As a private individual, I may not imprison, rob or mutilate a fellow citizen (or even a fellow resident); as a servant of the state, a policeman, guard or executioner, I *must* do all these things, in the service of the state.

The creation of officials, people who are assumed to act not in their private interest but the state's, is in many ways a marvel. In the beginning kings were perhaps no more than alpha males: they were obeyed, and flattered, because they had most power, and used it, unashamedly, in their own interest. Clans that had kings did better (so they thought) than clans without a single, final power, because they held together better: where there is no king, no final court, there is no way of avoiding feud and civil war. Better serve *one* king than a multitude; better have 'peace' than run the risk of being caught up in blood feud, even if the king is mad. The idea that the king himself is subject to a further law, and so may forfeit royalty, is a revelation. The king must make and enforce judgement, but not as a private individual for private gain. Consider again the birth of Israel's kingdom: Saul forfeits the throne because he spares the conquered king of the Amalekites and 'the best of the sheep

---

[80] Reinhold Niebuhr, *Moral Man and Immoral Society* (Scribners: London 1933).

and of the oxen, and of the fatlings, and of the lambs, and all that was good'.[81] In effect, he accepted a bribe to spare an evildoer. David in his turn chose to use his royalty to spare himself embarrassment, and keep the woman he wanted.[82] Kings (which is every ruler) should govern in the name of justice, and not for their own profit. As human individuals they are subject to the very same law as others, and may not use their powers for personal advantage. As kings, they must enforce the law even if this demands that they, and others, do particular acts that would not be allowed to them as individuals. As kings, they may not mourn as David did for Absalom:

And the victory of that day was turned into mourning unto all the people: for the people heard say that day how the king was grieved for his son. And the people gat them by stealth that day into the city, as people being ashamed steal away when they flee in battle. But the king covered his face, and the king cried with a loud voice, O my son Absalom, O Absalom my son, my son! And Joab came into the house to the king, and said, Thou hast shamed this day the faces of all thy servants, which this day have saved thy life, and the lives of thy sons and daughters, and the lives of thy wives and of thy concubines; in that thou lovest thine enemies and hatest thy friends. For thou hast declared this day, that thou regardest neither princes nor servants: for this day I perceive, that if Absalom had lived, and all we had died this day, then it had pleased thee well.[83]

Is there any prospect of a more 'loving' system? The impulses to defend one's own, to hold grudges against those who do us harm and to be 'generous' only as advertisement, are deeply rooted in the nature of any social animal. That generosity is often less than 'altruistic' even explains the oddity that we resent even those who do us *good*. If it is truly better to give than to receive, those always on the receiving end are being injured – and all the more since they are expected to be grateful. These impulses need to be controlled if we are to live at peace in a larger world, to which (perhaps) we are not yet accustomed.

---

[81] 1 Samuel 15.9ff. [82] 2 Samuel 11–12.
[83] 2 Samuel 19.2ff.; Absalom had attempted to usurp the throne, and been killed (by Joab, who made it his lifelong business to do the things that David had rather not). Joab won his point, but later backed the unsuccessful candidate for the succession, and was killed, by Solomon, on David's dying words (1 Kings 1.7ff.; 2.5, 28ff.).

The controls we have so far created demand obedience to a power that, in turn, employs the violent and demeaning tactics we have foresworn as subjects. Loving our enemies, it seems, is something that we can attempt as individuals, but not as state officials.

The way that Jesus proposed we should live does seem to be at odds with this – although He uses just the rhetoric of genuine self-interest that some moralists have deplored. We are to pile up credit in heaven, rather than on earth, and get the better of our 'enemies' by loving and forgiving them. Rebellion against established power has rarely any other reason than to *replace* that power. Jesus, apparently, requires us *not* to replace it, but to ignore it. By doing *more* than we are required to do we show the irrelevance of the requirement. By not caring to claim coin for ourselves, we make taxation irrelevant. 'Giving Caesar what is his' does not mean, as thousands of state apologists have supposed, that we should agree that Caesar has some authority, a claim that stands alongside God's, but that the money stamped with Caesar's head is *his*, and so not something we should want ourselves.[84] Paul similarly rebuked his congregations for supposing that they could go to law (to Caesar's law) to settle their disputes: 'Do you not know that we shall judge angels?'[85]

[84] Matthew 22.15ff.
[85] 1 Corinthians 6.3. 'Angels', in this context, are the institutional systems by which our lives are usually governed: society as a god, in the sense that Durkheim analysed.

CHAPTER 5

Human identities

NATURAL KINDS

Scientific racists in the nineteenth century convinced themselves that 'Africans' must be of a different species, whatever the Bible or tradition or experience said. They claimed for themselves and for their 'science' the right to ignore traditional opinion on this matter. No doubt their error, or their sin, was similar to that made by consciously 'biblical' theorists who supposed that the fable about Ham's descendants somehow justified Negro slavery.[1] The habit of inferring 'facts' from 'values' is usually blamed for this. Instead of trying to find out what is truly the case, we are inclined to insist on what *must* be the case, on the basis of our beliefs in what *should* be. Negroes, they thought, really *should* be slaves (whereas all *men* were created equal), and they must therefore insist that either Negroes were not quite *men*, or that the gift made at our creation had been withdrawn from some of us. But the fallacy is also committed by those on the other side. The body of social scientists and biologists who were called, in 1949, to lend their authority to UNESCO's moral and political ideals, declared firmly that 'man-kind is one: all men [i.e. all humans] belong to the same species'.[2] They were probably

[1] The fable (in Genesis 9) is concerned with *Canaanites*, those peoples whom the people of Israel conquered in their occupation of Palestine. If it has a larger, allegorical moral it has to do with the children of Ham in general – who, as Jacques Ellul has pointed out, were the politically powerful nations of that day: Egypt, Philistia, Babylon (*The Meaning of the City* (Eerdmans: Grand Rapids, Mich. 1970), pp. 10, 25); the moral to be drawn is that imperial power is slavish, as Aristotle also thought.
[2] Cited by J. R. Baker, *Race* (Clarendon Press: Oxford 1974), p. 65.

correct: our present evidence suggests, indeed, that we are a homogeneous species, perhaps because our common ancestry was not so long ago. But it may reasonably be doubted that any serious efforts had been made to discover if all sub-varieties of humankind are interfertile. If UNESCO's scientists had known that there was greater genetic variety amongst Africans than there was between Asians and Europeans (so that it is likely that the latter groups share common ancestors in emigrants from Africa more recent than the ancestors *all* human beings share), would they have begun to wonder if perhaps we were as likely to be different species as are *Pan paniscus* and *Pan troglodytes* (the bonobo and the common chimpanzee), or the species of Darwin's finches? What difference would it or should it have made if we were indeed of different species (that is, different breeding populations)? Why does it matter whether *Homo neanderthalensis* is the same species, or not, as *sapiens*? Would it matter if, in later years of interplanetary exploration, human populations drifted to become new species?

In UNESCO's mind it was important that all of us be conspecifics because we had to believe, and act on, the declaration that all creatures born of woman must be expected to have much the same fundamental wants and talents. Thus, the statement 'all members of our species are *human*' implies that they all need food, drink, shelter, culture and companionship if they are to be happy, and that all can contribute to the on-going enterprise of human life. As Whewell also insisted, we are not to suppose that obvious physiological and cultural differences will render any member of our species alien, or undeserving. But why does that require there be only one *species*? Is it not also true that 'mammalkind (primatekind, hominoidea) is one: all mammals (primates, hominoids) belong to the same class (order, superfamily)'? To be human at all is to be a member of a certain biological taxon, currently labelled *Homo sapiens*: creatures who did not belong would not be biologically human, though they might resemble many of us very closely. If mankind (i.e. humanity) exists as a distinguishable kind at all, it must be one (i.e. one species, genus or family), but it does not follow that 'humankind' could not name a higher taxon than the single species, and still be worth respect.[3]

In folk taxonomy, humankind must embrace that set of creatures who have a common nature, namely humanity. That nature need not always be actualized: physical and social injuries alike may leave their victim dumb or deformed, but it is axiomatic that the victim would have joined the human game, were it not for the injury. What is 'natural' to a given kind is what members of that kind would do, under 'normal' or 'ideal' circumstances. Those circumstances, in turn, are to be defined as the ones in which members of the kind would realize their natures. If a creature's nature is its genetic code, then there will be some born into our species whose nature is irrevocably unhuman, such that it was never an open possibility that they should grow up to be language-using, cultural, God-fearing mammals. To believe that, but for fortune, they too would have been like us is only reasonable if we think that they are really immortal souls, housed (to their cost) in damaged instruments. This belief may be useful practically: if we think that there is a 'real human' inside the apparent vegetable, we may expect (and so get) more of her, and treat her more as we would wish to be treated. It may also be a dangerous belief, encouraging the folk-taxonomic feeling that unusual creatures are *defective*. Seals are not merely deformed quadrupeds; our human-born monsters also have their own discoverable natures, their own contribution to the species pool.[4]

---

[3] I first raised the question whether humanity was a 'natural kind' in a paper intended for the World Archaeological Congress (and not delivered in person, in protest at what seemed to me to be a racialist exclusion of scholars from South Africa): 'Is Humanity a Natural Kind?': in T. Ingold, ed., *What is an Animal?* (Unwin Hyman: London 1988), pp. 17–34, and since reprinted in *The Political Animal* (Routledge: London 1999). Apartheid, I hasten to add, was a thoroughly repellent system, and such as to make the South African state a textbook example of an illegitimate regime – but why should we penalize all subjects of such a state? And why was South Africa so obviously much worse than other regimes, which treated their subject populations with even greater contempt? The Bantu populations of South Africa at least had some rights, in theory, to govern themselves, and prosper. Did Native American inhabitants of the United States, or Aboriginal Australians, or !Kung Bushmen, or European gypsies, or . . .?

[4] See David L. Hull, 'A matter of individuality', *Philosophy of Science* 45.1978, pp. 335–60, esp. p. 358; and also his *The Metaphysics of Evolution* (SUNY Press: New York 1989).

Where the folk taxonomist supposes that all humans have a common nature, whether that is genetic or Platonic or both, the biologist speaks rather of 'one great breeding system through which genes flow and mix in each generation'.[5] Wilson himself is inclined to speak as if the actual, historical features found within our species constitute a 'nature'. David Hull points out, more plausibly, that biological science does *not* support the idea that all humans have a common nature,[6] nor that there is a single 'norm'. Perhaps all reptiles have a three-chambered heart, and all birds (except the cassowary?) have feathers, but nothing says they *have* to: indeed, the moral of evolutionary theory is that there are always variations. Humankind can vary too, and does. So the unity of humankind (the biological taxon) does not rest in the possession of a common nature, but in being a breeding population such that my ancestors were, and my descendants may be, yours as well. Not every imaginable human pair can expect viable offspring, but we are all embedded in a lineage such that any pair might reasonably expect to be *able* to share great-grandchildren or the like. This may result in the continued existence of widely shared qualities, but it does not always have to; nor can we be absolutely confident that past conspecifics were altogether like us. In chapter 3, I suggested how domestic dogs might become two species, by the extermination of all dogs but Irish wolfhounds and chihuahuas. That is, in essence, how the hominoid, and perhaps the hominid, line became several species, by the death of those who bridged the gap between us.

Does our biological diversity, and even the possibility that there might, after all, be many human species, really give us good reason to despise the *other* species? Perhaps it is our good fortune that *sapiens* has not speciated (despite the advantages that this might bring). Even bigots find it a little difficult to despise those peoples who can justly claim to be close relatives, to share ancestors and perhaps descendants.[7] If some biologists

[5] E. O. Wilson, *On Human Nature* (Haravard University Press: Cambridge, Mass. 1978), p. 50.
[6] Hull, *Metaphysics*, pp. 11–12.
[7] Except, of course, that bigots will not *want* to share descendants, and our shared ancestry is only another excuse to hate each other.

are to be believed, we could not expect to be concerned for creatures outside our species, even if they talked to us. The fact that so many of us *are* concerned for creatures outside our species, even when they do not, is a puzzle to be deconstructed in the usual way. Any concern for those who could not give us any evolutionary advantage must have some other object. Perhaps we are just sentimental, overflowing with the affections that were fixed in us by ancestors who minded about their conspecific dependants. Maybe (a little more plausibly) those ancestors who, being righteous, had a care for their beasts,[8] left more descendants than the fools who neglected them. Perhaps being concerned for those who cannot pay us back is only a signal, like a peacock's tail, of our superior stamina, and earns points in the mating game. 'He who the Ox to wrath has mov'd, shall never be by Woman lov'd', remarked Blake, gnomically (and perhaps implausibly).[9] Without such an explanation, it is supposed, no such affections could be widely felt, nor any moral impulse to respect those whose children we could not share. *Rational* non-humans, in fact, would fare far worse than beasts, since we could not easily expect to patronize them.

Speciation is a function of isolation, whether by a literal river or by a shared distaste for any closer relationship. Once the populations have drifted far enough, and been selected for some subtly different life, any *sexual* bond between them is unlikely to be strong – though this does not stop creatures, human or non-human, finding sexual release through contact. But 'not fancying each other much' is hardly a sound foundation for removing each other from any moral consideration. The prurient descriptions common in nineteenth-century memoirs of the physique of 'Hottentots' now strike us as contemptible, but presumably have as good a reason as any imagined dislike of other rational species. Why is the 'yuk factor', regularly denounced by would-be scientific innovators, suddenly of such moment when it comes to considering creatures of another species? If species were, as once they were thought to be, true

---

[8] Proverbs 12.10.
[9] Blake, 'Auguries of Innocence' (*c.* 1803), *Complete Writings*, ed. Geoffrey Keynes (Oxford University Press: London 1966), p. 431.

natural kinds, then creatures of such different kinds need share no nature. Now that we think of ourselves as relatives (one genus, family or order), and know that there is no *nature* that all and only our conspecifics share, what grounds the conviction that our morals lie within a boundary we know is quite unreal?

The deconstruction of a uniquely human nature needs further commentary from Christian thinkers: after all, it is *our* nature that the Word took up, and that has been assumed to be a human one. If it was not *our nature* that He assumed, since – *qua* human beings – we have no nature,[10] what happened in the Incarnation that we need to recall and ponder? If others of our species need not share 'our' nature, then we lose even the standard humanistic reason to respect them all. In the old days those who despised another human showed contempt for *humanity*: coming to value ourselves as *human* we valued every-thing which shared that nature. Perhaps the respectably *human* creatures can be distinguished from mere human beings, crea-tures who are our kin? Perhaps we should only concern our-selves with 'rational beings' or 'persons', and treat non-rational or non-personal human beings as animals? There are plenty of moralists who have concluded so. But there is a biologically informed alternative that is also closer to the Abrahamic norm. In valuing our *kin*, because they are kin, we put aside respect for character or talent. Our kin are those of a common descent, with whom we may hope to work and play and worship. When Aristotle gave a penny to a beggar, his companions wondered why he would give to one so 'undeserving': he replied that he did not give to 'the man' ('the fellow'), but to humanity ('the human thing').[11] As kindred, it did not matter what the man himself was like. Aristotle's response to kindred was just *kind*, and kindness is a virtue that can cross class, racial *and intellectual*

---

[10] This claim is not the same as the – muddled – existential claim that 'human beings have no nature' because humanity consists in 'having to decide'. That was exactly, after all, what Aristotle said 'we' were, namely creatures who need reasons for their actions (*Nicomachean Ethics* 1.1098a3). The humanity of which he was speaking was the life of those who are asking the question 'what is the good life for human beings?', and he leaves open the possibility that there are biologically human beings who do not do that.

[11] Diogenes Laertius, *Lives of the Philosophers* 5.1.11.

barriers. John Paul II, in *Evangelium Vitae*, makes the point, in rebuking

the mentality which tends to *equate personal dignity with the capacity for verbal and explicit*, or at least perceptible, *communication*. It is clear that on the basis of these presuppositions there is no place in the world for anyone who, like the unborn or the dying, is a weak element in the social structure, or for anyone who appears completely at the mercy of others and radically dependent on them, and can only communicate through the silent language of a profound sharing of affection.[12]

Kindness is more than patronage. In such acts (not focused by the hope of profit), we catch a glimpse of what our nature might be. The nature we share in Adam is not shared just by our own conspecifics. It is the tendency of any living thing to grab things for itself, and harass those we have hurt. When 'God broke through the borders of our standard definition of what is human and gave a new, formative definition in Jesus',[13] He also and identically gave a new account of what it is to be alive. The beginning of evil was our self-assertion.[14] Its cure lies in laying hold on life.

HUMAN DIGNITY AND HUMAN NATURE

The horrors of modern war arise in part because every such war is *civil*. By insisting that all human beings, everywhere, are part of a single human community, we allow ourselves to feel for all of them the emotions that we variously feel for other classes in a class society. Animals are other nations: in the past, we hunted other *humans* in the same spirit as we hunted cattle. Ritual humiliation, degradation, hate are only appropriate responses to creatures who might challenge us for status within

---

[12] *Evangelium Vitae* (25 March 1995), taken from the Vatican's website (http://www.vatican.va), §19; it is a pity that John Paul is so concerned to maintain a decent status for all such *human* creatures that he continues to disregard the implications of this doctrine for the non-human.

[13] J. H. Yoder, *The Politics of Jesus* (Paternoster Press: Carlisle; Eerdmans: Grand Rapids, Mich. 1994), p. 99.

[14] Plotinus, *Enneads* v.i.i; the word Plotinus uses is *tolma*. See A. H. Armstrong, 'Plotinus' in A. H. Armstrong ed., *Cambridge History of Later Greek and Early Medieval Philosophy* (Cambridge University Press: Cambridge 1970), pp. 195–271, esp. pp. 242ff.

our own community. Correspondingly, we want them on the boundaries of our group because our status depends on having others to despise. 'Vermin' are to be destroyed – or rather crushed: if there were no vermin, after all, there would be less respect for vermin-catchers. Instead of seeing our racist insults to our human enemies as 'treating them as animals', or justifying that treatment, consider our account of rats (for example) as *vermin* as a way of reading animals as untouchables, the lowest of our human castes, included in the body politic by being excluded. Without untouchables, pariahs, vermin, we lack a proper sense of our own dignity. War then becomes the extension of *class* war.

It is implicit in the account I have been giving that universal humanism is not the only option. It is far too easy to assume that every human being must acknowledge all other human beings as equals, at least in dignity. Since it is all too obvious that we do not in fact treat other human beings like that, it is assumed that we need special excuses for ourselves, most notably the error of 'treating human beings as animals', 'dehumanizing' those we mean to hurt. It must be easy for us, it is supposed, to hurt, harm, kill 'animals', since they are of another species, so we pretend that humans of another race or culture must be 'animals', to help us hurt them. But the message of Darwinian theory is that we do not have characters or habits because they benefit the species: why should we expect a human lineage to preserve a general respect for any human creature? We care for our kin, and those who might be expected to do us good. Of course it has turned out that all human beings *are* our kin, but kinship has many degrees in any case. If there is no strong evolutionary reason why we should all respect our conspecifics, there is no need to postulate a special excuse for not respecting them. Giving more respect to dogs than foreigners may be a plausible adaptation, since we profit more, genetically, from earning the love of dogs.

Universal humanism, in short (that is, the doctrine that all and only members of our species merit serious, equal, benevolent concern), is a cultural artifact, and not a biological norm. That we are equal in our humanity (while obviously unequal in

wit, strength, skill, virtue, wealth and family connections) is
sometimes understood with reference to 'rights': none of these
obvious inequalities, it is said, gives any of us more *right* than
any other. Each of us has identical right to govern our lives both
singly and collectively, because every one of us is 'human'. The
historical fact is that neither now nor ever in the past has any
such right been recognized. We sterilize rather stupid women
(even if not now so brazenly as Oliver Wendell Holmes),
without their consent, 'for their own good'; we deny a vote to
any class we despise; we do not, in any real sense, accord an
equal respect to everyone. The most that could plausibly be
claimed is that decent societies allow all human beings *some*
dignity – except when our aim is to destroy that dignity (by
stripping, shaving, shouting, denying them names and treating
them 'like cattle'). At least such treatment is not casual, and
usually (not always) has a term.

Acknowledging a human dignity, and aiming to destroy it,
both assume that human beings 'naturally' are different from
non-human. Captives, remember, have traditionally lost that
claim: by being willing to live 'at any price', they have forfeited
the claim to dignity, or any say in what is done to them.
Prisoners in Japanese prison camps who baffled their captors by
claiming a human dignity they had forfeited – in their captors'
eyes – insist that their 'human rights' were violated. Only
'fanatics' and 'fundamentalists', it was said, could so forget an
ineradicable humanity: surely any of us can easily imagine
ourselves as captives, Jews, or stupider than we are, and thence
conclude that we should want better treatment (and so give it).
Attempts to make that argument universally compelling fail.
Either I cannot imagine being like that, or cannot imagine that
I would still feel as I do now if I were that, or see no reason why
someone's not *liking* treatment is a reason not to treat them so.
If I were guilty of a serious crime, I would not like being
punished, and probably (which is different) would not want to
be. I might even deny that I should be. So what? Why should
'being human' demand that I even have a say at all (let alone a
final say) in what is done to me? The historical fact is that
almost everyone who ever lived has been denied that say. And

even those who think they have a say have rarely succeeded in getting what they wanted. Why should not we not treat each other as cattle, since we always have?

The ethical revolution of the Axial Era was founded in the recognition, or creation, of humanity. Humans are those who use intelligible speech (though accents and local dialects ensure that we always know who is foreign), and whose facial expressions are not wholly unfamiliar. Human communities across the world acknowledge tears and laughter, and suffer from lust, hurt pride and indignation. We often find each other's ways absurd, or cannot conceive why anyone should feel the way, apparently, they do. Sometimes we can hardly grasp what emotion it is they feel. Plenty of intelligent and even decent people have doubted that others can be really human, as their appearance or their behaviour is so strange. The normal word employed for our own tribe means 'people', and all others are 'non-people'. Even within the tribe, it is the upper castes (especially the adult males) who are really people.[15] In the eighteenth and nineteenth centuries, it was almost entirely loyal Abrahamists who insisted that Negroes and Bushmen were indeed our brothers, while chimpanzees and orangutans were not.[16] 'Freethinkers', like Josiah Nott, felt themselves free to suppose that 'savages' could have no common ancestry with us, and Darwin expressed his horror at the thought of being related to the Fuegians. One reason why believers were suspicious of theories that suggested that we had a common ancestry with apes was just the thought that our common *human* ancestry might be in doubt, or at least our common nature.

Since species evolve . . . they should be treated not as classes whose members satisfy some fixed set of conditions – not even a vague cluster of them – but as lineages, lines of descent, strings of imperfect copies of predecessors, among which there may not even be the

---

[15] Indeed, we can almost *define* a tribe as a group of people who normally and publicly accept a particular class as 'proper people': if there are two or more such classes then there are probably different tribes.

[16] 'Neither the *Pongo* nor the *Longimanus* is your brother; but truly the American and the Negro are'; Herder, cited by Baker, *Race*, p. 22.

manifestation of a set of central and distinctive, let alone necessary and sufficient, common properties.[17]

Quite what paradoxical influence Darwin had in encouraging late nineteenth-century racism is uncertain; doubtless, like Aristotle, he only provided pretexts for policies preferred for other reasons. But there is a serious issue. Speciation is the transformation of varieties into reproductively isolated populations (and conversely, of reproductively isolated populations into discernible varieties). Members of such an isolated population do not necessarily share any particular property with all and only their own conspecifics (accept that they are indeed fellow members of that population). Nothing says that it is *wrong* to speciate: on the contrary, as I observed before, it may be highly desirable to speciate, and so to occupy more niches than one species could.[18] It follows that humanity, as the common essence of the present species, is of no biological significance: there is no common essence, and any species might as well be many.

One answer, implicit in the Platonism which was the chief evolutionary postulate until Darwin, is that 'humanity' names an ideal, the form to which our lineage approximates, as other lines have embodied forms like Vertebrate-at-Sea or Hunting Carnivore. On this account, there may have been, or may yet be, many *human* species, just in the sense that many populations may have members guided to humanity. Of course, that postulate explicitly allows that other populations than ours have or may have human members, and even that members of our species may fall so short of being human as properly to be something else. 'Throwbacks' and 'sports' and even 'hopeful monsters' may not share our *human* nature; perhaps not even 'savages' do, any more than the ogres, elves and goblins of our legendary past (echoes, perhaps, of other hominid species). So neither Platonism nor Darwinism give us grounds for the

[17] A. Rosenberg, *Sociobiology and the preemption of social science* (Johns Hopkins Press: Baltimore 1980), pp. 122–3.
[18] Humankind, of course, has been remarkably successful in occupying many different environmental and functional niches, without establishing significant barriers against gene flow (that is, without speciating), but this ignores the niches that we cannot occupy without larger physiological change.

absolute insistence that all and only our own conspecifics are significantly human. Quite how high we raise the barrier varies: according to some, no one can be human who cannot count or reason; others accept that even stupid people are still people, just as long as they can talk; others propose that anyone who recognizes human faces, smiles and burbles is a human being (maybe a young or damaged one, but human), united by 'the silent language of a profound sharing of affection'.[19] Perhaps this would not matter at all, except that being human is a ticket to somewhat better treatment. We should not treat *human* beings like cattle, or like any animal, because they are *human* (and by implication we may, or should, treat 'animals' like animals). The ticket, of course, is often torn up, unused.

'Personism', the suggestion that we should treat creatures better the more that they are 'persons', is not quite the Axial Era's creed, since many creatures born into our kind turn out to be not quite persons.[20] The more generous personists acknowledge that some non-humans might be personal (might recognize us and each other, and their own mirrored faces, and jockey for position and the best banana). Humanism then turns out to be a combination of such personism and a residual love of kin, whatever they might be like. 'Human rights', the right to be an equal, are properly 'persons' rights', but all human beings deserve a little courtesy, as kindred, even if they are not equals. That infants, imbeciles, lunatics and the senile *are not* our equals is not so certain on a dualist creed. For materialists whatever alteration or inadequacy in brain chemistry makes it impossible for someone to direct her life, communicate or reason, also makes it impossible to *be* what otherwise she might. If it were otherwise we might have to admit that someone *is* our equal, though unable to communicate or even realize that fact because she has no adequate tools to do so. Occasional stories of the

---

[19] John Paul II, *Evangelium Vitae*, §19. See Gavin Fairbairn, 'Complexity and the Value of Life', *Journal of Applied Philosophy* 8.1991, pp. 211–18. Far too many ethicists – and medics – assume that they themselves know better than 'disabled' persons and their immediate carers that such lives cannot really be worth much, and are therefore undeserving of any special care.

[20] See Jenny Teichman, 'Freedom of Speech and the Public Platform', *Journal of Applied Philosophy* 11.1994, pp. 99–106.

sometime paralysed who turn out to have been listening all the time to doctors saying that there was no one there, do something to restrain us. But those stories need not imply a real, dual being: the point may only be that sometimes part of the brain still works though its connections to the outer world are down. That is a sad enough scenario.

Can a modified personism (allowing credit to damaged human beings who are our kin, and *might* be really persons) be adequate for decent, or Christian, ethics? If human beings as such have no distinctive nature, what was the nature that God dignified in Adam, and took up to Himself in Jesus Christ? Once upon a time, we had no problem: humans were a special creation, and a fallen one; non-humans, though they shared the cosmic corruption, were innocent of sin, and made to serve us all. Treating them decently was demanded to save our dignity, not theirs. Perhaps they had feelings not unlike our own, and needed to be domesticated just as we needed to be disciplined, but they were not the subjects of their lives, nor meant for celestial glory. Perhaps all that is true – but it hardly fits the evolutionary story that we mostly now believe.

REASON AND MORAL JUDGEMENT

Commentators all too often assume that once a goal is specified there *must* be a 'best way to reach it', and that this, by trial and error, will be chosen. The claim is false. Aristotle identified the general form of practical reasoning as syllogistic: I need a cover; a cloak is a cover; so, I will take it. 'The conclusion,' he says, 'is an action'.[21] But even if I need a cover, there may be other things to serve. A 'practical' syllogism is not demonstrative, but reaches its conclusion quickly if no other premise (as 'a coat is a cover too', or 'this cloak belongs to George') intervenes. Even more rigorously practical syllogisms, which require a further premise about what is right (or fine or beautiful), are not demonstrative. The conclusion, that is, is not demanded by the premises, even if they are its reason. Courageous acts are noble;

---

[21] Aristotle, *De Motu Animalium* 701a8ff.

and *this* is a courageous act – but the act may also be discourteous, or greedy. At the least, it may not be the only courageous act on offer, let alone the only virtuous one. Moral reasoning is defeasible in a way that 'factual' reasoning is not. It may be true, in general, that saving life is good, and *not* be true that this particular way of saving life is good (say, killing someone else to get spare parts).

Evolutionary logic has the same explanatory, but non-demonstrative, air. Whatever common hereditary character exists we can be sure that it was not, or has not been, eliminated, and we may tell some story why. But that story only makes sense within a context that we cannot be sure was real, and would never allow us to predict results. Evolution does not deliver the only solutions possible, even within a fixed environment, nor does it eliminate all 'defects'. Darwin, in hinting that it did, was wrong, as Darwin should have known quite well. Consider Darwin's finches: the point after all was that a huge variety of recognizable finches now exist upon the Galapagos. Some have short beaks, others long. Some serve to pick out insects; others to crack nuts.[22] The story that they are all related is immensely plausible. But the very fact that they are different shows that there was not *one* solution to the first Galapagos finches' problem. There was not even *one* solution to the problem of eating insects. As soon as they were playing different games they were not *competing* with each other at all – and so, like the cichlids of the Rift Lakes, survived much better. The same lesson applies at every level. Those who breed the best are those who do not compete, but divide resources by dividing lives, and find new ways to help.

The dreadful error made by eugenicists was to suppose that they could tell what worked, and that the 'less perfectly adapted' (to the modern world) should be restrained from breeding (by malnutrition, sterilization, and murder).[23] The

[22] See David Lack, *Darwin's Finches: an essay on the general biological theory of evolution* (Cambridge University Press: Cambridge 1947). Darwin himself was actually more impressed by the tortoises.

[23] See P. M. H. Mazumdar, *Eugenics, Human Genetics and Human Failings: the Eugenics Society, its sources and critics in Britain* (Routledge: London 1992). In the USA, Oliver Wendell Holmes Jr, declaring that 'three generations of imbeciles are enough', saw

'logical' conclusion must be to allocate the licence to breed by competitive examination, with standards rising yearly. The alternative is to realize that we are not all playing the same game, since competition is disaster.

A cloak is not the only covering; covering oneself is not the only way to keep warm; and keeping warm is not the only way to live. That is one reason why we cannot strictly deduce what should be done from any array of facts, including facts about how creatures of our kind have prospered. Some strategies may be excluded (so long as we keep our eye on some particular goal), but any goal except the 'most complete' can be rede-scribed as a contentious means. This Aristotelian analysis of action rests on the claim that we all have such a final goal: to live well. Aristotle himself accepted that there are ways to qualify that claim. Non-human animals may have more local goals, which are not subsumed within a larger: they wish to eat, to sleep, to play, to walk outside, without conceiving that such passing wants together compose a life. Human beings of a 'slavish' nature are similarly moved, he thought, by fear or greed, but not by any wish simply to do right. Doctors, he also says, do not think about whether or not to try to heal a patient: by extension, any profession's goal has been selected as what constitutes 'doing the right thing' for that professional – and even the selection may not have been deliberate. Very often, we just find ourselves in a situation where our course of action follows smoothly on. Of course, we *could* do something else: there is no logical tie between our doing what is right and doing whatever it is it seems we are 'bound' to do here and now. There is also no psychological bar to changing one's mind, repenting or having second thoughts. But in doing what comes naturally we also do what generally we are 'bound' to do: no one is likely to live well who thinks of nothing but of living well, and never acts spontaneously.

We cannot *deduce* what we should do from any facts, even

fit to ruin the lives of innocents because, he supposed, they were not quite as clever as he thought he was (see Stephen Jay Gould, *The Mismeasure of Man* (W. W. Norton & Co.: New York 1981), p. 335). The law which licensed this oppression continued in action until 1972, and similar assaults have been perpetrated since.

from 'moral facts' about what should be done. One of the most virulent of mental microbes is that 'you cannot get an "ought" from an "is"'. David Hume offered an early version, expressing an ironical surprise that moral discourses so often and so swiftly moved from statements where 'is' was the favoured connective to ones including 'ought'.[24] What reason could there be to move? Hume's disingenuous question was also one he asked about identity and causality: however did we move from claims about what *had* happened to claims about what *would*? How do we move from saying that events of type A invariably follow events of type B to saying that token Bs *cause* token As (and what do we mean by that)? What is the connection between speaking of my memories of being a ten-year old and claims that I myself was him? Hume's answer, so it seems, was simply that we do. It is useless to invent some general premises to justify the movements, since we would have no better reason for them than for the particular judgements (and probably much less). It is a lot more plausible to claim that a particular match has caused a particular forest fire, than that *all* matches, suitably positioned, cause such fires, or that all *little* fires are followed by much larger ones. It is also a lot more plausible to claim that burning little Jo is wrong than that it is always indefeasibly wrong to injure anyone. Recognizing a wrong, in other words, is simply what we do, as naturally as we expect the noise of thunder. That recognition, and accompanying emotions of indignation or apology, does not depend upon obedience to a law of non-contradiction. We do not contradict ourselves when we admit that little Jo has been badly, and deliberately, burnt, but decline to blame the perpetrator: in that limited sense we are not being 'irrational'. We may be being thoroughly unreasonable, as we would be if we supposed that holding a red-hot poker to her head would not *hurt* (merely because there is no formal contradiction in that claim).

The other chief inventor of the plague (namely G. E. Moore) has also been misrepresented. The fallacy he identified ('the naturalistic') was to equate the meaning of 'good' with any of

[24] David Hume, *Treatise on Human Nature*, Book III.I, ed. L. A. Selby-Bigge (Clarendon Press: Oxford 1888; first published 1740), p. 469.

the things we see are good. 'Good' cannot mean just the same as 'pleasurable', or 'in human interests', or 'required by law' because we can all understand that it is possible to doubt that any such things are ever, or always, good. That such and such is good is always a substantive claim. Moore did not deny that it might also be a true one, and even that it be indefeasibly true, and obviously so. Whereas no moral argument as such is indefeasible, particular claims may be. It does not follow (as above) that acquiring a particular piece of knowledge must be good, merely because knowledge is, in the abstract, good, since the act in question might be treacherous, cruel or impertinent. There are also particular acts that are good 'no matter what': we do not withdraw our praise because some action, over the course of history, has a less than ideal outcome. A life well-lived, as Aristotle said, cannot be made a wretched one by anything that happens afterwards.[25] And also (as Aristotle also said), we find out what we seriously think is good by asking ourselves, in honesty, what we would prefer. Of course, our judgement may be wrong – as it may in any matter – but that is not to deny the possibility of moral reason.

Hume's version of moral judgement rests on shared senti-ments, but results in substantive claims about the social and legal order likeliest to win approval, over the long run, from social primates like ourselves. Moore's judgement – though he came to suspect that moral judgements expressed sentiments not unlike Hume's – was originally more Platonic. Our recogni-tion of an act, or an agent, as 'good' rests on our inner knowledge of the good. Our particular judgements, however, are not direct intuitions, but measured conclusions from long argument about what creatures like us prefer. It remains possible ('logically possible') that it would be better overall if there *were* no creatures like us, but this is a judgement that is unlikely to win large acceptance.[26]

---

[25] Aristotle, *Nicomachean Ethics* 1.1101b5f.

[26] G. E .Moore, *Principia Ethica* (Cambridge University Press: Cambridge 1903); see also his 'Reply to my Critics', in Paul Schilpp, ed., *The Philosophy of G. E. Moore* (North Western University Press: Evanston, Ill. 1942). See my 'The Lack of a Gap between Fact and Value', *Aristotelian Society Supplementary Vol.* 54.1980, pp. 245ff.; and 'Morals, Moore and Macintyre', *Inquiry* 26.1984, pp. 425–45.

As rational beings we recognize that there are many things that are, in the abstract, goods. We make particular decisions in the light of our best understanding of our own slightly shifting priorities, including our reputation among those who matter to us. If Aristotle is right, we also act 'for beauty's sake': not merely to acquire such goods as are compossible, but to be 'in the right', to walk in beauty. The question is, how such a love of 'beauty' can be given biological sense. Pursuing 'goods' is easy enough to understand: goods are just those possessions which evolutionary history has made it likely that we shall desire, simply because desiring (and obtaining) them has somehow allowed our ancestors to produce us.

We cannot be expected to want things that were very bad for us, or for our ancestors. Or rather, we cannot be expected to like things such that liking them would have led our ancestors to have fewer descendants than their cousins did, with different tastes. Or rather, we are likely to have the tastes we have (whatever they may be) because those tastes did help our ancestors of the not-too-distant past to outbreed those with different tastes (perhaps). Or rather . . . But none of this makes any convincing sense. The tastes that the first humans had were helpful enough to create an environment, a niche, in which our species could expand, whether or not we outbred our non-human cousins. Those tastes need not have been especially fine-tuned: indeed, the evidence is that they were not. All sorts of sexual, gastronomic and cultural practices have served us well enough. A fancy for eating earth, or excrement, will probably be a rarity (though not unknown); a fancy for eating caterpillars is likely to be a cultural variation within a larger fancy for nutritious food. Even what counts as nutritious has some genetic and some cultural aspects, which we can neither disentangle nor predict. A practice now widely established is probably one that someone once desired, and that has been flexible enough to allow its own transmission. Any such practice will involve *lost* opportunities as well as gains. None need be one that everybody likes, or ever liked, or ever was 'good' for us, or for our genes. Even widely established practices with a strongly genetic component may only be the present phenotype of a genotype that was selected when its *phenotype* (in a different context) was a different one. Some are merely responses to the practices of other kinds of thing, and carry no advantages for *us* at all. Is there any point in imagining what the genetic advantage is of catching colds? Why need we suppose that madness or immorality have any better reason? 'Organisms play the game because, and only because, their ancestors did not lose.'[27]

The point is not, as some have said, just 'metaphysical'. It is not only that getting what we want, or discovering a viable set of goods, may not be 'right'. We have no guarantee that any such 'goods' are good, even in the restricted sense that they are good for our survival, or our line's survival, or that they ever were. 'The survival of the fittest' does not guarantee that what survives is fit, still less that what has not survived had obvious flaws. All we can say is: such and such survived, in a context where there were alternatives, and perhaps because some character gave it an edge, in differential reproduction, above available rivals in that time and place and species. Some characters may have been fixed, by chance, within small populations.[28] Others worked well enough, and were not challenged. Others again survived some culling process, but for no reason that could guarantee a long success. We can suspect that species subjected to the harshest selective process will be most vulnerable to a sudden change: fitted all too closely to a single niche, they are lost when the pool dries up or the eucalyptus dies.[29] Conversely, species that can change their tune have not been rigorously pruned – or, what has been pruned is just the habit of settling down too soon. Genomes cannot respond quickly to

[27] M. H. Ghiselin, *The Economy of Nature and the Evolution of Sex* (University of California Press: San Francisco 1978), p. 41.

[28] Ernst Mayr's Founder Effect, whereby a population may have the traits it does solely because it was founded by a small group which just chanced to have them, perhaps having survived some catastrophe for no inheritable reason; it seems highly plausible that such small populations could preserve new variations while they are still vulnerable: without such havens, it is difficult to see how random changes that might eventually be 'fit' could avoid being culled.

[29] A recent study suggests that *Chlamydomonas* (a single-celled organism found in ponds) has the resources to adapt to light and (with more difficulty) dark environments: the light-adapted variety can then be bred back to the norm more easily than the dark-adapted, subjected to a harsher cull, can be (Kate Douglas, 'Replaying Life', *New Scientist*, 13 February 1999, pp. 28–33).

changed circumstances, so that it must pay most species to be incomplete at birth, picking up the necessary cues to invoke one of out many patterns of behaviour. This process may look Lamarckian: if a genotype allows for several pheno-types, depending on the circumstance, the realized phenotype of parents may itself give that phenotype a stronger chance of emerging sooner in the offspring (by hormonal influence or parental example).

Consider one example. Homosexual bias, it is said, should have been eliminated long ago, because a homosexually biased animal would 'obviously' leave fewer offspring. The claim rests on confusions. Plenty of homosexuals have bred, despite their tastes. Plenty of homosexuals could have been heterosexual, even if (which is doubtful) most homosexual males have a particular gene not widely known among heterosexuals.[30] All that need ever have been handed on genetically is a broadly sexual interest, focused by early experience and adolescent choice.[31] It has never been (in evolutionary terms) an especially damaging option to bond sexually with members of the same sex, either for young males exiled from the troop, or for young females passing the day together. In some species and some societies, the sexual impulse is entangled with dominance rituals; in others with hedonic practices, like grooming, that may or may not themselves have dominance overtones. That a few may find their sexual impulse incapacitated, at all ages, with the opposite sex, is no more surprising than the ends of any 'normal curve'. In species that mate once and die, the

---

[30] 'A gene' may be a single altered codon, or a stretch of codons reversed or transposed from the 'usual' order; in either case it may not be inherited at all, any more than is the doubled chromosome that leads to Down's syndrome. The assumption that there must be only one such 'gene' for 'homosexuality' is actually as gratuitous as the assumption that there is a single phenotypic trait ('being homosexual'). Does anyone suppose that there is a single gene (one codon or many) for 'taking a job having something to do with feet (footballer, chiropodist, acupuncturist, ballet dancer, shoe shop assistant)', such that all and only 'they' have that identical gene? Perhaps some extreme genetic determinist does, but not for any good reason (is there a gene for being an extreme genetic determinist?).

[31] Some mildly interesting research suggests that the preference is cued, in some, by exposure to particular smells in childhood: Philip Kitcher, *Vaulting Ambition: socio-biology and the quest for human nature* (Harvard University Press: Cambridge, Mass. 1985), p. 267.

impulse has to be focused; creatures that can mate at any time, and repeatedly, rely on early environment and choice to focus their desire. Some songbirds sing a species-specific tune without any cue or coaching. Others need to hear the relevant tune before they sing, although they can pick it out from several options. Others again learn singing from their peers, and develop the basic tunes in individual ways.[32] Even if some of those ways do not help to attract mates, there would be no problem with their existence. Neither is there a problem about gays, or celibates, or contraceptive users. Do we suppose that we are now selecting out the willingness to have abortions?

According to Wilson, moral philosophers are doing nothing more than consulting their limbic system when they compare their moral intuitions.[33] A properly informed biologist, it seems, can offer us a 'better' way. It seemed at first a strange claim. Moral and political philosophers when Wilson wrote were actually wary of all 'intuitions' or 'gut feelings'. No doubt, they had (like Wilson) some unconsidered thoughts, but the drift of moral exploration favoured claims that could sound sensible to *anyone*. Some commentators suspected, with good reason, that this 'anyone' concealed too much: did we have any reason to believe that everyone could agree on anything? Were we not inclined to exclude the thoughts of anyone who probably would not think or feel like us? 'Rational man', too often, was no more than 'Western, prosperous male'. 'Rationality', too often, simply meant the willingness and talent to obtain those things that our particular gender, class and tribe agreed were good. 'Gut feelings' and intuitions were classed as superstitions – unless they were those of 'rational man'. Government committees appointed to consider problems about new technology still often blame all popular objections on the 'yuk factor', and urge that the public needs to be educated and informed (so that it may, eventually, not feel so squeamish).[34] Why 'yuk factors'

---

[32] W. Thorpe, *Animal Nature and Human Nature* (Methuen: London 1974).

[33] E. O. Wilson *Sociobiology: the new synthesis* (Harvard University Press: Cambridge, Mass. 1975).

[34] The Banner Committee, appointed by the UK Minister of Agriculture to consider 'Ethical Problems about Emergent Technologies in the Breeding of Farm Animals' (1996), thanks to its chairman, Michael Banner, has set a helpful precedent in

should be less reliable than 'yum factors' (that is, the pleasure principle) they do not say.[35] Even less arrogant moralists than are usually found on government committees generally agree that moral debate involves comparisons between what general principles suggest and what our hearts commend in particular cases. In general, professionals prefer to act on *principles*, even if they seem to be refuted by their 'counter-intuitive' results. Presumably, our intuitive feelings (and maybe even our belief in intuition) were once 'fit'.[36] But why, philosophers enquired, should we accept the morals of the Stone Age, any more than its metaphysics?

Rhetorical distrust of 'intuition' or 'gut feeling' may conceal the biologically and historically contingent roots of 'reason', whether in philosophers or biologists. Is it possible to uncover them, and what do we do when we have? Our ancestors had to deal with practical and social problems long before they had much time (or chance) to *think*, and even before they were human. Perhaps there are intelligent life-forms somewhere who grow up in isolation, and must work out which company to join by abstract thought alone. Even they (presumably) are cued to recognize which companies are their own conspecifics, and it is difficult not to suppose that they will have appropriate emotions, talents and priorities. We may be *more* versatile than those imagined creatures, just because we are normally brought up in families that can supply appropriate suggestions. Feral children may reveal *how* versatile: apparently, we can survive, sometimes, as members of quite other mammalian tribes.[37] Empirical

---

acknowledging the authority of such moral judgements, and insisting that there are some acts that have no excuse.

[35] The most influential work of political philosophy in several decades insisted that the rules we should require were those that would be selected by anyone, irrespective of their personal ideals, attachments, status or ability (John Rawls, *A Theory of Justice* (Clarendon Press: Oxford 1971)). That those rules turned out to be remarkably like the ones that people with John Rawls's ideals, attachments, status and ability most probably would pick, was perhaps coincidental.

[36] As D. G. Ritchie suggested in *Darwinism and Politics* (Swan Sonnenschein & Co.: London 1891, second edition), p. 104.

[37] On feral children, see J. A. L. Singh and Robert M. Zingg, *Wolf-Children and Feral Man* (Archon Books: Hamden, Conn. 1965); Douglas K. Candland, *Feral Children and Clever Animals* (Oxford University Press: New York 1993). It would be wrong to confuse children like Genie, imprisoned in a cellar for her formative years, with such

evidence about our tendencies and talents is incomplete – and for reasons that I shall explore below, most probably always will be. Perhaps we can discover a little more from biological theory.

According to modern myth, theologians used to argue that there could never be biological complexity without a reasoning mind to make it so. Dawkins has indeed suggested that he would himself have been a theist before 1859, when it was realized that 'order' could emerge from 'chaos' without any reasoned plan.[38] The foundation of that argument, as David Hume showed, could never have been empirical: one premise (that there was never order without a designing mind) in fact being contradicted by the other (that there *was* order without any *other* sign of a designing mind).[39] The intelligence displayed in nature did not, for Plotinian theists at least, demand that any mind had nature in mind *before* it came to be. Forethought, and careful calculation, were devices *we* might use, but not an infinite intellect, whose image is displayed wherever there is any being at all. An infinite intellect does not make plans, revising them in the light of circumstance or discovering, just too late, that they have unforeseeable effects. In a real sense, *unconscious* artifice is far superior to our techniques.

In other words, why are we *conscious* of priorities, and racked by indecision? In the absence of such forethought, it is likely that different behaviours are excited by specific cues (including the completion of an earlier task). Ichneumon wasps perform the rituals of catching, paralysing, caching caterpillars, laying

children as seem to have been reared by non-humans. It is understandable that psychologists should rely on Genie's case (since it is far better attested than the other stories), but we should not assume that the non-humans treated the children quite so badly. See Susan Curtiss, *Genie: a psycholinguistic study of a modern-day 'wild child'* (Academic Press: New York 1977); cf. Jean Claude Armen, *Gazelle Boy*, tr. S. Hardman (Bodley Head: London 1974).

[38] Richard Dawkins, *The Blind Watchmaker* (W. W. Norton & Co.: New York 1986), pp. 6–7; see Alvin Plantinga, 'When Faith and Reason Clash', *Christian Scholar's Review* 21.1991, pp. 8–32, reprinted in David L. Hull and Michael Ruse, eds., *The Philosophy of Biology* (Oxford University Press: Oxford 1998), pp. 674–97.

[39] David Hume, *Dialogues concerning Natural Religion* (1779), *Hume on Religion*, ed. R. Wollheim (Fontana: London 1963); Hume did not play entirely fair, since his Demea, an orthodox theist, is driven from the dialogue too soon. The character who loses the argument, in most readers' view, is an unorthodox deist. I take this as a parable of sorts: the most convincing obstacles to 'natural religion' stand in the way of doctrines which are themselves opposed to actual, historical religion.

eggs in them and sealing up the cache, without, it seems, any further goals in mind. They do not vary the behaviour to achieve such distant goals in the face of obvious obstacles. This is not, or need not be, because they are *stupid*, but because that is not what they want. Even we, who pride ourselves on being rational,[40] may find ourselves enticed into behaviour that does not serve our final ends, nor even the functions that behaviour was 'selected' to fulfil. Folk psychology has recognized very well the possibility of sudden transformations, and the power in 'wearing different hats'. Some creatures not entirely unlike ourselves might live as fully divided minds, inhabiting quite different life-worlds and doing different things, as different modules leap into life. We can even imagine that each of these modules has a voice, a memory, and even a local plan. Perhaps we ourselves are a lot more like that than we now imagine. Where then is the Self?

It is not unknown, unfortunately, for a domestic dog who has been playing with a human child (as dogs have played with puppies) suddenly to shift into aggressive mode and treat her as a prey or plaything (as dogs have played with rats). The impulse to believe the dog a murderer is strong (that impulse itself, remember, may be one source of self: see above), but we could equally, and charitably, suppose that it never was relating to a continuing entity, the child. The object of its attention in one mode was not, for it, the *same* as the object of its attention in another. Correspondingly, it was never *the same dog* at all. Domestication may consist in simply suppressing those aggressive minds, or seeking to call them up on careful cue. But if there were a chance of a mind remembering lesser minds, and re-identifying entities encountered in successive minds, we could redeploy those lesser minds' resources. It would be premature to suppose that only our conspecifics manage that.

That suggestion has been made to account for our own ancestry. It seems likely that we possess different mental and behavioural circuits, modules, lesser minds: likely because there

---

[40] 'That vain animal who is so proud of being rational. . . and before certain instinct will prefer Reason, which fifty times for one does err', John Wilmot, Earl of Rochester, *New Oxford Book of English Verse* (Clarendon Press: Oxford 1972), p. 393.

are pathological conditions in which one sort of mind goes missing, and because we know ourselves, from inside, how our morals and memories shift. Coping with life is often a matter of summoning up the appropriate mentality, as professionals have especial cause to know: professionals, whether literally actors or not, need to be able to *perform*, and those performances are not just superficial. The larger modules currently identified have to do with language, employing tools, dealing with animals, and mathematics.[41] Competence in one does not require any competence in another; damage to one does not mean damage to another. But if these minds or modules come to be the possessions or the denizens of a larger mind, they can be mutually infected. We can treat people as if they were tools, and know that we are doing so. Conversely, we can animate machines.

There is a genuine question whether these different minds or modules are *real*, or only artifacts of the particular tests, both formal and informal, that we apply. Aristotle was probably right to say that the soul can be divided up in infinitely many ways: not because it is composed of infinitely many bits, but because continuums are not discontinuous![42] We have been seeking to identify the elements of conscious life since we first began, and named them as gods or demons. Those efforts cannot, in their nature, be merely 'objective': we alter ourselves by the theories that we compose about ourselves. Even the signs of the zodiac have more than an astronomical reality. What matters, in tradition, is that they should serve 'the human form'.[43] In the Olympian system gods have opposites, and all must be compelled to obey the law enforced by Zeus: that is, the laws of hospitality and sworn word.[44] Some hoped to satisfy their gods

---

[41] Steven Mithen, *The Prehistory of the Mind* (Thames & Hudson: London 1996); see R. Ornstein, *Multimind* (Houghton Mifflin: New York 1986).

[42] Aristotle, De *Anima* 3.432a25ff.; see Gould, *Mismeasure*, for a discussion of the search for mental factors, and psychometricians' tendency to reify unreals.

[43] 'They ought to be the servants, and not the masters of man, or of society. They ought to be made to sacrifice to Man, and not man compelled to sacrifice to them; for when separated from man or humanity, who is Jesus the Saviour, the vine of eternity, they are thieves and rebels, they are destroyers' (Blake, 'Descriptive Catalogue' (1809), *Complete Writings*, p. 571.

[44] It is significant that modern moralists are rarely exercised by duties such as these, which arise upon particular occasions as matters of personal honour.

by putting times aside for each to have their undivided attention, but there is no lasting hope (once we are conscious in a wider mind) of keeping those divisions. Once again, we do not just want *this* good (say, sex), then *that* (say, company): we are always liable to be conscious of the range of goods and want them with a single mind. The issue then becomes, how best to prioritize them, and whether to surrender any. Zeus, so Aristotle told us, is the *chief* god, not the only one.[45]

BEAUTY, ROMANCE AND PEDERASTY

The rituals of courtship, sex and possibly shared parental care are linked, in us (and rarely in other creatures), with rituals of grooming and shared comfort. They are also linked, in other creatures as well as us, with rituals of dominance and supplication. In parental species, the rituals of filial appeal and sexual offer may reflect each other. In a well-ordered species, no doubt, these similarities are no more than reflections: offspring are not sexual objects, and the young attract attention, but do not evoke *attraction* of the sexual sort. But once the barriers between our different minds come down, we cannot always distinguish what we feel. If natural selection were exact and ruthless (if it did 'fine tune' the product) we would only be sexually attracted to suitable co-parents. Anyone with different tastes would have been bred from existence long ago. But the confusion of roles and manners consequent on *not* being divided minds is not so desperate a state as (yet) to have extinguished us. On the one hand, we have invented romantic, heterosexual love as a composite of lust, mutual comfort, wish for children and fidelity. On the other, we have invented pederasty, seeking to complete our admiring attention to the young by copulation. Similar confusions (whether positive or not) result in homosexual love: the use of sensitive organs to cement the bond of friendship, irrespective of their use in generation.

Confusion is not necessarily a bad idea (it may, in fact, be the source of many *good* ideas). Love itself (by which I do not mean

---

[45] Aristotle, *Eudemian Ethics* 7.1244a12ff.; see *A Parliament of Souls* (Clarendon Press: Oxford 1990) for my earlier discussion of our multiple minds.

agape)[46] is a complex confusion of emotions and commitments, deeply informed by stories and cultural expectations. Lust (as we all know) passes. Love aspires to look beyond lust's passing and, though it takes doves, storks or gibbons as images of that enduring marriage, is probably quite unlike the sentiments and habits of those other creatures. Pederasty, on the other hand, is certainly a betrayal, an attempt to bring together sexual and parental feeling in an arrangement that cannot, of its nature, last, and is, of its nature, dominating.

These judgements are, it seems to me, well founded – though it might be argued that there could be (and perhaps, in Greek society, once were) social conventions about the relationships of sometime lovers which partly ameliorated the problem. Both practices depend on bringing different moods or minds together in a way not open to more divided minds. The romance of (heterosexual) love has shaped our civilization (both for good and ill); the romance of pederasty shaped the Greek.[47] For a cultured Athenian, pederasty was no more *certainly* abuse than marriage now is rape (though rape and abuse are possible). It was not even just the same as lust: the use of male or female slaves for sexual satisfaction is likely to be pervasive wherever there are slaves. The point about a freeborn boy was that he was not a slave, but must be wooed and cared for. Boys who were too 'easy', of course, were scorned, especially if they grew up to be 'effeminate'. The object was that boys should become men. Young male beauty excited admiration, lust and quasi-parental feeling: Athenian fathers (usually much older than

---

[46] Christian disputes about the connection between *eros* or *philia* and *agape* seem no longer to be in fashion. Anders Nygren, *Agape and Eros*, tr. P. S. Watson (SPCK: London 1953) and Denis de Rougemont, *Passion and Society*, tr. M. Belgion (Faber: London 1956) both took the view that they were not the same. Martin C. D'Arcy, *The Mind and Heart of Love* (Faber: London 1945) made more connections between the two. D'Arcy was probably the wiser philosopher, but I suspect that the distinctions should not have been forgotten.

[47] George Devereux, 'Greek Pseudo-Homosexuality and the "Greek Miracle"', *Symbolae Osloenses* 42.1967, pp. 69–92; see Kenneth Dover, *Greek Homosexuality* (Duckworth: London 1978) for a more detailed account of pederastic practice. To state what should be obvious: the Greek experiment has very little to do with the present-day gay scene, except by historical imitation. Michael Vasey, *Strangers and Friends* (Hodder & Stoughton: London 1995), gives a moving account of how an evangelical Christian can feel at home in gay society, or a gay in evangelical society.

their wives, and absent upon city-business) might 'love' their sons at a distance, but were not available 'to make men' of them. Boys, in effect, were to be apprenticed to an older lover, so that they should know what beauty it was that they should serve thereafter.[48]

Pederasty as a way of bonding young males to the military cohort or the citizen body is one possible, because actual, institution, and no more 'unnatural' than is romantic love as a way of bonding couples in the enterprise of procreation, child care and old age. Plato's attempt to spiritualize the bond (and make it clear that buggery is child abuse[49]) takes the underlying engine of procreation seriously. The children of our body carry our genes, and hosts of modern biologists have argued that parental (and perhaps avuncular) care is all that could be natural. Caring for other people's children is held to be, at best, an artificial virtue. A reply in kind is simple. In the first place, evolution is rarely so fine-tuned: few fathers throughout history have known which child is theirs, or even known that any was. It is enough that we are moved to care for children. The assumption that lions, or gorillas, who kill whatever cubs they find alive in the pride they have just joined, are acting 'in the interests of their genes' (because this makes the females available as mates) may be true, but the killers have not *recognized* that these are not their cubs.[50] More probably, what happens on those murderous occasions is a simple bonding failure: some

---

48 See Philip Slater, *The Glory of Hera* (Princeton University Press: New Jersey 1992).

49 Plato, *Gorgias* 494; *Laws* 636c. The attempt to find philosophical support for gays, by suggesting, as Nussbaum has done, that it has only ever been the Christian churches which condemned buggery, and that 'the Greeks' heartily approved of it, is utterly wrong-headed: see J. M. Finnis, 'Law, Morality, and "Sexual Orientation"', *Notre Dame Law Review* 69/5.1994, pp. 1049–76; Gerard V. Bradley, 'In the Case of Martha Nussbaum', *First Things* 44.1994. 'Being buggered' was felt to be a humiliation in ancient Greece (as it still is in much of the world), and those adults who consented to it were despised. It does not follow, of course, that same-sex friendships – even erotic friendships – should be despised. Still less does it follow that those who find companionship and meaning in their lives through such adventures deserve to lose their social status, their jobs, their health or their lives.

50 Nor is there any need to suppose that lions who kill cheetah cubs (though cheetahs do not even compete to catch the same prey as lions) are acting out a pattern established when lions' ancestors competed with *Dinofelis* (as Steven M. Stanley proposed, *Children of the Ice Age: how a global catastrophe allowed humans to evolve* (W. H. Freeman & Co.: New York 1996), p. 75). There has simply been no evolutionary

creatures – including females – fail to bond with their own cubs, perhaps because of some disruption in the process that leads from parturition. Nature, so to speak, is unlikely to program us only to love the young we *know* are ours. It will more plausibly rely upon our loving those we saw at an impressionable age or moment (our own and theirs). Accidents may happen either way: some of us are more impressionable, and some less. In the second place, children that we care for now are likely enough to grow to care for our grandchildren: even if they are not themselves our own close kin, they will be fathers and mothers of our kin, and kindlier because of our own care. In the third place, almost all the children we are likely to encounter are in fact our own close relatives.[51] Perhaps one or two might carry a mutant allele that somehow made them indifferent to others' children (by making them less impressionable, perhaps), and our care for them might therefore allow the gene pool to be invaded by uncaring, or more chauvinistic types. But there is no good reason to suppose that anything so important as parental love has been left to the mercies of a single gene, nor to suppose that emotionally retarded adults prosper.

The Darwinian hypothesis is that we have the impulses and feelings that we mostly do because these, by and large, have helped to support the actions we must take if we are to have a future, through our descendants and close relatives. They need not have been fine-tuned (in fact, those populations that have been subjected to so rigorous a cull as to be precisely adapted to one narrow range of possibility are usually now extinct). It would seem to follow that we ought to respect those impulses and feelings if we want to have a future: 'respect', not automatically obey, since times may now have changed. Times *may* have changed, but we might also be wary: such inhibitions or repugnancies as we now feel, exist precisely because we also feel attractions. They act as limits on what we might otherwise be

reason for the lions *not* to kill small objects such as these. Nor have they yet woken up to what they are doing.

[51] Steve Jones, *In the Blood: God, genes and destiny* (HarperCollins: London 1996), points out that almost everyone in these islands is my cousin, and probably at no more than five or six removes. And every human being is descended, if not from Adam and Eve, at least from someone living at the core of the Old World a few thousand years ago.

glad to do – and because they act as limits, we would be glad to disregard them, and dream up reasons why we have the right. Generations of young men and women have been glad to believe that sexual desire is fun, only to be forcibly reminded that sex has its price. The world we experience in the glow of lust is not necessarily one that others share, nor one that lasts, nor one we would wish to live in. If shame or fear or sudden revulsion kept them almost chaste, perhaps they should be glad. Such inhibitions are less *pleasurable* than lust, but they are just as much a product of our past. Why is it 'natural' to give way to lust, and not to shame instead? Why is 'the yuk factor' something to despise, and 'the yum factor' a good guide? How can we bring our worlds, our 'gods', together?

The dominant view amongst moralists has been that human beings, as animals, have many goals and feelings. A 'good life' is one that achieves some reasonable amount of what we want, at reasonable cost. We can, and should, accept some guidance from the past embodied in our common feelings, and our common lore, especially as it is those feelings which define, exactly, what we want or fear. The really radical option, of abandoning that past, is one I shall explore in chapter 7. The question here is whether this 'pluralistic', or polytheistic, theory of value works. It is certainly, empirically, true that we have many wants and fears, that our worlds change around us as we change. Our talents and our tempers are evoked by particular circumstances (like the dog's). Institutions of the sort I have described provide some patterns to enable us to cope with shifting worlds,[52] but are as various as the worlds themselves. According to modern common sense there is no one 'right way', nor any single goal deserving of our absolute devotion. All we can say is that some ways, some institutions, offer a more tightly knit assembly than some others, and that our sense of selfhood will be correspondingly diverse.

---

[52] And the dog's problem may not be innate: its failure to co-ordinate its worlds is a failure of social context, and not 'in its genes'. My use of the term 'worlds' to signify those ways that *the world* appears to us in different modes is owed, in origin, to Alfred Schutz *Collected Papers* vol. 1: *The Problem of Social Reality*, ed. M. Natanson (Nijhoff: The Hague 1971).

This account of practical reasoning is, nowadays, associated with the name of Aristotle, who is widely supposed to have disagreed with Plato by defining a human life as one lived here and now, in company with other human beings, and with no single good to serve.[53] Virtues, by this account, are just those states of character that enable us to achieve such goods, avoid such harms, as we are naturally disposed to want or fear. They include capacities for dealing with our companions, whether family, or friends, or fellow citizens, or strangers. 'One who is willingly solitary must be either a beast or a god'.[54] Impulses too distant from the norm for general sympathy are bestial. Failures to look far enough ahead, or to have a conception of a whole life to be lived, are slavishness or vice. The bourgeois dream is defined by the slogan 'Nothing in Excess'.[55] A far more plausible reading of the Aristotelian texts tells a different story. The best life is one lived 'in accordance with virtue, and if there is more than one such virtue, in accordance with the best and most complete'.[56] That most perfect virtue, in the end, is *wisdom*, and Aristotle is as convinced as any Platonist that there is one single strategy for life, by which we may transcend humanity. He did not applaud plurality: on the contrary, it is wicked people who are plural in themselves, and virtue is defined by having a single goal – the beautiful.

Plato taught that we desire to be immortal (in effect, to be a god). Desiring that (but knowing that this flesh is mortal) we desire 'to beget in beauty'. Some rely upon their literal children, others on their pupils and apprentices. We want them to be what we have failed to be, to carry the flame onwards. The all-too-easy error in this is to suppose that being like *us* is what we mind about: the only beauty that *can* be carried forward is not

---

[53] This is only one of the many spurious Aristotles; the other one of importance in this study is the one portrayed by scientists as a gullible authoritarian (witness Peter Medawar's foolish account in *From Aristotle to Zoos* (Weidenfeld & Nicolson: London 1984), pp. 24ff.). But that is by the way.

[54] Aristotle, *Politics* 1.1253a3ff.

[55] Cf. C. S. Lewis, *The Pilgrim's Regress* (Bles: London 1933), pp. 86–7: 'You cannot go too far in the right direction.'

[56] Aristotle, *Nicomachean Ethics* 1.1098a16–17. 'The end of mortal life was to put on immortality as much as might be'; Lewis, *Pilgrim's Regress*, p. 87, quoting *Nicomachean Ethics* 10.1177b33.

ours. Recognizing a friend as 'half of myself'[57] is to realize a larger self than *mine* – or else it is to absorb the friend as no more than a limb or organ, and to lose the friend.

Greek ethics – and the codes of most traditional peoples – are at once more realistic and more fanciful than the codes approved by recent moralists. Where modern moralists have tended to find virtue in what *everyone* should do, and *everyone* agree upon (though actually excluding many creatures from that universal class), Plato and Aristotle alike began from what particular individuals should do. This may explain why *honour* is an important category for them, but hardly at all for modern moralists.[58] On the other hand, they saw the possibility of transcending this world here, and all its occupations. Imagine yourself with lines ascending to your various goals; perhaps some of those goals can be arranged in order (so that you make money *to* get married, and marry *to* have children – or, of course, the reverse),[59] but most can only meet outside our sphere. Whatever it is that is worth everything is not a worldly goal, since any of those could, on occasion, be surrendered for another one. Without that transcendent goal, we have no *single* life, no unity.

The beauty of mind and body we admire and wish to nurture and recreate in others and ourselves is easily contaminated. On the one hand, it is an object that transcends the many different moods or modes that make us up. On the other, it may take its

---

[57] Augustine, *Confessions* (tr. T. Matthew, ed. R. Huddlestone (Burns & Oates: London 1923)) 4.6 (*dimidium animae*) had been anticipated by Aristotle (*heteros autos*: another self). The question whether such friendship is no more than an *egoisme à deux*, and something to be abjured by believing Christians is regularly reconsidered; see my 'Friendship in the Christian Tradition' (with Gillian Clark), in R. Porter and S. Tomaselli, eds., *The Dialectics of Friendship* (Tavistock Press: London 1989), pp. 26–44.

[58] '[Honour] must mean the honour of the concrete and therefore always the individual man, the dignity and estimation due to every man, but to each as this particular man, not merely as the specimen of the race, but directly, personally and exclusively', Karl Barth, *Church Dogmatics* vol. III/4, p. 655, cited by Stanley Hauerwas, *Despatches from the Front: theological engagements with the secular* (Duke University Press: Durham and London 1995), p. 63.

[59] The architectonic structure described by Aristotle (*Nicomachean Ethics* 1.1094a6ff.) is concerned with what we would surrender if we had to, and what we would use as a means. The supreme good should never be surrendered, and never used as a means. What will the whole world profit you, if you have lost your 'soul'?

flavour from just those moods or modes, particularly the sexual. Admiring beauty and desiring beauty (and sometimes, in reaction, killing beauty) are all available responses – available to us, if not, as such, to other animals. In them, the objects of desire, affection, filial piety, hunger and springtime exuberance are separate, as they may also be in us, with the help of ritual. In constructing a mind in which those lesser minds all merge, we can discover or create a single object. The beauty of children, lovers, music, sunsets, mathematics and gastronomy is grouped together despite the obvious difference.

Is this more than a tedious analogy? Is it anything but a dangerous evasion? Both pederasty and romantic love may seem like self-indulgence, deliberate narrowings of attention, at the cost of recognizing other goods – or even the good of the purported object. Baboon cubs, remember, may not get any benefit from being abducted by their would-be 'aunts' or 'uncles'. As institutions, romantic love and pederasty both claim a moral purpose, but this may be a mere excuse for sensual appetite. This is not just to say that pederasts, and families, may often do great harm. Even if there is no direct abuse they may do harm: witness the Sufi who paid a family to keep their son idle, because the Sufi wanted to admire his beauty.[60] The story does not say if the child, once grown, was grateful; he clearly had no cause to be. We are fortunate, perhaps, that our plans for our children are so often failures: if they grew up to be what we had wanted (or had thought we did) we would regret it. Luckily, thanks to Weismann's Law and their recalcitrance, each child is a new beginning (weighted down, no doubt, by sin and her elders' expectations).[61]

But the issue is not just with failure. Suppose the fantasies are real: a caring, non-abusive pederast; a loving family of healthy young. Even at their imaginable best, such love is narrow. We pardon bias on the part of parents and of lovers that we would scorn in industrialists or statesmen. What matters, it almost

[60] Fakhroddin Ibrahim al-Iraqi (1211–89), according to Peter Lambourn Wilson, *Scandal: essays in Islamic heresy* (Autonomedia: New York 1988), p. 134.

[61] Even the clones of adults whom some genetic engineers now promise will, we can be very glad to say, prove unamenable to being what their makers wish.

seems, is that we 'love', that we experience the emotion, not that the world continues or our beloveds prosper. Most likely, this is a relic of the ancient concern with *motive*, and the rightness of acting for the right reason, whatever the result. In the modern context, it can be misunderstood. On the one hand lies a merely sensual outlook, to enjoy the small occasions without exciting envy or hostility.[62] On the other lies a more dynamic view, the drive to create our own world in the future. Either form seems flawed, but is there any other way of living?

MANY MINDS AND THE SINGLE INTELLECT

We are all, in a way, made of many little minds, moods, modules – 'human' and 'animal' alike. In humans, and perhaps some other creatures, it is evident that there is a would-be mastermind, aware of itself as owning or pervading many such moods, and being able to retain its own self-known identity through many episodes. The obverse of that subject is the single world in which we recognize landmarks and friends, persisting through those episodes. There may be entirely other sorts of creature, capable of reason: indeed, we have often imagined just such creatures as angelic intellects and hoped that we were too. The modern biological picture of our being is in a way not far removed from the Platonic: the mastermind, or intellect, is fractured or reflected into many little modes, each capable of driving action on (desire, or fear, or shame, or righteous anger). In Aristotelian theory (which is more easily assimilated to the modern style), such modules are all functions of an organic whole, the living animal. In Platonic theory, which has been the common sense of centuries, the mastermind has been distinguished from the living animal.[63]

That this has actually been common sense is clear. Consider the fact that we can sensibly *imagine* ourselves as foreigners,

---

[62] John Cowper Powys, *In Defence of Sensuality* (Village Press: London 1974; first published 1930) offers an almost plausible account of this.

[63] As Aristotle himself also thought: *nous* is not a function of any particular bodily organ, though all kinds of other mental activity may be; see *De Anima* 3.429b25ff. Howard Robinson establishes Aristotle's dualist credentials in 'Aristotelian Dualism', *Oxford Studies in Ancient Philosophy* 1.1983.

imbeciles, or of the other sex. If each of us is just the animal we are (of *this* sex, *this* variety, *this* age and circumstance) imaging oneself as something else is fantasy. What would it mean to say that *this* exact table might have been *that* chair? Of course, the wood of which it is made could have been used to make a different thing, but then it would not have been *this* table, nor *that* chair. Switching the identity of table and chair is as mean-ingless as suggesting that the number seven might *be* the number ten. Imagining oneself as a Ruandan refugee is not – though it is an imagining that needs careful handling. If the soul were only the form of a living animal then it can be no one else's: which is why Aristotle dismissed the possibility that we, as human beings, might be 'reincarnated' as a rat or bee or bush. If on the other hand there is something that could without absurdity 'be' either this present person or a Ruandan – or a rat – then that thing cannot be just the form of any particular creature. So Aristotle, and not the Aristotelians, was right, that the 'intellect' is not the body's form. Once that step is taken, a fully Platonic account may have more appeal, and the thing, whatever it is, that knows itself as me, might as easily look out from any creature's eyes.[64]

The Platonic or Pythagorean account has not usually been the preferred account in Christian or even wider Abrahamic circles. It has been assumed instead that only *human* beings were subjects of a life, or agents. The elegance or intelligence in any animal 'action' was just the way they were. More careful observation makes it difficult to suppose that animals, even insects, are entirely dumb. If humans are required to take a larger view of things it is not because the others have no view of things at all. That theory was always so implausible that we have to suppose extraneous reasons for supporting it. Strangely, the chief such reason is often blamed on 'Platonism', namely, that what is most important in us is what transcends the flesh. If what was most important ('the immortal intellect') were some-thing shared with 'animals' and 'animals' were only interested

---

[64] See Zeno Vendler, *The Matter of Minds* (Clarendon Press: Oxford 1985); Geoffrey Madell, *The Identity of the Self* (Edinburgh University Press: Edinburgh 1981) for further expansions of this argument.

in the things of this world here, that most important thing must be, it was thought, this-worldly. Conversely, if it is not (and 'animals' *are* this-worldly), it cannot be something shared with them. From this in turn it follows that we cannot, consistently, imagine ourselves in their place, nor hear the voice of a friend, as Pythagoras said he did, in the howls of a beaten dog.[65] They lie beyond the reach of reason, friendship, justice.

So our beliefs about animals – and also about the intellect – have been conditioned by the conviction that we must transcend them: 'animal nature' exists to be transcended, and anyone with any sympathy for an animal must have degenerate morals.[66] This is a travesty of Plato's own position, and that of most Platonists. Until this century, the only work by something like a professional philosopher exhorting us to respect non-human animals (namely, Porphyry's *On Abstinence from Animal Flesh*[67]) was by a Platonist. Platonists sustained for centuries the tradition of sacramental theism, and a delight in animals. Each real type of creature revealed, they thought, real beauty, one aspect of the divine. If human beings might perhaps contain them all, it certainly was not by despising them. The intellectual grasp of things was not a way of leaving things behind, but of putting aside concupiscence. Sense and sensual desire are unreliable because they take things from one angle only, and encourage us to grasp at what must be left to be.

So consider 'animal' behaviour in another light. Much of it is indeed directed toward making use of mere material: a cat will usually only see a mouse as a moving object or a furry toy. But even cats, when not in hunting mode, let other creatures be. A cat may momentarily pursue a household hamster (say), but then halt, seemingly embarrassed, and permit the creature some outrageous liberty. 'Intellect', which is just letting things

---

[65] According to Xenophanes' mocking story, recounted in Diogenes Laertius, *Lives of the Philosophers* 8.36.

[66] This was explicit in much nineteenth-century discourse; I discussed the issue in *The Moral Status of Animals* (Clarendon Press: Oxford 1977), and more recently in papers reprinted in *Animals and their Moral Standing* (Routledge: London 1997).

[67] Gillian Clark's translation and commentary (Duckworth: London 2000) supersedes the familiar version produced by Thomas Taylor (who himself built on Porphyry's arguments to satirize the campaign for women's rights in *A Vindication of the Rights of Brutes* – quite what his own position was is now obscure).

be, is not a discursive faculty possessed by talkers. Talking is exactly what gets in the way of intellect. Letting things be, or the opening of the eyes, is a moment which may arise in any animal being: what is different in us is that we talk about it (and so often miss the point).

Similarly, the caste- and class-transcendent love which posits common 'humanity' is not a discursive bargain between desperate brigands,[68] to play halfway fair with other bargaining primates. It is the moment of seeing, with sudden joy, that some other being is not *material*, but a whole world wakening.

> How do you know but ev'ry Bird that cuts the airy way,
> Is an immense world of delight, closed by your senses five?[69]

The more we know about animals the easier it is to make that move, and realize that they may make it too – but it *is* a move: merely knowing *about* someone or something is not knowing them. This is not to adopt that other error, that animals are 'innocent': why should they be? All creatures that there are on earth are grasping for their own deliverance: sudden enlightenments or summons come to all alike. The fact that this seems foolish is a reminder of how pre-Darwinian our imagination often is: we constantly assume that animals do not change, although our modern theory is founded on the fact that they do. It is not just that variations gradually accumulate, but that which variations prosper is determined by the choice of life. The conditions under which we make those choices, and their net effects, are not for us to determine; that differences are made is certain.

Plato and Aristotle alike insisted that the intellect was not *intelligence*. Once grant the distinction, there seems no reason to

---

[68] The phrase is J. L. Mackie's, in *Ethics: inventing the difference between right and wrong* (Penguin: Harmondsworth 1977). As I pointed out in a review article on Ted Honderich, ed., *Morality and Objectivity: essays in honour of J. L. Mackie* (Routledge & Kegan Paul: London 1985), Mackie was at least aware that the older ethical tradition made a higher demand than this. Other modern moralists have actually forgotten what 'moral beauty' is (on which, see below). See my 'Mackie and the Moral Order', *Philosophical Quarterly* 39.1989, pp. 98–144, and 'The Better Part' in A. Phillips-Griffiths, ed., *Ethics* (Cambridge University Press: Cambridge 1993), pp. 29–49.

[69] William Blake *The Marriage of Heaven and Hell* (1790–3) plates 6–7, *Complete Writings*, p. 150.

insist that intellect is something only humans have. If intellect were intelligence, displayed in calculation or in games of chess, we would have to admit that humans have already been surpassed: there need be no upper limit (except perhaps the physical) to the speed or range or exactness of mechanical calculation.[70] Chess programs can already beat us all, at least at chess. Not one has yet the common sense of mice, nor ever 'opened its eyes' to see how strange things were. If ever they do, it will not be by their program. Any of us can now complete calculations, produce diagrams or sort out data that only the most gifted managed a few years ago: the difference of ordinary intelligence between one scholar or scientist is of increasingly little significance. The difference in insight or compassion may be as great as ever. It follows that we should find the most important element not where scholars and scientists have been accustomed (namely, amongst people much like them), but where that insight and compassion dwell.

> Then every man, of every clime,
> That prays in his distress,
> Prays to the human form divine,
> Love, Mercy, Pity, Peace.
> And all must love the human form,
> In heathen, turk or jew;
> Where Mercy, Love, & Pity dwell
> There God is dwelling too.[71]

The 'human' does not dwell only in our species, and in loving other particular creatures we are awakened to 'the human' in them:

[70] Though there may well be problems, even of a mathematical sort, which cannot be solved by calculation; see Roger Penrose, *The Emperor's New Mind: concerning computers, minds and the laws of physics* (Oxford University Press: New York 1989). Compare Blake's argument: 'As none by travelling over known lands can find out the unknown, so from already acquired knowledge Man could not acquire more: therefore an universal Poetic Genius exists' (Blake, 'All Religions are One' (1788), *Complete Writings*, p. 98).

[71] Blake, 'The Divine Image', in *Songs of Innocence* (1789), *Complete Writings*, p. 117. This is not to forget Blake's balancing proposition, in 'A Divine Image' (1794), ibid., p. 221
> Cruelty has a Human Heart,
> And Jealousy a Human Face;
> Terror the Human Form Divine,
> And Secrecy the Human Dress.

Each grain of Sand,
Every Stone of the Land,
Each rock & each hill,
Each fountain & rill,
Each herb & each tree,
Mountain, hill, earth & sea,
Cloud, Meteor & Star,
Are Men Seen Afar.[72]

So what *is* 'the human'? On this account, the dignity of human beings lies in the fact that some of us are saints. Being a 'saint' or even being a sage is not the same as being clever. What matters may be found as easily, more easily, amongst the unlearned or the 'animal'. What sanctity requires of cats, or mice, who knows? We can recognize all manner of callous, greedy conduct in others, and grudgingly acknowledge it in ourselves; by its occasional absence we catch sight of something more. In ordinary life, even our virtues are discrete: the way we behave, and think it 'right' and 'natural' to behave, is not the same at work, at home, at play, on holiday in 'foreign parts'. Our inconsistencies are sometimes challenged: we 'wake up' to realize that actions have effects, that strangers may be as sensitive as kin, that 'what we ought to do' is not one thing in Rome, and another in Piccadilly. That recognition is an escape from fragmentary life: the philosopher, so tradition says, is 'a citizen of the cosmos', not only of one particular city.[73]

Return for a moment to the 'Many Minds' idea. Some commentators have suggested that those who suffer from 'multiple personality disorder' reveal the human condition, and that we are all variously divided and at odds with our own selves. There has even been a fashion for equating different 'personalities' with the operation of the left and right hemispheres of the brain, so that *all* of us contain an alternate personality that is waiting for its chance. In fact, if the disorder exists at all, it

---

[72] Blake, to Thomas Butts (2 October 1800), ibid., p. 804–5; see also his annotations to Swedenborg's *Divine Love* (about 1789): 'think of a white cloud as being holy, you cannot love it; but think of a holy man within the cloud, love springs up in your thoughts, for to think of holiness distinct from man is impossible to the affections', ibid., p. 90.

[73] See Epictetus, *Discourses* 2.10.

involves far more than two discrete personalities, which cannot easily be linked to separate areas of the brain. *All* the personalities, after all, usually have access to all the bodily functions of the single entity we recognize from outside as a human being. The reading of such evidence as there is that I have advocated elsewhere suggests that the disorder rests on error: the error, perhaps, of those who seem to suffer, as well as the error of those who diagnose their problem.[74] What contemplative tradition suggests is that the intellect, the Self, can be distinguished from its passing moods and thoughts. The Self is the light into which our different actors step – as one victim recognized in his own self-description. Once we recognize that Self, the *nous* that thinks itself (as Aristotle put it), we can see that It is not the persons, or the masks, it wears. So why should we think it limited to ordinarily human masks?

The biblical and Koranic records both suggest that 'animals' can seek their food from God, rejoice in God, and give us good advice (or bad). It is customary to regard such claims as folklore, or as metaphor. Early Christians followed Stoic and Epicurean consensus in denying that 'animals' were ever part of the covenant: the texts they carried denied that common view, and had to be interpreted to their destruction. Even Paul was not guiltless – though too much should not be made of a passing trick of rhetoric. That we should not muzzle the ox that treads out the corn is, in its context, a clear denunciation of those who cheat their helpers – namely the oxen they have put to work for them. Paul chooses to suggest that God cannot really care about oxen, but that the command refers to *human* workers (and in particular to those who labour at spreading the good news of Christ).[75] The covenant God makes with all is to give them an opportunity. Sometimes new doorways open; sometimes a line is drawn. If none of us can be responsible for the talents with

[74] 'How many Selves make me?' in D. Cockburn, ed., *Human Beings* (Cambridge University Press 1991), pp. 213–33; 'Minds, Memes and Multiples', *Philosophy, Psychiatry and Psychology* 3.1996, pp. 21–8.

[75] 1 Corinthians 9.9. Paul goes on to disclaim any wish himself to take financial aid from his congregations. He must in fact have known that the command was, properly, taken to apply to the very creatures named in it, even if, like other commands, it had a wider meaning.

which we face the world, nor add an inch to our stature by any careful thought, perhaps we should indeed consider 'the fowls of the air, and the lilies of the field'.[76] Living by God's providence is living 'like an animal'. If we are worth more than many sparrows, Christ enquired, why do we not trust that God will feed us too? The text, of course, has been read to say that we *are* worth more than many sparrows, and may therefore blind and kill them: the reading is perverse.

No doubt Whewell was right to insist, in the passage I quoted in chapter 1, that any human being was 'more worthy of account, than millions of millions of mollusks and belemnites, lizards and fishes, sloths and pachyderms, diffused through myriads of worlds'.[77] He was contending, like Paul, with those who thought to diminish people, or people of another race or class than theirs, and sought to contrast the *thinking* creatures, conscious of their duties, with *unthinking* animals. Denys Cochin's claim that 'the mind that is conscious of itself and possesses the idea of good has no connection with the mind lacking these characteristics',[78] was similarly motivated. But we can now realize that thinking, or even consciousness of moral beauty, need not be confined within one breeding pool. The Church has been singing and praying for centuries in terms that clearly specify that all things have a voice; why not take that seriously?[79]

So what is it that shows us God? The Stoic view was that 'the sage' had the 'mind of God', enlightened through his recognition that all things were fated, and so knowing everything that can be known. Some moderns, long misled by the equation of the intellect and intelligence, suppose that 'having the mind of God' means knowing the theory that 'explains' – or at any rate fully describes – the world. The road to being, or perhaps

---

[76] Matthew 6.26–9; 12.6.
[77] William Whewell, *Of the Plurality of Worlds* (John W. Parker & Son: London 1854), p. 368.
[78] Cited by Harry W. Paul, *The Edge of Contingency: French Catholic reaction to scientific change from Darwin to Duhem* (University Presses of Florida: Gainesville 1979), p. 61.
[79] Those who base doctrine on liturgical demands (so that the *lex credendi* is the *lex orandi*: what we should believe is fixed by the way that we should pray) ought to take especial care, lest their words be empty.

making, God, lies through applied mathematics – but with no hint that mathematics itself depends on a vision of intellectual beauty. Having the mind of God is seeing things 'objectively', without affect – a condition more usually linked with psychopaths. 'Thought alone can make monsters, but the affections cannot.'[80] The alternative (and one that is truer to biblical and even Stoic thought) is to find the mind of God in insight and compassion. It is not the mechanically considered world – the world of Kipling's machines, that can 'neither love nor pity nor forgive'[81] – that is God's truth, but the world rejoiced in. Mortal creatures like ourselves never know very much of that rejoiced-in world, but the fragment our eyes are (sometimes) opened to is real. A cat's world *may* be smaller than my own (though all I really know is that the overlap between our worlds is small); it is still possible even for a cat to find that world a fragment of a larger, and to be changed by seeing it.

Jewish and Muslim writers acknowledge saints and prophets, and reckon that God can speak as easily through a donkey as a man. Christians have contended that Jesus is more than prophet. Whereas a prophet only speaks 'the word of God', Jesus is that Word. Whereas Jews and Muslims reckon that the Torah or the Koran is the uncreated Word, Christians identify that Word as the man Jesus. A variety of sensible heresies have sought to modify that claim, to mean that Jesus and the Word are different things, but that Jesus, as it happened, acted and thought and spoke just as the Word required. There are possible worlds, on that account, where he died as a jobbing carpenter, or a bandit, and Judas or Caiaphas or Pilate spoke the Word. Orthodox Christendom refused that option: from everlasting there is one Word only, and it is identically Jesus son of Mary. In him our human nature was remade – or rather it was in Him that this nature was first begun. Without Him we do not know what we are to be, and so do not know ourselves at all.

[80] Blake's annotations to Swedenborg's *Divine Love*, *Complete Writings*, p. 90. He was wrong to suggest – momentarily – that 'the affections' as we now experience them must be innocent.
[81] Rudyard Kipling, 'The Secret of the Machines', *Collected Verse 1885–1926* (Hodder & Stoughton: London 1927), pp. 675–6.

Some variously concluded that the Word is only Jewish, or only masculine, or only thirty-odd years old, and that whatever nature lies outside that range cannot represent or profit from His Incarnation. More sensible theorists, adapting metaphysics to sound ethical conclusions, have insisted that the very same nature transcends such small divisions: Jew or Gentile, male or female, slave or free, we are all one in Jesus Christ our Lord[82] – but Paul did not conclude that being 'human' or 'non-human' made no difference. We are now in a position to see what does or does not. If God's Word is incarnate in a human being, commonly so-called, it is also and necessarily incarnate in a mammal. A living creature bears the stamp of God: it is the very thing God speaks from eternity, and all other things are at once its echoes and companions. I have argued elsewhere that the Incarnation is itself Creation.[83] There would not be a world like this at all unless God uttered it; He could not utter it as He did (and does) without creating a biosphere to house and spell His Word. Nor can He create it without, in some sort, abandoning it to itself.[84] But whatever corruption or catastrophe we see around us we can be assured that God does not desert us. We exist because He speaks his Word, and accepts Himself the constraining context of our echoing choice. It is not only human nature, for there is nothing that is only human nature, that God takes up in Christ, but that of everything.

Popular tradition has always known as much, seeing God's grandeur, mercy, love – or anger – in all manner of animal stereotypes. It is no surprise that we went on treating 'animals' badly (and excusing ourselves on specious grounds for this): after all, we went on treating people badly too, although we had been warned that what we did to any of them we did to the Lord of Heaven. Our problem has been that we think such tales are metaphors, and so do not count. The friends of God, accordingly, are neither those who tame their 'inner beasts' nor

---

[82] Galatians 3.28.
[83] In *God's World and the Great Awakening* (Clarendon Press: Oxford 1991).
[84] S. Weil, *Gateway to God*, ed. David Raper (Fontana: London 1974), p. 48: 'Because he is the creator, God is not all-powerful. Creation is abdication. But he is all-powerful in this sense, that his abdication is voluntary.'

those who act like friendly animals, but those who are woken up to some new possibility, and act within the tangled residue of past awakenings. We can conceive, though not imagine, how the final wakening will spread through all those stiffened sinews, unfolding and releasing the true form of things, the company of all God's faithful people. Living in the anticipated light of that new world, we can afford a little courtesy to creatures caught, like us, in the coils of chance and time.

SUBSTANCES, QUALITIES AND CLONES

It is crucial to the account I have given – and probably to any decent ethical and sacramental theory – that we distinguish between *what* things are, and *how*, between their substance and their qualities. Without that distinction *how* things are determines how we think of them. 'Hating the sin but not the sinner' would be an impossible task, as sinners are only sins. Loving our fellow creatures would demand that we love what they do. If a thing were only the sum of its properties, then different properties would make a different sum, and so a different being. Seneca, visiting his old homestead, was taken aback (he says) to see a worn-down slave who turned out to have been his childhood playmate. That slave did not just happen to house vague memories of a happier day: he really was the boy.[85]

This would not be worth recalling, were it not that moderns (philosophers, theologians and sometimes biologists) have subverted the distinction. Some opposition rests on simple misunderstanding: a belief in substance is interpreted as a belief in static, unrelated entities, whereas reality is dynamic and relational. Really to be is to be doing something, with the help and in the context of a wider world. The core components of reality, it is said, are better reckoned *events* than *things*.

It is also widely asserted that a belief in substance rests on Indo-European grammar: as Quine wittily observed, 'ontology

---

[85] Seneca, *Letters* 12, Thomas Wiedemann, *Greek and Roman Slavery* (Routledge: London 1988; first published 1981), p. 129. The context is given by Seneca's self-mocking realization that he is himself quite old.

recapitulates philology'.[86] In 'other languages', it is said (though no example survives a long inspection), no subjects separate from events are mentioned. In those other (real or imagined) languages, grammatical structures do not distinguish nouns and verbs, and the nearest we can get to accurate translation is the impersonal coinage of 'there is' or 'it is': as in 'it's raining', when nothing and no one rains. Such vaguely Whorfian deductions are fallacious:[87] the question whether Inuit or Navaho or Mandarin allow their speakers to discriminate between substances and qualities (as in fact they do) is not well answered by examining grammatical forms. 'It's raining' does not imply, nor lead one to suppose, that some one thing is raining; 'there was a rustling and a scrabbling' does not suggest that nothing at all scrabbled. No matter what the grammatical form, no human speaker finds it difficult to distinguish entities and events, nor living individuals and artifacts and heaps. Of course we can all imagine that an artifact is living, or that a heap is Mister Heap: the point is that this *is* imagining. We know that headaches exist when someone's head is aching: that head, or better still that someone, is a real subject which sometimes is clear-headed. Such individuals are the same in many transformations; unless we think 'a headache' is a sprite, there is no single thing it always is.

It is true that there are some problems about substance (as Aristotle knew). All other sorts of being (quality, quantity, relationships, and so on[88]) require the prior existence of real

---

86 W. O. Quine, *Word and Object* (Wiley: New York 1960). Haeckel's original aphorism, that ontogeny recapitulates phylogeny, is not really true. We do *not* pass through successive evolutionary stages in the womb, and 'early humans' were *not* childish. See Stephen Jay Gould, *Ontogeny and Phylogeny* (Harvard University Press: Cambridge, Mass. 1977).

87 Benjamin Lee Whorf is responsible for one of those 'really cute' ideas that continue in service long after they have been utterly refuted: namely that our mother tongues unalterably condition how we feel and think, and that Western European languages are somehow less appropriate or less amiable than Inuit or Hopi (which, by hypothesis, he did not understand). 'No one is really sure how Whorf came up with his outlandish claims, but his limited, badly analyzed sample of Hopi speech and his long-time leanings towards mysticism must have contributed' (Steven Pinker, *The Language Instinct: the new science of language and the mind* (Allen Lane: London 1994), p. 63). What Pinker means by 'mysticism', I do not know.

88 Aristotle's list of categories is inexact, and changing, but a lot more plausible than later attempts to distinguish different 'categories' of being. Gilbert Ryle's use of the

entities; but equally there are no entities, in the ordinary sense, without such properties. There can be no relationships unless there are things related; but equally, there can be no things unless they are related, somehow. The notion of a single, unqualified thing is null. That metaphysical conclusion is mirrored in a physical: even the most seemingly essential properties of matter depend on there being things far away. And in the biological: there cannot be a *single* living thing, since all things living depend on other living things, as components and contributors. Again: what a thing characteristically does defines its being, so that if it were not to be doing that it would cease to be at all. That indeed is how Aristotle addresses the practical problem, how we are to live. To answer the question we need to know what 'we' are: the answer is that we are creatures who wonder what to do, and our life is one of action deliberately chosen. A creature that no longer lived like that would not be interested in the answer, and would, *qua* human being (in the sense he meant), no longer exist at all, any more than a hand cut from a living body is a hand. Whatever is left behind, it seems, is stuff that once was human – but in that case being-the-thing-one-is is no more than a property of some underlying matter. Living things, on this account, are only Plasticene, shaped into different forms by circumstance. The only ultimate subject, Aristotle began to wonder, is pure stuff, which is not a countable, individual thing at all. It seems to follow that there are no substances: the stuff is not a substance, and every putative example turns out to be no more substantial than a coloured shape.

One plausible distinction is the following: there are no substances that do not exist, but there are many qualities (in the sense that includes quantities and the rest) which do not *exist*, in the sense that they are not instantiated. 'Non-existent sub-stances' are not individuals, but only ways of speaking about whatever *real* individuals might have such and such properties. The (non-existent) fat man in the corner is neither the same nor not the same as the (non-existent) surgeon on the stool. It is not

expression 'category mistake', for example, is merely rhetorical (see my 'What Ryle meant by "Absurd"', *Cogito* 11.1997, pp. 79–88).

that there are real unicorns who *do not exist*, but only that the complex property (of having a horse-like body, cloven hooves, a single horn growing from the forehead, and a taste for lilies) is not, so far as we know, instantiated. If it were, then unicorns would exist; that is, there *would* be unicorns. Interestingly, this familiar solution to the question whether 'existence is a predicate', intended to subvert the ontological argument for God's existence, itself subverts a familiar argument *against* that God's existence. If there are no substances that do not exist there are equally no possible (non-existent) worlds with better or happier beings than ourselves. There are no other substances than the ones there are (ourselves amongst them), and *our* being is indeed inextricably bound up with all the other substances, and our history. Even God Himself cannot first contemplate all possible worlds and every possible substance, and select the 'best' compossible assortment of such substances, since we and our fellow creatures are the only substances there are, in roughly the only world that we can be.[89] If, on the other hand, 'being this substance' is only a matter of there being something with the relevant properties, then it ceases to be clear why we should believe that there are no properties that *must* be instantiated (as there are certainly others that cannot be). 'Being God' may be just that property, such that it is impossible that it should not be: there are no possible *godless* worlds, and some world there must be.

But this is not the context for a further study of the Being of God.[90] My present concerns are biological. How can there be *substances*, in the sense we seem to need, in the world described according to the modern theory? Each multicellular living organism develops from a single eukaryotic cell in accordance with the patchwork instruction in its genome. Any locus or set of loci, on its chromosomes may vary unpredictably from its parents' genomes. Some genes (that is some exons) seem to have

---

[89] I attempted to unravel some of these problems in 'On Wishing there were Unicorns', *Proceedings of the Aristotelian Society* 90.1990, pp. 247–65. This could certainly be a better world than it is at present, but there *are* no better worlds – unless it is the world of Platonic Forms, where The Unicorn Itself resides in bliss.

[90] See my *God, Religion and Reality* (SPCK: London 1998) for another attempt at the issue.

the same immediate biochemical effect in creatures very distantly related. Would-be genetic engineers seek to equip organisms with the phenotypic characters displayed in others by inserting genes from the latter into the former genome – though 'insertion' is too bland a term for the actual assault, in which the recipient cell is broken into, and bits of DNA mechanically inserted in the hope that some will stick, or viral vectors are employed to carry the bits in. To those who complain that 'species boundaries' should be respected, the engineers reply, with justice, that any genome is much more like a loose-leaf folder than a carefully stitched volume. Any DNA, in principle, can turn up or be inserted anywhere. There are no uniquely human codons. Just as species turn out not to be real classes, united by a single natural essence, so individual organisms are only constructs, which might have been put together otherwise. Perhaps, after all, we are only 'Mister Heaps'.[91]

In ordinary contemporary life we do not seriously suppose that human twins are truly 'identical' even when they grew from a single zygote. Clearly they are distinct particular creatures, perhaps with subtly different characters and certainly different experiences. We are still strangely receptive to strange stories about them: how even twins separate from birth have chosen the same lives, and endured the same diseases, for no reason that any of us can see. Confronted by the possibility of cloning adult individuals, we have immediately supposed that we could thus recreate lost children, or lost genius. When critics complain that this is to treat humanity as an artifact, they are mocked for thinking that identical twins are not fully human, and reminded that experience makes the difference: we will never get back the child we lost, nor have we any real chance of

---

[91] Science-fiction writers, as so often, have explored some possibilities: consider Vernor Vinge's multi-bodied intelligences, in *Fire upon the Deep* (Orion Books Ltd.: London 1992), or David Brin's *traeki*, in *Brightness Reef* (Orbit: London 1995) and its sequels. In both cases new agents are deliberately constructed from a common stock, and experience their own identity quite differently from the way we think we do. If we could construct our children by similarly deliberate action, or even infect existing constructs by viral or nanotechnological artifice with novel properties, how long could we convince ourselves that we were right to conceive ourselves as 'entities' at all?

recreating genius.[92] But in that case what is the point of cloning people?

The only likely medical advantage will be to clone spare parts. In a not-too-distant (and repulsive) future, rich families will no doubt keep a stock of manufactured twins, deliberately brain-dead, 'for the children's sake'. It may be less repulsive if distinct organs and tissues can be grown from cloned cells without the apparatus of a fully grown human body, but it is not clear that experiments will stop short of growing *nervous* tissue that might, in friendlier days, be someone's own. But those who imagine a kind of deathlessness by rearing genetic duplicates to develop the 'same' character or similar talents, deserve a clearer answer than has so far been given. If what we mind about, in ourselves and others, are our *qualities*, then maintaining and perfecting those is as good as never dying. My clone, on this account, is not my twin, but as much of Me as anyone, including me, could wish. It need not even be a perfect copy: in fact, much better if it were not.[93] Once we have found out what biochemical context allows what phenotypic variation, I may conclude that some slight alteration in the programmed childhood will make a better Me. The child, once he is stable enough to know what I have done, may actively resent the burden of being Me – but might, appropriately prompted, be quite happy to be a link in the unending chain.

This fantasy may offer its own cure. If all that matters is my qualities, it hardly matters whether they recur together. Most of my genes are shared with millions; none of my qualities can really be called unique (except of course the 'quality' of being Me, *ipseitas* – but that is in dispute). As long as the human lineage continues, so will all of me that matters. To those who

---

92 C. J. Cherryh's *Cyteen* (Hodder & Stoughton: London 1983) is probably the best evocation of such an attempt, and the best guess at what might be necessary to obtain a formal identity between distinct individuals; see also Cherryh's *Voyager in Night* (Methuen: London 1985), where computer simulation (of an alien kind) produces similar problems. I discussed this and related sorts of 'immortality' in *How to Live Forever* (Routledge: London 1995).

93 Why should I wish myopia or stress headaches on my clone, and why should I (or could I) subject him to successive childhood traumas, even if 'they made me what I am'? But the more I wonder about what *I might have been*, the closer I come to doubting that I *am* this particular dying animal.

say, 'But it will not be Me', the question must be 'What is this Me it will not be?' Trying to keep my qualities together is a foolish hope, for just the reason that asexual reproduction has been much less successful than the sexual: mixing the properties in every generation scatters the seed more widely.[94] As I said earlier, we do not even need to procreate to be sure that there will be many like us, yet not too like, in subsequent centuries. But creatures that have those qualities will not, after all, be what I think is Me.

What is offensive in deliberately producing replicas? The difficulty of so doing (and the many hideously failed experiments that will litter the path of progress[95]) is a good reason not to try. The burden on the replicas themselves to live their predecessors' lives will be even greater than the burden on all ordinary children. But the real offence – and the reason why our own children do resent being made to live *our* lives – is that real entities are more than qualities. To value ourselves or others only for what they do is to forget their quiddity. The reason why I should not live *your* life is that I am not you, however alike we are and however closely related. To seek to build a baby is to treat it as an implement of ours; kings make tools, or extra limbs, out of their 'friends' and therefore have no friends.[96]

This answer rests, dogmatically, on the conviction that individual organisms (such as babies) really are individual identities. Imagine instead that there were many-bodied selves, like Brin's *traeki*, whose consciousness of their own being depended on the

---

94 This probably is not the full truth about the success of sexuality: mixing the genes, by transduction or infection, does not *necessarily* require two sexes. The point is rather that two strategies of reproduction (infecting others with one's DNA, and providing the cell to be infected) each prosper when they are the rarer option. The result is that in most species there are as many males as females, even though there *need* be only a few. See Ghiselin, *Economy of Nature*, and John Maynard Smith, *The Evolution of Sex* (Cambridge University Press: Cambridge 1978).

95 One seemingly insurmountable problem is that the cells of adult organisms – even if they are returned to their original, polyvalent state and their DNA made ready to create an entire creature, and not just its parts – will have suffered damage over the years of copying. That is why, remember, the cells which will become new organisms are segregated and vigorously tested. So clones created with DNA from adult cells are more than likely to be deeply flawed: it is not just a fault in the techniques, to be remedied by further practice.

96 Aristotle, *Politics* 3.1287b29.

interaction of many such living bodies, each contributing some element to the whole's abilities. If psychological identity consisted only in a continuing character, or consistency, such many-bodied selves would differ only in degree from us. All multi-cellular creatures, in a way, are colonies or swarms; some swarms themselves give evidence of being managed by a single program, and might as well be entities if action is all that mattered. Similarly, if being a single self were only a way of speaking – as some modern writers say[97] – a similar unity of family line can be created, even without genetic engineering. In brief: if we are only what we do, or what we say, the construction of a line of clones may carry risks, and yet not be subject to an absolute ban; it would not involve a wrongful, disrespectful attitude to another self, but rather a continuance of the only sort of selves there are.

It is no surprise that material unity must be a matter of degree, or common speech. To be material at all is to be extended: each space–time *locus* is, by definition, different from every other; each *locus*, by definition, depends on every other. Boundary lines are always fuzzy, in physics as in society. If there are absolute identities they cannot be material. There are possible worlds, or seemingly possible worlds, no doubt, where real identities wake up in swarms, or packs, or lines of descent. An entity is unified (that is, an entity exists) where experience is brought, consciously or unconsciously, to a point. A nation, in our world, is not a unity, however well coordinated it may be; a human being is, however confused. Might we not create new sorts of creature by extending a single entity's grip through generations, or keeping lines of communication open between separate bodies? And if so, might not cloning be an element in that new world? Is that not what 'noogenesis' requires?

Once again, it may be that this outcome is simply not

---

[97] It should be noticed that the destruction of our sense of self which 'no-ownership' theories of perception and cognition entail has particularly horrific overtones in the context of the opposing heresies of Nazism and Communism. Kimberley Cornish, in *The Jew of Linz: Wittgenstein, Hitler and their secret battle for the mind* (Century: London 1998), makes a strong case for the thesis that Wittgenstein and Hitler shared this radical quasi-Buddhistic revelation, and at least raises a serious question about Wittgenstein's own loyalties.

allowed: no more a *real* possibility than other fantasies of avoiding death. But there may be one last argument against the attempt: namely that it is an attempt to keep things single that should be more diverse, and predictable that should be more uncertain. The cloning of adult organisms can only be intended to retain a good that we already know, at the expense of the unfamiliar. The bio-engineers are the real reactionaries, rather than those who oppose them. As above, sexual reproduction is better than asexual, because it allows more difference and diversity.

Difference and diversity – the 'dappled things' of Hopkins' poetry[98] – are properties of the whole that may be lost. On the one hand, it seems likely that we are living through a mass extinction which may cost as many species as the Permian crash. Those earlier extinctions cleared the way for new evolutionary radiations, as the survivors spread out into the empty places. Whether the present events will permit that outcome is uncertain; in the past, whatever did the damage went away. If we survive, it probably will not have done. On the other hand, some theorists have welcomed the collapse, preferring to imagine a domesticated world, in which no species exist except the ones we want, in their own place. The domesticated world is difficult: we do not yet know exactly what is needed to sustain a viable ecosystem – witness our failures to construct any genuinely self-contained biosphere of the sort that interplanetary colonists will need. Whether we shall find out in time, who knows? But if a seriously denuded biosphere *is* practicable, we may be glad of it. Perhaps it is all we have left to hope for, in this world; maybe it would, in some ways, be a better place – as any civilized community is a better place than savagery. If the lion lies down with the kid, it must be a tame lion.

Deserts (whether cold or hot) have their own beauty; so indeed does parkland. But it is noticeable that most of us think even gardens better if they are more diverse.[99] The more

---

[98] G. M. Hopkins, 'Pied Beauty', *Poems of Gerard Manley Hopkins*, eds., W. H. Gardner and N. H. Mackenzie (Oxford University Press: London 1970, fourth edition), p. 69.

[99] The opinion is certainly not universal: one of Haeckel's charges against Britain was that it had 'mobilized all the different races of man' instead of joining Germany in

creatures, and the more different sorts of creature, that there are the better. There being 'too many' of one sort will usually mean that other sorts are diminished; if too many sorts are diminished, even the originally excessive sort will perish too. That may be the situation in which we find ourselves: even if there is no 'balance of nature' to call a halt to our own multiplication, it may be that we will be involved in the general collapse of kinds that will result from the elimination of too many central species. But suppose – which is also possible – that we will be able to survive in a much diminished biosphere. We may have to take control of many processes that have happened automatically, and that control may itself have unwelcome political effects. But it could equally be argued that attempts to avoid that situation would require draconian controls – so the question remains, why a more variegated ecosystem would be better than a less.

'Biodiversity', as a label for the variegated ecosystem, may be what we welcome just because our ancestors needed that environment. What seem like deserts to the foreigner may have their unexpected bounties, their subtle microsystems and in-genious creatures. But in general the more sorts of thing there are, the greater the wealth of food and usable material. Any sensible pre-human forager would prefer the wider range of stuffs, and take delight in their variety. Any sensible forager who was also possibly prey would welcome a range of places to avoid more specialized predators. No doubt foxes also prefer variety. It takes no great imagination to provide such evolutionary pretexts for whatever tastes we have: small hills, running water, woods; islands, with lookout points and sheltered coves; forests with occasional clearings. Since tastes *do* differ (individually and culturally) the probability is simply that we prefer whatever set of differences are most familiar, but can extend that local liking to the general form.

exterminating them. 'The English were tragically oblivious to the fact that the "cultural and psychological differences that separate the highest developed Euro-pean peoples from the lowest savages are greater than the differences that separate the savages from the anthropoid apes"' (*Eternity* (Truthseeker: New York 1916) p. 107, cited by D. Gasman, *The Scientific Origins of National Socialism* (Macdonald: London 1971), p. 134).

Perhaps evolutionary excuses mirror a much older story. All the different forms of beauty present some aspect of the Beautiful. It is important to the completeness of material being that as many such forms as possible are represented over time.[100] Some need to be kept separate, by time or place, but all are contained, in principle, in the Beauty which is the eternal Intellect. It may be that some times and places are, relatively, desert, but the whole remains. Desiring things *not* to be desert here and now is, on the one hand, right (since we are bound to wish as many beauties as possible to be present), and on the other, wrong (since 'being desert' is itself a form of being, and beauty, which it would be ungrateful to despise). From all of which it follows that we certainly have practical, and may have metaphysical, reasons to prefer biodiversity, but cannot be absolutely sure that *this* region, of time or place, is not a properly desert one. If it is wrong (as surely it must be) to despise natural beauties, it cannot also be right to despise the beauty of desert or degraded land. What we welcome in all these cases is the triumph of new life. Even gardens and parkland, given the chance, would acquire their own diversity. Even 'wasteland' will soon be wild again. Even clones and genetic artifacts will not stay tame for ever.

---

[100] See A. O. Lovejoy, *The Great Chain of Being* (Harvard University Press: Cambridge, Mass. 1961; first published 1936).

CHAPTER 6

The goals of goodness[1]

NATURAL GOODS AND MORAL VIRTUES

What, so far, is the conclusion of this enquiry?

There is a conflict between current popularizations of biological theory and ethical – let alone spiritual – demands. The
problem is not posed merely by 'Social Darwinism' but by the
'Sociable Darwinism' that Darwin himself (and others) have
advanced, and that marches with other fashionable tendencies.
The goal of goodness, it is widely supposed, is to perpetuate
one's kind, and there can be no ethical standard beyond species
survival.[2] Since species are, of their nature, fissiparous (tending
to break up into other new species), this species relativism is
hardly distinguishable from cultural relativism: each sub-breed
of humanity might reasonably expect to be a species soon.[3]
Religion, if it is justified at all, is merely as a means to species –
or group – survival by social solidarity. Even religious leaders
increasingly speak of 'cultural traditions', find proselytism
vulgar, and praise particular rites simply as giving those familiar
with them a sense of belonging. The praise is paradoxical: those
who wish there to be Anglican Cathedral choirs (say), although
nothing that such choirs sing is 'true', must depend as much as

[1] Originally delivered at the Anglo-Indian Convivium in Panchgani in January 1998, to
an Anglo-Dutch forum in Rotterdam in March 1998, and to the Philosophy Society at
Durham University in March 1999. An earlier version was published in *Studies in
World Christianity* 4.1998, pp. 228–44.

[2] As Michael Ruse and E. O. Wilson, 'Moral Philosophy as Applied Science: a
Darwinian approach to the foundations of ethics', *Philosophy* 61.1986, pp. 173–92
suppose.

[3] See my 'The Lack of a Gap between Fact and Value', *Aristotelian Society Supplementary
Vol.* 54.1980, pp. 245ff.

tourists on there being 'naive believers' who will innocently maintain the traditions that 'sophisticated believers' (that is, unbelievers) merely relish. A tradition self-consciously maintained merely to allow us something to 'belong' to is as futile as any project self-consciously adopted to give us a 'sense of purpose' (stamp-collecting, fashion, or visiting old churches).

Certainly this respect for tradition, and community, is an advance on the high-mindedly ethical attitude that despises the real concerns of ordinary people in the name of a global ethic known only to the intelligentsia. Greek philosophers who admired the people of Israel as 'a nation of philosophers' automatically distinguished the properly 'ethical' aspects of the Law from the merely superstitious or ritualistic (and so misunderstood the whole, while confusing their own cultural traditions with merely and universally 'rational' ones).[4] There is a lot to be said for 'thick' ethical concepts as well as 'thin' ones, and ways of being that are peculiar to historically contingent peoples. Those who profess to despise those local codes in the name of a self-chosen set of supposedly rational rules are very rarely people anyone (except their class-mates) could admire – especially since they are usually blind to the superstitions and contingent rituals to which they themselves adhere.[5] But though a renewed concern for real communities and real traditions is an advance, it must also be admitted that a religious tradition founded in God's call to Abram to leave country, kinsmen and his father's house, cannot be easily equated with

[4] 'The average agnostic of recent times has really had no notion of what he meant by religious liberty and equality. He took his own ethics as self-evident and enforced them; such as decency or the error of the Adamite heresy. Then he was horribly shocked if he heard of anybody else, Moslem or Christian, taking *his* ethics as self-evident and enforcing *them*; such as reverence or the error of the Atheist heresy' (G. K. Chesterton, *St Francis of Assisi* (Hodder & Stoughton: London 1923) pp. 144–5).

[5] So Darwin: 'The strangest customs and superstitions, in complete opposition to the true welfare and happiness of mankind have become all-powerful throughout the world . . . It would be difficult to distinguish the remorse felt by a Hindoo who has eaten unclean food, from that felt after committing a theft; but the former would probably be the more severe' (*The Descent of Man* (Princeton University Press: New Jersey 1981; a facsimile of the 1871 edition), vol. 1, p. 99). That the limits of 'property' might themselves be arbitrarily and brutally enforced seems not to have occurred to him, nor that there might be reasons for Hindu feeling. In general, Darwin was clearly faintly surprised when any member of the 'inferior races' showed any 'sensible' moral feeling, and was quick to deprecate it (ibid., pp. 95–6).

an order to stay put. It may also be disturbing that popular religiosity now so often turns on bland injunctions to 'be comfortable with who you are', and recommendations that 'religious rituals' will accomplish this self-integration. A 'spiritual' atmosphere is a dreamily uplifting one. Those who respect tradition might perhaps show more respect for what tradition tells us – namely, that we have every reason *not* to be comfortable with who and what we are.[6]

The problem is not only with religious thinkers. Moral philosophers of a more secular kind, whether or not they give weight to 'thick' ethical concepts over 'thin', also equate morality with the rules necessary (or sufficient) for social life, which is axiomatically to be preserved and enhanced. 'The Worst Person in the World', in a familiar children's story, is simply someone who dislikes sugar, birdsong, company, and ball games.[7] Moralists identify the moral and the sociable. They vary in the breadth of their preferred society: some seek to discover rules that will be adequate to preserve humanity at large, or even the biosphere; others are content with local groups, families and nations. It is understandable that even universal humanists, in practice, usually prefer not to surrender their own nation's gains for the sake of distant beneficiaries. These fashionable, hardly noticed, tendencies to love our species (weakly) and our own immediate society (strongly), are supported by biological theorists. Our genes, it is said, allow us no goals, nor inhibitions, that conflict with inclusive genetic fitness. We must expect that we are ineradicably possessive, grudging, nepotistic, racist; that males are incurably unfaithful; that our belief in free will, and in objective morals, are alike

---

[6] A related issue is the common inference that we should be gentle with wrong-doers since any of us could easily have done as ill: if we can imagine ourselves doing it, it cannot have been that bad. The converse is more likely: it is because we could so easily have done it that we know – or should know – that we are sinners.

[7] Not that this lacks all moral insight: 'The worst person in the world . . . lived all alone in a terrible mess. Most of the day he sat in a very uncomfortable chair and listened to old records he did not like' (J. Stevenson, *The Worst Person in the World* (Penguin: Harmondsworth 1980)). It may be true that 'the worst person', if there is one, is not the one who 'does most harm', nor anyone her neighbours would bother to condemn. The easy assumption that Hitler is almost the only one we 'know' must be in Hell, is both ignorant and vulgar – but that too is another story.

illusions engineered as evolutionary successes. This does not mean, as I have pointed out before, that we are bound to be merely selfish. Genes have no reason to create 'selfish' breeders (for selfish breeders, preferring their own well-being and survival to those of any other, do not have many offspring). Altruism, in the ordinary sense, is an explicable device, and not made any less altruistic for being, in general, 'advantageous' to the genes that predispose their carriers to that behaviour.

But this clarification of the current rhetoric does not remove the moral and meta-moral problems. The characters that we are predisposed to have and to admire, as well as the rules those characters devise for us, will not be egoistic; it does not follow at once that they will have the form required by the Christian (or any genuinely spiritual) creed. The altruism we can expect to feel is, centrally, 'kin-altruism' (with, perhaps, some stray affection for those who look or smell like kin but are not), and 'reciprocal altruism' (offered in expectation of a quick return[8]). Any demand to care for an unprofitable stranger, or to love your enemy, is to be regarded as an offence to natural law: either we cannot 'really' acknowledge such a duty (and our professions to the contrary must have some natural goal), or it must be an evolutionary 'mistake', soon to be overtaken by more carefully discriminating lines.

There is a larger problem. On this account, our admiration for the 'socially useful' characters, and our willed obedience to 'socially useful' rules, are programmed into us solely because they have helped the relevant genes to propagate themselves. If that is why we value certain characters, or care for certain creatures, and we know that is why, how long can we avoid sheer disillusionment? Consider the programmed persons of C. J. Cherryh's stories,[9] whom she names 'azi'. Azi are cloned human beings, born from artificial wombs, and reared in carefully controlled circumstances that make them wholly loyal to their conditioning. They are the 'natural slaves' of Aristotle's

---

[8] Not necessarily from the immediate beneficiary: by being kind I promote an appropriate *atmosphere*, which may bring benefits to me and mine.

[9] See especially *Downbelow Station* (Methuen: London 1983), *40,000 in Gehenna* (Methuen: London 1986) and *Cyteen* (Hodder & Stoughton: London 1989).

imagining, with the exception that they have all the natural virtues we desire (unfailingly loyal, loving, courteous, courageous and the rest). But what must an intelligent azi feel once she has realized what makes her have the feelings, even the 'memories', that she does? Coming to realize that she loves her owner only because her owner had her bred and reared for that, must she not, in that moment, have to choose whether or not to mind about her feelings? The rush of 'affection', 'admiration', 'loyal obedience' are suddenly revealed as chemical events, and emptied of significance. Must that not also be the result of the 'discovery' that parental affection, deference and a belief in an objective ethics, on the one hand, and sibling rivalry, sexual jealousy and tribal violence on the other, are all alike the result of genetic engineering? We have been programmed for another's purposes. Waking up to realize that our goals are, strictly, fictions, what can we hold on to?

It will not do even to respond that we have at least our *own* good to attend to, once we realize that altruism is a device to spread our genes, even at our individual expense. It is just as easy to suggest that we have some notion of 'our own' because it has paid our genes to demand a longer service from an individual organism than in some other lines. What counted for us as 'our own' is just as much an artifact in the case of 'our own body' or 'our own future' as it is in 'our own children' or 'our country'. There need be no real thing, myself, nor any real good of *mine*, any more than there is a real 'Clark Family' or real 'Britain'. All such ideas are helpful illusions: helpful to our genes. Even immediate pleasures are no more than bribes to do what has generally propagated genes. We have the desires – and even the ordinarily 'selfish' desires – we do because something else has had an advantage from it.

THE DARWINIAN USE OF USELESSNESS

What lies on the far side of our disillusionment is something I shall address below. But first it is necessary to refine the argument. One great advantage of evolutionary theory (and of course a considerable failing) is that there seems no limit to what it can explain – most often, after the event. It is all too easy for theorists to identify their own experience as universal, and then offer arguments to prove it must be so: so E. O. Wilson finds reasons to expect that men 'go out to work' and women 'stay in the suburbs to maintain their home'; Stephen Pinker explains that men are prepared to buy, and women to sell, sexual favours because that is how all animal courtship works. It is not, of course, a fault *confined* to evolutionary theorists: almost all of us too easily believe that what *we* do and have seen is natural, and all others are perverse.

> All good people agree,
> And all good people say,
> All nice people, like Us, are We
> And every one else is They.[10]

Chesterton's defence of history: 'the whole object of history is to make us realize that humanity can be great and glorious, under conditions quite different and even contrary to our own.'[11] There can be a similar defence of speculation. Let us suppose that Hume was wrong: we do not only value, nor only encourage others to value, characters that are, in our view, 'useful to society'. People do pursue 'non-biological ends', even to their genetic disadvantage. Hume himself, in another moment, would admit as much, in scorn: priestly celibacy is valued, and the priests who practice it. How can that be?[12]

One possible answer is that genes are not the only replicators: there are also 'mental microbes' of the kind that Dawkins has called 'memes'. The idea preceded him. 'The ideas which rise in the minds of men with the same tendency to variation that we find throughout nature, compete with one another for

[10] Rudyard Kipling, 'We and They', *Collected Verse 1885–1926* (Hodder & Stoughton: London 1927), pp. 709–10.

[11] G. K. Chesterton, *Fancies versus Fads* (Methuen: London 1923), p. 176.

[12] Darwin, referring as acidly as Hume to the 'senseless practice of celibacy' as having been ranked amongst the highest virtues, blames this 'folly' on an exaggerated respect for self-control (*Descent*, vol. I, p. 96). According to Haeckel's followers it should be illegal to remain unmarried, and illegal for women to restrict their child-bearing – unless of course one was poor, sick or criminal (D. Gasman, *The Scientific Origins of National Socialism* (Macdonald: London 1971), p. 98).

sustenance and strength.'[13] But this account, however sugges-
tive, is unlikely to be really helpful. 'Parasitic memes' are, at the
moment, only metaphors: whereas the genes originally postulated as units of Mendelian inheritance have turned out to be
bits of DNA, there is no likelihood at all that memes will find
similar one-to-one correspondences with bits of RNA (or whatever other biochemical factors support our memories) that
might migrate from brain to brain, as though theories could be
spread by literal, viral infection. There are no neo-Mendelian
laws of rhetorical persuasion, and the main use of the notion (of
a 'meme' or a 'mental microbe') appears to be to categorize
ideas as false or foolish without the trouble of arguing for the
claim. For the moment, it seems better to manage without
memes, and solely within the neo-Darwinian framework of
genetic replication and selection. What neo-Darwinian explanation can we find for our (postulated, but also plausibly real)
admiration of things useless?

There are of course many such putatively useless objects of
care and admiration: fictions, flowers, crystal prisms, pet birds,
number theory and the light of stars. If Aristotle is right, virtues
themselves are valued, not for their 'usefulness' but for themselves alone: the highest goods must, technically, be pointless!
The particular useless objects that I choose to consider here are
the useless old. Why, in evolutionary terms, do we survive so
long past reproductive age, and why do the young take care of
us when old? Why do we not just lie down and die once we have
reared our young, and why are we not left to do so? My question
can be misunderstood. When Dawkins asked why mothers
(notably baboons) do not let others steal and rear their babies
(so releasing them from care, and allowing them to have
another, extra child,[14] he was not confessing, as David Stove

---

[13] D. G. Ritchie, *Darwinism and Politics* (Swan Sonnenschein & Co.: London 1891), p. 22.
Pearsall Smith's question is apt: 'How is one to keep free from those mental microbes
that worm-eat people's brains – those Theories and Diets and Enthusiasms and
infectious Doctrines that we catch from what seem the most innocuous contacts?
People go about laden with germs; they breathe creeds and convictions upon you
whenever they open their mouths' (Logan Pearsall Smith, *All Trivia* (Constable:
London 1933), p. 47). And *why*, as he also asks, should we resist them?

[14] Richard Dawkins, *The Selfish Gene* (Oxford University Press: London 1976), p. 110.

supposes, to a contemptible failure of imaginative sympathy.[15] The question was rather, how it has come about – despite the apparent advantages of allowing such adoptions – that mothers do not desire it. The answer in that case may be very simple: a species whose parents do not desire the company of their own young is unlikely to contain many would-be abductors. Cuckoos willingly abandon their own offspring – but not to other cuckoos. And even if abandonment did become an occasional strategy, other parents would have good reason to resent too profligate a use of it. There may be a similarly simple answer to my question – which is, in turn, not a confession that I do not myself wish to live on, nor that I find the 'useless old' disposable. But why are we a species that contains that possibility, of gladly living on past reproductive age, and caring for and admiring those who do?

If we do live on (and expect and wish to live), of course, we may have a reason to endorse the social rules that make us care for others while we are young. The price of our being cared for, once we are old, is that we set the precedent of caring, when we are young. We might even add that this need not be conscious strategy, any more than other cases of reciprocal altruism demand a calculation. But the problem remains: why should there be a *genetic* advantage in this practice? If the young devote attention to the old, they have less time and resources to spare for the younger still: they must have fewer offspring because the old are 'in their second childhood', and take up the space. A line whose elderly died easily, or were left to die, would have more offspring than the ones whose elderly were cared for. We should expect, accordingly, that in most human lines there would be neither wish to live, nor need to care. It is because we do, after all, live gladly on that we can even entertain the strategy of establishing precedents so we will be cared for too. Correspondingly, we may as well admit that care and admiration for the old is not experienced in such economic terms. If we can expect ourselves to live, we can also 'see ourselves' in others who are already old, and feel for them. That altruistic

---

[15] David Stove, *Darwinian Fairytales* (Avebury: Aldershot 1995), pp. 82–3; some of Stove's other criticisms are a great deal better.

feeling, though it seems to cost us scope for further reproduction, is just as much a datum as our own wish to live.

The commonest solution is self-congratulatory (since it is most often proposed by people who are themselves upon the edge of age). Those lines that preserve the elderly, it is said, preserve some valuable life experience. Because they have their elders to advise them, they will prosper more: the elderly, after all, are good investments, and have more great-grandchildren than do those who died abruptly when their children were grown up. The claim may be correct, but the reason offered has two disadvantages. First, what evidence is there that the young pay any attention to the elders' advice? Second, what evidence is there that this advice is good? What evidence is there that the young or middle-aged willingly do anything that 'the old fool in the corner' says? What evidence is there that the said old fool has any real idea of what to do, especially in an age (which is every age[16]) where life is changing rapidly? Is it not notorious, across all ages and all countries, that the young do not take advice, and that the old are probably out of touch (and may be simply loopy)?

Perhaps they have some use, as baby-sitters, while their own children work? Having a few such elders in the camp may relieve more active people of the chore of baby entertainment, and so preserve those babies and the chance of more? Second childhood is an advantage since it gives an insight into childishness, a little constrained by age and careful habits. Maybe that same childishness earns them respect: mammalian species need to care for the young, and are trapped into doing so by making the young, in their own helplessness, unbearably attractive. Falling so readily in love with babies, we have some love to spare for things *like* babies (puppies, kittens, grandad). But as grandchildren grow the problem comes again: why would anyone live, or want to live, or be wanted, beyond the point of

---

[16] The notion that Europe changes rapidly, whilst Cathay, or Amazonia, or the Australian Deserts are unchanging, and the elderly more useful in such unprogressive places, is the effect on the one hand of pride in our own accomplishments, and on the other of ignorance about what has been going on elsewhere. That the Bedouin are just like nomads back in Abraham's day, or that Australian Aboriginals have lived unchanged for forty thousand years, is exceedingly unlikely.

usefulness, or cuteness? There are of course some modern
moralists who will conclude that economic (and genetic) reason
rules: if we do care for our useless old, it is by mistake, and
everyone should work against that 'error'. It seems hard luck –
to some – that an inheritance is squandered to preserve the life
and comfort of an aged person when it could be used for toys,
or holidays, or education, or a brand new car (all useful
objects). To others – and to tradition – it is the useless old who
show us what to value.

What is the advantage to genetic lines of creating and
admiring elders (that is, useless old fools)? It has been argued
that we believe (or have been made to believe) in an objective
moral order because we are thereby much more likely to obey
that order (which in fact improves our 'inclusive genetic
fitness'). For as long as we keep promises (say) just when it seems
to suit us, we cannot make – or trust – such promises: only they
can promise, and trust a promise, who will keep them solely
because they gave their binding word. Believing that this is an
objective duty, we can reap advantages. Believing that we only
do it because it is mostly 'advantageous' (and to others) we
begin to lie, and so lose any advantage from the institution. So if
our genes require us to believe that there are other reasons for
moral obedience than what is 'useful', what better mechanism
can there be to get us to believe this than to make us value
things we think are useless? We value the useless old – along
with other useless things – *because* they are useless; we value
what is obviously useless because otherwise it would be obvious
we only valued useful things (and especially what gave advantage to our genes, not us). At the same time, by valuing the
useless and decrepit we may lessen our own attachment to
transitory gains in a way that makes it possible for more young
to be born. If we only valued health and strength and youth,
how could we allow our own diminution for the sake of yet
more struggling young? If we only valued what we can enjoy
while young, who would have children (and surrender youthful
dreams to them)?

The ethical significance of this is obvious. By letting ourselves
believe that only what is directly 'useful' or 'productive' is of

value, we deny old age has value, and so resist the steps that lead from youth to age. By only valuing what is productive, we make it difficult to *be* productive. Producing children, running a household, holding down a job are the first steps to age: if age is not worth having, who could endure – unless compelled – those steps? *Growing up depends on growing old.* Only those prepared themselves to be, in their turn, the useless elderly, can ever be really useful.

There are, of course, a range of other factors. It may be, for example, that elderly fathers (and their damaged sperm) may produce occasionally useful – and very many damaging – variations in the lineage. It may be that women who survive childbearing and the menopause emerge from years of mothering to be such terrifyingly active figures that the whole clan prospers. My concern is with our valuation of what seems most useless, and to show that, on sound evolutionary terms, we only get advantages by valuing such useless things. There is no need to pretend that fools are useful: it is enough that we can love them in their uselessness without offending evolutionists.

INDIFFERENCE TO THE COMMON GOOD

We do, as a matter of fact, often admire folly, weakness and indifference to earthly gain. Though we *say* that only action for the common good is admirable, in practice we acknowledge that this common good includes the presence of creatures utterly indifferent to it, and careless of the means. Children are the obvious example, but the elderly 'renouncer'[17] (whether by her own will, or Another's) is another. It is time to take the story a little further. One constant phenomenon in evolutionary history is pre-adaptation: the reason dinosaurians once developed feathers (we may guess) was that they gave an advantage for temperature control. Having feathers, their descendants flew. Similarly, let us suppose, evolutionary logic has created a

---

[17] I draw the term from Hindu social philosophy, which distinguishes the four stages of life as student, householder, forest-dweller and renouncer; see Heinrich Zimmer, *Philosophies of India*, ed. J. Campbell (Routledge & Kegan Paul: London 1952), pp. 155–6. This seems to neglect the existence of children.

place in our hearts for the holy fool, or the Buddha.[18] Rather than admire the useful it is open to us to admire the 'useless'. Similarly, Rudolf Steiner's followers have proposed, Down's syndrome children need not be 'defective', but intimations of an evolutionary future.[19] As long as we only admit to admiring technical or intellectual competence, they have less value: once we realize that there are 'useless' values, we may also realize that they are very much nicer people than the rest of us. Longing to be valued as profitable citizens are valued, we miss the moment when we might escape.

> An aged man is but a paltry thing,
> a tattered coat upon a stick, unless
> soul clap its hands and sing, and louder sing,
> for every tatter in its mortal dress.
> Nor is there singing school but studying
> monuments of its own magnificence.
> And therefore I have sailed the seas and come
> to the holy city of Byzantium.[20]

So 'second childhood', and the singing soul, is our ideal? There are obviously quite plausible responses: we may appreciate children, but who – as Aristotle says – would make childishness her way of life?[21] Is not regression to 'second childhood' exactly what most – especially – of *us* most fear? When Samuel Johnson had his stroke, he composed a Latin verse to test his wits: it was not a very good verse, he noted, but at least he knew it was not, and was reconciled to physical damage that fell short of what he feared.[22] The merely *ad hominem* riposte, that I myself have

---

[18] Since a 'Buddha' is, by hypothesis, 'enlightened', it may seem strange to couple one with a 'fool'. But the enlightenment that is intended is not worldly cunning, and a holy fool is not exactly stupid.

[19] K. König, 'The Mystery of the Mongol Child' in A. C. Harwood, ed., *The Faithful Thinker: centenary essays on the work and thought of Rudolf Steiner* (Hodder & Stoughton: London 1961), pp. 179–91.

[20] W. B. Yeats, 'Sailing to Byzantium', *Collected Poems* (Macmillan: London 1950), p. 217.

[21] *Nicomachean Ethics* 10.1174a2–3. Cf. Matthew 17.3.

[22] 'I was alarmed, and prayed God, that however he might afflict my body, he would spare my understanding'; James Boswell, *Life of Samuel Johnson* (Clarendon Press: Oxford 1953), p. 1241 (19 June 1783). Johnson was actually himself not merely *tolerant* of such infirmities in others, but loving: of Christopher Smart, confined in a madhouse, he had remarked 'I did not think he ought to be shut up. His infirmities

shown no sign of admiring ignorance – or holy poverty – is not really to the point: I admit to being comfort-loving, bourgeois and ordinarily (non-heroically) humanitarian, but I am not the measure of virtue. It is not necessarily hypocritical to praise a character I do not have (rather the reverse)! But I can admit to qualms. Who profits from extolling 'noble stupidity' except the powerful? Perhaps there is indeed a selective value in such folly – because our masters want us to be fools. If enlightenment about the manufactured goals of life leads to disillusionment – and possibly disobedience – there is an advantage, for our masters, in our preferring ignorance (whether those masters are our human lords, or the mad molecules, our genes). Conversely, the folly of second childhood just is that disillusionment with worldly goods.

Nothing in the evolutionary or social evidence can help us to break out from this circle. Evolutionary transformation has made up creatures (us) who value useful things, and also useless ones: our very valuing of what is useless turns out, by a complex chain, to be genetically advantageous. Not caring only about our worldly goods is necessary if we are to keep those goods, but also sufficient reason not to want to. The goal of goodness need not be social value: social values lead us to the moment where we recognize the good.

Without some input from outside, gene talk leads either to an empty optimism or to disillusionment. Either everything is for the best (since we could not think anything was good unless that thought had been selected as the fittest for the time), or nothing at all is for the best (since all we think is good is what our masters make us think). Either way the end is often conservative. Those who despair of any good have no good reason to exert themselves against the present; those who endorse the goods thrown up in time have no good reason to expect a better. The nepotism of Sociable Darwinism decrees, in either case, that those we feel are 'ours' demand our loyalty, at any expense to others. The energetic Anglo-Saxon of Darwin's dreams will

were not noxious to society. He insisted on people praying with him; and I'd as lief pray with Kit Smart as any one else' (ibid., p. 281 (24 May 1763)).

cherish his own kin, and look with equanimity on the elimination of savage races, or the sterilization of the 'unfit'.[23]

Darwin's examples, echoed in many early twentieth-century
writings, of 'the lower orders of mankind' are Negroes, the poor
and the Irish, who are all disturbingly 'fit' (that is, prolific). It is
understandable that those who were described as weak or
stupid (namely, the poor, the savage, the Irish or the Catholic)
regarded Darwinism as an excuse for tyranny. But we can look
past Darwin's own prejudice to see what actually follows: once
again, there seem to be good reasons why a disregard for
worldly advantage may be preserved in the gene pool, and
thereby open the door to an unworldly vocation. We can take it
further: part of worldliness (as above) is to be concerned for
'one's own' and for the 'useful' (and this has issued in the racist
and imperialist designs to which Darwin himself, and other
heroes of 'enlightened thought' lent colour). But once again,
Darwinian theory can explain just about anything. Suppose it is
true (as Darwin also thought it was) that 'man's noble qualities'
include 'sympathy which feels for the most debased, benevolence which extends not only to other men but to the humblest
living creature, [and] his godlike intellect which has penetrated
into the movements and constitution of the solar system.'[24]
How can it possibly have come about that we feel such
sympathy and benevolence for such 'debased' and unassuming
creatures? How can we, for that matter, have any such godlike
intellect, if we have only those intellectual qualities as have been
needed for our genes' proliferation? That second question is
another story. The first perhaps has an answer. After all, 'our'
genes are in almost every case also the genes of other creatures.
Why should we suppose that genes, as it were, much care what
species they inhabit? By encouraging us all to care for everything that is likely to be a carrier of some copy of themselves,
our genes can ensure more copies of themselves, even if in

[23] Haeckel similarly expected 'the Indo-Germanic race' to exterminate all others: 'it
would be easier to train the most intelligent domestic animals to a moral and civilized
life than the majority of natives' (*The History of Creation* (Appleton: New York 1876),
vol. II, p. 366, cited by Gasman, *National Socialism*, p. 127).

[24] Darwin, *Descent*, vol. II, p. 405.

another line.[25] Even if this were not true, it is enough that our common ancestors were all one species, once upon a time, and were bred to recognize each other as potential friends as well as rivals. Whether rivalry or friendship wins must be a matter of local management: there seems no reason to expect that friendship must win amongst our present conspecifics and rivalry outside. On the contrary, the more closely we are related the more likely we are to be competing for our worldly gains; the more distantly, the more it is possible for us to look past rivalry. Once we accept that we can reasonably expect to value the non-human, and to delight in their life, we may be relieved of worldliness. The more we are relieved of worldliness (and so of envious competition), the more we can value others in their otherness. 'Consider the lilies of the field: they toil not, neither do they spin.'[26] Of course, it could be said, they do compete – but not in a way that denies another creature its own chance of life.

It follows that despite popular rhetoric to the contrary, it is possible for creatures to admit affection and admiration for the whole of life, and not to demand the elimination of the weaker or more feckless. Holy fools who recognize all other creatures as their kin have just as much good reason for their view as H. G. Wells for his: as good a reason, and a much better heart.

In one way, appreciation of the holy fool, the innocent non-human, even the 'feckless poor', amounts to a grand disillusionment. The idols of our time and place lose their attraction once we realize how they are made. What is to stop that disillusionment going further? If admiration of the holy fool, as I have suggested, is just as explicable on neo-Darwinian terms, and just as much a way of making us obedient, what then? Cleanthes prayed to follow willingly where Zeus led – but if he were disobedient and rebelled, he would follow just the

---

[25] F. von Schilcher and N. Tennant point out that 'genealogically unrelated [or very distantly related] individuals can nevertheless (as far as the genetic theory is concerned) turn out to be kith and kin, simply by sharing a significant number of alleles' (*Philosophy, Evolution and Human Nature* (Routledge & Kegan Paul: London 1984), p. 29).

[26] Matthew 6.28.

same.[27] Suppose we do despair: depression, suicidal disillusionment and even 'anti-natural' perversions have also been engineered to dispose of those who will not follow where God
leads (and so they follow willy-nilly). There is, in the end, no
choice about obedience, but there may be some faint choice of
how we obey (as Epictetus said).

When worldliness prevails a life is judged worth living, a
creature worth admiring, and a nation well 'developed', by the
number of its worldly goods. Those who have those goods are
better developed than those who do not, and even when they
wish to show their genuine benevolence by seeking to share
those goods with others (or at the least encourage others to
obtain them somewhere), it is with the clear conviction that the
undeveloped are inferior. What else could they be, as lacking
what makes a life worth living? Unproductive lives are worth-
less; unused land belongs to those who would make 'better' use
of it. Whatever your image of the 'better life', the Exxon
advertisement declares, *you need more oil*. Economic orthodoxy
advocates the inculcation of desires: if only the poor, the Irish,
the aboriginal could *want* a little more, they would work the
harder to obtain it.[28] Occasional mavericks prefer to advocate
the 'Zen' solution to the problem of scarcity (which is also the
traditionally philosophical), namely, to want only what can
easily and justly be obtained, to live in a way that is alert to our
dependence on a fruitful world, and on the grace of God.[29]
Rather than value things or people for what can be produced
from them, the holy fool will value them for what they are –
which is, expressions of God's bounty.

Biologically, we have, as it were, our feathers because – in
devious and unexpected ways – they made our ancestors 'fitter'.
Because we have them, we can – on occasion – fly.

Or to end with a different, and more familiar, story. Plato's

[27] A. Long and D. Sedley, eds., *The Hellenistic Philosophers* (Cambridge University Press:
Cambridge 1987), vol. 1, p. 386, 62B, citing Epictetus, *Encheiridion* 53.
[28] This was indeed George Berkeley's advice to the Roman clergy of Ireland, that they
should encourage their flocks to *want* a little more (though not too much); see the
various essays on his economic theory in *Berkeley: Money, Obedience and Affection*, ed.
S. R. L. Clark (Garland Press: New York 1989).
[29] Marshall Sahlins, *Stone Age Economics* (Tavistock Press: London 1972).

cave is a more complex and labyrinthine place than he admitted.[30] Those who break their chains and wander off from
where they were first bound may find themselves in darkness.
Some return to their first home. Others follow any distant speck
of light (not infrequently blocking that same light off from
others). Some, self-consciously modern, huddle together, and
explain past legends of the warm, bright place as simply ways of
saying that people huddled together often feel quite warm, and
can see coloured images if they press their eyeballs gently. Just a
few in wandering through the tunnels may at last – by accident
– enter a new cave that opens on the world outside. If they
come back into the labyrinth to say what they have seen, they
are mocked as sad, unworldly fools. Strangely, they do not seem
to mind.

[30] Plato, *Republic* 7; I owe this elaboration of the metaphor to Celia Green, *The Human
Evasion* (Hamish Hamilton: London 1969).

CHAPTER 7

The end of humanity

THE PLEASURE PRINCIPLE

By older standards, we are all hedonists. The only respectable reason for any act is the pleasure that it brings, or the suffering it avoids. Even those who take account of pains and pleasures that are not their own do so because they are *pleased* by others' pleasures, and sympathetically pained by others' pains. Even those who take some pleasure in the thought of leaving the world a 'better place' intend no more than that the world will have more pleasure for less pain. Our welfare, or the welfare of the world, is measured in the pleasures and the pains we can count. It does not follow that we are all 'utilitarians'. Utilitarians believe, or hope to believe, that there are 'best outcomes overall', or even *one* best outcome. They may disagree as to whether the value of those outcomes rests upon the total net enjoyment of life, or on the average or median enjoyment. Is a smaller 'happier' human population better than a larger 'happy' one?[1] They may be more or less ruthless in their calculations: few professed utilitarians in fact consider whether it *might* be right (for example) to breed pretty imbeciles for pederasts or babies for gourmet restaurants, or to have everyone 'put down' before they achieve the last, seventh, age

---

[1] Those who conclude, a little unwillingly, that every additional happy individual is an improvement, and that we should therefore aim for the largest 'happy' population rather than the smaller, 'happier' one (as Derek Parfit, *Reasons and Persons* (Clarendon Press: Oxford 1984)) have neglected the obvious truth that adding as many different *sorts* of happy creature as possible will use the world's resources better. A world that is packed tight with organisms of one sort (say, human) will still have indefinitely many spaces left for other things. The *largest* populations are the most diverse.

of man. Being decent folk, professed utilitarians will usually, if challenged, think of some specious reason why those programmes *would not* achieve 'best outcomes', while similar programmes (which they happen to approve of) *would*. Less dogmatic moralists will usually doubt that we can assess whole outcomes in this way. Even if we could, in principle, count up the pains and pleasures of alternative world histories or discover what the actions were that lead to those alternatives, the pains and pleasures themselves would often depend on what we already find agreeable or obnoxious. The utilitarian calculus either takes account of *all* our feelings or it does not. If it does, then the loathing that the programmes I mentioned will excite in any 'decent' agent must count against their being chosen. But in that case, the calculus adds nothing much to our previous, *moral* judgement. If, however, the calculus is intended to replace such 'primitive' moral judgements, then utilitarians cannot avoid the thought that, pleasure for pleasure, those programmes might work out. The public, of course, would need to be 'educated', slowly, to accept them (and it would be naive to think that this will take very long).

That paragraph was, I hope, revolting. But nothing except the programmes that I specified was in any way unusual. If 'yuk factors' are irrational, and the only proper concern of policy is to avoid pains and multiply pleasures in the relevant constituency, why should we not consider them? This too is not, strictly, a utilitarian goal. Utilitarians dedicate themselves to the whole picture: not just the happiness (net pleasure) of their countrymen, but of the sentient creation. Sensibly enough, they may suppose that net happiness overall is best preserved by everyone's dealing only with what they, realistically, can manage. The duty of government is best conceived as liberals do: a matter of safeguarding the arena, or the market place, where creatures manage their own affairs, with whatever degree of violence and fraud that most of them desire. But this is just to say that none of us, whether private or political agents, can act as good utilitarians: we cannot be swayed from the tasks we *can* (perhaps) perform by thoughts of what the 'good overall' might be, even if there were such a good. Excuses, of course, abound for our discounting of pleasures and pains experienced by those not in our care. Most honestly, we can agree that it would cost us individually and corporately 'too much' to let ourselves be worried by the pleasures and pains, whatever they may be, of Amazonian Indians, or whales, or honey-bees. Whether the greatest net pleasure, or the highest average or median net pleasure, is to be found in a world like ours, or in one where humankind is only one species amongst many, we are in no position to know. Are dolphins happier than hyenas, overall? Are hyenas happier than antelopes? How many happy antelopes are 'worth' how many happy hyenas? Does any of that make useful sense?

Utilitarian rhetoric, in brief, is rhetoric, and little more. The real work is done behind the scenes, in judgements about the importance, to us, of different creatures, and the value we place on different policies. The pleasure that may be taken in skinning a cat alive is judged enough to validate that act if the *cat's* experience is not thought relevant, and sadistic pleasure is counted just as pleasure. The pleasure that is taken in catching and hurting sadists may also be a factor in rebuking sadistic acts – though the pleasures of homophobia, strangely enough, are rarely reckoned relevant. We do not in fact decide on what to do by reckoning up the 'total outcomes' of our acts. We do not know what those outcomes are, nor how to rank them against alternatives. Instead, we work from our immediate likes and dislikes, remembering the dangers involved for us in 'liberty' and 'government control' alike. The rhetoric still has its influence: 'yum factors' are reckoned serious, 'yuk factors' not. The only acceptable reason – amongst such moralists – for forbidding something is that it will do more harm (i.e. cause more pain to significant entities) than good (i.e. pleasure to other significant entities). The pains of mental distress, or moral revulsion, are thought transient, reasons (at best) for delaying, not forbidding, action.

Older rhetorics persist. It is widely affirmed that human life is sacred, even though we no longer have any well-grounded reason to suppose that the lives of *humans*, just as such, are significantly different from the lives of hominids, primates,

mammals or animals in general. Some moralists subvert even
that restriction, and argue that *non-persons* lie outside the class of
beings who must properly be protected: it is not clear what
reason, other than caution, they could have for rejecting the
programmes I listed in an earlier paragraph. Perhaps by extending 'rights' to imbeciles we put a fence around the law, and
save ourselves misjudgements about who is, or is not, 'really'
imbecile. Again: we honour 'liberty' without acknowledging
that it has painful costs (except when seeking reasons to object
to traditional 'free-will' theodicies). If God the Creator, as some
say, should not create 'free beings' if the costs in suffering were
high, so neither should sensible hedonists approve of liberty for
all. The notion that 'paternalism' is a bad idea rests on the
value of self-chosen lives, irrespective of the pleasures they
accrue (on which see chapter 3). Without these antique notions,
present policies might be a lot more like the programmes that I
sketched even than they are.

How could it be otherwise? 'Do not you see that that dreadful
dry light shed on things must at last wither up the moral
mysteries as illusions, respect for age, respect for property, and
that the sanctity of life will be a superstition?'[2] The 'dry light' to
which Chesterton refers is the objectifying vision that denies the
existence of any transcendent value. We have not *discovered*,
through science, that there are no such values, but stipulated
that *science*, which is 'true knowledge', is defined by its disregard
of value. What science does not know about is nothing real.
This notion, remember, is quite unlike the original, originating
principles of science: when we began being 'scientific', it was
because we recognized the beauty of even the basest and most
trivial seeming things, and thought to climb towards a god's eye
view of beauty. Our error, mythologically, has been to prefer
Apollo's view to God's,[3] and at last to lose even that god's view
of things.

[2] G. K. Chesterton, *The Poet and the Lunatics* (Darwen Finlayson: London 1962; first
published 1929), p. 70.
[3] Apollo is the god of *distant* views, of destiny, and hygiene: in his pursuit of what he
loves he transforms the beloved into an object which can no longer please him; see
W. F. Otto *The Homeric Gods*, tr. M. Hadas (Thames & Hudson: London 1954),
pp. 61–80.

If the universe is valueless, life only a self-sustaining chemical reaction and belief in objective beauty a once-convenient illusion, what is left but pleasure and avoiding pain? Concern for the pains and pleasures even of significant others cannot be anything but pragmatic: the protection and comfort blankets that we cannot win by ourselves, as individuals, we might secure for each of us by winning them for all (or for the most stable group, containing us, that we can manage). Perhaps that open, egoistic hedonism will at least avoid hypocrisy, and confusion. Once we realize exactly what we want, we have some chance of getting it. As long as we confuse the issue with our talk of rights and duties, we do not know what we are bargaining about, or with whom. Perhaps the children of this world *are* wiser in their generation than the children of light,[4] because they know what it is they want.

But there is a real difficulty in this. Why, as I have asked so often before, is the 'yum factor' so much more sensible than the 'yuk'? Pleasure is a device that gets us to do what once our genes required. Pain is a device to stop us doing things that are inconvenient for our masters. No doubt neither device works perfectly. The pleasure that we get from sugary things was once, perhaps, a help in keeping alive. That same pleasure now just helps to ruin teeth. Once we appreciate that we are puppets, what role can pain or pleasure have but as illusions? Pain, perhaps, lasts longer: whatever the cause may be, and whatever we think of things, pain *hurts*. Pleasure always was more transient: a sudden exultation that convinces us that we are gods – or at least that we are not nothings. Knowing, or believing, that we are puppets, what is left of pleasure? Orgasm is a brief convulsion which concludes an act once necessary for reproduction, and desired because those creatures who were not strongly motivated to the act did not have many descendants. It is the sweetie which persuades a child to undertake a disagreeable task with unforeseeable consequences. So also is parental love. The question is not just why we should attend to the past meanings of parental, filial or sexual love, but whether

---

[4] Luke 16.8, in the parable of the unjust steward.

in fact we will feel them at all once we know their 'purpose'. Why bother to multiply pleasures when we know they are bribes? Will they be bribes any longer once we know their worth? Once we took pleasure in activities we knew or believed were well worth doing anyway; if only the pleasure gives them worth, then anything at all can be used for pleasure's sake, with steadily diminishing returns.[5] Is there actually empirical evidence that the disillusioned young desire sex as much, or still enjoy it? They *do* it a lot, no doubt.

There is perhaps some reason to suspect that this is not simply a theoretical worry. It is no doubt easy to believe that the sheer weight of pain and eager desire will be enough to keep us moving. But the main effect of pornographic images of the kind now all too familiar, on the web as well as on the upper shelves of newsagents, is to diminish desire of the older sort. Pain is at least an intense and possibly lasting feeling – though the drift of post-Wittgensteinian philosophy has been to deconstruct even *that* inevitable datum – but pleasure is of its nature transient. Even the *painfulness* of pain depends, in part, on how we take it: in particular, how we feel about the destruction of our bodies. But if the wholeness of our bodies is no longer a clear good, no longer an echo of some celestial beauty, why should it matter to us whether our bodies are 'whole' or 'clean' or not? Desire was once our route to immortality (mystical or merely reproductive). Do we still think it is, and do we care? What is left but 'fun'? The older rhetoric could emphasize the importance of keeping our bodies 'clean' and 'straight' and 'strong', so that we could do our duty: does that rhetoric now have any meaning, and can we retain our older attitude to pain? Decadence is that state in which only pleasure makes an activity worth while. Whereas our predecessors distinguished the pleasure that we take in something that would in any case be worth doing well and

---

[5] Perhaps the Catholic Church has seemed unnecessarily rigid in rejecting ways of keeping copulation clear of procreation, but there was a point in this: if copulation is valued *only* as a present pleasure, then any other form of sensual enjoyment must, in principle, be just as 'good'. Good liberals may believe they think this true, but how about auto-erotic suffocation, necrophilia, or shagging sheep? The usual response is that copulation is to be welcomed as a *shared* pleasure, an escape from solitude, but this is already to import moralistic judgements into the assessment of 'mere pleasure'.

'mere pleasure', modern hedonists deny that anything is worth doing at all apart from the pleasure it brings. Is it certain that such decadence is pleasurable for long? Notoriously, tedium demands more graphic and more stimulating images and experiences. Pain gives a buzz no less than pleasure, and a more lasting one.

No doubt such rhetoric has less effect on toothache than on more exotic or romantic pains. No doubt a saving cowardice prevents most of us from sliding down the destructive path. But it is not clear how we could distinguish, in principle, between the buzz of danger or 'the burn' and the buzz of mutilation, masochism, drugs. None of these sensations are anything more, we are to suppose, than bribes. Knowing that they are bribes, we begin to play with them.

ENGINEERING ETHICS

If our bodies and minds have been constructed from chance innovations by evolutionary selection, without any regard to Beauty or the Good, it may be true that most minor deviations will be less 'fit' – that is, will have fewer copies in all later generations – than is the average or median character (leaving aside, for now, all quibbles about the likely survival of 'less fit' variations, genetic drift, and changes in the phenotypic expression of underlying genotypes). But their 'fitness' is of no serious concern to any disillusioned eye. Why should we not rearrange things to secure whatever it is we still find we want? Our predecessors, even if they made use of cows or lambs or slaves, did seriously believe that all these creatures expressed a valuable beauty. We might use them, or even abuse them, and still think it important that there should be such 'natural' shapes. But if these shapes are no more significant than any chance-abraded pebble, what does it matter if they exist or not? If we retain a residual, 'superstitious' belief that *pain* (not just my pain) is 'bad' we might even reckon it better to extinguish living creatures and their pain together. We might reasonably (if 'reason' now means anything) construct animal-artifacts that are no more than tissues or usable organs without any central selves. After all, we have sought to consider cows as *beef* or sheep as *mutton* for millennia: why not create 'pure beef', rather than farm cattle?

'Pure beef' would be an answer to the animal welfarist's concerns: mere, self-propagating, muscular tissue, from which we could carve slices as we pleased. There would be no need for any such artifact to have sensations, or any sense of self. The fact that it would, in essence, be *cancerous* tissue might give us pause – but only until 'yuk factors' were re-educated. Once 'pure beef' is established, we could also have 'long pig'. But there are even more repugnant artifacts.[6] Pain, after all, is only a sort of stimulus which has served to put animals off less 'fit' activities, and is no more an 'evil' than any other intense stimulus. Once we abandon any sense that there are valuable forms of being, what counts except intensity of feeling? And amongst such feelings is the pleasure of control. Was Orwell's O'Brien so implausible?[7] Why would the engineers not take pleasure in the creation of intensely *feeling* artifacts, pro-grammed to respond 'delightfully' to their masters' touch? *Decent* engineers, no doubt, with laudably limited imaginations, may prefer to construct things that take *pleasure* in their masters' touch – but is there any sense in that distinction, once we have abandoned beauty? Pain and dependence run together: we cling, as children, to the very despots that injure us. If any of our responses can be engineered, so can that. So alongside 'pure beef' we shall have 'toys', *designed* to have no dignity. 'In the late medieval and early modern period, most towns had a rule making it *compulsory* to have a bull baited before it was slaughtered by the butcher.'[8] And so far from its being right to

---

[6] See my 'Making up Animals: the view from science fiction' in Alan Holland and Andrew Johnson, eds., *Animal Biotechnology and Ethics* (Chapman & Hall: London 1997), pp. 209–24.

[7] He suggested (G. Orwell, *Nineteen Eighty-Four* (Secker & Warburg: London 1949)) that the future was to be a boot upon a human face, for ever, echoing in this Jack London's *The Iron Heel* (1907). My edition of the latter was published by the Co-Operative Publishing Society of Foreign Workers in the USSR in Leningrad in 1934. The editor seems to have seen no irony. See 'Orwell and the Anti-Realists', *Philosophy* 67.1992, pp. 141–54.

[8] Keith Thomas, *Man and the Natural World* (Penguin: Harmondsworth 1984), p. 93 (my italics). Such legislation is no more irrational than the rules that demand that

kill such creatures *quickly*, it was supposed that they must be killed *slowly*, because they would taste better. The wish not to make food-animals or toys suffer is simple squeamishness, with no more weight than a wish to make them tasty or 'delightfully squirmy'.[9]

Neither 'pure beef' nor 'toys', it will be argued, are any different 'in principle' from the products of selective breeding since the Neolithic. We have certainly bred our cattle and domestic pets to respond as we would wish them to. We have also selected and bred *ourselves* to be childishly inventive and obedient. Darwin's conviction that we are weeding out the criminal or lunatic genotypes was foolish. But way back in the early days there were few enough of us for breeding plans to have some power: we are all descended from people who, consciously or unconsciously, chose humanity. So why, it is argued, should we not act faster? Either we and our domestic animals (and crops) are only what has happened accidentally, or else we are (in part) the products of past ideals; why not remake us all? The chances are that those of us *without* ideals (because convinced that ideals are illusions) might even do *less* harm (by older standards of harm) than those with utopian visions. Perhaps we might more easily trust engineers with little local goals (even if they are to produce 'pure beef' or 'toys') than ones with a passion to remake the world.

We can be confident, of course, that there will always be glitches, bugs, and unforeseen conclusions. The idea that we could wholly control the world, or our descendants, is laughable. We do not even control our children, our household pets, or our own dreams and feelings. Every effort of control creates new monsters.[10] Even in the old days, when there were few enough of us to make a breeding programme possible, we could

medicines, household products and cosmetics be 'tested' on non-human animals before they are tried out on any humans.

[9] My apologies again for inducing nausea, but that response to evil may now be one of the only reminders of transcendent virtue we can still evoke. See Peter Berger, *A Rumour of Angels: modern society and the rediscovery of the supernatural* (Penguin: Harmondsworth 1969), pp. 84ff. on the 'argument from damnation'.

[10] See my 'Tools, Machines and Marvels' in Roger Fellows, ed., *Philosophy and Technology* (Cambridge University Press: Cambridge 1995), pp. 159–76.

not halt all emigration, nor all immigration. Nor could we seriously suppose that our descendants would have more respect for *us* than ever we did for our progenitors. Those who plan to bequeath their own ideals, along with other legacies, are seriously deluded, especially if those ideals include disdain for everything that went before: what else are children for, but to reject their parents (even if they do it kindly)? Even if Orwell's Newspeak *were* taught to all our children, at the expense of any natural tongue, they would transform it in a generation. Even if the masters of the world sought out and killed all those who would stand against them, a single generation would be enough to raise new rebels up.

Some idealists respond to this challenge by adapting their own ideals to the supposed ideals of anyone: by willing only what, they think, their successors *must* desire, they hope to secure their future. Perhaps they only give themselves excuses to *imagine* that the future might be theirs: it is certain that they will have no power to amend it. Maybe they would be happier, as Aristotle saw, if they did not invest their hopes in something that another could, and probably will, correct. Living only to leave a legacy that our children will despise or hate or casually ignore is folly. Others believe that they have power to ensure that our successors will be what we wish: in the old days, neither ancestry nor education guaranteed success, but perhaps engineering will. Moral exhortation is like magic: it turns on the conviction that the world at least of human character can be changed and fixed by *words*. Just as we have learnt that there are swifter, more reliable and even more commendable means than magic or than moralizing to heal the sick in body, so may we heal the sick in soul. That, after all, was Augustine's own conviction: the *natural* or *physical* effects of potions might properly be used for healing, while the *symbolical* effects were only magic, and for that very reason wrong.[11] Why should we not expect a similar success in matters 'moral'? *Telling* people not to sin is as absurd as telling them not to be sick.

A merely 'eugenic' engineer expects to eliminate 'bad social

---

[11] Augustine, *De Doctrina Christiana*, ed. R. P. H. Green (Clarendon Press: Oxford 1995), p. 109 (2.111).

habits' by allowing only the 'best' stock to breed, and usually identifies that 'best stock' with people of his or her own race and class. Even if there were clear correlations between identifiable bits of DNA and clearly characterized social tendencies (as there are not), the task would be impossible. We cannot (and certainly do not) control the context within which genes do their highly various work. The very same genes that make someone 'a master criminal' (whatever that may be) might equally have made them master of some more respected trade, or none. The very same genes that earn someone a place as gamete-donor in a fashionable bank might just as easily have led to jail. All natural virtues have their corresponding vices: all natural virtues, indeed, *are* vices, although splendid ones. Modern gene engineers have a better case, just in that (they hope) they need not rely on gradual, assortative matings to discover the 'best' genes. The ideal, eventually, must be to excerpt 'the genes for genius' (in whatever craft is wished) and substitute them for the common genes at those particular *loci*. The game, eventually, will be to *design* our children with the characters, talents, and features that we wish, and guard them from 'misuse' of what we give them. What would be the point of making them smart, alert, charming and energetic if we thereby bred our bane? What would be the point if it did not even 'make them happy'? If anything at all can be made 'to make them happy', their *happiness* does not give us a reason to choose one set of talents or another. So all that remains is that we would act to make *us* happy, taking the contingent nature of our happiness for granted. And why should we take even that as fixed? We make our ordinary choices within a relatively stable context: being male (for example) we could choose to be less masculine. Perhaps we can also choose, more easily than our ancestors, to stop being male, because we *want* to be female. But what if we can also choose whether to *want* to be female? Or whether to *want* to be anything else? Is there any basis for such choices, except the toss of a coin?

Some gene engineers may contend that species survival (or their line's survival) will provide a firm criterion of judgement. Let us select, in our descendants and ourselves, exactly that range of temperaments and talents that has most chance of doing best. Where there are doubts, let us engineer competing options, all equally our descendants but all different. The answer is no answer. Once we have discovered how contingent our identification with a particular line or population is, and how easily altered, the survival or partial survival of 'our line' has no greater authority than any other superstitious goal. Perhaps we could bribe ourselves and others to pursue that aim (by making ourselves enjoy it), but we could equally bribe ourselves and others to do the opposite, or nothing. Which aim is likelier to succeed, 'in the long run', is not as easy a guess as some suppose. Current fantasies sometimes suggest that living things, and maybe our descendants, will remake the worlds, and that one day life will be 'for ever'. The vindication of religion's 'opium dream' will be the creation of a world immune to death or radical diminution. But these fantasies demand that we believe more probable impossibilities than religion ever did. If the universe, despite appearances, is founded in good will, we may hope that all shall be well. If it is founded only upon chance and time, we have no reason to suppose that 'life' (whatever that may be) will 'win', nor any reason to think its victory will be what 'we' (whoever that may be) desire. 'The universe does not give a damn one way or the other about the special wants and ultimate welfare of mosquitoes, rats, lice, dogs, men, horses, pterodactyls, trees, fungi, dodos, or other forms of biological energy.'[12]

Such fantasies are worth confronting. But perhaps there is a little more to say about more ordinary, local, engineering hopes. At the moment, talk of eliminating our genetic faults is usually euphemism. Once someone has been conceived with this, or another, genetic fault, which cannot be controlled by dietary or other environmental measures, the only solution offered is abortion. Most modern moralists, being covertly dualist, insist

---

[12] H. P. Lovecraft (1929), quoted by S. S. Prawer 'Allurements of the Abyss', *Times Literary Supplement*, 19 June 1981, pp. 687–8. Lovecraft was certainly an execrable (and often execrated) writer, but at least he had the courage, and the craft, to face a world entirely stripped of value without recourse to fantasies about an eventual human triumph that we have no worldly reason to expect.

upon distinguishing the bodily life of such unfortunates from their 'personal' life and dignity. Apparently it must be all right to kill an embryo to save it future pain, even though it would be wrong to kill an infant for the selfsame reason. A few, more robust 'personists' also approve infanticide, as being a better option than merely 'to let the infant die'. Both schools, the cautious and the more robust, deny that their approval of abortion or infanticide has any implications for the dignity and worth of *people* with those handicaps. People who actually have the handicaps think differently. If people are to be given more or less protection because their lives are judged to be more or less worth living, it is difficult not to suspect that they are valued only for what they produce. If it is reasonable to kill a child to spare it pain, because its life can never be one the judges think worth living, why is it reasonable to sustain such lives, at public expense, once they are being lived? If abortion or infanticide of the 'disabled' is permissible, can their own later judgement, that they choose to live, be granted any reasonable weight? Personists reply that *later* disabled people have their wills, and judgement: earlier they have no wills at all, and therefore are not frustrated. Only those who know what they would be missing have a right, or any capacity, to claim their lives – but no one believes them when they say that lives *like* theirs are worth preserving.

It is unjust to suggest that personists are disingenuous in this: their sincere judgement is that the judgements of rational people rule, and that those who are not, at the moment, rational people must be subject to our judgement (that is, to the judgement of those who are *not* disabled). It is up to adults to decide for themselves whether their lives are worth living – and a decent society, it is tacitly assumed, will accept their decision, and pay for it. At the same time, we must decide for those incapable of the decision what they would, most probably, decide – and a decent society, it is assumed, will leave that decision to those biologically most likely to consider the creature's feelings. Personists are perhaps, however, unduly optimistic in their view that there is any such biological prejudice: leaving the decision to the parents, or the mother, is not necessarily in any infant's interests. The fact of the matter is that parents *may* love their children, if appropriately cued, but do not necessarily do so without the cues, or in any sense that tracks the infant's genuine welfare or its likely wishes. The difference between parents and state-officials as responsible decision-makers is not as clear as liberal personists suppose. Parents may well reflect fashionable opinion, and the clear advice of those supposed to be either medical or moral experts. Those experts, even when they say they will respect the judgement of those who think that their own 'disabled' lives are still worth living, routinely insist that the lives in prospect for disabled embryos are *not* worth living. The disabled, in other words, are not acknowledged as good witnesses. Our present attitudes to the helpless are not just biological, but stem from centuries of ideological concern. John Paul II's reference to the 'silent language of a profound sharing of affection'[13] is to the point. That language may be proleptic, directed towards what embryos and infants (and others) may yet be. It may also be a very present fact, delighting in the actual, present properties of creatures without ordinary human speech.

Might we be able, soon enough, to alter the arrangement of our own genes? In that case, we shall no longer need to avoid or to abort those likely to suffer because of their genetic flaws. Instead we might be able to repair the errors, whether by actually excising or replacing a dangerous allele, or just by turning it off. Once we can do that much, the temptation will be there to extend the range of characters that we think are faults. If we can spare our children, it is said, the 'pains' of milk-intolerance, myopia, clumsiness or cowardice or mild stupidity, why should we not? We should be careful, of course: many of the traits we count as flaws may turn out to be associated with the ones we think are virtues. Disentangling darnel from wheat is best left to the end of days[14] – especially if there might be occasions when it is darnel that we really need. But let us, unrealistically, imagine that we know enough to take that care,

---

[13] *Evangelium Vitae* (25 March 2995), taken from the Vatican's website (http://www.vatican.va), §19.
[14] Matthew 13.24ff.

and still to engineer the traits we wish. Let us suppose that we can really manufacture people, as we have hoped to manufacture cattle. Where is the harm in that – especially if we then treat such products 'well'?

Treating them 'well', of course, may be a vacuous project, if we ourselves determine what it is they wish. It might be a great deal cheaper to create new people with fewer wishes, or ones more cheaply satisfied. We cannot all live as richly as modern, middle-class Americans – and had therefore better ensure that very few of us have any wish to do so. We cannot all live as richly as my readers, or myself. So the engineered humanity of later days is likelier to be small, brown, clever at sums and verbal jests, playful, vegetarian, content and courteous. Or at least, if it is not these things, it probably will not have much future.

The route to that imagined world, of course, is likely to be littered with our failures. At the present time the failures will, most certainly, outnumber the 'successes', even if we know who the latter are. And maybe there will be many more than one such engineered humanity, even when the failure rate goes down. My gesture at what we actually need to be, after all, may easily be rebutted. Some will insist that large, blue-eyed Caucasians with milk, meat and coffee addictions must be just the thing, even though they cost the earth. Engineering may bring us, in fact, exactly the many human species we have so far avoided, including many hominoid hybrids, perhaps equipped with pidgin or (more probably) with useful, manual skills and an engineered obedience.

Is this what we desire, and what we should? What will become of 'old humanity', and should we mind?

PRESSING THE FLESH

The 'real' or 'physical' world presents an unimaginable expanse where discrete (but related) entities compete for space. In that world magic and good intentions do not work. Spiritual maturity, indeed, is partly founded in the discovery that magic does not work – or rather (since it certainly *does* work as far as our ordinary human world is concerned) *should not* work or be made to work.[15] Whatever mood we evoke, or invoke, the great world goes its way. 'Accepting facts' may sometimes be a cynical device to damage love or loyalty, but it may also be the proper acknowledgement of a world we do not control. The fantasy that we could win a war with 'nature', and so transform the waking world into our dream, *is* fantasy. It is therefore not entirely surprising that an alternative fantasy is now widespread. When William Gibson composed *Neuromancer* he knew little about 'information technology', and intended only to write a dystopian fiction.[16] To his horrified surprise, readers welcomed his vision of 'cyberspace' as a consensual delusion within which data could be represented as caverns, fortresses and treasure-troves. The travellers in 'virtual reality' could be whatever they chose to be, and grow up to be 'gods':

> Real are the dreams of gods, and smoothly pass
> Their pleasures in a long, immortal dream.[17]

The catch, as many writers from Gibson onwards have acknowledged, is that the consensual hallucination will in the end prove as intractable as the real waking world, as it will be the incalculable result of many different rebellious wills at work (just like 'the real waking world'). 'Virtual reality' will be as flawed, as *fortunately* flawed, as this, and as the memory even of a single person.

Behold, in those fields and caves and innumerable dens of my Memory, innumerably full of innumerable kinds of things, whether they be brought in as images, as all bodies are, or by the presence of the things themselves, as the arts are, or by I know not what notions or impressions as the affections of the mind, which the memory holds even when the mind feeleth them not, since whatsoever is in the mind

---

[15] Deuteronomy 18.10ff.; Kimberley Cornish, *The Jew of Linz: Wittgenstein, Hitler and their secret battle for the mind* (Century: London 1998), pp. 141ff. gives a clear account of what 'magic', as the evocation and fixation of emotion in the sorcerer and his victims, has involved.

[16] William Gibson, *Neuromancer* (Gollancz: London 1984); Ed Regis, *Great Mambo Chicken and the Transhuman Condition* (Penguin: Harmondsworth 1990) describes the thoughts of those who took Gibson seriously.

[17] John Keats, 'Lamia', part I, lines 127–8, *Poetical Works*, ed. H. W. Garrod (Oxford University Press: London 1956, p. 164).

is also in the memory, behold, I say, how through all these I run about and flutter on this side and that, and I penetrate into them as deeply as I can, but without finding of any bottom.[18]

There is an obvious moral for our present life. But it may also be useful to consider in more detail why the dream is popular, and what it means.

John Keats's sympathies lay with Lamia, rather than with the sharp-eyed philosopher who recognized the serpent beneath the lovely woman (but signally failed to recognize her real good will).

> Philosophy will clip an Angel's wings,
> Conquer all mysteries by rule and line,
> Empty the haunted air, and gnomed mine –
> Unweave a rainbow, as it erewhile made
> The tender-person'd Lamia melt into a shade.[19]

On the one hand Apollonius stands for that objectifying gaze which strips reality of memory, of charm, of meaning, and which must at last eliminate itself as well. If nothing is real except what can be weighed and measured then even the objectifying gaze itself is unreal. There can be no *problem* about relating 'mind' and 'matter' since there is no Mind. In the face of that nonsense it may be as well to carry on insisting that we all experience a world far greater, and that Apollonius is a bigger fool than Lycius. But on the other hand, *we are not gods*, and the world is not our dream. Retreating to the world of dreams we miss the greater beauty. One sort of fantasist imagines that the cosmos will, some day, be wholly controlled by 'our' intentions: everything that was once 'matter' will at last be 'mind', in the sense that there will be nothing unintended, undomesticated, uncontrolled. Another sort of fantasist imagines that we shall invent a cosmos, 'virtual reality', which is, by definition, *better* than the old. In either case, all things that matter will be what we wish, and there will be no *Other* to alarm us. Fantasy, in short, imagines that we shall at last achieve the

[18] Augustine, *Confessions*, tr. T. Matthew, ed. R. Huddleston (Burns & Oates: London 1923), 10.17: p. 285.
[19] Keats, 'Lamia', part II, lines 234–8, *Poetical Works*, p. 177.

world that religion posited, the world without division, the world where magic works.

But is this really what Christians, Abrahamists, theists or even decently religious people had in mind? No doubt some versions of the fantasy will sound more 'religious': imagined worlds where all our basest fantasies are played out will look like *hell*, not heaven, whereas the mind-impregnated, 'fully humanized' cosmos of other fantasists depends on our having 'higher' aims and characters than that. But even those higher characters may not be what religious people favoured. Popular discourse nowadays confuses magic, spirituality and righteousness. 'Spiritual' music is more or less 'uplifting', a device to control our moods and manners. 'Spiritual' people have access to powers that make things run the way we wish them to. For some, the moods they control are purely internal; for others, they are 'spiritual beings' in their own right, whom we invoke. Older theorists were suspicious of such beings, and such moods. Not all spirits are *good* spirits. In this context bodily existence comes to seem a necessary refuge from the realm of magic. It is not unreasonable to think of our bodies as 'prisons' or 'tombs', since they do indeed prevent our doing many things that we would wish. But for that very reason we may often be glad that we have been imprisoned. A world in which our every wish, or every passionate wish, was granted would be one we could not seriously welcome. Current fantasies about 'abandoning the meat' amount to wishing that our dreams should come true – without remembering what those dreams often are.

Bodies at least are welcome guardians against fantasy, but it may be that they are more than that. The corporeal world resists our wishes, but it may also realize them. Wishing to escape corporeality is the wish to be omnipotent – and so to be alone. Bodies are the medium through which, however feebly, ignorantly or wilfully, we encounter genuine others. Bodily embraces may be dangerous, since they encourage those desires that tradition names concupiscence to eat up and control. But they are at the same time strong reminders of our real presence, and the presence of our friends. It is understandable that moralists should urge us to be 'pure', and to stand back from fond embraces which may prove less *fond*. But the messy, smelly, rough, resistant presence of real bodies may also be essential to our spiritual health. One day we may live as angels, but any present attempt to live like that will probably only result in living like *fallen* angels.

Mahatma Gandhi's apparent obsession with cleanliness was a response to Hindu (and all too human) attitudes to dirt. Those charged, in Hindu culture, with laundry or latrines become, literally and anagogically, filthy. By taking responsibility for his own excrement, Gandhi was making a symbolic point.[20] On the one hand, we do need, for our own physical health, to keep our distance from our bodily excretions, but we must also seek to transcend the easy opposition between the pure and the polluted.[21] Even those legendary saints of Western tradition who showed their holiness by not washing were not quite as absurd as modernists suppose. By embracing in their own person what is, naturally, considered and felt as filth (including beggars, lepers and the working poor) they acted out a transcendent hope.

> The shepherds' hovels shone, for underneath
> The soot we saw the stone clean at the heart
> As on the starting-day. The refuse heaps
> Were grained with that fine dust that made the world;
> For he had said, 'To the pure all things are pure.'[22]

False spirituality seeks to escape from bodies, and sets up a global opposition between purity and pollution which in turn encourages contempt. A related falsehood then deliberately employs 'filth' in magical operations. But both errors remain contemptuous of this best of bodily worlds. Whatever true spirituality may be, it demands that we see *through* the dust and dirt to what it signifies, and welcome it as our right way home.

20 See Ved Mehta, *Mahatma Gandhi and his Apostles* (Penguin: Harmondsworth 1977), pp. 243ff.; see also Margaret Chatterjee, *Gandhi's Religious Thought* (Macmillan: London 1983), pp. 143ff.

21 See Louis Dumont, *Homo Hierarchicus*, tr. M. Sainsbury (Weidenfeld & Nicolson: London 1970); Mary Douglas, *Purity and Danger* (Penguin: Harmondsworth 1966).

22 Edwin Muir, 'The Transfiguration', *Collected Poems* (Faber: London 1960), p. 199.

'RAMPANT PRIMATEMIA'

Sensualism, egoism and false spirituality all threaten an end to humanity, since all encourage us to despise the given, natural world. Strangely, a similar threat emerges from the opposite wing of geo-politics. Humankind can all too easily be considered cancerous.

Our species retains hereditary traits that add greatly to our destructive impact. We are tribal and aggressively territorial, intent on private space beyond minimal requirements, and motivated by selfish sexual and reproductive drives. Cooperation beyond the family and tribal levels comes hard. Worse, our liking for meat causes us to use the sun's energy at low efficiency.[23]

Patently, our present existence and civilized lifestyle constitute a threat to the integrity of the whole living world. As in chapter 3, we are living through, and causing, the sixth mass extinction. From the point of view of the planet, so to speak, the explosive growth of the 'third chimpanzee' is a destructive fever, 'rampant primatemia'.[24] Perhaps the living earth is more resilient than some doom-watchers have supposed. It has, after all, survived those earlier mass extinctions, as well as the first and greatest of pollution incidents, the spread of photosynthesizers and their poisonous by-product (oxygen). Living things have managed to maintain a climate bearable by living beings, and so made sure that the climate has not arrived at the chemically stable conditions found on Venus or on Mars. Whether they can survive the very rapid changes that we cause may be a different matter. In one imaginable future, the climate and biochemical condition of the earth will be controlled by

[23] E. O. Wilson, *In Search of Nature* (Allen Lane: London 1992), p. 184.
[24] The phrase is James Lovelock's, in *The Ages of Gaia* (Oxford University Press: Oxford 1988); see also Alan Gregg, 'A Medical Aspect of the Population Problem', *Science* 121.1955, reprinted in Garrett Hardin, ed., *Population, Evolution and Birth Control* (Freeman & Co.: San Francisco 1969, second edition), pp. 89–92, who describes humankind as a cancer within the 'federation of community of interdependent organs and tissues that go to make up [the planetary physician's] patient'. See also the poems of Robinson Jeffers (e.g. *What Odd Expedients, and Other Poems*, ed., R. I. Scott (Archon Books: Hamden, Conn. 1981)). I discussed this attitude further in *How to Think about the Earth* (Mowbrays: London 1993),especially in chapter 3 on 'Blood and Soil'.

conscious, human or post-human engineers to produce such stuffs as they require. In another, the whole enterprise of human or post-human engineering will have been destroyed, and any descendants that we have will live, as once our ancestors lived, upon the margins of a world that does not need them. In other possible futures, the fever, cancer or devouring parasite has killed its host, and left no more than a dreadful warning to any galactic visitors who may one day come.

It is unlikely that philosophers or theologians are competent to guess which future is more likely. It is unlikely, indeed, that any of us are competent to guess. Unfortunately, incompetence is no excuse. We have to choose what future to believe in if we are to *live* at all. Like William James's mountaineer, we cannot *prove* that there is a foothold except by reaching for it, at the risk of failure.[25] We must believe what we cannot prove except by believing without proof. We may even have to *believe* that we are in danger in order to avoid the danger (and so be proved wrong).[26] The question is: which foothold shall we hope for? Shall we have confidence in our technical abilities, and aim for the engineered future? Shall we instead prefer the living earth even at the cost of our own species' spread? It is implicit in my argument so far that there is no *obvious* value in *our species* that cannot be found elsewhere. Those who prefer humankind above all others, and the humanized world above the manifold environments and life-worlds of the living earth, are only acting out a limited egoism. One might as well insist that the world should only be Anglo-Saxon, or only Serbian. Personally, I do not believe that we have the technical ability to run a world, nor do I find that human beings, by themselves, contain all value. It follows that the foothold I desire to find is one that allows as many living kinds as possible a chance of living, in the world we are given. The temptation to control and conquer, even when it is partly guided by a beautiful ideal, is always to be resisted. We

---

[25] William James, 'The Will to Believe', in *The Will to Believe* (Longmans, Green & Co.: New York 1919).

[26] Jonah, the only really successful prophet (and the most obviously fictional), told Nineveh that it was doomed – and the people of Nineveh believed God and repented (Jonah 3.4–5). When God spared the repentant people, 'it displeased Jonah exceedingly, and he was very angry. . ..' (Jonah 4.1).

may love our children just because they are *ours* – but loving them requires that we do not own them, and that we welcome their first happy steps away. We may be glad to have encouraged beauty, but that beauty must develop past our vision of it.

Can we live lightly on the lovely land? Or is the only actual future to be one of plague and war, until the heavenly city descends? Good moderns, until recently, have expected that our only dangers were those of total war. If only we could avoid such atavistic hatreds, we could hope to improve our power over nature until we *built* the City: the place where everything has a human purpose. Tradition warns us, of course, that the attempt is always halted by a divine intrusion. We shall not be allowed to finish building Babel. Tradition also warns us that in 'the last days' we shall be asked to choose between our mortal comforts and the word of God. Antichrist is not a Hollywood horror, but the best that human culture can devise. In Solovyev's story he offers everyone what they, as mortal beings, most want: security, comfort, and 'spiritual uplift'.[27] Everything, in fact, except the word of God.

Early Christians were accused of hating the human race. Radical environmentalists have often earned a similar accusation. Both sects have suggested that the love of money, our desire for luxury and earthly comfort, lie at the root of evil. Both sects urge us not to mind about possessions, and suggest that only a remnant will be 'saved'. Both sects, to function in a civilized society, themselves acquire wealth, and work out ways in which their members can earn a living. The days when any large number of us could live as wandering primates, hunter-gatherers, are gone. Extremists may suppose that only those who practise the wandering life will be found worthy of the coming kingdom; more prudent believers continue to live 'responsible', settled lives, in the hope that the Day of the Lord will be delayed, or that they will be admitted to the coming age for the sake of their good intentions. As a settled, 'responsible' householder and citizen, I share that hope.

[27] V. Solovyov, 'A Short Story of the Anti-Christ' in *War, Progress and the End of History*, tr. Alexander Bakshy and Thomas R. Beyer Jr (Lindisfarne Press: New York 1990), pp. 159–84.

But it is still worth trying to face the possibility that the extremists have it right. Every 'reasonable', civilized person will agree that we ought to live as adults: we ought to take out insurance policies, plant crops and prepare for winter.[28] We ought to guard against the unexpected, and consider the expectable effects of present acts. Radical environmentalists especially will urge us to stop playing silly games, and remember that our actions have effects. Adults accept responsibilities – and especially the responsibility of trying to make a world their children can grow up in without fear. But at the same time those same prophets urge us not to care about the very things that *adults* mind about: status, property and comfort are no more than games. On the one hand, spiritual progress rests in 'growing up'; on the other, it rests in becoming 'like a child'. It is natural that I, and any readers of this book, will wish that God preferred grown-ups, and that He wants us to accumulate *enough* to prosper (even if He also issues worrying rebukes about riches). It is natural to hope for progress, and to believe that this will result in greater human control of nature (even if we worry whether we *could* control it well). But all the great religious traditions, as I have remarked before, suggest instead that we should claim *nothing* as our own, and that salvation is a new beginning. It is not the *adult* who reveals what God would have us be, and neither need it be the *adult* (or the intelligent citizen) who is the heir of ages. 'Which is the essential dragonfly – the long-lived crawling larva, or the ephemeral winged imago?':[29] the species could equally be represented by the child, the adult being dismissed as the degenerate modification in the later part of life to reproduce and do the necessary work. As I remarked some years ago, instead of thinking of our young as marginal to the real interests and concerns and habitual practices of adult society, it is worth noticing the extent to which the rest of our society even now is centred on the needs and delights of the

---

[28] As Paul said of those who were taking too little thought for the future: if they will not work, let them not eat (2 Thessalonians 3.10).

[29] T. Gibson, 'Youth for Freedom' (Freedom Press: London 1951), reprinted in L. I. Krimerman and L. Parry, eds., *Patterns of Anarchy* (Doubleday: New York 1966), pp. 436ff., esp. p. 438.

young.[30] On the one hand, perhaps that is a symptom of derangement, of a failure to live up to our demands, and relapse on fun. On the other, at the far side of radical disillusionment, we can perhaps catch glimpses of another way.

Once upon a time all serious hominids expected to live their lives among the trees. Once upon an even earlier time, all serious wrigglers expected to settle down as sedentary molluscs. What happened instead, for some of them, was that their young refrained from 'growing up' as serious creatures should, and instead grew into humankind (or, earlier, vertebrates). God's call, or the chances of evolution, is to grow up without abandoning childhood. Those of us who have already grown should hope to find a better life suggested in our young: instead of thinking that they should grow up to be like us, we may entertain a fantasy of growing to be like them. When the final line is drawn beneath humanity, perhaps it will be the children who live on.

Chesterton remarked on the inconsistency in modern habits: on the one hand we deprecate the older praise of virgins; on the other, we worship – it is hardly too strong a term – the particular beauty of children in the moments before puberty, and know very well that this is virginal.[31] In the kingdom of heaven, Jesus told us, there is no marriage, and also that we must be children there. Sexuality, no doubt, and parenthood are also ordained by God. The deliberate refusal of that vocation, which is to lose one's very own childhood in the care of others', may itself be sin.[32] But perhaps the time has come to reconsider modern habits. Good liberals urge believers to be tolerant of blasphemy, but are themselves affronted by any apparent insult to Aphrodite. Perhaps they are wise; but let us briefly consider that sex exists to encourage parenting, and parents to care for children. 'The creation of a new creature, not ourselves, of a new conscious centre, of a new and indepen-

---

[30] 'Children and the Mammalian Order' in G. Scarre, ed., *Children, Parents and Politics* (Cambridge University Press: Cambridge 1989), pp. 115–32, reprinted in *The Political Animal* (Routledge: London 1999).

[31] G. K. Chesterton, *Orthodoxy* (Fontana: London 1961; first published 1908), p. 155.

[32] A sin committed not by monks or nuns but by those dedicated to the gods of fashion.

dent focus of experience and enjoyment, is an immeasurably more grand and godlike act even than a real love affair; how much more superior to a momentary physical satisfaction? If creating another self is not noble, why is pure self-indulgence nobler?'[33] Chesterton might add that even pure self-indulgence, pure enjoyment, might be nobler than the queasy blend of sentiment and pseudo-mysticism which treats sex as a sacrament. There is something comic, as well as tragic, about the recent rediscovery of child abuse: what on earth did we expect? If we tell a generation that shared pleasure is the proper route to heaven, and old taboos are dead, why be surprised that paedophiles think so too? The real value of sexuality lies not in transient sensation and particular 'acts of love', but in the long-drawn-out business of procreation, in the constant recreation of a virginal beauty – a beauty that we destroy by lust. But that is another story.

[33] G. K. Chesterton, 'Blasphemy and the Baby', *G.K.'s Weekly* 27.9.1930, reprinted in Alvaro da Silva, ed., *Brave New Family* (Ignatius Press: San Francisco 1990), pp. 169–71, esp. p. 171.

CHAPTER 8

The covenant with all living creatures[1]

BEGINNING FROM THE BEGINNING

The Bible's claim is that our possession of the land (and anything else we think we own) is conditional on our keeping to the covenant, whose conditions are listed in Deuteronomy chapter 28.[2] Those conditions are regularly ignored. We easily believe that we can avoid all consequences for our sin: 'You keep saying "This place is the temple of the Lord, the temple of the Lord, the temple of the Lord!" This catchword of yours is a lie; put no trust in it. Mend your ways and your doings, deal fairly with one another, do not oppress the alien, the orphan, and the widow, shed no innocent blood in this place, do not run after other gods to your own ruin'.[3]

There have been many attacks on the Scriptures as being 'anti-environmentalist'. On the contrary, so I contend, the Scriptures emphasize our duties – not as 'stewards', but as neighbours. It is true that Baal, in some sense a nature god, is not approved[4] and some critics suspect – not *entirely* without reason – that modern pantheistic environmentalism, and New Age ideas, are exactly that sort of Baal worship.[5] But from the

---

[1] Much of this chapter was originally delivered as a Chaplaincy Lecture at the Anglican Chaplaincy of the University of Liverpool, and published in the collection of those lectures; parts have also been tried out on environmentalists at King's College London.

[2] Deuteronomy 29.1 says this Moab covenant is in addition to the one at Horeb.

[3] Jeremiah 7.4.

[4] see 2 Kings 11.17–18: Jehoiada's covenant against Baal.

[5] A more plausible analogy for Baal worship, of course, is simply 'establishment religion' – the assumption that those with power have a *right* to what they want, even if it belongs to someone else (see 1 Kings 21). 'The worshippers of Moloch were not

very first chapter of Genesis it is affirmed that 'being' itself is good. 'God could not have created a thing had he hated it, as the Wisdom says, and the mere fact that he keeps it in being is the proof that he loves it.'[6] After the flood God makes a covenant with all living creatures.[7] The Lord rejoices in His works.[8]

Some modernist theologians explain the apparent failings of our present world as God's chosen way of creating rational individuals. Everything, by their account, exists for us to use. The God of orthodoxy has no need of secondary causes of this sort. Whatever He creates, He creates for its own sake, because He chooses to. Some have held that He created every possible creature; others that He actualizes only some real possibilities; others again that even God the Omniscient cannot inspect all possible, non-existent, beings (because there can be no criteria for their identity beyond what God makes real in creating some 'of them'). Whatever the truth of this, we can be confident that He creates exactly what He wants, for its own sake or 'for His glory'. Nor does the God of orthodoxy need to make particular creatures co-existent: as far as we can see He may have randomized creation, since His chosen must, in any case, relate to anyone at all who is their neighbour, irrespective of their nature or their merits. Nor does He select for special treatment just those creatures that a finite observer might expect: nothing in the long ago determined Him to raise up mammals, hominids, or Abram. So orthodox theocentrism is far less committed to the notion of a 'visible plan' than atheistic critics have supposed.

Granted that things exist 'for their own sake', because God wishes just those things to be, then they are not simply 'for us'. From this beginning we can see that the commandments have a

gross or primitive. They were members of a mature and polished civilization, abounding in refinements and luxuries . . . And Moloch was not a myth; or at any rate his meal was not a myth. These highly civilized people really met together to invoke the blessing of heaven on their empire by throwing hundreds of their infants into a large furnace' (G. K. Chesterton, *The Everlasting Man* (Hodder & Stoughton: London 1925), p. 169). We do things more quietly now.

[6] E. Cardenal, *Love*, tr. D. Livingstone (Search Press: London 1974; first published as *Vida en el amor*, 1970), p. 43, after Wisdom of Solomon 11.24–5.

[7] Genesis 9.8ff.   [8] Psalm 104.

wider message than simple social solidarity. Consider the Sabbath rules:[9] the Sabbath is not just the seventh day; it is also the tenth day of the seventh month; and in the seventh year land is left for the poor and the wild things.[10] Amos links the sabbath requirement explicitly to a ban on the commercial exploitation of the poor.[11] Jeremiah makes possession of the land conditional on obedience.[12] There are related commandments about Jubilee, and about the rules of war: Leviticus says that no land is to be sold outright (lest land accumulate in the hands of the rich);[13] Deuteronomy requires us not to burn fruit-bearing trees in war;[14] Isaiah makes it clear that violation of the eternal covenant leads to disaster.[15]

Or as another said:

These were the words of the Lord to me: Prophesy, man, against the shepherds of Israel; prophesy and say to them, You shepherds, these are the words of the Lord God: How I hate the shepherds of Israel who care only for themselves! Should not the shepherd care for the sheep? You consume the milk, wear the wool, and slaughter the fat beasts, but you do not feed the sheep. You have not encouraged the weary, tended the sick, bandaged the hurt, recovered the straggler, or searched for the lost; and even the strong you have driven with ruthless severity. . . I will dismiss those shepherds: they shall care only for themselves no longer; I will rescue my sheep from their jaws, and they shall feed on them no longer.[16]

Ezekiel, or the Lord, here takes it for granted that true shepherds care for sheep. 'A righteous man cares for his beast, but a wicked man is cruel at heart.'[17] Literally, of course, shepherds care for sheep only that they may profit from them in the end, but perhaps this was not so in the beginning, and need not be wholly so even now.

For any man who is just and good loves the brute creatures which serve him, and he takes care of them so that they have food and rest and the other things they need. He does not do this only for his own good but out of a principle of true justice; and if he is so cruel toward

---

[9] Exodus 16.23ff., 20.8–9.   [10] Leviticus 25.6.   [11] Amos 8.5.
[12] Jeremiah 11.3.   [13] Leviticus 25.23.   [14] Deuteronomy 20.19–20.
[15] Isaiah 24.5; so also Jeremiah 4.23, and 5.25: 'your wrongdoing has upset nature's order'.
[16] Ezekiel 34.1–4, 9–10.   [17] Proverbs 12.10; cf. 27.23ff.

them that he requires work from them and nevertheless does not provide the necessary food, then he has surely broken the law which God inscribed in his heart. And if he kills any of his beasts only to satisfy his own pleasure, then he acts unjustly, and the same measure will be measured out to him.[18]

The covenant of peace lies on the far side of a transformation, for God 'will create new heavens and a new earth, and the past will not be remembered, and will come no more to men's minds'.[19] So what is the effect of this belief, that 'from the beginning until now the entire creation . . . has been groaning in one great act of giving birth'?[20] In the new world no one will hurt or harm; here, it often seems, we – which is all of sentient creation – are condemned to hurt and harm each other. 'You bring darkness on, night falls, all the forest animals come out: savage lions roaring for their prey, claiming their food from God.'[21] If, as so many people hasten to insist, 'animals were given to us', it is only because we have all been 'given' to each other: given, in part, that we may care for, and respect, each other. We should care for the weak and helpless, 'champion the widow, defend the cause of the fatherless, give to the poor, protect the orphan, clothe the naked'.[22] Even when we have done that, we shall be in the wrong, and need forgiveness; but perhaps we need not trouble ourselves to do much more. In the new world, there will be no marriages, no temples and no courts of law. There, we shall call no man 'father'. There, we shall be naked and unashamed. But it does not immediately follow that we should try to live by those laws here and now. Vegetarians, according to Karl Barth, are trying, like conscientious nudists, to anticipate the Kingdom – though the case would be more convincing if it were not so easy for us (I say nothing about lions, nor yet the Inuit) to be vegetarian.

Some of those who live in expectation of an imminent *parousia*

[18] Anne Conway, *Principles of the Most Ancient and Modern Philosophy*, eds. A. P. Courdert and T. Corse (Cambridge University Press: Cambridge 1996), p. 35; the book was originally published, posthumously, in 1690.
[19] Isaiah 65.17; see Revelation 21.1.
[20] Romans 8.22; see Isaiah 26.17ff.
[21] Psalm 104.20–1; see Job 38.39ff.
[22] 2 Esdras 2.20ff.; see Isaiah 1.16ff.

have seemed to conclude that, being in the image of God, we are now entitled to do as we please with things. After all, some say, if this world here is due for demolition, then God himself must think it is garbage. But 'those who boast of the dignity of their nature and the advantages of their station and thence infer their right of oppression of their inferiors, exhibit their folly as well as their malice'.[23] Nebuchadnezzar learnt the hard way that 'God has power to humble those who walk in pride.'[24] 'Let that mind be in us that was also in Christ Jesus, who being in the form of God did not think to snatch at equality with God.'[25] A few of us may manage to make appropriate vows of poverty, chastity, non-violence, obedience, and to greet each other – which again is all of us – as the children of God we hope to be considered. We may strive to see that 'garbage' is only in the eye of the beholder, that to *be* at all is to be something, to be informed, illuminated, by a real form, an aspect of God's grandeur.[26] Because this is indeed a radical alternative, which few of us adopt, we usually console ourselves by thinking of it, rather than attempting it. As Orwell commented: 'we all live by robbing Asiatic coolies, and those of us who are "enlightened" all maintain that those coolies ought to be set free; but our standard of living, and hence our "enlightenment", demands that the robbery shall continue'[27] – so we are satisfied with saying that we *wish* to stop. The world we actually inhabit is not that real world we say we believe in, but one constructed around the life we actually live.

Pigs, according to Chrysippus, should be reckoned locomotive meals, with souls instead of salt to keep them fresh. The bloated turkeys bred for Christmas tables are incapable of natural reproduction, so they must be artifacts: 'There is a price to be paid for fabricating around us a society which is as

---

[23] Humphrey Primatt, *The Duty of Humanity to Inferior Creatures* (Centaur Press: Fontwell 1990; second edition edited by A. Broome 1831), p. 22.

[24] Daniel 4.34.   [25] Philippians 2.5ff.

[26] See G. M. Hopkins, 'God's Grandeur', *Poems of Gerard Manley Hopkins*, ed. W. H. Gardner and N. H. Mackenzie (Oxford University Press: London 1970, fourth edition), p. 66.

[27] George Orwell, cited by Wendell Berry, *What are People for?* (Rider: New York 1990), p. 201.

artificial and as mechanized as our own; and this is that we can exist in it only on condition that we adapt ourselves to it. This is our punishment.'[28] Once we have abandoned anthropocentric fantasies we should ask instead how God, the transforming God, would have us think of pigs, of turkeys, of Nature, and how, in expectation of the Coming, we should treat them. Nothing is 'just garbage'; nothing is 'just a pig'; even of a fish it is blasphemy to say it is *only* a fish, or of a flower that it is 'only a growth like any other'.[29]

The Noahic covenant permits us to make use of other creatures, in a ruined world, so long as we do not use their blood, which is their life.[30] The Mosaic law lays down further, explicit principles: we may not, for example, muzzle the oxen that tread out the corn,[31] nor take mother and young from any nest,[32] nor take a calf, lamb or kid from its mother until seven days after its birth,[33] nor boil a kid in its own mother's milk,[34] nor leave a beast trapped in a well on the pretext that today is holy,[35] nor yoke ox and ass together,[36] nor plough up all the fields, in every year, and so deprive the wild things of their livelihood.[37] I am aware, before you tell me so, that many of these laws may once have had a ritual or anagogical significance. 'Does God care for oxen? Or is the reference clearly to ourselves?'[38] I see no reason not to answer: 'Both'. 'For all existing things are dear to thee and thou hatest nothing that thou hast created – why else wouldst thou have made it?'[39] That is certainly how they have been taken, in Rabbinic, Christian and Islamic commentary. They may indeed have their beginnings in religion rather than human morals, in the

---

[28] P. Sherrard, The *Eclipse of Man and Nature* (Lindisfarne Press: West Stockbridge, Mass. 1987), pp. 71–2.

[29] G. K. Chesterton, *The Poet and the Lunatics* (Darwen Finlayson: London 1962; first published 1929), pp. 54, 58; see also pp. 68ff.

[30] Genesis 9.3ff.; see also Leviticus 17.13–14, Deuteronomy 12.15–16. Traditionally, it is the Noahic covenant that is held to bind *all* human peoples: the Mosaic covenant binds only the people of Israel. Israel's self-styled inheritors have varied in their attitude to those laws, and in their obedience.

[31] Deuteronomy 25.4. [32] Deuteronomy 22.6–7; see Leviticus 22.28.

[33] Leviticus 22.26–7. [34] Deuteronomy 14.21.

[35] Deuteronomy 22.4; see Luke 14.5. [36] Deuteronomy 22.10.

[37] Leviticus 19.9–10, 23.22; 25.6–7. [38] 1 Corinthians 9.9.

[39] Wisdom of Solomon 11.24–5.

vision of what shall be rather than the plan to do as well as we can here and now. But perhaps that is where the love even of humanity begins: not in the bargains struck by desperate brigands which modern moralists sometimes identify as the real form of morals, but in the revelation that we may yet be gods.

All these laws are regularly broken now, and all the laws that echo or put fences round them. Later prophets make it clear that even permitted sacrifices, which are the only source of lawful meat, are not approved: 'I am sick of holocausts of rams and the fat of calves. The blood of bulls and goats revolts me.'[40] Once again, I am aware that these condemnations are sometimes said to be merely provisional, and that Isaiah, or the Lord, was only objecting to sacrifices made 'with unclean hands'; are our hands clean? But in any case, all such sacrifices ended, for those who follow Christ, at the Crucifixion. Paul accepted that Christians need not fear to eat the meat of beasts sacrificed to idols, but only on the assumption that by doing so they did not worship demons, and on condition that this 'liberty' did not become a pitfall for the weak.[41] Those tempted to continue eating meat – and doing all the other things that amount to that – should perhaps now wonder what it is they worship, and refrain. Everything God made is good, no doubt;[42] but that is a very strange reason to treat it just as 'useful', or to suppose that everything it does, or has done to it, must be perfectly all right. I am told that Islamic commentators have also argued that animal sacrifice, and meat eating, is permitted, or even required – but the assumption is still made that the animals have really been treated justly. If (as I suppose) they have not, then the sacrifice is unclean.

Turning aside from the mechanized, anthropocentric world to the world promised by the prophets (even if we cannot get there by ourselves, or swiftly) is a wakening.

We live in a world of unreality and dreams. To give up our imaginary position as the centre, to renounce it, not only intellectually but in the imaginative part of our soul, that means to awaken to what is real and eternal, to see the true light and hear the true silence. A trans-

---

[40] Isaiah 1.11.   [41] 1 Corinthians 8.12–13; cf. Revelation 2.14; 2.20.
[42] 1 Timothy 4.4; see 1 Corinthians 10.25.

formation then takes place at the very roots of our sensibility, in our immediate reception of sense impressions and psychological impressions. It is a transformation analogous to that which takes place in the dusk of evening on a road, where we suddenly discern as a tree what we had at first seen as a stooping man; or where we suddenly recognize as a rustling of leaves what we thought at first was whispering voices. We see the same colours, we hear the same sounds, but not in the same way. To empty ourselves of our false divinity, to deny ourselves, to give up being the centre of the world in imagination, to discern that all points in the world are equally centres and that the true centre is outside the world, this is to consent to the rule of mechanical necessity in matter and of free choice at the centre of each soul. Such consent is love. The face of this love which is turned towards thinking persons is the love of our neighbour: the face turned towards matter is love of the order of the world, or love of the beauty of the world which is the same thing.[43]

Weil here draws too rigid, too Cartesian a distinction between thinking persons and matter: there are innumerable grades of being, tradition tells us, 'below' and 'above' the thinking person. 'The moral consequence of faith in God', so Niebuhr tells us, 'is the universal love of all being in Him . . . This is [faith's] requirement: that all beings, not only our friends, but also our enemies, not only men but also animals and the inanimate, be met with reverence, for all are friends in the friendship of the one to whom we are reconciled in faith.'[44] How can we be reconciled to God, if we show no mercy to our neighbour? 'If a man nurses anger against another, can he then demand compassion from the Lord?'.[45]

BARGAINS WITHIN THE COVENANT

But is this possible? Is the argument against any attempt to 'immanentize the *eschaton*' simply that it is quite beyond our power, and therefore that the rules we live by must indeed be different? Is it (as hosts of moralists have held) impossible to

---

[43] Simone Weil, *Notebooks*, tr. A. Wills (Routledge & Kegan Paul, 1956) vol. 1, p. 115.
[44] H. Richard Niebuhr, *Radical Monotheism and Western Culture* (Harper & Row: New York 1960), p. 126.
[45] Ecclesiasticus 28.2–3.

reach an agreement with non-humans of a kind that gives sense to talk of 'justice between man and beast'?

The real oddity of the Stoic (Augustinian, Thomist, Cartesian and modern) claim that we can make no bargains with the animals, and that they therefore lie beyond the sphere of justice,[46] is that we have been making bargains with them for millennia.

Does not daily observation convince us that they form contracts of friendship with each other, [and] with mankind? When puppies and kittens play together is there not a tacit contract that they will not hurt each other? And does not your favourite dog expect you should give him his daily food, for his services and attention to you?[47]

If human beings are, specifically, talking animals, it is worth noting that we have also talked *to* animals, and understood their answers. By this I mean nothing fabulous, or sentimental. We communicate with non-humans (and with humans) at a non-verbal level, understanding each other's moods and intentions. Most of our alliances have been exploitative – either of the non-humans we persuade into our keeping, or of those we prey on in the wild. Domestication is a process employed on humans as well as non-humans, and as open to manipulation, on both sides. Dogs manipulate their humans, thereby displaying their grasp of their own and their humans' status in the pack. Domestic animals, human and non-human, are bred and reared to know their limits; philosophers and political theorists, meditating on those limits, construct imaginary compacts to explain, and to constrain, what happened naturally. It is even possible – although the great age of innovative domestication was the Neolithic – for human beings to come to tacit agreements with wild creatures: Jane Goodall lived amongst the Gombe chimpanzees more equably than Colin Turnbull did amongst the human Ik.[48] Understanding our limits, and what

---

[46] An inference for which I have yet to see a single decent argument.

[47] Erasmus Darwin, *Zoonomia* (1794–6), vol. I, p. 169, cited by Keith Thomas, *Man and the Natural World: changing attitudes in England 1500–1800* (Penguin: Harmondsworth 1984), p. 121.

[48] Jane van Lawick-Goodall, *In the Shadow of Man* (Collins: London 1971); Colin Turnbull, *The Mountain People* (Cape: London 1973).

motivates creatures of different kinds in social situations, is vital to the construction of enduring communities.

There are indeed limits to our understanding, and to the possibilities for friendly association, though they are not necessarily the ones we commonly imagine. Language does not always unite us, but divides. Even Augustine acknowledged that it was easier for dumb animals of different species to get on together than two humans who did not know each other's language, and easier to get on with one's dog than with a foreigner![49] Our ethical relationship to creatures that we can be friends with, will be different from that to those we cannot: but it does not follow that we should think of the latter only as un-friends, or enemies, or mere material.

Amongst the loyalties we actually and historically form are ones toward domestic or working animals. A child's affection for a cat or dog or horse is not much different from her affection for her human friends and family. She values its company and reciprocal affection, demands that others care for it, and could easily resent occasional bids for solitude or independence. Those who work with 'animals' are usually, and naturally, attached to them even when they have put 'childish things' away. They come to see, more or less knowledgeably, with the others' eyes, and allow them more or less of liberty to go their own way when it suits them. Dogs, cats and horses are the commonest non-human creatures to elicit, and partly reciprocate, affection, in the settled West. But cows, pigs, hawks, snakes and spiders all have their admirers, here and elsewhere. It seems indeed to be a species characteristic that we readily adopt small (smallish) creatures and rear them in our midst, expecting them to learn enough of our ways to be called 'tame'. It is no contradiction to add that we frequently betray what trust they have in us.[50]

So the claim that we cannot make bargains with non-human animals is simply false. How detailed the bargains that we make

[49] Augustine, *City of God* 19.7.
[50] See further my 'Enlarging the Community' in Brenda Almond, ed., *Introducing Applied Ethics* (Blackwell: Oxford 1995), pp. 318–30; reprinted in *The Political Animal* (Routledge: London 1999).

can be, and what motivates us all (human and non-human) to keep them, will vary. Many such bargains will be marginal to the central interests of each of the bargaining tribes; others will be so significant as to change the natures of those who enter them, or are brought up in them. Most, as I remarked, are exploitative: even the bargain with dogs, which was once almost of equals, has long since been rewritten to allow 'us' civilized humans liberty to do very much as we please with them – while at the same time reserving the right to sneer at other human tribes who have a different use for them, as food. That the bargain was, or is, exploitative does not mark it off as any different from the social compacts that political theorists more usually debate. The sort-of-contracts that lie, in historical reality, behind the modern state are just as forced. Some of the peoples that the people of Israel encountered when they invaded Palestine chose to bind themselves and their descendants to be hewers of wood and drawers of water, rather than be destroyed.[51] A similar choice, or something like a choice, was made, back in the Neolithic Age, by several species (and, perhaps significantly, by hardly any since). Dogs, horses, cattle, sheep and camels 'chose' to be domestic, and have paid a savage price since then. Creatures that 'chose' freedom (including people who turned their backs on 'civilized' society) risk extinction in a world controlled by 'civilized' people.[52]

The original sort-of-compact that was made guarantees their species' survival, and better medical care than they would have as wild things; the price is that they are available for use, as food, amusement or laboratory material. That there were literal, individual, informed choices, way back then, is not required – any more than such actual choices are required by social contract theorists. It is, some say, quite reasonable to agree to give up natural, risky liberties, for the state's care and protection: perhaps our ancestors did not do this of their own volition (and we have had no choice), but state authority is

---

[51] Joshua 9.3ff.
[52] I am aware that the event probably owed more to chance, as it is called, than these words might suggest: the ancestral dogs came closer by degrees, and those who grew up to resent domestication either left or died. Much the same happened to people.

thereby justified, because we *could* have consented. So could domestic animals – though we may surely have some doubts that they would, that anyone would, consent to the conditions under which they live at present. Might there not be a better, fairer bargain? Is it not already obvious that whatever contract of care and protection we, perhaps, proposed, has long been broken?

That the bargain is broken when, for example, we ship living cattle over many miles and hours to be slaughtered amongst strangers for meat that no one really needs, has seemed obvious to many who had not previously worried about the plight of cattle, and who might still think nothing wrong, as such, in killing 'animals' for food. Similar incidents during the slave trade began to awaken a suspicion that it was not the passing incidents, but the trade itself, that should be banned – despite the obvious truth that every civilized society until then had licensed slavery. Breeding, rearing, mutilating, imprisoning, torturing and killing non-human animals are all questionable practices, even if those animals are not themselves in any position to rebel (any more than serfs have been for most of human history). The growing perception that serfs and slaves and foreigners deserve respect, and the corresponding thought that there are other social forms which could accommodate our friendship, has changed our moral consciousness: we can no longer comfort ourselves with the thought that people who are poor, casteless, 'primitive' (or Irish) are so unlike 'us' that we need not fear that we are doing them wrong. A similarly changing perception of non-human animals makes it impossible, in good faith, to think that an impartial judge would vindicate our conduct towards them.[53]

The thought at which some humane commentators stop (as I

[53] 'Ask it for once without presupposing the answer of the egotism of our species, as God might ask it about his creatures: Why should a dog or a guinea pig die an agonizing death in a laboratory experiment so that some human need not suffer just that fate?': Erazim Kohak, *The Embers and the Stars* (University of Chicago Press: Chicago 1984), p. 92. Arthur C. Clarke posed the question in more secular terms: if superior extraterrestrial intelligences turned up, might we not be judged on our treatment of our fellow terrestrials (see *The Deep Range* (Muller: London 1957), and *Childhood's End* (Sidgwick & Jackson: London 1954))?.

already hinted) is that it is wrong to hurt non-humans, but not wrong to kill them. Ending their lives does them no harm, because they have – it is said – no general plan of life, nor any expectation of their ends. That much the same can be said of many human animals is either accepted (and the ban on killing infants, imbeciles, the ordinarily feckless, or the elderly, judged less significant than the ban on 'real murder') or hurriedly disguised. Killing such human 'marginals' is judged wrong because of its effect on general morale, or as an offence of the same order as violating unconscious human bodies. It might as well be argued that killing non-humans is also a desecration: an open declaration that their lives are not valued. If the principle on which liberal zoophiles depend (that hurting is wrong, but not killing) were as obvious as some suppose, we would not disapprove of people who have their pets 'put down' for trivial reasons. Instead, we think such 'pet lovers' have betrayed their trust, and shown most clearly that they did not *love* at all. Even utilitarians, who place the value of an entity in its utility, may reasonably say that a living animal has more utility, more value, than a dead one: the value its flesh adds to the lives of others is rarely as great as the value it adds to its own. Non-utilitarians, who reckon that an entity may be valued 'in itself' and irrespective of the quality of life dependent on it, will have more reason to think that killing things requires a defence.

One argument against allowing murder is, of course, simply the self-interested one, that I am likely to live more safely amongst people who condemn homicide, and even defend each other against offenders. 'Animals', it is said, will not be affected either way by our forbearance, and may therefore be safely killed. The claim is dubious, since a non-aggressive lifestyle is as effective in avoiding most aggression in the case of animals as well as humans. But it is even more doubtful that the ethical argument against killing really depends on bargains of that sort. Those who are bound only by the laws of brigandage are not generally well regarded. Even liberals will think it wrong to kill off Amazonian tribes to get their land, even if there is not the slightest risk that the tribesmen could kill us instead (and if there is, the sooner – I suppose – that they are killed the better).

The same good reason not to kill non-human tribes is just that they have lives of their own to live, that we have no God-given privilege to take away what God has given them. What is astonishing is that good liberals, at this point in the argument, so often fall back on ideologies that are otherwise associated with paradigmatic enemies of liberal values. Non-aggression is all very well, they say, but we are living in the jungle, and at war with every other kind of creature. Radical zoophiles, so it seems, are traitors.

If we catch sharks for food, let them be killed most mercifully; let anyone who likes love the sharks, and pet the sharks, and tie ribbons round their necks and give them sugar and teach them to dance. But if once a man suggests that a shark is to be valued against a sailor, or that the poor shark might be permitted to bite off a Negro's leg occasionally; then I would court-martial the man – he is a traitor to the ship.[54]

Chesterton was right to suspect that those who claimed to care for 'animals' were sometimes less than courteous or just to *human* beings of a class or race that they despised. It is our very own conspecifics, after all, that we are likelier to fear or loathe (as Darwin loathed the Fuegians). The Ik were driven to their dreadful state in part because more powerful people wanted to preserve the landscape and its animals for their own pleasure, and therefore excluded the Ik from their ancestral land.

How we are to love those who mean us harm, and whether we may rightly defend ourselves – and those we love – against such harm, are genuine problems. There are those who, making themselves available as prey to any others, somehow disarm those others. It does not immediately follow that *princes* should make their people prey to any enemy, nor that we should stand mute and 'harmless' when an enemy approaches to harass and kill the poor. But is it really true that sharks, or other predators, intend to harm us? And why, if they do, does this have anything to say about our treatment of harmless beasts? 'If a wolf will seize upon a man, is a man therefore warranted to

[54] G. K. Chesterton, 'Christmas', in *All Things Considered* (Methuen: London 1908), p. 215: my thanks to gkchesterton@cwix.com for the reference.

whip a pig to death? . . . What is this but to say that cruelty in Britain is no sin because there are wild tigers in India?'[55]

There is a difference between creatures bred and reared to be a part of 'our' community, and those outside. The rights that radical zoophiles demand for domestic and other 'cultured' animals need not be ones that every wild thing has, or can be assumed to have. It is for this reason, amongst others, that the suggestion that such zoophiles do not 'really' believe that animals have rights, or they would be out defending blackbirds against foxes, and worms against blackbirds, as well as foxes against hunters, is misplaced. The truth is that we do not feel ourselves obliged to defend even all human beings against assault. In most cases it is enough that we do not ourselves assault them, and defend and nurture only our own dependents – though there may come a moment when the offence is simply too great to be borne, and we must create (most often in bloody war) a new civil order to prevent recurrence. Domesticated creatures (including us) have been, hamfistedly and hypocritically, creating a community that sometimes serves as a model for a larger, global order – but that is an order that we cannot ourselves create. They will not hurt or destroy on all God's holy mountain – but the best that we can manage here and now is to care for our own, and not attack the others.

'THINGS ARE GOD'S LOVE'

Awakening to realize the real beings of the creatures amongst whom we live, we have the opportunity to forge new images, new ways of living, that accommodate the interests of all. In attempting this, we have all art and literature to draw upon. For the mistake too often made has been to think that we should dispense with all such historical or mythological or personal associations if we are to realize the truth. 'Enlightenment' has been equated with a decently modern emancipation from superstitious reverence or compassion – but even Spinoza (who

[55] Primatt, *Duty of Humanity*, pp. 30, 36.

followed Stoic argument in holding that only a 'womanish and sentimental pity' stood in the way of using everything non-human as we pleased) would have drawn the line at irreverence. It is true enough that an amorous adolescent would do well to distinguish the real being of his inamorata from the dramatic and emotional fictions in which he cloaks her. It is quite untrue that he should therefore think of her as no more than bare, forked animal: that would itself be a dramatic and emotional fiction. What matters is that he, that they, should wake up to the possibility of friendship. That friendship is incompatible with the 'knowingness' that is too often inculcated. A foolish work of elementary English criticism, examined by Lewis, sought to 'debunk . . . a silly piece of writing on horses, where these animals are praised as the "willing servants" of the early colonists in Australia' (on the plea that horses are not much interested in colonial expansion). Lewis comments that its actual effect on pupils will have little to do with writing decent prose: 'some pleasure in their own ponies and dogs they will have lost: some incentive to cruelty or neglect they will have received: some pleasure in their own knowingness will have entered their minds' – but 'of Ruksh and Sleipnir and the weeping horses of Achilles and the war-horse in the Book of Job – nay, even of Brer Rabbit and of Peter Rabbit – of man's prehistoric piety to "our brother the ox" they will have learnt nothing'.[56]

Treating our friends, or our potential friends, as merely flesh – which is, merely material – is no advance at all on treating them as characters, even if the characters and parts that we impute to them are faulty. 'Do not you see that that dreadful dry light shed on things must at last wither up the moral mysteries as illusions, respect for age, respect for property, and that the sanctity of life will be a superstition? The men in the street are only organisms, with their organs more or less displayed. For such a one there is no longer any terror in the touch of human flesh, nor does he see God watching him out of the eyes of a man.'[57] Even of a fish it is blasphemous to say that

[56] C. S. Lewis, *The* Abolition *of Man* (Bles: London 1946, second edition), pp. 12–13.
[57] Chesterton, *The Poet and the Lunatics* p. 70.

it is only a fish.[58] We do not know what fish are meant to be, nor what, in the restoration, they will be – except that God will reckon they are 'good'. We can go further: 'Picasso was right when he said that we do not know what a tree or a window is. All things are very mysterious and strange and we only overlook their strangeness and their mystery because we are so used to them. We only understand things very obscurely. But what are things? Things are God's love become things.'[59]

So we should live as non-violently as we can manage, building up our friendships and respecting the limits that are needed to allow each kind its place. Let us live according to those rules that will allow as many creatures as possible, of as many kinds, their best chance of living a satisfactory life according to their kind. Let us acknowledge our particular duties of care and forbearance to those creatures who have been part of our society for millennia. Let us acknowledge that, as the Koran told us, there are other nations in the world, with whom we should not expect to be at war. Until the nineteenth century, every civilized society kept slaves. Until the twentieth, every civilized society believed that property could be acquired by military conquest (brigandage). There are still brigands, and slave-runners, in the world, but no one else acknowledges their claims.

In the twenty-first century (I live in hope), we might begin to acknowledge that we have no right, no general entitlement, to treat our kindred as no more than means. The robbery will, no doubt, continue. Particular legislation, in particular times and places, may be required to identify some acts as crimes. The global commonwealth may need to lay down minimal conditions of common decency in the treatment of non-humans.[60] It is one thing to recognize that 'animals' have feelings, and lives of their own to live, and so to include their interests in any

---

[58] Ibid., p. 58.

[59] Cardenal, *Love*, p. 43; see also my *God, Religion and Reality* (SPCK: London 1998).

[60] The Universal Declaration of Animal Rights, presented to UNESCO back in 1978, may be a beginning (see *The Universal Declaration of Animal Rights: comments and intentions*, eds. Georges Chapouthier and Jean-Claude Nouët (Ligue Française des Droits de l'Animal: Paris 1998)). So may be the occasional agreements forged in the European Union and elsewhere about the proper care of animals on the way to death.

impartial calculation of the greater good. It is another to acknowledge that this recognition demands of us that we not think them merely means to an end, even so benign an end as that same 'greater good'. It is yet another to seek to live in ways that we can bear to remember when we meet our kindred in the *eschaton*.

The covenant God made, we are told, in the beginning and affirmed since then, is to grant all things their space. 'The mere fact that we exist proves his infinite and eternal love, for from all eternity he chose us from among an infinite number of possible beings.'[61] Every thing we meet is also chosen: that is a good enough reason not to despise or hurt it. Whether it will be a strong enough reason to prevent us, I do not know. God knows.

[61] Cardenal, *Love*, p. 40; though this way of putting it perhaps imputes to Him more information than even the omniscient can have, since there are no criteria for the identity of all those *merely* 'possible' beings.

CHAPTER 9

Conclusion: cosmos and beyond

THE OPEN AND CLOSED COSMOS

One of the many oddities of late twentieth-century environmentalist rhetoric has been the insistence that we need to abandon the old, monotheistic metaphysics in favour of a more pantheistic sensibility.[1] Monotheists, it is supposed, believe that the wholly admirable, the Divine, is Somewhere Else than here, and that we human beings need not consider anything thisworldly worth respect. Pantheists, on the other hand, suppose that God, the wholly admirable, is Here, and that we cannot detach our *human* kind from earth. The charge against monotheists is at least unproved. Pagan and Abrahamic monotheists have repeatedly affirmed the value, to God and to His saints, of this world here. Nor is there any good reason to believe that other peoples, far away or long ago, have ever behaved much better. But what is really odd about the rhetoric is that, through all the centuries of Western domination which environmentalists most often blame for our present crisis, it has been a *pantheistic* metaphysics that has had most influence.[2]

Benedict Spinoza, it can plausibly be argued, was the first

---

[1] A topic I have explored in *How to Think about the Earth* (Mowbrays: London 1993), and also, more theologically, in 'Pantheism' in David E. Cooper and Joy A. Palmer, eds., *Spirit of the Environment* (Routledge: London 1998), pp. 42–56; see also *The Political Animal* (Routledge: London 1999).

[2] This is one reason why Europeans with any historical sense have often mistrusted environmentalists: that they remember what the effects of pantheism were before. See Anna Bramwell, *Blood and Soil: Richard Walter Darré and Hitler's Green Party* (Kensal Press: Abbots Brook 1985); R. A. Pois, *National Socialism and the Religion of Nature* (St Martin's Press: New York 1986); D. Gasman, *The Scientific Origins of National Socialism* (Macdonald: London 1971).

modern philosopher. He was traditional in seeking scriptural excuses for his claims, and finding ways of making a traditional (largely Stoic) philosophy plausible. He was modern in insisting that there was no distinction between God and Nature, no wider field of explanation than the cosmos itself, nor any higher value than could be found therein. The cosmos (being everything that is) must be a single, closed system. There can be no miracles, nor any escape from universal law. Quite why this revelation – that there is no escape – should ever have been considered a release from tyranny, a basis for 'free thought', requires a sociological explanation. It is customary to assert that the 'closed cosmos' of medieval speculation was broken open when Giordano Bruno saw the implications of Copernicus' theory. Suddenly the sphere of the fixed stars, the shell of a cosmic egg, dissolved into an infinitely extended space. But Olbers' paradox – that the sky is dark at night – makes it clear that the universe of stars is *not* infinitely extended: if it were, each point in the sky would be filled by a star, and the whole would be ablaze. The material cosmos is, on current theory, a finite whole, ruled by a single law. What goes on 'outside' is scientifically unknown (though that has not stopped speculation about unending streams of cosmoi, from which our little world buds off).[3] The reason for that speculation is not to assure us of liberty, but to find some way of insisting that everything is really as it *must* be. Bruno's infinite vacancies are replaced by the Stoics' single, necessary universe.

If there is no escape, and human beings like us are only and entirely what can be evolved within the cosmic prison, we may as well settle down in comfort (if we can agree on comfort). To ask more of ourselves than creatures like us could reasonably give is folly. The moral effects of laxity are all around us, but cannot be corrected. The epistemological effects are usually ignored. There is nothing special about the little sliver of the electromagnetic spectrum that our eyes happen to see best. But the very people who emphasize this point will rarely enquire, in that case, why our *intellectual* apparatus must be supposed to be

---

[3] See Lee Smolin, *The Life of the Cosmos* (Weidenfeld & Nicolson: London 1997).

more accurate or more inclusive than our sensory. Our ways of thinking, just as much as our ways of seeing or hearing or tasting, have been evolved as *adequate* for past survival purposes. Nothing at all in that Darwinian story gives us reason to believe that they will be adequate to unravel the whole cosmos, any more than are the mental maps and stratagems devised by squirrels. That belief, historically, was founded on Renaissance Platonism, which chose to emphasize the divinity of human intellect. The Church, with proper caution, doubted that we could outguess God: the systems we devised were not necessarily those that God had chosen to employ. As Descartes, at his cautious best, well knew, no physical systems *have* to be what they are, and none *have* to exist at all. Nothing is explained by saying that things *like* that always happen: not even an apple falls 'because all apples – or all middle-sized objects – fall'. They fall because God wills it so – and might, if He chose, transform them into pigeons.

The man of science says 'Cut the stalk, and the apple will fall', but he says it calmly as if the one idea really led up to the other. The witch in the fairy tale says, 'Blow the horn and the ogre's castle will fall'; but she does not say it as if it were something in which the effect obviously arose out of the cause . . . The scientific men . . . feel that because one incomprehensible thing constantly follows another incomprehensible thing the two together somehow make up a comprehensible thing . . . A tree grows fruit because it is a *magic* tree. Water runs downhill because it is bewitched. The sun shines because it is bewitched.'[4]

This is not to disparage reason. Chesterton himself insisted that there could be no contradictions in reality, that the Laws of Non-Contradiction, Identity and Excluded Middle, were demanded for a sane intelligence. Like Chesterton, I also think it possible to prove that God exists: that is, that there is a necessary cause of everything, present in its entirety at every point, which demands our entire allegiance. The existence of

[4] G. K. Chesterton, *Orthodoxy* (Fontana: London 1961; first published 1908), pp. 50–1; Chesterton uses the term 'magic' here to mean those brute and unexplainable conjunctions that we sometimes mistake for explanations. Why 'A *always* follows B' is somehow less astonishing than the fact that *this particular* A follows *that* B, is itself obscure. In reason, it should be a lot more surprising, and so no explanation.

that cause, that is, is necessary, but its action free. If the pantheistic model popular since Spinoza were enough, we should have instead to admit that everything is only as it must be, and that our only comfort lay in learning to live with it. If pantheism, as I believe, is wrong, we may instead consider whether monotheism is right. Correspondingly, 'this' world need not be all we hope for.

Monotheists, while agreeing that God sustains a world we might, in part, unravel, have no particular reason to deny to God the right, and power, to intervene or do things differently. Christians in particular are bound to admit that 'if such an event [as the resurrection] has happened in history, then history is not a closed system of immanent causes and effects'.[5] If we are serious in contending that Jesus is both perfect Man and God, then we have to acknowledge that we did not know, until Him, what Man amounted to. The first Adam is of the earth, but the second is the Lord from heaven.[6] It is in that Lord from heaven that we discover what it is to be human, or to be animal. The distorted version found in this world of change and chance and competition is not the 'normal' form.

THE PLATONIC VISION

Darwin annoyed Richard Owen by refusing to acknowledge that there was any other possible explanation for evolutionary novelty than 'random mutation'. His reason – though he did not trouble to defend it – was that talk of ideal forms or limits could not be reckoned 'scientific'. Ideal forms, perhaps he thought, can only be identified through their supposed effects, and so are not amenable to any independent check. Or he supposed that any properly causal relationship must involve an interchange of energies: hot water warms cold hands, but only because it loses heat to them (and to the surrounding air). And

---

[5] Richard B. Hays, *The Moral Vision of the New Testament* (T. & T. Clark: Edinburgh 1997), p. 166.

[6] 1 Corinthians 15.47; Paul is probably conscious of Rabbinic glosses on the first and second chapters of Genesis, which might be held to distinguish, first, the heavenly Adam, and then the Adam created from the dust of the earth.

heat is 'really' molecular motion. Formal explanations, perhaps he thought, could have no real significance, since they only repeat the explanandum.

None of those suggestions really does the job. After all, scientists since Galileo had been using *geometrical* explanations. The properties of a geometrical figure turn out, very often, to be effects of its construction. If a plane figure has three straight sides, it will also have three internal angles, with a sum of 180 degrees.[7] An alteration in one property will alter others. Galileo applied this reasoning to physical systems. On the one hand, his demonstration that everything must fall, at least in a vacuum, at the very same speed, implicitly ignores the possibility that *shape* or *essential nature* or even, magically, a *name*, can make a difference: falling objects can properly be conceived as aggregates of smaller, lighter objects, without regard to anything that, as real wholes or humanly significant things, they are.[8] To that extent Galileo may seem to support the Enlightenment rejection of formal and final causes. But on the other hand, Galileo himself considered himself a Platonist – and with good reason.[9] The structures which he conceived intellectually were really operative in the world of sense, even if experience was always fuzzier and less exact than the intellectual theorem. In the world we actually, sensually, inhabit things *do not* fall at the same speed, and balances are always inexact. But it remained a real possibility for scientists inspired by Galileo that the different properties of living creatures would turn out to be connected as rigorously as the properties of geometrical shapes. To be *this* they must also be *that*.

Certain shapes, so Whewell thought, would prove to be

[7] The fact that such a plane figure could be inscribed upon the surface of a sphere and then have different properties is a warning that we should be alert to the possibility of hidden premises. *Logic* cannot wholly determine truth, and odd results must be expected.

[8] If physical objects are material, then if heavier things fell faster, wholes would fall faster than their parts: which is absurd.

[9] 'Fundamental laws of motion and of rest are laws of a mathematical nature. We find and discover them not in Nature, but in ourselves, in our mind, in our memory, as Plato long ago has taught us'; Galileo, cited by A. Koyré, *Metaphysics and Measurement* (Chapman & Hall: London 1968), pp. 13, 42. See also my *A Parliament of Souls* (Clarendon Press: Oxford 1990), pp. 36ff.

inevitable, even if we could not now see why. Owen too expected that we might eventually find biology as lucid as ballistics. And that is indeed what has happened in some areas: we no longer wonder why or how bees can construct their honeycombs so well. That is how they are *bound* to build them if they build at all. An alteration in one part of a living form demands some matching alteration elsewhere, or the whole falls down or falls apart. Human beings were *political* animals, so Aristotle had said – and also animals that need reasons for what they do, that talk, and that walk upright. These features, in an Aristotelian philosophy, all hang together,[10] though Aristotle himself entertained the possibility that there could be humans who *were not* featherless bipeds.[11] Platonists can be still more flexible.

In a way, Darwinian 'explanation' was a strategy of despair, a reaction against the extreme *Aristotelian* hope of finding 'biometrical' explanations for everything. Reptiles do not *have* to have three-chambered hearts, even if they do. Birds do not *have* to have feathers. People do not *have* to be able to speak. Even in geometrical ballistics, after all, a good many features of the beams and missiles are not required. Nothing in the geometry demands that they be painted blue, or made of steel (though they cannot be made of butter, at least at ordinary temperatures). By Darwin's most extreme account, just about every feature of a living thing is 'accident'. Living creatures are mere assemblies of chance properties, that work well enough together. The older hope – of scientists far more than theologians – was that they had those properties because they must, because they were demanded by the way things had to be constructed. More recent studies attempt to locate geometrical patterns in

---

10 See my *Aristotle's Man: speculations upon Aristotelian anthropology* (Clarendon Press: Oxford 1975), pp. 24, 29, 46: Aristotle tries to wrap all the observably unique features of humanity together (language, practical thought, upright posture, hairlessness) in the hope of showing that 'Man is the most characteristic, most polar and most living form of life', as Chardin was to put it (Teilhard de Chardin, *Man's Place in Nature*, tr. R. Hague (Collins: London 1966), p. 17). My readers will recognize that I do not agree – but the theory is still an influential one.

11 Aristotle, *Metaphysics* 7.1036b3–4, 8.1043b11; see Clark, *Aristotle's Man*, p. 25: 'hydrocarbon arachnoids from Jupiter are men as well as we, if they can converse with us and we with them'.

the way things grow. Plants do not *happen* to grow by the Fibonacci numbers,[12] but because that sequence governs more things than just plants. No one has yet managed to show how *every* feature, say, of the vertebrate skeleton is required. There are lots of other ways a skeleton *could* be put together. There are even many ways in which the double helix of DNA itself could be put together, although the way it is displays a real elegance. That there are some geometrical or mathematical constraints on living creatures *still* seems a plausible suggestion. That those constraints determine all the ways they are is very much less certain. There are many possible ways of being, and many that we have not yet developed.

The more extreme, and non-Darwinian, suggestion is that the real constraints upon those possibilities are also powerful enough to evoke something like the variations that we see. A broadly Darwinian theory can accommodate some notion of the physical (and so geometrical) laws that determine how things grow. If those laws or limits can also make mutations of an appropriate kind more likely,[13] Darwinian theory falters, but still retains some force. The difference is that a more 'Galilean' universe guides living growth, and perhaps evokes good candidates for selection. What reasons might we have to agree or disagree?

If all available variations are represented in a multi-dimensional 'morphospace' we need not be surprised if there are distinctive clusters, and many empty spaces. The Darwinian explanation is that 'natural selection' concentrates populations at the 'peaks of adaptive fitness'. In the absence of such selection the population would in the end be scattered evenly across all morphospace, like the stars of an infinite universe. The alternative is to suppose that even in the absence of selection, there would be clusters of associated variations, and that not all

---

[12] Various solutions to this puzzle are discussed by Ron Amundson, 'Two Concepts of Constraint', *Philosophy of Science* 61.1994, pp. 556–78, reprinted in David L. Hull and M. Ruse, eds., *The Philosophy of Biology* (Oxford University Press: Oxford 1998), pp. 93–116.

[13] As Asa Grey, in effect, suggested: see Peter J. Bowler *The Eclipse of Darwinism: anti-Darwinian evolution theories in the decades around 1900* (Johns Hopkins University Press: Baltimore and London 1983), p. 211.

imaginable combinations of properties would ever be realized. At the moment this can only be a thought-experiment.[14] In the absence of an empirical resolution it seems reasonable to suspend judgement.

The standard argument now used against such geometrical constraints and goals is that they are unnecessary. Darwin's reply to Grey was, first, that such guided variation would make selection superfluous. It is an odd answer, since Darwinians usually point out that natural selection is an *inevitable* consequence of three primary conditions, whatever the source of the variations with which it deals. The sloppy use of Occam's razor is endemic. As I observed in chapter 2, the fact (if it is one) that the butler *could* have done the murder by himself does nothing to prove he did, even if he was *bound* to be involved somehow. If the butler and the housemaid could have done it more easily together, perhaps they did. We have no actual proof, in fact, that merely Darwinian evolution works. We simply do not know if there can be sufficient random changes in any particular genome to provide the phenotypic variations amongst which 'nature' can select. We do not know if 'nature' selects the very same thing for long enough to have the effects we see. Attempts to calculate how long it would take for so many different creatures to emerge from any particular lineage lack any serious basis. Even related attempts to discover how long it would take to pass from one collection of genetic bases to another, by piecemeal alterations in the genome, are mathematically absurd.[15] All that we can be certain of is that it would certainly be easier and swifter if there were life-friendly con-

---

[14] See Amundson 'Two Concepts', after P. Alberch, 'Developmental Constraints in Evolutionary Processes' in J. T. Bonner, ed., *Evolution and Development* (Springer Verlag: New York 1982), pp. 313–32.

[15] A useful analogy is the sort of game where one word (ROPE) is transformed, by single letter stages, to another (HANG), so that every stage is a real word. Perhaps there is a route involving the least possible number of stages (though we cannot always know it), but nothing at all suggests that this is the route that is travelled on a particular occasion. What grounds the assumption that the least possible number of changes must have connected the common ancestor of chimpanzees and people with present people? On the contrary, it would seem very unlikely that the minimal route was followed, without diversion or dead ends (unless, of course, the Lord raised Adam up). Cf. Christopher Wills, *Exons, Introns and Talking Genes* (Oxford University Press: Oxford 1992), pp. 43ff.

straints on what occurs. Darwin's second reply to Grey was that, as far as we can see, most actual variation is pointless: it bears no observable relationship to any present or future good of the organisms concerned. But this too seems a strange reply. We can have no notion of what the *future good* of anything will turn out to be, nor what the Lord will summon from bare dust. Each variation is an opportunity. Perhaps most of them will have no future that we can see. Perhaps some *should* have no future. But we do not actually observe that all possible changes in the bases of a genome actually occur with equal frequency, nor that all possible changes result in phenotypic variations. Nor do we actually observe the route from one change to another. Even when we know that one particular codon leads synergetically to a particular protein, we are as far from understanding in detail how that protein, at an appropriate moment, helps to create a frog, a beetle or a dandelion. The conviction that a merely piecemeal chemical reaction is *all* that ever occurs is not an empirical claim at all, but an ideological one.

Scientific explorations of those possible constraints continue. But the chief reason why we should consider this a serious possibility is the one I have explored so far. If there really are no forms of beauty, no constraints at all on what can happen or the way it grows, then there are no real values. In fact, as I have tried to show, the historical inference was the reverse. It was because we began to assume that there were no values, that we came to believe in Darwin. The problem would be serious enough if this merely meant that there was nothing really to choose between Stalin and Teresa. It is still worse – at least for the future of science – that there is nothing to choose between 'true science' and 'superstition'. If there are no real values, then 'science' is no more than one, very various, institution, struggling to survive. Its mental microbes may (or may not) be more resilient. Its claim to grasp true explanations by thought or by experiment is vain.

Is this no more than the argument I painted in less glowing colours in chapter 5, that we might seek to infer 'facts' from 'values'? We are almost bound to believe that if something

should be, then it *is*. That, after all, was the original reason for
Copernican heliocentrism, that the sun *should* be the centre.
More generally, great scientists will often say that it is a theory's
beauty that attracts them, long before it is 'proved' true by
merely empirical methods. Our problem is to distinguish
passing tastes from genuine intellectual insights. 'Genius is
revealed in a delicate feeling which *correctly* foresees the laws of
natural phenomena.'[16] Descartes got the laws of motion *wrong*.

Actually, there are other reliable feelings than those attribu-
table to genius. A theory which entails that my wife is mer-
cenary or unfaithful or a Martian spy is plainly and
immediately false. There are things I know without experiment,
and without any need to justify myself to my academic peers.
Which is just as well. If we had to offer scientific proofs of the
postulate that scientists are honest and trustworthy witnesses to
what they say, we could never even begin – since scientific
demonstrations rest upon the assumption that most scientists do
not lie about experiments. The discovery that they sometimes
do can only be absorbed without collapsing science because it
remains the case that most of them, we think, do not. People
who seriously think that institutional science is part of a grand,
military-industrial, conspiracy, cannot themselves do science,
because they cannot sensibly rely on anything that 'scientists'
say. Similarly, there is no need to offer 'scientific' proof of the
real existence of God and His Word, as though there were
possible worlds in which He does exist, and others, subtly
different in ways discernible by experiment, where He does not.
On the contrary, the conviction that there is a rational and
discoverable order, and therefore any chance of scientific proof
at all, is historically, and I believe philosophically, dependent on
orthodox theism. Imagining that 'God does not exist' amounts
to denying that there is discoverable truth, or any truth worth
discovering. In the place of science, we could only have mental
microbes. 'Theories spring up as if at random, and there is
survival of the fittest (i.e. of those that catch the fancy of the

---

[16] Claude Bernard, *Introduction to the Study of Experimental Medicine*, tr. H. C. Greene
(Macmillan: New York 1949), p. 43 (my italics).

village of savants). Such a science as this can well be a form of *élan vital*, but certainly not a form of the search for truth'.[17]

I conclude that it is wise to accept a less Darwinian theory, while still agreeing that there may be many features of the living world which merely *happen* to be so, and that we are unlikely ever to have a full understanding of why present living forms *must* be as they are. It is indeed often rash to reach a conclusion about what *must* be on the basis of what we think *should* be. For that very reason, we should often be less credulous when Darwinists insist that there *cannot* be altruists, or God, or very good reasons for believing that there are good reasons. The evidence that there often is a reason to accept some element of Platonism is, on the one hand, observational: despite catastrophe and isolation, creatures seem to display some very similar forms, in whatever lineage. On the other hand, it is transcendental: if there were no forms of beauty, we could not do science. We could not even live.

THE WORLD AS BRIDGE

'Jesus, on whom be peace, has said: this world is a bridge. Pass over it, but build not your dwelling there.'[18] So far from excusing any disrespectful treatment of this-worldly things, the creatures passing over the bridge beside us, this is a proper rebuke to *worldliness*. Similarly, when Leo XIII in his bull *Rerum Novarum* (1891) insisted that 'God has not created man for the fragile and transitory things of this world, but for Heaven and eternity, and He has ordained this earth as a place of exile, not as our permanent home',[19] he was not excusing oppression but denouncing it.

---

[17] Simone Weil, *The Need for Roots*, tr. A. F. Wills (Routledge & Kegan Paul: London 1987; first published 1952), p. 247.

[18] Joachim Jeremias, *The Unknown Sayings of Jesus*, tr. Reginald H. Fuller (SPCK: London 1964) p. 112, quoting the inscription ordered by Akbar in 1601, on the mosque at Fathpur-Sikri. Jeremias traces the saying to an original saying of Jesus, recorded in the Gospel of Thomas (logion 42): 'Become passers-by.' The author of Hebrews made a similar point, that 'here we have no lasting city' (13.14). So also did Aristotle.

[19] *Rerum Novarum* (15 May 1891), §33, taken from the Vatican website: <http://www.vatican.va>.

This same image of a *bridge* has been applied to humankind itself. Nietzsche's disdain for the 'last men' who desire their comforts, and complacently believe themselves the goal of history,[20] has much to commend it, even if his own idea about what comes next is flawed. The Nietzschean Darwinism that is now widely influential posits an unknown post-human, free to create a new reality – if only we could find a reason for any one creation. Post-humanists need acknowledge no authority in any past successes, nor devote themselves to doing what our past decrees. Post-humans are a new creation: in H. G. Wells's *Star Begotten* they are, perhaps, created from the seed of Martians; in Olaf Stapledon's *Last Men in London*, they are the minds of our remote descendants travelled back to observe our tragi-comic fate. Here, and in other science fiction, we are asked to conceive of alien or angelic minds peering out from our own eyes, in benign puzzlement at our bizarre preoccupations. The image is one that the religious should find familiar.

Of course – as my analogies suggest – it may not be only *God* or the Word of God that looks out of our eyes: we are familiar with the possibility of gods who are not God. When we see things in the way that a god would see them (with Apollo's eyes, or Aphrodite's) we need to remember how the opposite god would see (as it might be, Hermes, or Artemis). The claim that Jesus is the one true Word of God amounts to denying that there is any other worthy to take His place: the only alternative to Jesus, in the end, is Satan. 'Let this mind be in us that was also in Christ Jesus, who being in the form of God, thought not to snatch at equality with God, but took the form of a servant, being obedient unto death, even the death of the cross.'[21]

Those who believe that humankind itself, as well as the world, is no more than a bridge between one state of being and another, higher, form (which is to say, the mass of educated, secular opinion) can all too easily despise the 'ordinary' folk with whom they do not wish to identify. Intellectuals especially are inclined to believe that *they* are early examples of the

---

[20] F. Nietzsche, *Thus Spake Zarathustra*, tr. A. Tille and M. B. Boxman (Dent: London 1933), pp. 9ff.: 'the most contemptible man, which can no longer contemn himself'.
[21] After Paul, Philippians 2.5ff.

Coming Race. Perhaps that is why they hope for an age when merely 'physical' achievements are delegated to machinery, and we can engage in suitably 'mental' pastimes (whether these are mathematical, imaginative or sensual). In the face of this predictable absurdity it is well to recall that God has different tastes, and that it is those same 'ordinary people' for whom Christ died, and not for some future (self-styled) supermen. But if 'ordinary people' (and their predictably ordinary tastes) are the proper object of ethical attention, what becomes of the idea that this world is a bridge? Do not 'ordinary people', precisely, want the ordinary goods of food, drink, shelter and companionship? When the law does finally go forth from Zion, 'Nation shall not lift up a sword against nation, neither shall they learn war any more. But they shall sit every man under his vine and under his fig tree, and none shall make them afraid.'[22] That is a simple enough goal to satisfy almost all of us, and its occasional, partial realization has always been enough to make that age an image of the golden.[23] What else will Antichrist offer us, except perhaps the sly conviction that we shall enjoy those goods 'as of right', and without the trouble of praising God for them, or sharing them with anyone 'undeserving'? In the Old Golden Age, so Greek theorists said, death and senility were unknown – but only because no one lived to be senile, and no one expected death.[24] In the New Golden Age promised by Antichrist, we shall similarly redescribe our condition. Philosophers, psychologists and political theorists will insist (as they do already) that there are no *selves* to perish or pass on, but only an on-going narrative that trembles on the edge of farce. Being satisfied with that story is to miss the moment when we might wake up. That moment, most likely, has less to do with speculative philosophy or New Age mystery making, than with the simple recognition of a child's cry, a duty to be performed here and now, a blinding

---

[22] Micah 4.3–4.

[23] For example, 'Judah and Israel dwelt safely, every man under his vine and under his fig tree, from Dan even to Beersheba, all the days of Solomon' (1 Kings 4.25) – despite the fact of Solomon's crimes and follies, culminating in the attempted murder of his appointed successor (see 1 Kings 11.40).

[24] So Tzetzes, cited by T. Cole, *Democritus and the Sources of Greek Anthropology* (American Philological Association Monograph 25.1967), p. 10.

headache. 'Jesus said: "Cleave a piece of wood: I am there. Raise up the stone, and you shall find me there." ' [25]

This world is a bridge – but we cross it step by step. There is another world than this, but the way to it is through the details of our daily lives, and not by fantasizing futures. We are transitional beings, but what we shall become is given already, in the person of Jesus Christ. 'When he shall appear, we shall be like him; for we shall see him as he is.'[26]

LIVING IN THE WORLD GOD MAKES

At a synod of Catholic Bishops in November 1998, Manuel Valarezo Luzuriaga, Bishop of Questoriana, and Apostolic Prefect of Galapagos, spoke as follows:[27]

The Holy Bible speaks to us on many occasions of the love of God for animals, plants and nature. In the same way, by starting off from their beauty and goodness, it teaches us to discover the Creator. Genesis tells us that God blessed them. Jesus tells us how God was concerned about the birds in the fields and richly adorned the lilies. Paul teaches us to discover the imprints of God in them. There have also been numerous saints in the history of the Church such as Saint Francis of Assisi, who have loved animals.

With the advance of technology our century has witnessed the destruction of natural riches, woods and the pollution of water and atmosphere and the disappearance of hundreds of species of animals and plants. There is no doubt that numerous movements defending ecology have come into existence in all nations. There is no doubt that movements exist, such as the Franciscan Order, which, following the spirit of its Founder, promote justice and peace and above all, respect for Nature.

I would like our Catholic Church to guide these movements. May I be allowed to suggest with all due respect to the Holy Father that, as

---

[25] Gospel of Thomas, logion 77; Jeremias, *Unknown Sayings*, p. 107. Jeremias goes on to disentangle this saying from its later, pan-Christic interpretation, and suggest that it was originally intended, exactly, as a blessing on *work*, in disagreement with Ecclesiastes 10.9 ('he who quarries stones is hurt by them; and he who splits logs is endangered by them') and the usual, gloomily realistic view of labour.

[26] 1 John 3.2.

[27] Drawn from the website for the Eighth Congregation, held on 27 November 1998, via the Vatican website: <http://www.vatican.va>. I have made another attempt at answering Luzuriaga's plea in 'Conducta decente hacia los animales: un enfoque tradicional', in the Spanish journal *Teorema* 18/3.1999, pp. 61–83.

he taught us to defend human life, in the same way he may teach us to respect every form of life existing on earth. May he give us a pontifical document, addressed to all men of good will, furnishing a doctrinal foundation of love and respect for life existing on the earth. Also, a document that promotes, in our naturalistic and secularized society, the knowledge and contemplation of God in the beauty and in the goodness of creatures.

So far as I know, there has as yet been no such pontifical document. John Paul II has preferred to reaffirm, along with Vatican II, the thesis that man is 'the only creature on earth whom God willed for its own sake'.[28] Everything else, presumably, is intended only for our good. While I can applaud the Pope's insistence that human beings are not to be treated merely as we commonly treat plants and animals, as material for our use, I must challenge the associated thought that God has no other intention in the creation of the living world than what we may want or need.

Though there is no pontifical document to this effect, there are of course many other Christian or Abrahamic texts which ask us to appreciate the value-in-themselves of living things. Unfortunately, that admiring rhetoric is rather rarely joined to any practical conclusion. Theological conferences devoted to the beauty of nature, or the admirable qualities of animals, are punctuated by meals at which those same animals are eaten up, after lives that are far from beautiful. Lewis's imagined devil, Screwtape, remarks that he knows of cases where men turn from praying devotedly for their wives and children to beating up those same, real, wives and children.[29] We are all too ready to dissociate the *imagined* object of our supposed affections and the real creatures. Until we open our eyes to see them our professions of 'love' are hollow.[30]

Fantasy is not our only error. Another is to mistake a sense of

---

[28] In the *Letter to Families*, given in Rome, at Saint Peter's, on 2 February, 1994; drawn from the Vatican website: <http://www.vatican.va>.

[29] C. S. Lewis, *The Screwtape Letters* (Fontana: London 1955; first published 1942), pp. 21–2.

[30] One frequent response is to claim that *only* human beings have any chance of opening their eyes, and seeing other creatures as anything more than material for their own aims, and that we are therefore, somehow, excused from actually doing so. I do not understand the logic of this claim.

unity for love. Believing that we are all 'one', that there is only a single, turbid stream of being, life and consciousness, we transform everything into material. Maybe that would be excusable if we were equally 'objective' about our very own purposes. In practice, objectifying visionaries consider their own purposes and selves inviolate while making everything else – especially things that cannot answer back – material. Fortunately – or providentially – our own sense of self, and our sense of significant others as individual selves, keeps breaking in. Our attention is always being drawn to individuals as something more than episodes or anecdotes within a single story. Instead of *one* world, there are, in a way, very many, though each unitary world experiences itself as a fragment or an echo of the wider realm. That spiritual tension is echoed in the biological.

And finally, what does Beauty demand of us? The traditional picture laid it down that there were special forms of beauty, forms of life, more or less well maintained by creatures in this world. There was never any need to suppose that every form of beauty could exist, in this world here, in a single generation. The splendour of the changing world exactly was that *different* forms were seasonally, or millennially, displayed. Nor did we ever *have* to believe that hybrids were impossible, or even ugly. To that extent the gradual accumulation of good reasons to believe in different life-forms from the ones here and now should have made no important difference to theistic views of life. Perhaps they were wholly different forms, or maybe they were just the earthly shapes that much the same forms took on in different ages. We could even live with loss: the sad discovery that fairyland had gone away did not imply that there were no fairies, only that there were none here and now. Our children live quite happily with the knowledge that their favourite prehistoric monsters are 'extinct'. Nothing in the 'facts' – whether of the fossil record, or of present DNA – makes it unreasonable to believe in Beauty: to believe, that is, that there are genuine forms of being to which our changeful world approximates. We may not now be able to conceive exactly how those different forms can live together: for the moment, indeed, we may suppose they cannot. Finding the way in which God's peace can rule our hearts, as it does not, now, entirely rule the world, will always be a challenge to our will and imagination. Occasionally we catch a glimpse of that kind world.[31] Uncovering it, as the ancients uncovered images in rock, demands that we show patience. There is a difference between the art that *uncovers* truth, and the art that seeks to mould or cut the world into the shape we – that is, articulate humans – wish.

We – that is, lifekind – are not only all related to each other: we are actively and ineradicably involved with one another.[32] Our present inability to reproduce a viable environment for humankind (whether on space stations or on a damaged earth) is not just an engineering problem: it is indeed like imagining that we could live without our heart, our liver or our brain. Sustaining the living earth (and us) requires the unconsciously cooperative work of many millions of species. 'This is the assembly of life that took a billion years to evolve . . . It holds the world steady.'[33] Human civilization itself is not constructed only by deliberate human action: it is a product of the unconscious, short-term choices of innumerable domesticable creatures, and movement by other animals, plants, fungi and bacteria into the newly created niches. Dogs adopted us as much as we adopted them; cereals and rootcrops grew in our middens long before we thought to help them on. Marvellously, this process has created what never naturally existed earlier: the realm of fantasy in which possible futures, and long-distance gains, can be evaluated. Unfortunately, one particular fantasy took root: the supposition that 'we humans' are unlike all other creatures because we expect to adapt our environment to us, rather than passively adapting to the given world. Given that delusion, we forget that every living creature seeks to create a world. The very soil and water we poison was made and is sustained by living creatures; we are all, as it were, inhabitants

[31] 'Buried like a mass of roses under many spadefuls of earth'; W. B. Yeats, *Mythologies* (Macmillan: London, 1959), p. 104.

[32] The point is made by Georges Chapouthier and Jean-Claude Nouët, eds., *The Universal Declaration of Animal Rights: comments and intentions* (Ligue Française des Droits de l'Animal: Paris 1998), p. 87.

[33] E. O. Wilson, *The Diversity of Life* (Harvard University Press: Cambridge, Mass. 1992), p. 15.

of a coral island, and live among and in and by the things that 'we', lifekind, have made and make.

It does not follow that the living world has any centrally coordinated plan – except the inherited command to multiply and build. It is enough that creatures who take advantage of the structures others build (and do not damage them) live far more fruitfully than those who seek to build things up from scratch. It is enough that, in proliferating across the globe, lifekind does open up new possibilities for its variants to try new games, or old games in a novel setting, but still holds them firm within the pattern of unconscious choices made long since. Because each new generation builds within a world already old, and on the basis of genetic information already copied and corrected many billions of times, complexity and diversity do continually increase despite sporadic catastrophes. Even if nothing at all was 'really valuable' until valuers emerged, those valuers emerged long since. Values exist 'out there' simply because there are so many and so diverse creatures who find themselves, and other things, important. If we – late twentieth-century Anglophones – were to value something incompatible with the values that we, lifekind, have already created, the full weight of our own disapproval would descend.

Evolutionism often results in the image of an integrated future, rid of unsightly blemishes and dedicated to the pursuit of intellectual excellence. The God at the End of Time, we are assured by otherwise sober scientists, will be able and even willing to reach back and resurrect the patterns of lost lives. Our duty, they tell us, is to work to produce that God, at whatever cost here and now to creatures with a different dream or demon (and keep the research grants rolling). Why the God should bother to recover creatures whose only effort was to make It what It is (and who have therefore nothing else to give), they do not explain. If I were that God (absurdly), I would be more inclined to recover what my creators had forgotten, namely the living, diverse world that we are damaging here and now. If, as I suppose, there is no need, nor chance, nor reason, to 'make God' (because God is already), I must suppose that He hates nothing He has made: why else would He have made it?

Why should He prefer some things, even the things He has made (maybe) to take care of others, to all those others He has handed to our care? The Stoics supposed that a good man was God's equal (though they were commendably disinclined to identify good men); Platonists and Hebrews have been wiser.

Recovering our natural sense of unity, and diffidence, we may perhaps have time to weed out mental microbes. Even if we do not, and the world changes, it is some consolation – perhaps a very great consolation – that the living world will continue, that lifekind, all of us, endures. The Good, and our understanding of the Good, if it is accessible at all, does not lie at the end of any world-conquering imperial project, but close at hand.

If the – broadly – Platonic account of our biology that I have hinted at is true, we have some reason, and some right, to rely on our best insights into the world of beauty. If it is not, and the most extreme of Darwinist theory rules, there are no forms of beauty, and no reason to expect that any particular way of life or thought will win. In the absence of any world-transcendent standards we shall have to rely instead on craft: the craft especially of making things up as we go along, and without any assurance that our works will last. We remain what we always have been, 'spiritual amphibia', children of earth and heaven. Whichever story turns out to be true it is not unreasonable to share Augustine's hope – and on that hope, I end.

I am confident that God in His mercy will make me steadfast in all the truths which I regard as certain, but if I am minded otherwise in any point, He Himself will make it known to me, either by His own secret inspirations, or through His own lucid words, or through discussions with my brethren. For this I do pray, and I place this trust and this desire in His hands, who is wholly capable of guarding what He has given and of fulfilling what He has promised.[34]

---

[34] Augustine, *The Trinity*, tr. S. McKenna (Catholic University of America Press: Washington D.C. 1963), p. 9 (I, 5)).

Index